General Editor

C.R. Webb M.A., F.S.G.

SOCIETY OF GENEALOGISTS
14 Charterhouse Buildings
Goswell Road

Published by
Society of Genealogists
14 Charterhouse Buildings
Goswell Road
London EC1M 7BA

© 2001 Society of Genealogists

ISBN 1 903462 33 9

Volumes of the National Index of Parish Registers already published

CONTENTS

ACKNOWLEDGEMENTS

The original work on the National Index of Parish Registers for Hampshire and the Isle of Wight was undertaken by Arthur J Willis in the early 1960s. A draft was completed by 1965, but was never published.

After a lapse of more than twenty years, the task of compiling the volume was taken over by Fred Edwards, former Treasurer of the Hampshire Genealogical Society. In parallel with Mr Edwards' work, I had started to compile my own guide to Hampshire parish registers, and we subsequently agreed to collaborate on the production of the National Index. Following Mr Edwards' death, the task passed to me.

I am indebted to the Reverend Francis Isherwood for information about Roman Catholic registers. Thanks are also due to Lt Col Ralph Nye and Bridget Stockhill, formerly of the Royal Army Chaplains' Department, who allowed me access to the Department's collection of registers, and to Kay Day of the Roman Catholic Records Office at Aldershot who supplied details of the military registers held there.

Of the many archivists and librarians who have assisted, special thanks must go to Heather Forbes of the Hampshire Record Office, who dealt with many queries during the early stages of compilation. I am also indebted to Sarah Farley and Pat Floyd at Winchester; Diana Gregg and Paul Raymond at Portsmouth; Andrew George and Sue Woolgar at Southampton; Sue Oatley, Richard Smout, and Liz Street at Newport.

ABBREVIATIONS

A	Arranged alphabetically
B	Burials
Bn	Banns
Boyd	Boyd's Marriage Index (at SG, SLC)
BRO	Berkshire Record Office
BT	Bishops' Transcripts
C	Christenings (Baptisms)
CMI	Clench Hampshire Marriage Index
Cop	Modern copies
CRS	Catholic Record Society Publications
D	Deaths
DRO	Dorset Record Office
FRC	Family Records Centre
HBI	HGS Burial Index
HGS	Hampshire Genealogical Society
HMI	HGS Marriage Index
HRO	Hampshire Record Office
I	Indexed
IGI	International Genealogical Index
Inc	Incumbent of the Parish, or Minister of the Church
IWCI	Isle of Wight Card Index (at IWRO)
IWRO	Isle of Wight County Record Office
LDS	Latter-day Saints
M	Marriages
Mfc	Microfiche copies
Mfm	Microfilm copies
Ms	Manuscript
OR	Original registers
Pallot	The Pallot Index (at the Institute of Heraldic & Genealogical Studies)
Pc	Photocopies
PCI	Portsmouth Card Index (at PCRO)
PCRO	Portsmouth City Records Office
PR	Parish Register
PRO	Public Record Office
Quigley	Isle of Wight indexes published by David Quigley
RACD	Royal Army Chaplains' Department
RCRO	Roman Catholic Records Office, Aldershot
RO	Record Office
SCA	Southampton City Archives
SCI	Southampton Card Index (at SCA)
SG	Society of Genealogists
SHC	Surrey History Centre
SLC	Salt Lake City (Church of Jesus Christ of Latter-day Saints)
Ts	Typescript
VMI	Victorian and Edwardian Marriage Indexes 1837-1910 (Isle of Wight)
WRO	Wiltshire and Swindon Record Office
Z	Births

covers the Isle of Wight and much of south east Hampshire. The Diocese of Guildford, created in the same year, includes several parishes in the north east of the county.

The diocesan boundaries have changed several times in recent years. Of the 414 mainland parishes and chapelries with registers commencing before 1900, 301 are now in the Diocese of Winchester, 87 in the Diocese of Portsmouth, 14 in the Diocese of Guildford, seven in the Diocese of Salisbury, and five in the Diocese of Oxford.

For each ancient parish, the parish listing shows the 1831 population and the Poor Law Union or Incorporation in which the parish was situated. Hundreds are not shown. The boundaries of Hampshire Hundreds changed substantially, and it would be misleading to show the Hundred in which a parish lay in a particular year. For information on Hundreds, reference should be made to The Victoria County History of Hampshire and the Isle of Wight (5 volumes, 1900-1914).

RECORD REPOSITORIES

The following repositories have been designated Diocesan Record Offices for the deposit of parish registers:

The Hampshire Record Office holds registers for the Diocese of Winchester (except Southampton parishes), and for the deaneries of Bishops Waltham and Petersfield within the Diocese of Portsmouth. The office also holds the registers of seven Hampshire parishes within the Diocese of Salisbury.

The Portsmouth City Records Office holds registers for the deaneries of Alverstoke, Havant, and Portsmouth within the Diocese of Portsmouth.

Southampton City Archives holds the registers of parishes within the City of Southampton.

The Surrey History Centre at Woking holds the registers of Hampshire parishes within the Diocese of Guildford.

The Isle of Wight County Record Office holds the registers of Isle of Wight parishes.

The Berkshire Record Office holds the parish registers of Combe, Stratfield Mortimer, Mortimer West End, and Beech Hill.

The Wiltshire and Swindon Record Office holds Bishops' Transcripts and marriage licence records for Bramshaw, Damerham, Martin, Plaitford, and Stratfield Mortimer.

PARISH REGISTERS

For each parish, the listing shows the location and dates of deposited parish registers. Separate dates are given for baptisms, marriages, burials, and banns. In the case of registers retained locally, a start date is given followed by a plus sign (+), indicating that the registers are continuous from that date. Information on local holdings has been taken from the parish record surveys undertaken by the Diocesan Record Offices. Parishes which have not deposited registers are listed only if their registers commence before 1950.

Three ancient parishes (Christchurch, Wonston, and Woodcott) have elected to keep their registers, but microform copies of these are available at the Hampshire Record Office. At the time of writing, the only pre-1813 registers which are not available at a record office as originals or photographic copies are the registers of Winchester College. It is possible that pre-1813 registers exist for St Ann Portsea (the dockyard church).

Approximately 44% of the ancient parishes on the mainland and 25% of those on the island have registers dating from the sixteenth century. A further 44% of mainland parishes and 50% of island parishes have registers dating from the seventeenth century. A comprehensive guide to the registers of Hampshire, excluding the Isle of Wight, was published in 1909:

> W A Fearon & W E Williams: Parish Registers and Parochial
> Documents in the Archdeaconry of Winchester.

A survey of parish registers was undertaken at the time of the 1831 census. It is clear from the 1831 returns and from Fearon & Williams that there have been a number of losses. The registers of Northington and North Stoneham now date from 1579 and 1640 respectively; in 1831 both had registers dating from 1538. Whitwell registers for the period 1559-1663 were listed in 1831 but are now missing. A sixteenth century register for St Thomas Portsmouth existed in 1819 when brief extracts were made, but was missing in 1831.

There have been losses by fire at Grateley (1643), New Alresford (1678, 1689, 1736), Stratfield Mortimer (1681), St Mary Southampton (1706), Leckford (1769), Ashmansworth (1810), and Chalton (1970). The Yateley registers survived the fire which destroyed the church in 1979, but many other parish records perished. Losses by theft have occurred at St Lawrence Winchester (1760) and Chawton with Farringdon (1978). Enemy action during World War Two caused losses at Dibden, Southampton, Southsea, and Shanklin.

Other parishes where losses are apparent include Bramshott, East Stratton, Linkenholt, Shipton Bellinger, Steep, Tufton, Vernham Dean, and Calbourne. The earliest Eastrop register has gone missing since 1931, though transcripts had previously been made.

Damage by damp is evident at Hannington and East Wellow, and also at Combe, where an iron chest containing the registers was thrown into a pond in 1832. The registers of East Worldham were placed in an underground chamber for safekeeping in 1940, and when recovered were found to be immersed in water. The first volume is now illegible, but a transcript had previously been made.

There have also been several recoveries. A Hartley Wespall register was discovered at Pentonville in 1852, and a Bentworth volume was restored to the parish in 1903. An eighteenth century register for Worting, listed as missing by Fearon & Williams, is now in the Hampshire Record Office. Early volumes for Swarraton and Preston Candover were discovered in 1975 and 1978 respectively. The Otterbourne register 1747-1805, missing for many years, was left outside the Vicarage in 1999.

MARRIAGE CENTRES

Until 1753 any marriage conducted by a priest was valid in law even if performed without banns or licence, and some incumbents were prepared to dispense with such formalities and marry all-comers. As a result, several parishes became notable marriage centres.

The registers of Empshott, Gosport Holy Trinity, Monxton, Newtown, Rowner, Sherborne St John, Winchfield, and Winslade all contain a high proportion of marriage entries where both parties were strangers to the parish. Tichborne and Up Nately also attracted a high proportion of non-residents, though the total number of marriages involved was much smaller.

Lord Hardwicke's Marriage Act of 1753 put an end to the activities of the marriage centres, and the marriage rate fell substantially in the parishes concerned. Monxton had already lost its popularity by 1725.

A few parishes flourished as marriage centres during the Commonwealth period. Andover, Bentley, and Elvetham were particularly notable.

BISHOPS' TRANSCRIPTS

Bishops' Transcripts (BTs) for the Diocese of Winchester are held at the Hampshire Record Office and have been microfilmed by the Church of Jesus Christ of Latter-day Saints. Few transcripts survive for the period before 1780.

The churchwardens' accounts for Wootton St Lawrence provide evidence that annual returns of parish register entries were being made to the Bishop's Registrar from 1565 to 1596 and from 1631 to 1633. Similar references occur in the records of Kingsclere (1562), Kingsworthy (1573), and Blendworth (1602). See Fearon & Williams, page 11.

Individual seventeenth century transcripts survive for Alton (1672), Bentley (1692), Farnborough (1665), Havant (1663), Hawkley (1697), Longparish (1678), Minstead (1687), Nursling (1687), Portsmouth (1682), Rockbourne (1677), Selborne (1677), and Newport (1681). Those for Rockbourne and Selborne survive as wrappers for Quarter Sessions records, and that for Farnborough is on the back of a Churchwardens' Presentment. More than seventy parishes have transcripts for single years or groups of years during the period 1700 to 1780.

The main series of transcripts dates from 1780, and most parishes have a good run from this year to 1858 or later. The parish listing shows the individual years which are available for each parish. The listing is based on the catalogue of Bishops' Transcripts at the Hampshire Record Office, which is inaccurate in some respects, and is currently being revised. For example the catalogue shows some parishes as having no returns for the years 1816 and 1817, but on inspection these are often present, sometimes bundled separately; they were added to the main series after cataloguing took place.

Bishops' Transcripts for Bramshaw, Damerham, Martin, Plaitford, and Stratfield Mortimer are held at the Wiltshire and Swindon Record Office. Post-1835 transcripts for Stratfield Mortimer and Mortimer West End are at the Oxfordshire Record Office.

MICROFORM COPIES AND PHOTOCOPIES

Most of the Hampshire parish registers deposited at Winchester, Portsmouth, Southampton, Woking, and Reading are available on microfiche at the Hampshire Record Office. Several undeposited registers are also available on fiche. The record offices at Portsmouth and Southampton hold microfiche copies of their own holdings, and copies of some Hampshire parish registers are available at the Society of Genealogists. The parish listing shows the coverage for each parish.

Major libraries within Hampshire hold microfiche copies of parish registers for their local areas, but it has not been possible to include library holdings in the parish listing.

The Church of Jesus Christ of Latter-day Saints has been active in microfilming church registers throughout the world, and has filmed many of those deposited at Winchester, Portsmouth, Southampton, Woking, and Newport. In addition, the Hampshire Record Office has filmed many of its own holdings. The coverage and location of microfilms for each parish is shown in the listing. Films held at the Genealogical Library in Salt Lake City (marked SLC in the listing) may be ordered for viewing at any LDS Family History Centre.

Photocopies of several parish registers are held at Winchester, Portsmouth, and Newport.

MARRIAGE LICENCES

Allegations and bonds for marriage licences issued by the Bishop of Winchester are held at the Hampshire Record Office. Abstracts and indexes have been published as follows:

> A J Willis: Hampshire Marriage Licences 1607-1640 (1960)
>
> A J Willis: Hampshire Marriage Licences 1669-1680 (1963)
>
> W J C Moens: Hampshire Allegations for Marriage Licences 1689-1837, Harleian Society Volumes 35 & 36 (1893) (Covers 1689-1693, 1701-1711, 1713-1837)
>
> A J Willis: Hampshire Allegations for Marriage Licences 1689-1837 (1962) (Supplement to the Harleian Society Volumes; reprinted from The Genealogists' Magazine Volume 14 Nos 2 & 3)

A microfiche copy of the Harleian Society Volumes and the supplement may be purchased from the Hampshire Record Office.

Marriage licence records for the parishes of Bramshaw, Damerham, Martin, Plaitford, and Stratfield Mortimer are held at the Wiltshire and Swindon Record Office.

PARISH REGISTER TRANSCRIPTS

92 mainland parishes and seven island parishes are included in the Phillimore series of Hampshire Marriage Registers published between 1899 and 1914, and available for purchase on microfiche from the Hampshire Record Office. The series is supplemented by a separately published volume of marriages 1776-1812 for St Thomas

Portsmouth. The registers of Ashe, Colmer, East Wellow, East Worldham, Hartley Mauditt, Priors Dean, and West Worldham are also available in printed form. Copies of all printed transcripts are held at the Society of Genealogists, and all but the Portsmouth volume are available at the Hampshire Record Office.

Substantial collections of parish register transcripts relating to Hampshire and the Isle of Wight are held by the Hampshire Record Office, the Society of Genealogists, and the Hampshire Genealogical Society. Local collections are held at Portsmouth, Southampton, and Woking. All transcripts held at the Society of Genealogists and at the record offices in Winchester, Portsmouth, Southampton, and Woking have been examined to check their coverage.

THE INTERNATIONAL GENEALOGICAL INDEX

The International Genealogical Index (IGI) is a computer-generated index of baptisms and marriages, published on microfiche by the Church of Jesus Christ of Latter-day Saints. Some LDS Family History Centres hold the IGI on CD-ROM, and visitors are permitted to download selected entries onto floppy disk for personal use. It has only been possible to show the coverage of the 1988 edition, but the coverage of the current 1992 edition does not appear to be substantially different.

Entries in the IGI have been extracted primarily from microfilm copies of parish registers and Bishops' Transcripts. Many of the registers deposited at Portsmouth are included, but coverage of the rest of Hampshire is patchy. There are few entries for the Isle of Wight.

Although the IGI is a valuable finding aid, it should be used with caution. Entries should always be checked in the source documents, and it should not be assumed that extraction is complete and accurate for the stated parishes and periods. It has been noted that the 1992 edition of the IGI omits some entries which appeared in the 1988 edition; also that the coverage of CD-ROM versions differs from that of microfiche versions.

MARRIAGE INDEXES

Several marriage indexes offer substantial coverage of Hampshire. The parish listing shows the years covered for each parish.

The HGS Marriage Index 1538-1837 (Hampshire Genealogical Society) has been compiled by HGS members from printed sources, modern transcripts, original registers, and Bishops' Transcripts. Both males and females are indexed. The index covers mainland parishes only, and is complete for the pre-1895 county of Hampshire. Some marriages in the former Wiltshire parishes of Damerham and Martin are included, but it has been decided not to complete the coverage of these parishes.

The Clench Hampshire Marriage Index 1538-1881 (Hampshire England Ancestry, 907 South, 100 East, Orem, Utah, USA 84058) has been compiled by Mrs Aubrey Mary Clench from original registers and Bishops' Transcripts, and is more than 90% complete. Marriages are indexed by males, but much of the index has now been computerised and can be searched for females also. The contents are shown in the parish listing.

Boyd's Marriage Index (at the Society of Genealogists) includes 109 mainland parishes and 28 island parishes; 92 mainland and seven island parishes are taken from the printed Phillimore transcripts. The marriages are included in the two miscellaneous series of Boyd's Index (red and blue bindings). Both males and females are indexed, though many marriages in the period 1701-1750 appear to be indexed by males only. Microfilm copies of the index may be ordered for viewing at any LDS Family History Centre.

The Victorian Marriage Index 1837-1900 and Edwardian Marriage Index 1901-1910 (published on microfiche by Barry Hall, 1a Hungerberry Close, Shanklin, Isle of Wight, PO37 6LX) index Anglican and Roman Catholic marriages on the Isle of Wight. Isle of Wight marriages 1539-1900 are included in the Isle of Wight Card Index, which is described below under "Other Indexes".

Pallot's Marriage Index (Institute of Heraldic & Genealogical Studies, 79-82 Northgate, Canterbury, Kent, CT1 1BA.) contains entries from 93 mainland and 22 island parishes, mostly for the period 1790-1812, but sometimes for a much longer period. All but seven of the parishes are also in Boyd, and six of these seven are available in printed or typescript form. The exception, Alverstoke, is included in the International Genealogical Index (IGI).

The Nimrod Index of Wiltshire Marriages (1 Lansdown Road, Swindon, SN1 3NE) includes marriages at Bramshaw, Damerham, East Wellow, Martin, and Plaitford.

OTHER INDEXES

The Isle of Wight County Record Office holds a card index to the parish registers and Nonconformist registers (originals and copies) held at the office. Baptisms, marriages, and burials are indexed from 1539 to 1900. The coverage is shown in the parish listing.

Southampton City Archives holds a card index of post-1837 parish register entries for many parishes within the city. The index is still being added to, and its contents are shown in the parish listing.

Volunteers at the Portsmouth City Records Office are compiling a card index of baptism, marriage, and burial entries from the registers held at the office. The current contents are shown in the parish listing.

The HGS Burial Index 1538-1837 (Hampshire Genealogical Society) has been compiled by HGS members from original registers, Bishops' Transcripts, and modern transcripts. The index covers mainland parishes only, and is complete for Anglican parishes. Some Nonconformist burials are included. The contents are shown in the parish listing.

NONCONFORMISTS

The Huguenot congregation at Southampton was established in the sixteenth century, but the main Nonconformist activity in Hampshire dates from the mid seventeenth century when congregations of Baptists, Independents, Presbyterians, and Quakers were established.

Until 1844, it was a requirement that Nonconformist meeting places be registered with the Diocesan Registrar. "Hampshire Miscellany III, Dissenters' Meeting House Certificates in the Diocese of Winchester 1702-1844" (A J Willis, 1965) lists about 1,400 registrations, though these include multiple registrations of the same meeting. From 1844, registration was transferred to the Registrar General.

An attempt has been made to list all Nonconformist congregations founded before 1940 which existed for more than a few years. Sources used to identify chapels include the 1851 Religious Census, denominational yearbooks, directories, and a Parliamentary Paper of 1882/3 "Registrations of Nonconformist Chapels". House meetings have been excluded unless a chapel was subsequently established.

Each Nonconformist chapel is listed under the name of the Anglican parish in which the chapel was situated. Where the chapel was known by the name of a place within the parish, a suitable cross-reference has been inserted. Dates of foundation and closure are given where possible.

Following validation in 1837, many Nonconformist registers were surrendered to the Registrar General, and these are now at the Public Record Office; registers of the Society of Friends (Quakers) are in class RG 6 and the remainder are in class RG 4. A few further registers were surrendered in 1858. The RG 4 Class List includes a "Topographical Index to the Whereabouts of Protestant and Catholic Dissenters" which provides a partial index of place names mentioned in the registers.

All surrendered registers have been microfilmed by the Church of Jesus Christ of Latter-day Saints, and most of them are available on film at the Hampshire Record Office. Those for the Isle of Wight are available at the Isle of Wight County Record Office. Registers in class RG 4 are available on film at the Family Records Centre. Many of the entries are in the International Genealogical Index.

The volumes at the Public Record Office form the main collection of Nonconformist registers, but a substantial number of pre-1837 registers and other records for Hampshire chapels are held elsewhere. These include records of Baptist congregations at Andover, Broughton, Longparish, Lymington, Portsea, Whitchurch, and Newport, Independent congregations at Alton, Fareham, Ringwood, Southampton, and Whitchurch, and Presbyterian congregations at Portsmouth and Ringwood.

See: J A Vickers: The Religious Census of Hampshire 1851 (1993)

ROMAN CATHOLICS

Following the Reformation, Catholicism in Hampshire, as elsewhere, survived largely through the support of landed Catholic families who were able to support priests and provide mass centres. In 1582 the official number of Recusants in Hampshire was the third highest of all the English counties, being surpassed only by Yorkshire and Lancashire. Chapels were maintained during the penal period at Brambridge, Gosport, Havant, Tichborne, Winchester, and at various locations in the Avon valley, though Catholicism was virtually eliminated in the Isle of Wight. Following the Second Catholic Relief Act of 1791, chapels were established at Portsea, Southampton, Cowes, and Newport. Hampshire also provided refuge for priests and other Catholics fleeing the French Revolution.

Pre-1837 registers are known for Brambridge (now Eastleigh parish), Gosport, Havant, Lymington (including Rook Cliff House, Milford), Portsea, Sopley (now Christchurch parish), Southampton, Tichborne, Winchester, Cowes, and Newport. Only Lymington surrendered registers to the Registrar General. Registers kept by French Émigré priests at Lymington, Southampton, and Winchester were thought to have been burned during World War Two, but they have recently been rediscovered at the Centre des Archives Diplomatiques, Nantes.

The early registers of Brambridge and Tichborne are missing, but transcripts exist. Those of Portsea are at the Portsmouth City Records Office, and those of Havant and Newport are in the Portsmouth (Catholic) Diocesan Archives. The Tichborne register 1837-1863, missing for several years, was discovered in 1989 among papers stored in the stable block at Tichborne House, and is now at the Hampshire Record Office. Twentieth century marriage registers for Bordon (Headley) and Purbrook have been deposited, but other Catholic registers remain in the custody of parish priests.

The Hampshire Record Office holds microfilm copies of registers for Lymington and Winchester. The Isle of Wight County Record Office holds photocopies of several Catholic registers.

All early Catholic registers except those of Southampton, and those kept by Émigré priests at Southampton and Lymington, have been printed by the Catholic Record Society. The Southampton register and the Southampton Émigré register are available as typed transcripts.

Registers of Roman Catholic military churches and chapels are held at the Roman Catholic Records Office, Aldershot. The office is not open to the public, but transcripts of the earlier registers are available at the Society of Genealogists. The parish listing includes Roman Catholic military churches and chapels at Aldershot, Alverstoke (Royal Naval Hospital, Haslar), Bulford (Wiltshire), Headley (Bordon Camp), Hound (Royal Victoria Hospital, Netley), Portsmouth, and South Tidworth.

See: G Dwyer: Diocese of Portsmouth, Past and Present (1981)

        R E Scantlebury: The Catholic Story of the Isle of Wight (1962)

HUGUENOTS

The register of the Walloon and French Protestant congregation of St Julien, Southampton, dating from 1567, is the earliest extant register of a Huguenot church in Great Britain. The volume is at the Public Record Office, and a transcript has been published by the Huguenot Society. A second congregation, formed by a breakaway group, existed in Southampton for several years, but no records are known.

SOCIETY OF FRIENDS (QUAKERS)

The Hampshire Quarterly Meeting of the Society of Friends was established in 1668 and included the Monthly Meetings of Alton, Ringwood, Southampton (1668-1756), Andover (1691-1737), Portsmouth & Isle of Wight (1681-1687), and Isle of Wight (1695-1752). Each Monthly Meeting comprised several Meeting Houses. The Dorset Quarterly Meeting and the Hampshire Quarterly Meeting amalgamated in 1804 to form the Dorset & Hampshire Quarterly Meeting.

All pre-1837 Quaker registers for Hampshire were surrendered, and are now at the Public Record Office in class RG 6. Microfilm copies are held at the Hampshire Record Office. Registers exist for the Hampshire Quarterly Meeting, for the Monthly Meetings of Alton, Ringwood, and Southampton, and for Bramshott, which formed part of the Alton Monthly Meeting. All date from the seventeenth century. In addition, registers exist for the Dorset & Hampshire Quarterly Meeting and the Poole & Ringwood Monthly Meeting, both of which were formed in 1804.

Before the registers were surrendered, an alphabetical digest of all birth, marriage, and burial entries was compiled from the registers of meetings within Dorset and Hampshire. Copies of the digest are held at Friends' Library in Euston and at the Hampshire Record Office. A microfilm copy is held at the Society of Genealogists.

The records of the Hampshire Quarterly Meeting and its successor, the Dorset & Hampshire Quarterly Meeting, are held at the Hampshire Record Office. The records are extensive, and reference should be made to the general article on Quaker records in Volume 2 of the National Index of Parish Registers. A paper on early Quakers in Hampshire is planned for publication in the Hampshire Papers series.

BAPTISTS

There is evidence of Baptist activity in Portsmouth as early as 1645, but the first Baptist church in Hampshire was established in 1651 as a joint church, meeting at Broughton in Hampshire and Porton in Wiltshire. By the end of the seventeenth century, churches had been established at Lymington, Lyndhurst, Portsmouth, and Whitchurch. Of these, only Lyndhurst and Portsmouth surrendered registers. The records of Lymington and Whitchurch are now at the Hampshire Record Office, and those of Broughton are at Regents Park College, Oxford.

Of the congregations founded in the eighteenth century, Portsea Meeting House Alley, Portsea White's Row, Romsey, and Newport General Baptist Chapel surrendered registers; by the time of surrender the Newport congregation had become Unitarian. The records of Clarence Street Chapel, Portsea are now at the Portsmouth City Records Office, and those of Brockenhurst are at Regents Park College, Oxford. Those of Beech Hill, Lockerley, and Mottisfont, are presumably still in church hands. The location of records for Southampton East Street Chapel is unknown.

About thirty congregations were founded between 1800 and 1837. Of these, Andover, Anmore (in the parish of Hambledon), Forton, Portsea Ebenezer Chapel, Newport Castlehold Chapel, and Wellow (in the parish of Shalfleet) surrendered registers. The register of Ripley Independent Chapel at Sopley includes entries for Baptists. Records of the Marylebone and Lake Lane Chapels at Portsea are now at the Portsmouth City Records Office, those of Andover are at the Hampshire Record Office, those of Fritham (in the parish of Bramshaw) are at the Wiltshire and Swindon Record Office, and those of Longparish are at the Gospel Standard Baptist Library.

Church record books for Baptist churches sometimes include records of adult baptism. Membership lists usually record dates of admission to the congregation by transfer or adult baptism, and dates of removal by transfer or death.

In the listing, General Baptist and Particular Baptist congregations have been distinguished where possible, but it should be noted that some chapels changed their allegiance during their lifetime.

See: R R Chambers: The Strict Baptist Chapels of England, Volume 1, Surrey and Hampshire (1952)

F Ridoutt: The Early Baptist History of Portsmouth (1888)

INDEPENDENTS (CONGREGATIONALISTS)

The term Independent, and later Congregational, was applied to churches which were self-governing. The Hampshire Union of Protestant Dissenting Ministers was formed in 1781, and subsequently became the Hampshire Congregational Union. The Congregational Union of England and Wales was formed in 1831. In 1972 the Congregational churches amalgamated with the Presbyterian Church of England to form the United Reformed Church, though some churches chose to remain outside the new organisation.

Because of their self-governing nature, the most important records of Independent churches are church record books, which record many aspects of church administration and membership. Membership lists usually record dates of admission to the congregation and dates of removal by transfer or death.

Of the congregations founded in the seventeenth century, Alton, Andover, Basingstoke, Christchurch, Fordingbridge, Gosport, Lymington, Odiham, Romsey, Southampton, Tadley, Winchester, and Newport surrendered registers, though only those of Gosport date from the seventeenth century. Southampton surrendered registers dating from 1783 but retained church record books containing baptism entries from 1674; these are now at Southampton City Archives. The records of Fareham and Whitchurch are now at the Hampshire Record Office.

Of the congregations founded in the eighteenth century, Burley, Crondall, Havant, Mortimer West End, Petersfield, Portsea Orange Street, Ringwood, Rowlands Castle (in the parish of Chalton), and Titchfield surrendered registers. No records appear to survive for Portsea Bethel Chapel or for Netley Chapel, Hound, which was possibly in existence by 1800. A register of deaths dating from 1835 was formerly held at Cadnam Chapel, Eling, but the chapel is now closed and the present location of its records is unknown.

More than sixty congregations came into existence between 1800 and 1837, though some of these were served from existing chapels and would not have kept separate registers. Bishopstoke, Emsworth, Gosport New Independent Chapel, New Alresford, Ripley (in the parish of Sopley), Stockbridge, Totton (in the parish of Eling), Cowes, East Cowes, Newport Nodehill Chapel, and Ryde surrendered registers.

PRESBYTERIANS

In the seventeenth century, the terms Presbyterian and Independent were used somewhat interchangeably. The congregations at Ringwood Upper Meeting House and High Street Portsmouth remained Presbyterian, but like most chapels of that denomination, became Unitarian. Both surrendered registers.

A separate denomination, the Presbyterian Church in England, was founded in 1836, and subsequently became the Presbyterian Church *of* England. Congregations were established at Aldershot, Bournemouth, Holybourne, Liss, Portsea, Southampton, and Totton (in the parish of Eling). Church of Scotland Military Churches were established at Aldershot, Bulford (Wiltshire), Over Wallop, and South Tidworth.

In 1972 the Presbyterian Church of England amalgamated with the Congregational churches to form the United Reformed Church.

UNITARIANS

The Presbyterian congregations at Portsmouth and Ringwood, and the General Baptist congregation at Newport became Unitarian. Further congregations were established at Bournemouth, Romsey, and Southampton. A church established at Ryde in 1876 was short-lived.

COUNTESS OF HUNTINGDON'S CONNEXION

The Countess of Huntingdon's Connexion had its roots in Calvinistic Methodism, but later became affiliated to the Congregational Union of England and Wales. Chapels were established at Basingstoke, Brockenhurst, and Lymington. The Independent Chapel at Mortimer West End became associated with the Connexion in 1826. Basingstoke and Mortimer West End surrendered registers.

METHODISTS

Wesleyans

Methodist chapels are organised into circuits, with one or more ministers allocated to each circuit. Hampshire was within the Salisbury Wesleyan Circuit until 1790, when a separate Portsmouth Circuit was formed. Circuits were subsequently established centred on Aldershot, Alton, Andover, Basingstoke, Bournemouth, Christchurch (originally known as Ringwood), Eastleigh, Fareham, Gosport, Petersfield, Romsey, Southampton, Southsea, Winchester, Newport (originally known as the Isle of Wight Circuit), Ryde, and Ventnor. The entry for each circuit gives details of the circuit formation and the chapels within the circuit.

Entries are included for the New Forest Wesleyan Mission, the South Hampshire Wesleyan Mission, and the Surrey & North Hampshire Wesleyan Mission; also for the Farnham, Guildford, Newbury, Poole, Reading, Salisbury, Sandhurst, and Wimborne Circuits, which included Hampshire chapels.

Primitive Methodists

The Primitive Methodist movement originated in Staffordshire about 1812, and had reached Hampshire by 1835 when the Andover and Micheldever Primitive Methodist Circuits were formed from the Shefford (Berkshire) Circuit. A separate mission covering Portsmouth, Southampton, and the Isle of Wight was formed as a mission of the Hull (Yorkshire) Circuit. Circuits or missions were subsequently established centred on Aldershot, Basingstoke, Bournemouth, Christchurch, Droxford, Hurstbourne Tarrant, Petersfield, Portsmouth, Romsey, Silchester, Southampton,

Winchester, Newport & Cowes, and Ryde & Sandown. An entry for each of these is included in the listing.

Entries are also included for the Chichester, Guildford, Newbury, Reading, Salisbury, Shefford, Wilton, and Woodfalls circuits, which included Hampshire chapels.

Bible Christians

The Bible Christian or O'Bryanite Church was founded in Cornwall in 1815, and had reached Hampshire by 1823. Circuits were established centred on Crondall, Farnham (Surrey), Liphook, Portsmouth (originally Portsea), and Southampton (originally the Botley Mission). The cause was particularly successful in the Island, giving rise to circuits for the Isle of Wight, Newport, Shanklin, and Yarmouth. An entry for each circuit is included in the listing.

Other Methodist Denominations

The Winchester Circuit of the Wesleyan Methodist Association was formed in 1835 by a breakaway group of the Winchester Wesleyan Society, and was joined by the Wesleyan societies of most villages in the Winchester area. On union of the Wesleyan Methodist Association with the Wesleyan Methodist Reformers in 1857, the circuit became the Winchester Circuit of the United Methodist Free Church. Other Association chapels were established at Gosport, Portsea, Southampton, and Wickham.

Congregations of Wesleyan Methodist Reformers and "Free Wesleyans" (presumably the United Methodist Free Church) were established at Cowes, Newport, Ryde, St Helens, Seaview (St Helens), Swanmore (Ryde), and Wootton Bridge (Arreton).

A linked group of Independent Methodist congregations was established at Boarhunt, Chalton, and Clanfield.

Methodist Union

In 1907 the Bible Christians united with the United Methodist Free Church and the Methodist New Connexion to form the United Methodist Church. In 1932 the Wesleyan, Primitive Methodist, and United Methodist Churches united to form the Methodist Church.

Records and Registers

The records of Methodist circuits and chapels are extensive, and many have been deposited at county and city record offices. Records other than registers are frequently closed for 30 years after the date of the last entry, so it is advisable to check their availability before visiting the appropriate record office.

Deposited Methodist records are usually catalogued under the name of the present Methodist circuit. Places of deposit for each circuit are as follows:

Hampshire Record Office:	Aldershot Farnborough & Camberley, Andover, Basingstoke, Christchurch & Lymington, Droxford, Eastleigh, Farnham & Alton, Gosport & Fareham, Petersfield Liphook & Haslemere, Romsey, Winchester

Portsmouth City Records Office:	Portsmouth
Southampton City Archives:	Southampton
Berkshire Record Office:	Newbury, Reading, Silchester
Isle of Wight Record Office:	East Wight, West Wight
Dorset Record Office:	Bournemouth, Poole, Wimborne
Wiltshire & Swindon Record Office:	Salisbury
Surrey History Centre:	Surrey & North Hampshire Mission

Methodist chapels frequently did not keep individual registers; baptisms were entered in a single register for the circuit. Where separate chapel registers exist, they often include entries for other chapels in the circuit. It is therefore advisable to check all registers for the relevant circuit.

All Wesleyan circuits in existence in 1837 (Andover, Christchurch, Gosport, Guildford, Newbury, Portsmouth, Reading, Salisbury, Southampton, Newport) surrendered registers either for the circuit or for the chapel at the head of the circuit. Registers were also surrendered by the Micheldever and Reading Primitive Methodist Circuits, Shefford Primitive Methodist Chapel, and the Farnham, Portsea, and Isle of Wight Bible Christian Circuits.

Most of the present Methodist circuits have deposited substantial numbers of post-1837 circuit and chapel registers. Exceptions are the Aldershot Farnborough & Camberley Circuit, the Basingstoke Circuit, and the Bournemouth Circuit, for which many registers are still in church hands. Military Methodist chapels are listed for Over Wallop and South Tidworth.

See: J A Vickers: Early Methodism in South East Hampshire (Portsmouth Archives Review Volume 4, 1979/80)

E R Pillow: Two Centuries of Winchester Methodism (1985)

W D Cooper: Methodism in Portsmouth (1973)

Henry Smith: Wesleyan Methodism in Portsmouth (1894)

J B Dyson: Methodism in the Isle of Wight (1865)

J Woolcock: A History of the Bible Christian Churches on the Isle of Wight (1897)

H L Calkin: Catalog of Methodist Archival and Manuscript Collections, Great Britain and Ireland. Part 6, Section 3a: Circuits and Societies, Southern England (1991)

A History of Methodism in Hampshire, compiled in 1827 by John S Stamp, was never published, but survives in manuscript at the Methodist Archives Centre, Manchester.

JEWS

Synagogues were established at Portsmouth, Southampton, and Bournemouth. A temporary Synagogue existed for some time at Aldershot. Records are presumably held by the congregations. A circumcision register for Portsmouth has been printed, but few surnames are recorded.

See: A Weinberg: Portsmouth Jewry (1985)

OTHER DENOMINATIONS

Congregations of the Catholic Apostolic Church were established at Lymington, Portsea, Southampton, Newport, and Ryde.

Congregations of Latter-day Saints were established at Aldershot, Froyle, Gosport, Portsea, Portsmouth, and Southampton.

Many congregations of Brethren and Plymouth Brethren were established, most of them meeting in rooms or halls. The listing includes only those congregations which established permanent chapels.

A congregation of the New Jerusalem (Swedenborgian) Church existed at Winchester, and a Sandemanian chapel existed at Romsey. A congregation of Universalists is recorded at Dock Row, Portsea; see National Index of Parish Registers Volume 2 page 792.

MILITARY RECORDS

In 1782, the 37th and 67th Regiments of Foot became the North Hampshire Regiment and the South Hampshire Regiment respectively, though neither had a permanent depot in the county until 1873. In 1881 the two regiments amalgamated to form the Hampshire Regiment, with the 37th forming the First Battalion, the 67th the Second Battalion, and the Militia the Third Battalion.

Before the establishment of its own county regiment, Hampshire had long provided garrisons for the Army, and entries for regular soldiers and militiamen are to be found in many parish registers, including those of Winchester, Portsea, Portsmouth, Gosport, Wymering, and Newport. The military camp at Aldershot was established in 1854.

Growth in the number of military depots led to the establishment of garrison churches. The parish listing includes Army churches and chapels at Aldershot, Barton Stacey, Bramley, Bulford (Wiltshire), Cove, Crookham, Gosport, Greatham (Longmoor Camp), Headley (Bordon Camp), Portsea, Portsmouth, South Tidworth, Winchester, Wymering (Hilsea Barracks), and Carisbrooke (Parkhurst Barracks). The listing also includes Royal Navy churches and chapels at Portsea and Rowner, the Royal Marine Artillery church at Portsea (St Andrew Eastney), RAF churches and chapels at Cove, Fawley, and Over Wallop (RAF Middle Wallop), and Military Hospital chapels at Aldershot, Alverstoke, and Hound.

A large collection of military registers is held at the Royal Army Chaplains' Department, but the Department is not open to the public and the registers are inaccessible at present. Other military registers are held at the record offices in Winchester, Portsmouth, Woking, and Newport.

The Royal Garrison Church at Portsmouth has burial registers dating from 1741, and the Royal Naval Hospital, Haslar, Alverstoke, has baptisms from 1829 and burials from 1827. No other known military registers for Hampshire commence before 1849. Marriages in military churches are conducted under the Marriage (Naval, Military, and Air Force Chapels) Act of 1932, and most of the churches have no marriages before this date. Exceptions are four churches at Aldershot, which have marriage records dating from the nineteenth century.

See: C T Atkinson: Regimental History, The Royal Hampshire Regiment,
        Volume 1 To 1914 (1950), Volume 2 1914-1918 (1952)

        D S Daniell: Regimental History, The Royal Hampshire Regiment,
        Volume 3 1918-1954 (1955)

        T S Cave: History of the First Volunteer Battalion Hampshire Regiment
        1859-1889 (with notes for 1890-1903) (1905)

CEMETERY REGISTERS

Most cemetery registers are held by local authorities, but microform copies or photocopies of many of them are held at the record offices in Winchester, Portsmouth, and Newport. These are included in the parish listing. Indexes to many Isle of Wight cemetery registers have been published by David Quigley, and can be obtained from the Isle of Wight Family History Society.

See: D Jacobs: The Cemeteries of Hampshire: Their History and Records (1997)

MONUMENTAL INSCRIPTIONS

Monumental inscriptions inside most Hampshire churches are recorded in one or more of the following:

        A J Jewers: Heraldic Visitation of Hampshire Churches (British Library,
        Egerton Ms 2364)

        J B Whitmore: Hampshire Church Notes (a manuscript collection at the
        Society of Genealogists)

        Collectanea Topographica et Genealogica, Volumes 7 & 8 (1841, 1843)

        J S W Gibson: Monumental Inscriptions in Sixty Hampshire Churches (1958)

The book by Gibson lists the churches included in each of the above compilations.

Monumental inscriptions in the churchyards of all the ancient parishes of mainland Hampshire, and many of the modern parishes, have been recorded by members of the Hampshire Genealogical Society. Copies are being deposited in the HGS Library, the Hampshire Record Office, and the Society of Genealogists, though none of these yet has a complete set. Some have been published on microfiche. Copies of monumental inscriptions in many Isle of Wight churchyards are available at the Isle of Wight County Record Office, but some churchyards remain unrecorded.

SOCIETIES AND ORGANISATIONS

The Hampshire Genealogical Society (founded 1973) publishes a quarterly journal. Other publications include A Catalogue of Members' Interests (several editions), A Guide to Genealogical Sources for Hampshire (updated annually), Index to the 1851 Census of Hampshire and the Isle of Wight (68 volumes 1980-1990), Index to the 1891 Census of Hampshire (in progress), Hampshire 1851 Census Surnames Index (a master surname index to the 1851 census volumes), and various monumental inscription transcripts on microfiche. Projects include a marriage index and a burial index. A baptism index is planned.

The Isle of Wight Family History Society (founded 1985) publishes a quarterly journal. Other publications include Directory of Members' Interests (several editions) and 1891 Isle of Wight Census Name Index - West Wight (2 volumes 1993).

The Hampshire Archives Trust (situated at the Hampshire Record Office) surveys and lists collections of archives, and advises on their conservation and storage. The Trust organises exhibitions, conferences, and presentations, and publishes a twice-yearly newsletter and an annual report.

The Hampshire Record Office publishes a series of booklets and leaflets describing its own holdings. Subjects include Sources for Genealogy, Parish Registers, Maps and Plans, Quarter Sessions Records, Diocesan Records, Medieval Sources, and Estate Records of the Bishops of Winchester.

The Hampshire Archivists' Group has published guides to Poor Law Records (1970) and Education Records (1977). The Hampshire Record Office holds reference copies which have been updated to show current holdings at Winchester.

SERIAL PUBLICATIONS

Catalogues, calendars, and transcripts of Hampshire records have been published in several serial publications:

Hampshire Record Society	(1889-1899)
Southampton Record Society	(1905-1939)
Hampshire Record Series	(1976 to date)
Portsmouth Record Series	(1971 to date)
Southampton Record Series	(1951 to date)
Isle of Wight Record Series	(1981 to date)

Titles of interest to genealogists include:

C R Davey: The Hampshire Lay Subsidy Rolls 1586 (1981)

E Hughes & P White: The Hampshire Hearth Tax Assessment 1665 (1991)

A J Willis & A L Merson: A Calendar of Southampton Apprenticeship Registers (1968)

E Roberts & K Parker: Southampton Probate Inventories 1447-1575 (1992)

P D D Russell: The Hearth Tax Returns for the Isle of Wight 1664 to 1674 (1981)

Hampshire Papers (1991 to date), Portsmouth Papers (1967 to date) and Southampton Papers (1961-1978) are monographs on historical aspects of Hampshire.

ABBOTTS ANN St Mary (562) (Andover Union)
OR   C1561-1986 M1561-1985 B1561-1989 Bn1754-1820,1824-1944 HRO
BT   1780-1867 HRO (Mfm SLC)
Mfc   C1561-1986 M1561-1985 B1561-1989 Bn1754-1820 HRO
Mfm   C1561-1875 M1561-1875 B1561-1875 Bn1754-1820,1824-1876 HRO, SLC
Cop   C1561-1882 M1561-1857 B1561-1883 Bn1754-1820 (Ts,I) SG, HRO
      M1561-1837 HMI; M1561-1881 CMI; B1561-1837 HBI
      Extracts C1561-1877 IGI

ABBOTTS ANN (Independent) (Founded c1821, probably closed c1900)

ABBOTSTONE
      A decayed parish, consolidated with Itchen Stoke in the year 1589.

ALDERHOLT [Dorset] (Independent) - See FORDINGBRIDGE

ALDERSHOT St Michael the Archangel (665) (Farnham Union) (Chapelry of
      Crondall; separate parish 1828)
OR   C1571-1887 M1590-1893 B1581-1891 Bn1754-1757,1889-1892 SHC
BT   1780-1781,1783-1816,1818-1855,1857-1863 HRO (Mfm SLC)
Mfc   C1571-1887 M1590-1893 B1581-1891 Bn1754-1757 HRO
      C1571-1875 M1590-1879 B1581-1859,1870-1875 Bn1754-1757 SHC
Mfm   C1571-1875 M1590-1879 B1581-1859,1870-1878 Bn1754-1757 SLC
Cop   M1590-1812 Phillimore Vol 2 and Boyd; C1796-1833 (Ts) SHC
      M1754-1837 B1796-1859 (Ts,I) SG, HRO, SHC; M1590-1837 HMI
      M1590-1856 CMI; M1790-1812 Pallot; B1581-1837 HBI
      Extracts C1572-1879 M1594-1876 IGI

ALDERSHOT Ascension (Daughter church to St Michael, established 1945; replaced
      the chapels of St Aidan and St Alban)
OR   C1943+ M1945+ Inc

ALDERSHOT Holy Trinity (Formed 1878 from St Michael)
OR   C1878-1951 M1878-1966 Bn1878-1956 SHC
Mfc   C1878-1951 M1878-1966 HRO
Cop   M1878-1881 CMI

ALDERSHOT St Augustine (Mission church to St Michael; separate parish 1958)
OR   C1907-1966 M1944-1975 Bn1945-1958 SHC
Mfc   C1907-1966 M1944-1975 HRO

ALDERSHOT All Saints (Royal Garrison Church) (Established 1863)
OR   C1855-1974 B1856-1895 RACD; M1896+ Inc (The registers date from the
      establishment of the South Camp Garrison Church, and include entries for
      Presbyterians. Burials took place in Aldershot Military Cemetery. It is
      possible that an earlier marriage register exists)

ALDERSHOT North Camp Garrison Church, Marlborough Lines (within the parish
      of Farnborough) (Erected 1856, dedicated to St Alban 1949, demolished c1964)
OR   C1889-1964 Bn1933-1940,1946-1964 RACD

ALDERSHOT South Camp Garrison Church - See St Michael & St Sebastian

ALDERSHOT St George (Garrison Church) (Established 1892) (In 1973 the church was transferred to the Roman Catholics and became St Michael & St George)
OR   C1889-1973 M1894-1973 B1895-1911 at the church (Entries prior to 1893 are for the "Iron Church". Burials took place in Aldershot Military Cemetery)

ALDERSHOT Garrison (unspecified church)
OR   C1928-1951 RACD

ALDERSHOT Cambridge Military Hospital (St Luke's Chapel, closed 1996) & Louise Margaret Maternity Hospital (Closed 1995)
OR   C1925-1971 RACD (One marriage took place in St Luke's Chapel in 1994)

ALDERSHOT (Roman Catholic) St Michael & St Sebastian, Stanhope Lines, South Camp (Garrison Church) (Erected 1855 as a multidenominational church, Catholic from 1863; closed 1973, destroyed by fire c1982)
OR   C1855-1969 M1856-1871,1922-1949 B1855-1916 RCRO (Including C1859-1863 in the North Camp. Burials took place in Aldershot Military Cemetery)
Cop   C1855-1920 M1856-1871,1922-1939 B1855-1873 (Ts,I) SG

ALDERSHOT (Roman Catholic) St Patrick (St Louis prior to 1913), Marlborough Lines, North Camp (Garrison Church) (within the parish of Farnborough) (Services originally took place in the multidenominational North Camp Church; separate church erected c1913, closed 1973, destroyed by fire)
OR   C1863-1972 M1861-1971 B1861-1882 RCRO (For C1859-1863 see St Michael & St Sebastian. Burials took place in Aldershot Military Cemetery) M1934-1977 Inc of St Michael & St George, Aldershot
Cop   C1863-1935 M1861-1935 B1861-1882 (Ts,I) SG

ALDERSHOT (Roman Catholic) St Joseph, Queen's Road (Founded 1869 at Cambridge Road, present site 1872)
OR   C1869+ M1871+ B1869+ Inc

ALDERSHOT (Baptist) Upper Elms Road (Pastor appointed 1874, Church founded 1883, active)

ALDERSHOT (Particular Baptist) Trinity Chapel, Victoria Road (Opened 1862, now closed)

ALDERSHOT (Presbyterian) Victoria Road (Founded 1862, church erected 1864, closed 1976, now the New Testament Church of God) (Records 1864+ HRO)
OR   M1911-1974 HRO (133M89/1/1-4); C1865-1974 United Reformed Church History Society, but likely to be transferred to HRO

ALDERSHOT (Presbyterian, Church of Scotland) St Andrew (Garrison Church) (Presbyterians attended the Iron Church at Thorn Hill and the North Camp Church; in 1866 the Iron Church was moved to Cranbrook Road (now Queen's Avenue) and became exclusively Presbyterian in 1893; present church erected 1927)
OR   C1872+ M1950+ B1872-1946 Inc (Burials took place in Aldershot Military Cemetery) (For earlier Presbyterian C and B see Aldershot All Saints)

ALDERSHOT Wesleyan Circuit (Formed 1857 to serve the camp and town; became part of Aldershot & Farnham Circuit in 1891; a separate circuit continued to serve the army. Included chapels at Aldershot and Farnborough) (Records 1881+ HRO)

ALDERSHOT (Wesleyan) Grosvenor Road (Aldershot Wesleyan Circuit, Aldershot & Farnham Wesleyan Circuit from 1891) (Founded 1857 in Cambridge Road, Grosvenor Road Chapel erected 1876, closed 1988 and amalgamated with Stone Street) (Records 1891+ HRO)

ALDERSHOT (Wesleyan) West End (Aldershot Wesleyan Circuit, Aldershot & Farnham Wesleyan Circuit from 1891) (Existed by 1880, closed c1977, demolished) (Records 1909+ HRO)

ALDERSHOT Primitive Methodist Circuit (The Bagshot Mission existed by 1858, became Guildford Circuit in 1871, and was renamed Aldershot Circuit in 1879. A new Guildford Circuit separated from this in 1883. Became part of Aldershot & Camberley Methodist Circuit in 1933. Included chapels at Aldershot, Cove, and Farnborough. Possibly included Binsted) (Records 1858+ HRO)

ALDERSHOT (Primitive Methodist) Rotunda Church, Victoria Road (Guildford Primitive Methodist Circuit, Aldershot Primitive Methodist Circuit from 1879) (Founded by 1873, chapel erected 1876, closed and demolished)

ALDERSHOT (Primitive Methodist) Ebenezer Chapel, Ash Road (Guildford Primitive Methodist Circuit, Aldershot Primitive Methodist Circuit from 1879) (Founded by 1876, chapel c1886, moved to Stone Street c1956, active) (Records 1951+ HRO)

ALDERSHOT (Reformed Episcopal) St George's Road (Founded 1901, amalgamated with the Rotunda Primitive Methodist Church in 1932)

ALDERSHOT (Brethren, now Evangelical) Park Hall Church, Lower Farnham Road (Moved to the former Roman Catholic church of St Saviour in 1994, active)

ALDERSHOT (Latter-day Saints) (Records c1900+ in Church archives at SLC)
Mfm   Membership records c1900-1944 SLC

ALDERSHOT (Jewish) (Worship at 14 High Street by 1867, temporary Synagogue for military personnel established at Barrack Road by 1899)

ALDERSHOT Redan Road Cemetery (Records - Rushmoor Borough Council)
OR   B1861+ Borough Council; B1870-1930 (consecrated) B1875-1928 (unconsecrated) (Ministers' registers) HRO (23M74/HY/3b,4-16)
Mfc   B1861-1951 HRO

ALDERSHOT Military Cemetery (Established 1856)
OR   B1856+ were registered at All Saints, St George, St Michael & St Sebastian, St Patrick, and St Andrew
       B1886+ Aldershot Garrison Adjutant
       Burial notes 1870-1955 Aldershot Military Historical Trust
Cop   B1875-1885 plus applications for memorials 1870-1885 (Ts,A) SG, HRO, SHC

ALDERSHOT & FARNHAM Wesleyan Circuit (Formed 1891 by union of the Aldershot and Farnham Circuits; became part of Aldershot & Camberley Methodist Circuit in 1933. Included chapels at Aldershot, Crondall, Ewshot, Farnborough, and Rowledge) (Records 1891+ HRO)

ALRESFORD - See NEW ALRESFORD, OLD ALRESFORD

ALTON St Lawrence (2,742) (Alton Union)
OR   C1615-1960 M1629-1942 B1616-1975 Bn1809-1851,1914-1929,1971-1997 HRO
BT   1677,1780-1785,1787-1848,1850-1861 HRO (Mfm SLC)
Mfc C1615-1875 M1629-1902 B1616-1901 HRO
Mfm C1615-1875 M1629-1876 B1616-1876 HRO, SLC
Cop C1615-1711 M1629-1711 B1616-1711 (Ms,I) HRO, Inc
     C1711-1757 M1711-1753 B1711-1759 (Ts,I) SG, HRO, Inc (Index reported to be defective); Card index to M1754-1837, CB c1750-1850 Inc
     M1629-1837 HMI; M1654-1881 CMI; B1616-1837 HBI

ALTON All Saints (Chapelry established 1875)
OR   C1875-1973 M1875-1977 B1882-1959 Bn1875-1990 HRO
Mfc C1875-1973 M1875-1977 B1882-1959 HRO
Cop M1875-1881 CMI

ALTON (Roman Catholic) St Mary, Normandy Street (Founded 1911 at Albert Road, present site 1938)
OR   C1911+ M1914+ B1911+ Inc

ALTON (Society of Friends) Monthly Meeting (see also Bramshott) (Established 1668; became part of the Alton, Southampton, & Poole Monthly Meeting in 1870. Comprised meetings at Alton, Alresford, Andover, Basingstoke, Baughurst, Bramshott, Crondall, Whitchurch, and Winchester) (Records 1659+ HRO)
OR   Z1728-1837 M1694-1837 B1728-1837 PRO (RG 6/197,277,351,396, 397,579,1006,1029,1030)
     Z1837-1877 B1825-1834,1838-1881 HRO (24M54/62-68,247,248,266)
Mfm Z1728-1837 M1694-1837 B1728-1837 HRO
Cop Index see Hampshire Quarterly Meeting; M1694-1837 HMI; B1728-1837 HBI

ALTON (Baptist) (Existed by 1889, new chapel erected 1891, active)

ALTON (Particular Baptist) - See ROPLEY

ALTON (Independent, later United Reformed) Normandy Street (Founded 1662, closed 1994) (Records 1807+ HRO)
OR   C1788-1837 B1834-1835 PRO (RG 4/397)
     C1788-1899,1909-1971 M1837-1844,1949-1983,1990 B1834-1835, 1838-1844,1967-1977 D1809-1899 HRO (31M93/2,3,54,55, 89M86/1,2)
     (Entries prior to 1837 are copies; D are in membership lists in 31M93/2)
Mfc M1949-1983 HRO
Mfm C1788-1837 B1834-1835 PRO, HRO, SLC
Cop M1837-1847 CMI; B1834-1835 D1809-1837 HBI; Extracts C1788-1837 IGI

ALTON Wesleyan Circuit (Formed 1860 from Guildford Circuit; became part of Surrey & North Hampshire Wesleyan Mission in 1900; re-established 1917. Included chapels at Alton, Binsted, East Worldham, Farringdon, Froxfield, Froyle, Holybourne, and Liss) (Records 1923+ HRO)
OR   C1845-1981 HRO (80M78/NMR5-6)

ALTON (Wesleyan) High Street (Guildford Wesleyan Circuit, Alton Wesleyan Circuit from 1860, Surrey & North Hampshire Wesleyan Mission from 1900, Alton Wesleyan Circuit from 1917) (Minister appointed 1844, chapel erected 1846, new church erected 1977, active) (Records 1876+ HRO)
OR   M1928-1976 HRO (80M78/NMR1-4)
Mfc   M1928-1976 HRO

ALTON (Wesleyan) Beech (Surrey & North Hampshire Wesleyan Mission, Alton Wesleyan Circuit from 1917) (Established c1902, closed by 1939) (Records 1902+ HRO)

ALTON Cemetery (Records - East Hampshire District Council)
Mfc   B1856-1995 HRO (Includes index)

ALTON Union Workhouse
OR   D1849-1915 HRO (PL5/2/62-63)
       Z1866-1931 (closed until 2007) HRO; D1915-1942 (closed until 2018) HRO
       C1923-1925 HRO (with the parish records of St Lawrence)

ALTON, SOUTHAMPTON, & POOLE (Society of Friends) Monthly Meeting (Formed 1870 by union of the Alton and the Poole/Southampton Monthly Meetings) (Records 1870+ HRO)
OR   Z1869-1909 B1867-1935 HRO (24M54/249,250,259-265)

ALVERSTOKE St Mary (12,637 including Gosport) (Alverstoke Incorporation) (See also Anglesey, Elson, Forton, Gosport)
OR   C1559-1995 M1559-1996 B1560-1975,1983-1998 Bn1948-1999 PCRO
BT   1780-1782,1784-1854,1857-1875 HRO (Mfm SLC)
Mfc   C1559-1975 M1559-1834,1837-1992 B1560-1975 HRO, PCRO; C1559-1738, 1820-1911 M1559-1710,1754-1783,1819-1905 B1560-1714, 1813-1875 SG
Mfm C1559-1875 M1559-1875 B1560-1876 PCRO, SLC
       C1559-1875 M1559-1893 B1560-1843 HRO
Cop C1559-1579 M1559-1579 B1560-1569 (surnames only) (Pc of a printed book at the British Library) SG; Index to PR c1559-1842 (A-Ferg only; possibly defective) (Ms) HRO (on film), PCRO (CHU42/1F/1); M1780-1837 Pallot CMB 1560-1686 (Ms,A) PCRO (CHU42/1F/2); M1813-1840 CMI C1559-1850 M1559-1686,1711-1777 B1560-1686,1711-1754 PCI M1559-1837 HMI; B1560-1837 HBI; Extracts C1750-1875 M1559-1875 IGI

ALVERSTOKE St Faith (Mission church)
OR   C1902-1956 PCRO
Mfc   C1902-1956 HRO, PCRO

ALVERSTOKE St Luke's Chapel, Royal Naval Hospital, Haslar (Established 1756) and Royal Naval Cemetery, Clayhall
OR   Royal Naval Hospital, Haslar
BT   1831-1853,1855-1882 HRO (Mfm SLC)
Cop   C1829-1862 B1827-1852 (Ts,I) SG; B1827-1837 HBI
       C1829-1862 B1827-1852 (Ts) PCRO (CHU42/11L/1), (Ms,I) HGS
       Index to B c1856-c1994 in Clayhall Cemetery (Ts) PCRO

ALVERSTOKE (Wesleyan) Children's Home
OR   C1898-1924 HRO (69M73/NMR20)
Mfc   C1898-1924 HRO
Pc   C1887-1983 HRO (Photocopy 699)

ALVERSTOKE Cemetery, Ann's Hill Road (Records - Gosport Borough Council)
Mfc   B1855-1953 HRO

ALVERSTOKE Workhouse (Alverstoke Incorporation)
OR   No registers survive. Other records at HRO.

AMBERSHAM - See STEEP

AMPFIELD St Mark (Formed 1841 from Hursley; see also Chandlers Ford)
OR   C1841-1984 M1842-1993 B1841-1951 Bn1842-1973 HRO
BT   1841-1874 HRO (Mfm SLC)
Mfc   C1841-1984 M1842-1984 B1841-1951 HRO
Cop   M1842-1881 CMI

AMPFIELD (Primitive Methodist) (Romsey Primitive Methodist Circuit) (Chapel erected 1897, closed c1946) (Records 1897+ HRO)

AMPORT St Mary (713) (Andover Union)
OR   C1665-1902 M1665-1975 B1666-1994 Bn1754-1812,1937-1955 HRO
       (Burials 1680-1761 are a 19th century copy from a register now missing)
BT   1782-1785,1787-1811,1813-1838,1840-1858,1860-1861,1867-1869 HRO
       (Mfm SLC)
Mfc   C1665-1902 M1665-1975 B1666-1994 Bn1754-1812 HRO
Mfm   C1665-1876 M1665-1876 B1666-1876 Bn1754-1812 HRO, SLC
Cop   M1665-1812 Phillimore Vol 2 and Boyd; M1665-1837 HMI
       C1665-1772 M1665-1751 B1666-1681 (Ts) HRO; M1665-1881 CMI
       M1790-1812 Pallot; B1666-1837 HBI; Extracts C1665-1876 IGI

AMPORT (Wesleyan) (Society existed by 1829, no references located after 1851)

AMPORT (Primitive Methodist) (Andover Primitive Methodist Circuit) (Chapel erected 1846) (Records 1846+ HRO)

ANDOVER St Mary (4,748) (Andover Union) (See also Charlton, Foxcott, Hatherden, Smannell)

OR   C1588-1996 M1587-1996 B1588-1995 Bn1754-1769,1853-1900,1920-1997 HRO

BT   1703,1780-1823,1826-1827,1830-1831,1841-1865,1872-1874 HRO (Mfm SLC)

Mfc   C1588-1981 M1587-1980 B1588-1983 HRO
      C1588-1853 M1587-1837 B1588-1876 SG

Mfm   C1588-1875 M1587-1875 B1588-1876 Bn1754-1769 HRO, SLC

Cop   Index to C1798-1914 M1781-1919 (males) B1784-1843 (Ms) HRO
      M1769-1781 Bn1769-1781 (Ts,I) HRO; M1587-1837 HMI; M1687-1881 CMI
      B1588-1837 HBI; Extracts C1700-1812 (BT) IGI; Extracts M1692-1812 IGI

ANDOVER St Michael & All Angels (Formed 1955 from St Mary)

OR   C1937-1982 M1956-1982 Bn1956-1984 HRO

Mfc   C1937-1982 M1956-1982 HRO

ANDOVER (Roman Catholic) St John the Baptist (Mission founded 1886, church in Weyhill Road opened 1921, present church opened 1958)

OR   1913+ Inc

ANDOVER (Society of Friends) (Meeting House erected 1713, sold 1880, burial ground attached) - See ALTON

ANDOVER (Particular Baptist) High Street, now Charlton Road (Founded 1824, chapels erected 1824 & 1866, active) (Records 1825+ HRO)

OR   Adult baptisms 1815,1839,1858-1893,1962-1969 D1830-1840, 1853-1858, 1864-1893,1955-1969 HRO (The entries occur in membership lists 1838-1893,1911,1918,1954-1969 in 122M87/1-3,8)

ANDOVER (Baptist) Smannell (Founded c1835)

ANDOVER (Independent, now United Reformed) East Street (Founded 1662, active) (Records 1814+ HRO)

OR   C1739-1837 B1807-1837 PRO (RG 4/709,710,2298) (Gap 1790-1806; includes dates of parents' marriages)
      C1871-1887 M1871-1875 B1872-1887 D1922-1970 (plus a few deaths 1819-1877) HRO (42M83/3) (The death entries occur in membership lists 1807-1889,1922-1977 in 42M83/1,2,3,32)
      C cert counterfoils 1923-1954, D certs 1838-1883 HRO

Mfm   C1739-1837 B1807-1837 PRO, HRO, SLC

Cop   B1807-1837 HBI; Extracts C1739-1837 IGI

ANDOVER (Independent, now United Reformed) Harroway Road, Picket Piece (Founded 1908, branch of Andover until 1957 when name changed to Picket Piece, active) (Records 1923+ HRO, with East Street records)

ANDOVER Wesleyan Circuit (Formed 1818 from Winchester Circuit; became Andover Bridge Street Circuit in 1932. Included chapels at Andover, Hurstbourne Priors, Longparish, Nether Wallop, Overton, St Mary Bourne, Thruxton, Vernham Dean, Wherwell, Whitchurch; possibly included Faccombe) (Records 1817+ HRO)

OR   C1815-1837 PRO (RG 4/1390); C1840-1934 HRO (96M72/NMC/R1-4) (Includes C1814-1820,1846-1854 in Whitchurch area, C1806-1813 at Southampton)

Mfc   C1840-1934 HRO (Includes Whitchurch & Southampton entries as above)

Mfm   C1815-1837 PRO, HRO, SLC

Cop   Extracts C1815-1837 IGI

ANDOVER (Wesleyan) Winchester Street, Bridge Street (Andover Wesleyan Circuit) (Meetings from 1761, room registered 1780, Winchester Street Chapel erected 1824, replaced by Bridge Street Chapel 1906) (Records 1815+ HRO)

ANDOVER (Wesleyan) Wildhern (Andover Wesleyan Circuit) (Founded 1818, probably purchased by Primitive Methodists) (Records 1818 [only] HRO)

ANDOVER Primitive Methodist Circuit (Formed 1837 from Shefford Circuit; renamed Andover East Street Circuit 1932. Included chapels at Amport, Andover, Appleshaw, Ashmansworth, Combe, Faccombe, Goodworth Clatford, Hurstbourne Tarrant, Kings Somborne, Leckford, Longstock, St Mary Bourne, Stockbridge, Upper Clatford, Vernham Dean, Weyhill, Wherwell) (Records 1837+ HRO)

OR   C1834-1951 HRO (96M72/NMC/R7-9) (C1904-1951 are in the register of Ludgershall [Wilts] chapel)

Mfc   C1834-1873 HRO

ANDOVER (Primitive Methodist) East Street (Andover Primitive Methodist Circuit) (Chapel erected 1838, closed 1967, demolished) (Records 1907+ HRO)

ANDOVER (Primitive Methodist) Charlton (Andover Primitive Methodist Circuit) (Meetings from c1838, Chapel erected 1855, closed 1969) (Records 1932+ HRO)

OR   C1961-1968 HRO (96M72/NMC/R16)

Mfc   C1961-1968 HRO

ANDOVER (Primitive Methodist) Wildhern (Andover Primitive Methodist Circuit) (Existed by 1871) (Records 1871+ HRO)

ANDOVER (Elim Pentecostal Church)

OR   M1987 HRO (One entry only) (31M92/1)

ANDOVER Cemetery (Records - Test Valley Borough Council)

Mfc   B1868-1970 HRO (Includes index 1916-1976)

ANMORE (Particular Baptist) - See HAMBLEDON

ANDOVER Union Workhouse

OR   No registers survive. Other records at HRO.

ANGLESEY St Mark (Chapelry of Alverstoke, established 1844, demolished 1911)

OR   None. Burials in Anglesey churchyard were registered at Alverstoke.

APPLESHAW (Not dedicated) (356) (Andover Union) (Chapelry of Amport; separate parish 1864)
OR   C1695-1920 M1709-1979 B1744-1995 Bn1824-1940 HRO
       (Gaps in C 1745-1779, M 1709-1718, B 1772-1783)
BT   1781-1796,1798-1831,1833-1867 HRO (Mfm SLC)
Mfc   C1695-1920 M1709-1979 B1744-1995 HRO
Mfm   C1695-1920 M1709-1979 B1744-1816 Bn1824-1940 HRO
Cop   M1709-1837 HMI; M1756-1882 CMI; B1744-1837 HBI

APPLESHAW (Primitive Methodist) (Andover Primitive Methodist Circuit) (Chapel erected 1869) (Records 1900+ HRO)

APPLESHAW Cemetery (Records 1889+ Appleshaw Parish Council)

ARNEWOOD (Baptist) - See HORDLE

ASHE Holy Trinity & St Andrew (146) (Whitchurch Union)
OR   C1607-1939 M1606-1989 B1618-1991 Bn1824-1992 HRO (The registers
       begin in 1729 but include a transcript, made in 1732, of an earlier register)
BT   1780,1782-1833,1835-1837,1842,1844,1846-1871 HRO (Mfm SLC)
Mfc   C1607-1939 M1606-1989 B1618-1991 HRO
Mfm   C1607-1876 M1606-1876 B1618-1812 HRO, SLC
Cop   C1607-1887 M1606-1886 B1618-1887 Printed in "A History of Esse or Ashe,
       Hampshire" by Rev F W Thoyts (1888); M1606-1836 HMI; M1606-1892 CMI
       Index to C1607-1887 M1606-1886 B1618-1887 (Ms) SG, (Ts) HRO
       Index to C1607-1887 HGS; B1618-1837 HBI; Extracts M1606-1719 IGI

ASHFORD HILL St Paul - See KINGSCLERE WOODLANDS

ASHFORD HILL (Methodist, Primitive Methodist) - See KINGSCLERE

ASHLEY St Mary (93) (Stockbridge Union) (Redundant 1976)
OR   C1725-1980 M1732-1941 B1725-1970 Bn1826-1953 HRO
BT   1780,1782-1785,1787,1789-1801,1803-1804,1806,1808-1811,1813-1856,
       1858-1874 HRO (Mfm SLC)
Mfc   C1725-1980 M1732-1941 B1725-1970 HRO
Mfm   C1725-1811 M1732-1812 B1725-1811 HRO
Cop   M1732-1837 HMI; M1732-1889 CMI; B1725-1837 HBI

ASHLEY (MILTON) St Peter (Daughter church to Milton)
OR   M1957-1988 Bn1957-1993 HRO
Mfc   M1957-1988 HRO

ASHLEY (MILTON) (Baptist) - See MILTON

ASHMANSWORTH St James (222) (Kingsclere Union) (Chapelry of East Woodhay; separate parish 1884)

OR   C1811-1965 M1813-1970 B1811-1993 Bn1814-1818,1824-1939 (plus copy burial register 1841-1857) HRO (Earlier registers destroyed by fire in 1810)

BT   1810,1812-1822,1825-1840,1842-1844,1846,1848-1849,1851-1854,1856-1867 HRO (Mfm SLC)

Mfc   C1811-1965 M1813-1970 B1811-1993 SG, HRO

Mfm   C1811-1965 M1813-1836 B1811-1812 Bn1814-1818,1824-1939 HRO

Cop   M1813-1836 HMI; M1813-1881 CMI; M1813-1836 Boyd; B1811-1837 HBI

ASHMANSWORTH (Primitive Methodist) (Andover Primitive Methodist Circuit, Hurstbourne Tarrant Primitive Methodist Circuit from 1910) (Chapels erected 1845 & 1888, closed 1964) (Records 1939+ HRO)

AVINGTON St Mary (191) (Winchester Union)

OR   C1610-1920 M1611-1981 B1609-1991 Bn1754-1811,1824-1986 (plus copy register 1841-1857) HRO (Gaps in C 1660-1673, M 1656-1686, B 1660-1671)

BT   1780-1781,1783-1787,1789-1794,1797,1804-1805,1807-1858,1862-1864 HRO (Mfm SLC)

Mfc   C1610-1920 M1611-1981 B1609-1991 Bn1754-1811 SG, HRO

Mfm   C1610-1920 M1611-1837 B1609-1812 Bn1754-1811 HRO

Cop   M1754-1811 (Ms,I) HRO (HGS holds index only)
       M1611-1837 HMI; M1611-1913 CMI; B1609-1837 HBI

AWBRIDGE All Saints (Formed 1877 from Michelmersh & Romsey)

OR   C1877-1970 M1878-1982 Bn1877-1963 HRO; B1878+ Inc

Mfc   C1877-1970 M1878-1982 HRO

Cop   M1878-1888 CMI

AWBRIDGE (Independent) (Founded 1819)

AWBRIDGE (Wesleyan) (Chapel erected 1847; 1851 Religious Census)

BADDESLEY - See NORTH BADDESLEY, SOUTH BADDESLEY

BAGSHOT [Surrey] Primitive Methodist Mission - See ALDERSHOT Primitive Methodist Circuit

BARTLEY (Particular Baptist) - See ELING

BARTON ON SEA (Wesleyan) - See MILTON

BARTON STACEY All Saints (623) (Andover Union)

OR   C1713-1986 M1713-1985 B1713-1985 Bn1824-1979 HRO

BT   1780-1802,1804,1806-1807,1809-1843,1845-1870 HRO (Mfm SLC)

Mfc   C1713-1986 M1713-1985 B1713-1985 HRO
       C1713-1861 M1713-1838 B1713-1896 SG

Mfm   C1713-1861 M1713-1838 B1713-1896 HRO

Cop   C1713-1812 M1713-1750 B1713-1812 (Ts,I) HRO (HGS holds index only)
       M1713-1837 HMI; M1713-1884 CMI; B1713-1837 HBI

BARTON STACEY St Peter (Garrison church)
OR   C1949-1960 RACD

BARTON STACEY (Primitive Methodist) (Micheldever Primitive Methodist Circuit)
(Chapel erected 1844, closed c1942) (Records 1953+ HRO)

BASING - See OLD BASING

BASINGSTOKE St Michael (3,581) (Basingstoke Union)
OR   C1638-1978 M1638-1985 B1638-1919 Bn1754-1786,1807-1995 HRO
BT   1701,1708,1780-1838,1840-1863 HRO (Mfm SLC)
Mfc C1638-1978 M1638-1985 B1638-1919 Bn1754-1786 HRO
     C1638-1916 M1638-1921 B1638-1919 Bn1754-1786 SG
Mfm C1638-1875 M1638-1875 B1638-1875 Bn1754-1786,1807-1872 HRO, SLC
Cop M1638-1812 Phillimore Vol 5 and Boyd
     C1638-1812 M1807-1812 B1638-1812 (Ts,I) SG, HRO
     C1675-1735,1798-1812 M1807-1812 B1638-1687,1739-1812 (Ms, Ts) HRO
     M1638-1837 HMI; M1813-1882 CMI; M1790-1837 Pallot
     B1638-1837 HBI; Extracts C1638-1812 M1838-1875 IGI

BASINGSTOKE All Saints (Daughter church)
OR   C1917-1971 M1917-1988 Bn1917-1986 HRO
Mfc C1917-1971 M1917-1988 HRO

BASINGSTOKE Christ the King, Brighton Hill (Daughter church)
OR   Bn1977-1992 HRO; C1972+ M1977+ Inc

BASINGSTOKE St Peter, South Ham (Daughter church)
OR   C1958-1969 M1965-1976 Bn1965-1988 HRO
Mfc C1958-1969 M1965-1976 HRO

BASINGSTOKE (Roman Catholic) Holy Ghost (Founded 1877; the area was
previously served from Woolhampton, Berkshire)
OR   1881+ Inc

BASINGSTOKE (Society of Friends) Wote Street (Meeting House erected 1828 on
the site of an earlier one; burial ground attached) - See ALTON, BRAMSHOTT

BASINGSTOKE (Particular Baptist) Ebenezer Chapel, Church Street (Meetings from
1825, chapel opened 1868)

BASINGSTOKE (Baptist) Sarum Hill (Chapel erected 1908)

BASINGSTOKE (Independent, now United Reformed) London Street (Foundation
date claimed as 1663, but probably founded 1686, Cross Street Chapel opened
1695, London Street Chapel erected 1710, active)
OR   C1739-1837 D1711-1727,1779,1791,1793 PRO (RG 4/1071,2106)
Mfm C1739-1837 D1711-1727,1779,1791,1793 PRO, HRO, SLC
Cop D1711-1727,1779,1791,1793 HBI; Extracts C1739-1837 IGI

BASINGSTOKE (Independent) New Road (Erected c1846, probably closed by 1900)

BASINGSTOKE (Independent) Worting Town End (A branch of Basingstoke 1862-1961)

BASINGSTOKE (Independent) May Street (Founded 1913)

BASINGSTOKE (Countess of Huntingdon's Connexion) Wote Street (Founded 1755)
OR   C1784-1836 B1784-1788,1790,1795 PRO (RG 4/398,714)
Mfm   C1784-1836 B1784-1788,1790,1795 PRO, HRO, SLC
Cop   B1784-1788,1790,1795 HBI; Extracts C1784-1836 IGI

BASINGSTOKE Wesleyan Circuit (Formed 1872; became part of the Surrey & North Hampshire Wesleyan Mission in 1900; re-established 1917. Included chapels at Basingstoke, Bramley, Cliddesden, Greywell, Odiham, and Wootton St Lawrence) (Records 1924+ HRO)

BASINGSTOKE (Wesleyan) Church Street (Basingstoke Wesleyan Circuit, Surrey & North Hampshire Wesleyan Mission from 1900, Basingstoke Wesleyan Circuit from 1917) (Chapels erected 1875, 1906, St Andrew 1965, active) (Records 1924+ HRO)
OR   M1903-1965 HRO (57M77/NMR1-6)
Mfc   M1903-1965 HRO

BASINGSTOKE (Wesleyan) Kempshott Village (Surrey & North Hampshire Wesleyan Mission, Basingstoke Wesleyan Circuit from 1917) (Erected 1913, active) (Records 1912+ HRO)

BASINGSTOKE Primitive Methodist Circuit (Formed 1848 from Micheldever Circuit. Included chapels at Basingstoke, Crookham, Dummer, Fleet, Hartley Wintney, Newnham, Odiham, Old Basing, Rotherwick, Sherfield on Loddon, and Wootton St Lawrence) (Records 1835+ HRO)

BASINGSTOKE (Primitive Methodist) Flaxfield Road, later Sarum Hill (Basingstoke Primitive Methodist Circuit) (Chapels 1847 & 1902, active) (Records 1883+ HRO)

BASINGSTOKE South View Cemetery (Records - Basingstoke & Deane Council)
Mfc   B1858-1994 HRO

BASINGSTOKE Worting Road Cemetery (Records - Basingstoke & Deane Council)
Mfc   B1914-1963 HRO

BASINGSTOKE Union Workhouse (situated in Old Basing parish)
OR   No registers survive. Other records at HRO.

BASSETT St Michael & All Angels (Chapelry of North Stoneham)
OR   C1899-1968 M1918-1978 Bn1961-1986 HRO
Mfc   C1899-1968 M1918-1978 HRO, SCA

BATTS CORNER (Bible Christian) - See BINSTED

BAUGHURST St Stephen (491) (Kingclere Union) (See also North Tadley)
OR   C1678-1953 M1678-1992 B1678-1898 Bn1754-1812,1938-1977 HRO
BT   1780-1811,1813-1865 HRO (Mfm SLC)
Mfc   C1678-1953 M1678-1992 B1678-1898 Bn1754-1812 HRO
Mfm   C1678-1811 M1678-1812 B1678-1811 Bn1754-1812 HRO
Cop   M1678-1812 Phillimore Vol 5 and Boyd, M1678-1836 HMI
      C1678-1837 M1678-1836 B1678-1837 (Ts,I) SG, HRO, Inc
      M1678-1881 CMI; M1790-1812 Pallot; B1678-1837 HBI

BAUGHURST (Society of Friends) - See ALTON

BAUGHURST (Baptist) (Existed by 1878, now closed)
OR   Church record books 1909-1940 Angus Library, Regent's Park College, Oxford

BAUGHURST (Wesleyan) (Newbury Wesleyan Circuit) (Chapel erected 1795,
probably closed by 1895)

BAUGHURST (Primitive Methodist) (Reading Primitive Methodist Circuit,
Silchester Primitive Methodist Circuit) (Chapels erected 1845 & 1872, closed
c1986) (Records 1872+ BRO)

BAUGHURST (Primitive Methodist) Haughurst Hill (Silchester Primitive Methodist
Circuit) (Founded 1905, active) (Records 1905+ BRO)

BAYBRIDGE (Primitive Methodist) - See OWSLEBURY

BEAULIEU The Blessed Virgin and Holy Child (1,298) (New Forest Union)
OR   C1653-1992 M1654-1994 B1653-1993 Bn1754-1813,1838-1839,1847-1986
      HRO (Gap in burials 1735-1745)
BT   None
Mfc   C1653-1992 M1654-1994 B1653-1895 Bn1754-1813 HRO
Mfm   C1653-1812 M1654-1812 B1653-1812 Bn1754-1812 HRO
Cop   C1653-1754 M1654-1745 B1653-1734 (Ts,I) SG (Rearranged chronologically
      from an alphabetical transcript, but not collated with the original register)
      C1654-1705 M1654-1753 B1654-1705 (Ts,A) HRO
      M1654-1837 HMI; M1654-1881 CMI; B1653-1837 HBI

BEAULIEU St John the Evangelist, Park (District established 1906)
OR   C1906-1962 HRO
Mfc   C1906-1962 HRO

BEAULIEU Cemetery
OR   B1963-1982 HRO
Mfc   B1963-1982 HRO

BEAUWORTH St James (Chapelry of Cheriton; separate parish 1879)
OR   C1841-1991 M1841-1964 B1842-1991 Bn1841-1982 HRO
BT   1841-1868,1870-1872 HRO (Mfm SLC)
Mfc   C1841-1991 M1841-1964 B1842-1992 HRO
Mfm   C1841-1876 M1841-1872 B1842-1879 Bn1841-1879 HRO, SLC
Cop   M1841-1883 CMI; Extracts C1841-1876 M1841-1872 IGI

BEDHAMPTON St Thomas a Becket (537) (Havant Union) (See also Cowplain, Leigh Park)

OR   C1688-1987 M1689-1989 B1688-1982 Bn1948-1990 PCRO
BT   1780-1781,1783-1866 HRO (Mfm SLC)
Mfc   C1688-1972 M1689-1977 B1688-1982 HRO, PCRO
Mfm C1688-1875 M1689-1875 B1688-1875 PCRO, SLC
Cop   C1688-1902 M1689-1837 B1688-1886 PCI
       M1689-1837 HMI; M1689-1882 CMI; B1688-1837 HBI
       Extracts C1688-1876 M1689-1759,1813-1876 IGI

BEDHAMPTON (Independent) (Founded c1844; 1851 Religious Census; no other references located)

BEDHAMPTON (Primitive Methodist) (Portsmouth Primitive Methodist First Circuit) (Opened 1875) (Records 1906+ PCRO)

BEECH (Wesleyan) - See ALTON

BEECH HILL St Mary the Virgin (Formed 1868 from the Berkshire portion of Stratfield Saye)

OR   M1868-1978 BRO; C1868+ B1868+ Bn1868+ Inc
Mfc   M1868-1978 BRO (also on Mfm)
Cop   M1868-1883 CMI

BEECH HILL (Baptist) (Founded 1796, active)

BENTLEY St Mary (728) (Alton Union)

OR   C1539-1974 M1541-1958 B1538-1943 Bn1754-1786,1823-1960 HRO
BT   1692-1693,1717,1729,1800-1818,1820-1862 HRO (Mfm SLC)
Mfc   C1539-1928 M1541-1958 B1538-1943 Bn1754-1786 HRO
Mfm C1539-1885 M1541-1875 B1538-1874 Bn1754-1786,1823-1875 HRO, SLC
       C1539-1885 M1541-1837 B1538-1874 Bn1754-1786 SHC
Cop   M1541-1812 Phillimore Vol 9 and Boyd
       C1539-1838 M1541-1837 B1538-1838 Bn1823-1838 (Ts,I) SG
       C1539-1812 B1538-1812 Bn1754-1786 (Ts) HRO, Inc
       Index to C1539-1838 M1541-1837 B1538-1838 Bn1823-1838 (Ts) HRO
       Index to C1539-1812 M1541-1812 B1538-1812 Inc; C1846-1885 (Ts,I) HRO
       Index to C1813-1838 M1813-1838 B1813-1838 Bn1823-1838 HGS
       M1541-1837 HMI; M1541-1881 CMI; M1790-1812 Pallot; B1538-1837 HBI
       Extracts C1539-1877 M1541-1875 IGI

BENTLEY (Wesleyan) (PO Directory 1855, no later references located)

BENTLEY (Bible Christian) Zion Chapel (Farnham Bible Christian Circuit, Crondall Bible Christian Circuit from 1863) (Existed by 1836, probably closed by 1939) (Records 1855+ HRO)

BENTWORTH St Mary (592) (Alton Union)

OR   C1599-1920 M1603-1989 B1599-1888 Bn1754-1810,1824-1972 HRO
       (Gaps 1599-1603, 1687-1695)
BT   1780-1808,1810-1866 HRO (Mfm SLC)
Mfc   C1599-1920 M1603-1989 B1599-1888 Bn1754-1810 HRO
Mfm C1599-1812 M1603-1753 B1599-1812 HRO
Cop   M1603-1837 Phillimore Vol 11 and Boyd; M1603-1837 HMI
       M1603-1881 CMI; M1790-1837 Pallot; B1559-1837 HBI

BENTWORTH (Independent) (Chapel c1825, church founded 1896, closed by 1929)

BIGHTON All Saints (290) (Alresford Union)

OR   C1573-1924 M1581-1980 B1580-1992 Bn1824-1957 HRO
       (Several gaps prior to 1688; only two marriages before 1589)
BT   1780-1868 HRO (Mfm SLC)
Mfc   C1573-1924 M1581-1980 B1580-1992 HRO
Mfm C1573-1876 M1581-1837 B1580-1812 HRO, SLC
Cop   C1573-1804 M1581-1754 B1580-1805 (Ms & Ts,I) HRO
       M1756-1812 Bn1756-1812 (Ts,I) HRO, HGS; M1581-1837 HMI
       M1581-1886 CMI; B1580-1837 HBI; Extracts M1581-1837 IGI

BIGHTON (Primitive Methodist) (Winchester Primitive Methodist Circuit) (Chapel established 1888 in part of a malthouse, probably ceased c1915)

BINSTED Holy Cross (960) (Alton Union) (See also Rowledge) (Chapelry of Alton; separate parish 1853)

OR   C1653-1964 M1653-1966 B1653-1860 Bn1754-1770,1823-1837,1917-1959
       HRO (The BTs for 1811-1812 contain marriages which are not in the register)
BT   1780-1782,1784-1786,1788-1805,1807,1809-1867,1872,1887 HRO
       (Mfm SLC)
Mfc   C1653-1964 M1653-1945 B1653-1685,1813-1860 Bn1754-1770 HRO
Mfm C1653-1864 M1653-1837 B1653-1860 Bn1754-1770,1823-1876 HRO, SLC
Pc   B1860-1983 HRO
Cop   M1653-1767,1798 B1663-1812 (Ms,I) SG; C1653-1660,1784-1813 (Ts,I) SG
       M1653-1837 HMI; M1653-1882 CMI; B1653-1837 HBI
       Extracts C1653-1864 M1653-1768 IGI

BINSTED (Wesleyan) (Alton Wesleyan Circuit, Surrey & North Hampshire Wesleyan Mission from 1900, Alton Wesleyan Circuit from 1917) (Existed by 1882, closed c1951) (Records 1882,1910+ HRO)

BINSTED (Primitive Methodist) (Existed by 1867) (Guildford Primitive Methodist Circuit?, Aldershot Primitive Methodist Circuit from 1879?)

BINSTED (Bible Christian) Batts Corner (Farnham Bible Christian Circuit, Crondall Bible Christian Circuit from 1863) (On the border of Binsted with Frensham, Surrey) (Chapels erected 1830 & 1876, closed) (Records 1949+ HRO)

OR   Some baptisms were registered at Bramshott (Liphook Chapel)

BINSTED (Bible Christian) Blacknest (Farnham Bible Christian Circuit, Crondall Bible Christian Circuit from 1863) (Chapel erected c1835, closed c1954)

BINSTED (Unsectarian) (Chapel existed by 1880)

BISHOPS SUTTON St Nicholas (527) (Alresford Union)
OR   C1711-1981 M1711-1980 B1711-1912 Bn1890-1971 HRO
BT   1728,1734-1735,1780-1781,1783,1785-1797,1800-1803,1805-1808,
      1810-1859,1864-1869 HRO (Mfm SLC)
Mfc   C1711-1981 M1711-1980 B1711-1912 HRO
      C1711-1855 M1711-1837 B1711-1912 SG
Mfm C1711-1876 M1711-1876 B1711-1876 HRO, SLC
Cop C1711-1812 M1711-1754 B1711-1812 (Ts,I) HRO, HGS
      C1813-1855 (Ts,I) HRO; M1711-1837 HMI; M1711-1881 CMI
      B1711-1837 HBI; Extracts C1711-1855 M1711-1837 IGI

BISHOPSTOKE St Mary (1,026) (Winchester Union) (See also Fair Oak)
OR   C1657-1985 M1661-1983 B1657-1941 Bn1754-1812,1871-1988 HRO
      (Only two burial entries prior to 1661)
BT   1780-1785,1787-1818,1821,1828-1837,1839-1868 HRO (Mfm SLC)
Mfc   C1657-1985 M1661-1983 B1657-1941 Bn1754-1812 HRO
Mfm C1657-1812 M1661-1812 B1657-1812 Bn1754-1812 HRO
Cop C1657-1837 M1661-1837 B1657-1837 Bn1754-1807 (Ts,I) SG, HRO, SCA
      C1657-1812 M1661-1812 B1657-1812 Bn1754-1807 (Ts,I) HGS
      M1661-1837 HMI; M1661-1881 CMI; B1657-1837 HBI

BISHOPSTOKE (Baptist) Horton Heath (Founded 1862, active)

BISHOPSTOKE (Independent) Union Chapel, Horton Heath (Erected 1820, closed)
OR   C1817-1828 PRO (RG 4/2039)
Mfm C1817-1828 PRO, HRO, SLC
Cop C1817-1828 (Ts,I) SG, HRO, SCA; Extracts C1817-1828 IGI

BISHOPSTOKE (Wesleyan) Crowd Hill (Southampton Wesleyan Circuit,
    Winchester Wesleyan Circuit from 1862, Eastleigh Wesleyan Circuit from 1891,
    South Hampshire Wesleyan Mission from 1900) (Society founded 1774, Meeting
    House registered 1791, chapel erected 1817, closed 1979) (Records 1909+ HRO)
OR   C1918-1975 HRO (19M73/NMC/R11)
Mfc   C1918-1975 HRO

BISHOPSTOKE (Bible Christian) Providence, Stoke Common (Southampton Bible
    Christian Circuit) (Founded 1848, Sedgwick Road Church erected c1958) (Records
    1914+ HRO)

BISHOPSTOKE (Bible Christian) Spring Lane (Southampton Bible Christian
    Circuit) (Established c1896, closed and amalgamated with Sedgwick Road)
    (Records 1931+ HRO)

BISHOPS WALTHAM St Peter (2,181) (Droxford Union) (See also Curdridge, Swanmore)

OR   C1612-1987 M1612-1992 B1612-1974 Bn1754-1816,1849-1984 HRO
BT   1780-1848 HRO (Mfm SLC)
Mfc   C1612-1987 M1612-1992 B1612-1974 Bn1754-1816 HRO
Mfm C1612-1876 M1612-1876 B1612-1876 Bn1754-1816,1849-1876 HRO, SLC
Cop C1737-1812 M1737-1754 B1737-1812 (Ms,I) HRO (HGS holds index only)
      M1780-1812(BT) (Ts,I) SG, HRO; M1612-1837 HMI; M1700-1883 CMI
      B1612-1837 HBI; Extracts C1612-1812 M1612-1876 IGI

BISHOPS WALTHAM (Roman Catholic) Our Lady Queen of Apostles (Priory Chapel founded 1912, parish formed 1931, present church erected 1977)

OR   C1931+ M1932+ B1932+ Inc

BISHOPS WALTHAM (Independent) Lower Lane (Founded 1836, demolished 1979 and united with the Methodist Church) (Records 1879+ HRO)

OR   C1879-1975 M1867-1887,1939-1971 B1881-1885,1939-1970 D1884,1890, 1895 HRO (128M88/1,23-24, 58M75/NMR2) (The death entries occur in membership lists 1863-1900 in 128M88/1)

BISHOPS WALTHAM (Primitive Methodist) Waltham Chase (Hambledon Primitive Methodist Branch from 1885, Droxford Primitive Methodist Circuit from 1892) (Chapel erected 1869) (Records 1919+ HRO)

BISHOPS WALTHAM (Primitive Methodist) Bank Street, Basingwell Street (Droxford Primitive Methodist Circuit) (Chapel existed by 1889, Basingwell Street Chapel erected 1910, united with the Independent Church in 1979 to form the United Free Church, active) (Records 1908+ HRO)

BISTERNE St Paul (Chapelry of Ringwood)
OR   Bn1864-1934 HRO; C1874+ M1864+ B1874+ Inc

BISTERNE (Wesleyan) Crowe - See RINGWOOD

BITTERNE - See SOUTHAMPTON Bitterne

BITTERNE PARK - See SOUTHAMPTON Bitterne Park

BLACKFIELD COMMON (Baptist) - See FAWLEY

BLACKMOOR St Matthew (Formed 1867 from Selborne)
OR   C1869-1972 M1869-1970 B1869-1940 Bn1869-1979 HRO
Mfc   C1869-1972 M1869-1970 B1869-1940 HRO
Cop M1869-1881 CMI

BLACKMOOR (Independent) Whitehill (Founded 1920, chapel opened 1921, demolished 1979) (Records 1921+ HRO)
OR   C1921-1974 M1933-1965 B1924,1932-1952 HRO (14M85/1,22-23)
Mfc   C1921-1974 M1933-1965 B1924,1932-1952 HRO

BLACKMOOR Whitehill Cemetery (Records - East Hampshire District Council)
Mfc   B1987-1995 HRO (Includes index)

BLACKNEST (Bible Christian) - See BINSTED

BLENDWORTH St Giles (246) (Catherington Union) (Replaced by Holy Trinity in 1851)
OR   C1586-1965 M1587-1953 B1587-1963 Bn1854-1946,1971-1987 PCRO
BT   1780-1781,1783-1784,1786-1835,1837-1868,1871-1872 HRO (Mfm SLC)
Mfc   C1586-1965 M1587-1946 B1587-1963 HRO, PCRO
Mfm   C1586-1875 M1587-1875 B1587-1875 PCRO, SLC
      C1586-1914 M1587-1836 B1587-1791 HRO
Cop   C1780-1812 M1780-1812 B1780-1871 (BT) (Ts,I) SG, HGS, PCRO
      (CHU40/3/7); C1780-1812 M1780-1812 B1780-1871 (BT) (Ts) HRO
      C1586-1914 M1587-1929 B1587-1963 PCI; M1587-1836 HMI
      M1700-1882 CMI; B1587-1837 HBI; Extracts C1586-1875 M1587-1876 IGI

BOARHUNT St Nicholas (225) (Fareham Union)
OR   C1654-1803,1813-1909 M1654-1989 B1654-1805 Bn1824-1905 HRO
      C1803-1812,1909+ B1803+ Inc (Gaps in C & M 1662-1681, B 1657-1681;
      Boarhunt C and B 1803-1812 are entered at Southwick, and vice versa)
BT   1813,1815-1827,1830-1831,1835-1838,1841,1844-1845,1851-1857,1860-1874
      HRO (Mfm SLC)
Mfc   C1654-1988 M1654-1989 B1654-1988 HRO, PCRO
      C1654-1909 M1654-1836 B1654-1805 SG
Mfm   C1654-1876 M1654-1876 B1654-1805 Bn1824-1878 HRO, SLC
Pc   C1803-1812,1909-1988 B1803-1988 HRO
Cop   C1654-1998 M1654-1998 B1654-1998 (Ts,I) HRO, PCRO
      M1654-1836 HMI; M1654-1882 CMI; B1654-1837 HBI

BOARHUNT (Independent Methodist) Ebenezer Chapel (Chapel erected 1830; associated with the chapels at Catherington and Clanfield; 1851 Religious Census)

BOARHUNT (Wesleyan) (Existed by 1867, new chapel erected 1924, possibly the same chapel as the Independent Methodist Society)

BOCKHAMPTON (Independent) - See CHRISTCHURCH

BOLDRE St John the Baptist (2,111) (Lymington Union) (See also East Boldre, South Baddesley, Sway)
OR   C1596-1970 M1596-1974 B1596-1992 Bn1754-1756,1777-1805,1870-1991
      HRO
BT   1780-1784,1786-1880 HRO (Mfm SLC)
Mfc   C1596-1970 M1596-1961 B1596-1926 Bn1754-1756,1777-1805 HRO
Mfm   C1596-1840 M1596-1813 B1596-1813 Bn1754-1756,1777-1805 HRO, SLC
Cop   M1596-1813 Phillimore Vol 11 and Boyd; M1790-1813 Pallot
      C1596-1880 B1595-1812 (Ts) HRO
      M1601-1812 (Ms,A) HGS; M1596-1837 HMI; M1813-1881 CMI
      B1596-1837 HBI; Extracts C1813-1840 M1777-1813 IGI

BOLDRE (Baptist) - See EAST BOLDRE

BOLDRE (Independent) East End Chapel - See EAST BOLDRE

BOLDRE (Independent) Pilley Green, Pilley (Founded 1858 as a mission station of Lymington, joint church with Lymington East End formed 1913, closed after 1985) (Records 1913+ HRO, with records of Lymington Independent)

BOLDRE (Primitive Methodist) East End (Southampton Primitive Methodist Circuit, Romsey Primitive Methodist Circuit from 1880) (Erected 1859, closed c1885)

BORDON St George (Garrison church) - See HEADLEY

BORDON (Roman Catholic) - See HEADLEY

BOSCOMBE (Independent) - See BOURNEMOUTH

BOSSINGTON St James (47) (Stockbridge Union) (Chapelry of Broughton)
OR   C1763-1989 M1763-1975 B1764-1990 Bn1763-1775,1901-1989 HRO
        (Some entries occur at Broughton)
BT   1782-1783,1791-1792,1799-1819,1822-1826,1828-1830,1835,1837-1838,
        1841-1854,1858,1861 HRO (Mfm SLC)
Mfc   C1763-1989 M1763-1975 B1764-1990 Bn1763-1775,1901-1989 HRO
        C1763-1989 M1817-1832 B1764-1812 SG
Mfm   C1763-1887 M1817-1852,1892-1901 B1764-1895 HRO, SLC
Cop   M1763-1832 HMI; M1799-1901 CMI; B1764-1837 HBI
        Extracts C1763-1879 M1817-1852 IGI

BOTLEY St Bartholomew (Replaced by All Saints in 1836) (722) (South Stoneham Union) (See also Hedge End)
OR   C1679-1975 M1680-1986 B1679-1972 Bn1754-1812,1866-1909,1940-1987
        HRO
BT   1781-1784,1786-1809,1813-1828,1853,1855-1879 HRO (Mfm SLC)
Mfc   C1679-1975 M1680-1986 B1679-1972 Bn1754-1812 HRO
Mfm   C1679-1875 M1680-1876 B1679-1875 Bn1754-1812 HRO, SLC
        M1754-1875 B1813-1875 Bn1754-1812 DRO
Cop   C1679-1837 M1680-1837 B1679-1837 (Ts,I) SG, HRO, SCA
        C1813-1837 M1813-1837 B1813-1837 (Ts,I) HGS
        M1813-1843 (Ms) HRO; M1680-1837 HMI; M1680-1881 CMI
        B1679-1837 HBI; Extracts C1679-1875 M1680-1876 IGI

BOTLEY (Roman Catholic) - See WINCHESTER

BOTLEY (Baptist) - See HEDGE END

BOTLEY (Independent) (Founded 1806)

BOTLEY Bible Christian Circuit - See SOUTHAMPTON Bible Christian Circuit

BOURNEMOUTH All Saints (Chapelry of St James Pokesdown, established 1915; replaced St James as Pokesdown parish church in 1930)
OR   C1915-1963 M1915-1986 Bn1930-1986 HRO
Mfc   C1915-1963 M1915-1986 HRO

BOURNEMOUTH Christ Church, Westbourne (Chapel to St Peter; originally The Holy Spirit, then St Nathanael & St John; Christ Church from 1908)
OR   C1898+ M1917+ Bn1918+ Inc

BOURNEMOUTH Holy Epiphany (District formed 1938 from St John Moordown & Holdenhurst)
OR   C1938-1978 M1941-1990 B1968-1978 Bn1941-1983 HRO
Mfc   C1938-1978 M1941-1990 HRO

BOURNEMOUTH Holy Spirit - See Christ Church, Westbourne

BOURNEMOUTH Holy Trinity (Formed 1867 from St Peter & Holdenhurst; closed 1973; demolished)
OR   C1867-1973 M1870-1973 Bn1870-1973 HRO
BT   1867-1871 HRO (Mfm SLC)
Mfc   C1867-1973 M1870-1973 HRO
Cop   M1870-1883 CMI

BOURNEMOUTH St Alban (Formed 1914 from St Augustin, Holy Trinity, & St John Moordown)
OR   C1909+ M1909+ Bn1909+ Inc

BOURNEMOUTH St Ambrose (Chapelry of St Peter; separate parish 1921)
OR   M1906-1986 Bn1938-1994 HRO; C1908+ Inc
Mfc   M1906-1968 HRO

BOURNEMOUTH St Andrew, Bennett Road (Chapel to Holy Trinity; parish 1919)
OR   Bn1908-1950 HRO; C1887+ M1909+ Inc

BOURNEMOUTH St Andrew, Boscombe (Chapelry of St James Pokesdown; separate parish 1929)
OR   C1908-1948 M1908-1977 Bn1947-1986 HRO
Mfc   C1908-1948 M1908-1977 HRO

BOURNEMOUTH St Augustin (Formed 1900 from St Stephen, St John Moordown, & Holy Trinity)
OR   C1893+ M1894+ Bn1929-1954,1962+ Inc

BOURNEMOUTH St Christopher (District formed 1933 from All Saints; separate parish 1949)
OR   M1934-1965 Bn1934-1983 HRO; C1933+ Inc
Mfc   M1934-1965 HRO

BOURNEMOUTH St Clement (Formed 1871 from St Peter)
OR   C1871-1941 M1874-1945 B1871-1945 Bn1928-1988 HRO
Mfc   C1871-1941 M1874-1945 B1871-1945 HRO
Cop   M1874-1882 CMI

BOURNEMOUTH St Francis of Assisi (District formed 1929 from St Alban, St John Moordown, & Holdenhurst)
OR   C1929+ M1931+ Bn1930+ Inc

BOURNEMOUTH St James The Greater, Pokesdown (Formed 1859 from
Christchurch)
OR   C1860-1979 M1861-1992 B1860-1956 Bn1952-1987 HRO
Mfc   C1860-1950 M1861-1980 B1860-1956 HRO
Cop   M1861-1881 CMI

BOURNEMOUTH St John the Baptist, Moordown (Formed 1874 from St Peter &
Holdenhurst)
OR   C1873-1991 M1874-1999 B1874-1960 Bn1934-1968,1986-1992 HRO
Mfc   C1873-1983 M1874-1983 B1874-1960 HRO
Cop   M1874-1882 CMI

BOURNEMOUTH St John the Evangelist, Boscombe (Formed 1890 from
St Clement)
OR   C1891-1959 M1895-1963 B1951-1963 Bn1925-1979 HRO
Mfc   C1891-1959 M1895-1963 B1951-1963 HRO

BOURNEMOUTH St John the Evangelist, Surrey Road (Formed 1891 from St Peter,
St Stephen, & Kinson [Dorset])
OR   C1889-1942 M1891-1989 Bn1891-1991 HRO; B1980+ Inc
Mfc   C1889-1942 M1891-1982 HRO

BOURNEMOUTH St Katharine, Southbourne (Formed 1887 from St James
Pokesdown)
OR   M1887-1982 Bn1887-1967 HRO; C1887+ B1982+ Inc
Mfc   M1887-1982 HRO

BOURNEMOUTH St Luke (Chapelry of St John Moordown; separate parish 1917)
OR   C1915-1951 M1915-1952 Bn1953-1991 HRO
Mfc   C1915-1951 M1915-1952 HRO

BOURNEMOUTH St Mary the Virgin (District formed 1922 from St Clement,
St Peter, St James Pokesdown, & Holdenhurst; separate parish 1934)
OR   C1922-1952 M1930-1994 Bn1930-1995 HRO
Mfc   C1922-1952 M1930-1963 HRO

BOURNEMOUTH St Michael & All Angels (Formed 1874 from St Peter)
OR   C1874-1941 M1876-1990 B1983-1991 Bn1933-1995 HRO
Mfc   C1874-1941 M1876-1958 HRO
Cop   M1876-1882 CMI

BOURNEMOUTH St Nathanael & St John - See Christ Church, Westbourne

BOURNEMOUTH St Paul (Formed 1890 from Holy Trinity; moved to a new church
at Throop in 1984)
OR   C1874-1983 M1890-1992 Bn1890-1984 HRO
Mfc   C1874-1983 M1890-1983 HRO
Cop   M1890-1893 CMI

BOURNEMOUTH St Peter (Formed 1845 from Christchurch & Holdenhurst)
OR   C1846-1951 M1845-1970 B1846-1974 Bn1946-1966 HRO
Mfc   C1846-1951 M1845-1946 B1846-1974 HRO
Mfm   C1846-1875 M1845-1875 HRO, DRO, SLC
Cop   B1846-1974 (Ts) HRO; B1846-1963 DRO; M1845-1881 CMI
        Extracts C1846-1876 M1845-1875 IGI (indexed as Holdenhurst)

BOURNEMOUTH St Saviour, Iford (Chapelry of St James Pokesdown)
OR   M1934-1940 B1934-1960 Bn1934-1992 HRO; C1934+ Inc

BOURNEMOUTH St Stephen (Formed 1882 from St Peter)
OR   M1902-1973 Bn1902-1941 HRO; C1882+ Inc
Mfc   M1902-1973 HRO

BOURNEMOUTH St Swithun (Chapelry of St Peter)
OR   C1908-1991 M1906-1994 B1952-1963 Bn1949-1994 HRO
Mfc   M1906-1962 B1952-1963 HRO

BOURNEMOUTH (Roman Catholic) Corpus Christi, Christchurch Road, Boscombe
   (Chapel founded 1887, present church erected 1896)
OR   C1897+ M1898+ Inc

BOURNEMOUTH (Roman Catholic) Our Lady Queen of Peace, Southbourne
   (Chapel founded 1916, present church erected 1939)
OR   C1934+ M1934+ B1934+ Inc

BOURNEMOUTH (Roman Catholic) Sacred Heart, Albert Road, Richmond Hill
   (Founded 1869 at Anstey Lodge, St Stephen's Road; present church erected 1875)
OR   1875+ Inc

BOURNEMOUTH (Roman Catholic) St Thomas More, Iford (Founded 1939, served
   from Corpus Christi until 1949)
OR   C1949+ Inc

BOURNEMOUTH (Society of Friends) Avenue Road (Meeting House erected 1871)

BOURNEMOUTH (Baptist) Palmerston Road, Boscombe (Founded 1875, closed
   after 1985)

BOURNEMOUTH (Baptist) North Street, Westbourne (Founded 1867, active)

BOURNEMOUTH (Baptist) Lansdowne Road (Chapel erected 1875)

BOURNEMOUTH (Baptist) West Cliff Tabernacle, Poole Road, Westbourne
   (Founded 1879, active)

BOURNEMOUTH (Baptist) Harcourt Road, Pokesdown, later Christchurch Road,
   Rosebery Park (Founded 1891, active)

BOURNEMOUTH (Particular Baptist) Mount Zion, Wootton Mount (Founded 1888
   in a room, chapel opened 1927)

BOURNEMOUTH (Baptist) Cardigan Road (now Cardigan Avenue), Winton (Founded 1910, active)

BOURNEMOUTH (Baptist) Old Bridge Road, Iford (Founded 1935, active)

BOURNEMOUTH (Baptist) The Avenue, Moordown (Founded 1935, active)

BOURNEMOUTH (Independent, now United Reformed) Southbourne Road, Pokesdown (Founded 1820, chapels erected 1835 and 1858; united with Boscombe in 1985 to form Pokesdown & Boscombe Church; active) (Records at DRO)
OR   C1841-1853 registered at Christchurch Independent Chapel (DRO NP4/RE1)
Mfm   C1841-1853 SLC

BOURNEMOUTH (Independent, now United Reformed) East Howe Lane, East Howe (Founded 1834, active)

BOURNEMOUTH (Independent, now United Reformed) St Stephen's Road, Richmond Hill (Temporary chapel opened 1849 in Orchard Street, Church founded 1856, Richmond Hill Church opened 1859, active)

BOURNEMOUTH (Independent, now United Reformed) Priory View Road, Moordown (Founded 1860, active)

BOURNEMOUTH (Independent, now United Reformed) Wimborne Road, Luther Road, Winton (Founded 1868, active)

BOURNEMOUTH (Independent, now United Reformed) East Cliff Congregational Church, Holdenhurst Road (Founded 1877, active)

BOURNEMOUTH (Independent, later United Reformed) Christchurch Road, Boscombe (Founded 1887, united with Pokesdown in 1985) (Records 1886+ DRO)
OR   C1889-1891,1957-1979 M1889-1892,1953-1962 B1969-1978 DRO (NP10/MR1/1, NP10/RE1)
Mfm   C1889-1891,1957-1979 M1889-1892,1953-1962 B1969-1978 SLC

BOURNEMOUTH (Independent) Poole Road, Westbourne (Iron church opened 1891, permanent church opened 1898) (Records 1891+ HRO, in 127M94)
OR   C1892-1910,1930-1932,1935 M1896-1925 B1901-1909,1924-1925 D1899 HRO (in 127M94/79) (The death entry occurs in a membership list)

BOURNEMOUTH (Independent) Charminster Road (Founded 1901)

BOURNEMOUTH (Independent, now United Reformed) Immanuel, Southbourne Road, Southbourne (Founded 1910, active)

BOURNEMOUTH (Independent, now United Reformed) Sutton Road, Charminster (Founded 1928, active)

BOURNEMOUTH (United Reformed) Ropley Road, Iford (Founded 1934, active)

BOURNEMOUTH (Presbyterian, now United Reformed) St Andrew, Exeter Road (Iron church at foot of Richmond Hill erected 1857, stone church on same site erected 1872, demolished 1886, present church opened 1888, active)
OR   M1921-1923 DRO (NP31/RE2/1-2)
Mfm   M1921-1923 SLC

BOURNEMOUTH (Presbyterian) St Mark, Bath Road (Founded 1898, church erected 1902, closed by 1939)
OR   M1923-1936 DRO (NP30/RE2/1-2)
Mfm   M1923-1936 SLC

BOURNEMOUTH (Unitarian) West Hill Road, now at Hinton Road (Founded 1882, church erected 1891, united with Poole 1968 and Ringwood 1975, active) (Records 1882+ DRO)
OR   C1887-1960 M1981-1986 DRO (NU4/RE1/1, NU4/RE2/1)

BOURNEMOUTH (Denomination not stated) Nathaniel Church, Seamoor Road, Westbourne (Existed by 1899, possibly closed by 1930)

BOURNEMOUTH Wesleyan Circuit (Formed 1873 from Poole Circuit; later known as Punshon Memorial Circuit; became part of Bournemouth Methodist Circuit in 1950. Included chapels at Bournemouth, Christchurch, and Milton) (Records 1873+ DRO, 1962+ HRO)

BOURNEMOUTH (Wesleyan) Victoria Place, Springbourne, Boscombe; Holdenhurst Road, Springbourne (Poole Wesleyan Circuit, Bournemouth Wesleyan Circuit from 1873) (Meeting established 1865, chapel erected in Victoria Place 1867, Wesley Church in Holdenhurst Road erected 1908)

BOURNEMOUTH (Wesleyan) Punshon Memorial Wesleyan Church, Richmond Hill (Poole Wesleyan Circuit, Bournemouth Wesleyan Circuit from 1873) (Chapel erected 1866-7 next to the Tregonwell Arms, replaced 1886 by Punshon Memorial Church, bombed 1943, Exeter Road Church erected 1958) (Records 1897+ DRO)
OR   M1938-1943 DRO (in NM1/K)

BOURNEMOUTH (Wesleyan) Ashley Road, Boscombe (Bournemouth Wesleyan Circuit) (Existed by 1875, church erected 1893, new church at Portman Road, St George's, erected 1931) (Records 1875+ DRO)

BOURNEMOUTH (Wesleyan) Winton (Bournemouth Wesleyan Circuit) (Chapel existed by 1872, Alma Road Chapel erected 1906, church in The Avenue erected 1927, amalgamated with the former Primitive Methodist Winton Wimborne Road Society in 1965, new church in Avenue Road 1968) (Records 1956+ DRO)

BOURNEMOUTH (Wesleyan) Southbourne, formerly Pokesdown (Bournemouth Wesleyan Circuit) (Churches erected at Darracott Road 1874, Seabourne Road 1907, Southbourne Road 1926) (Records 1896+ DRO)

BOURNEMOUTH (Wesleyan) Poole Road, Westbourne (Bournemouth Wesleyan Circuit) (Society formed 1886, school chapel erected 1877, church erected 1900)

BOURNEMOUTH Primitive Methodist First Circuit (Later known as Curzon Road Circuit; became part of Curzon Road & Winton Methodist Circuit in 1937. Included chapels at Bournemouth and Highcliffe) (Records 1907+ DRO)

BOURNEMOUTH Primitive Methodist Second Circuit (Later known as Winton Circuit; became part of Curzon Road & Winton Methodist Circuit in 1937. Included a chapel at Bournemouth)

BOURNEMOUTH (Primitive Methodist) Commercial Road (Bournemouth Primitive Methodist First Circuit) (Meetings by 1878, chapel erected by 1889, probably closed by 1923)

BOURNEMOUTH (Primitive Methodist) Herridge Memorial Chapel, Curzon Road, Springbourne (Bournemouth Primitive Methodist First Circuit) (Formed as a mission of Commercial Road; early meetings in Boscombe Grove Road, Malmesbury Park Road, Nortoft Road; Herridge Memorial Chapel erected 1909; amalgamated with Springbourne Wesleyan in 1956) (Records 1905+ DRO)
OR   M1934-1953 DRO (in NM1/M)

BOURNEMOUTH (Primitive Methodist) Wimborne Road, Winton (Bournemouth Primitive Methodist Second Circuit) (Society formed 1888, school chapel opened 1892, Wimborne Road Church opened 1905, sold after society joined with The Avenue in 1968) (Records 1961+ DRO)
OR   M1908-1967 DRO (in NM1/S)

BOURNEMOUTH (Primitive Methodist) Hannington Road, Pokesdown (Bournemouth Primitive Methodist First Circuit) (Originally met at Cromwell Road, Hannington Road Chapel erected 1897, sold 1955 and joined with St George's, formerly Ashley Road, Boscombe) (Records 1930+ DRO)

BOURNEMOUTH (Primitive Methodist) Arnewood Road, Southbourne (Bournemouth Primitive Methodist First Circuit) (Society formed 1907 at Avon Road, Christchurch, moved to Arnewood Road 1914, joined with the former Wesleyan Southbourne Society in 1956)

BOURNEMOUTH Curzon Road & Winton Methodist Circuit (Formed 1937 by amalgamation of the two Bournemouth Primitive Methodist Circuits. Became part of Bournemouth Methodist Circuit in 1950) (Records 1937+ DRO)

BOURNEMOUTH Methodist Circuit (Formed 1950 by amalgamation of the Punshon Memorial and Curzon Road & Winton Circuits) (Records 1950+ DRO)

BOURNEMOUTH (Apostolic Faith Church) Muscliffe Road, Winton (Records 1931+ DRO)

BOURNEMOUTH (Jewish) Synagogue, Wootton Gardens (Congregation established 1905 meeting in the Assembly Rooms, Synagogue in Wootton Gardens erected 1911, active; burials take place in Kinson and Boscombe Cemeteries)

BOURNEMOUTH (Jewish) Reform Synagogue, Christchurch Road (Established 1947, active; burials take place in Kinson Cemetery)

BOURNEMOUTH Wimborne Road Cemetery (Established 1878)

BOURNEMOUTH East Cemetery, Gloucester Road
BT   B1898-1916 HRO

BOURNEMOUTH North Cemetery

BOWYERS (Primitive Methodist) - See STEEP

BRADFIELD [Berkshire] Union Workhouse (Union included Stratfield Mortimer)
OR   Z1836-1862 C1845-1930,1944 D1835-1842 B1845-1917 BRO
Mfm   Z1836-1862 C1845-1930,1944 D1835-1842 BRO, SLC

BRADLEY All Saints (103) (Basingstoke Union)
OR   C1725-1994 M1730-1987 B1725-1992 HRO; Bn1824+ Inc
BT   1781-1794,1796-1807,1809-1810,1812-1866,1868,1870 HRO (Mfm SLC)
Mfc   C1725-1994 M1730-1987 B1725-1992 HRO
Mfm   C1725-1812 M1730-1812 B1725-1812 HRO
Cop   C1725-1812 M1730-1753 B1725-1812 (Ms,I) SG (Transcribed from British
        Library Add Mss No 39,962 Vol 4 ff 247-257); M1730-1835 HMI
        C1725-1812 M1730-1753 B1725-1812 (Ts,I) HRO, HGS
        M1730-1887 CMI; B1725-1837 HBI

BRAISHFIELD All Saints (Formed 1855 from Hursley, Michelmersh, & Romsey)
OR   C1855-1922 M1856-1989 HRO; B1856+ Bn1856+ Inc
BT   1855-1862,1867 HRO (Mfm SLC)
Mfc   C1855-1922 M1856-1989 HRO
Cop   M1856-1902 CMI

BRAISHFIELD (Independent, now United Reformed) (Founded 1818, active)

BRAISHFIELD (Wesleyan, Wesleyan Methodist Association) Pucknall
     (Southampton Wesleyan Circuit, Winchester United Methodist Free Church Circuit
     from 1835) (Existed by 1825, probably lapsed by 1840, re-formed and chapel
     erected c1887, closed c1910)

BRAMBRIDGE (Bible Christian) - See TWYFORD

BRAMBRIDGE & HIGHBRIDGE (Roman Catholic) - See EASTLEIGH

BRAMDEAN St Simon & St Jude (215) (Alresford Union)
OR   C1573-1948 M1576-1973 B1578-1992 Bn1775-1812,1824-1994 HRO
BT   1780-1781,1783-1870 HRO (Mfm SLC)
Mfc   C1573-1948 M1576-1973 B1578-1992 Bn1775-1812 HRO
Mfm   C1573-1876 M1576-1876 B1578-1875 HRO, SLC (Omits M1775-1824 in
        Volume 2 of the registers)
Cop   C1573-1948 M1576-1973 B1578-1876 (Ms,I) HRO; M1576-1837 HMI
        C1774-1826 M1775-1824 B1774-1826 (Ms,I) HGS; M1576-1881 CMI
        B1578-1837 HBI; Extracts C1573-1876 M1576-1776,1813-1876 IGI

BRAMLEY St James (429) (Basingstoke Union)
OR   C1580-1970 M1580-1984 B1580-1902 Bn1824-1952,1963-1974 HRO
      (Several gaps, notably 1615-1643, M 1705-1724, B 1678-1714)
BT   1705,1781-1854,1856-1867 HRO (Mfm SLC)
Mfc   C1580-1970 M1580-1984 B1580-1902 HRO
Mfm   C1580-1875 M1580-1875 B1580-1875 HRO, SLC
      C1580-1875 M1580-1837 B1580-1812 DRO
Cop   M1580-1812 Phillimore Vol 1, Boyd, Pallot; Extracts M1580-1837 IGI
      C1580-1812 M1580-1754 B1580-1812 (Ms) SG; M1580-1837 HMI
      C1580-1812 M1580-1812 B1580-1812 (Ts) HRO; M1580-1882 CMI
      C1580-c1812 M1580-c1812 B1580-c1812 (Ms,A) HRO; B1580-1837 HBI

BRAMLEY St Barbara (Garrison church)
OR   C1956-1975 RACD

BRAMLEY Wesleyan (Basingstoke Wesleyan Circuit) (Records 1923+ HRO)
OR   C1959-1975 HRO (57M77/NMR7)

BRAMSHAW St Peter (482 in Hampshire, 357 in Wiltshire) (New Forest Union)
      (The Wiltshire portion was transferred to Hampshire in 1895)
OR   C1597-1964 M1597-1966 B1614-1993 Bn1775-1818,1822,1916-1967 HRO
      (Several gaps prior to 1700)
BT   1620-1624,1632-1633,1637,1666-1682,1686,1689-1691,1706-1708,1711,
      1714,1718-1730,1735-1741,1747-1752,1755,1762-1766,1793-1880 WRO
      (Mfm SLC)
Mfc   C1597-1964 M1597-1966 B1614-1993 Bn1775-1812 HRO
Mfm   C1597-1812 M1597-1812 B1614-1812 Bn1775-1812 HRO, SLC
      C1784-1812 M1775-1812 B1784-1812 Bn1775-1812 DRO
Cop   C1597-1812 M1597-1812 B1614-1812 Bn1779-1808 (Ms on film) WRO
      M1597-1835 (Ts,I) WRO; C1597-1775 M1597-1760 B1614-1777 (Ms) HRO
      M1597-1835 (Ts,I) SG (catalogued under Wilts); Index to B1800-1837 SG
      M1597-1835 HMI; M1597-1965 CMI; M1597-1835 Nimrod Index
      B1614-1837 HBI; Extracts C1597-1812 M1597-1812 IGI

BRAMSHAW (Particular Baptist) Fritham (Chapel erected c1842, iron chapel erected
      1878, became the United Free Church in 1904) (Records WRO)
OR   Adult baptisms 1842-1851,1858,1877 B1846-1921 D1876-1941 WRO
      (1458/8-9) (Includes entries for Rehoboth Chapel, Downton, Wilts)

BRAMSHAW (Wesleyan) (Romsey Wesleyan Circuit, South Hampshire Wesleyan
      Mission from 1900) (Chapels erected c1839 & c1884) (Records 1883+ HRO)

BRAMSHAW (Primitive Methodist) Furzley (Southampton Primitive Methodist
      Circuit) (In Wiltshire until 1895) (Existed by 1850, probably closed by 1880)

BRAMSHILL (Baptist) - See EVERSLEY

BRAMSHOTT St Mary the Virgin (1,210) (Headley Incorporation, Petersfield Union from 1869)

OR   C1560-1972 M1560-1956 B1561-1951 Bn1754-1793,1916-1987 HRO
(Gap 1652-1665; a register for this period once existed, but is now missing)

BT   1780-1781,1783-1789,1791-1795,1797-1870 HRO (Mfm SLC)

Mfc   C1560-1972 M1560-1956 B1561-1951 Bn1754-1793 HRO

Mfm   C1560-1876 M1560-1875 B1561-1876 Bn1754-1793 HRO, SLC

Cop   C1560-1729 M1560-1812 B1561-1812,1893-1936 (Ms & Ts) HRO
M1560-1836 HMI; M1560-1881 CMI; B1561-1837 HBI
Extracts C1560-1876 M1560-1875 IGI

BRAMSHOTT (Roman Catholic) The Immaculate Conception, Headley Road, Liphook (Chapel at Woolmer Lodge founded 1870, present church erected 1911)

OR   C1869+ B1891+ Inc

Cop   C1870-1908 (Ts,I) B1891-1902 (Ts) SG

BRAMSHOTT (Society of Friends) (Bramshott & Headley) (part of Alton Meeting)

OR   Z1638-1693,1722 M1664-1729,1741 B1661-1739 PRO (RG 6/1028) (Includes entries for Alton, Alresford, Basingstoke, Romsey)

Mfm   Z1638-1693,1722 M1664-1729,1741 B1661-1739 HRO

Cop   Z1638-1693,1722 M1664-1729,1741 B1661-1739 (Ts) SG; B1661-1739 HBI
For index, see Hampshire Quarterly Meeting; M1664-1729,1741 HMI

BRAMSHOTT (Bible Christian) Queen Street, Liphook (Farnham Bible Christian Circuit, Liphook Bible Christian Circuit from 1863) (Preaching Room established 1842, chapel subsequently erected, active) (Records 1882+ HRO)

OR   C1874-1975 M1907,1933-1966 HRO (89M72/NMR18-23) (Includes baptisms at Lindford [Headley], Standford Hill [Headley], and Batts Corner [Binsted])

Cop   C1874-1975 M1907 (Ts,I) SG, HRO (in 89M72/NMR18)

BRAMSHOTT (Bible Christian) Passfield Common (Farnham Bible Christian Circuit, Liphook Bible Christian Circuit from 1863) (Chapel erected 1831, possibly the same chapel as Standford Hill Chapel, Headley)

BRANSGORE St Mary (Formed 1874 from Christchurch & Sopley)

OR   C1822-1956 M1876-1975 B1822-1993 Bn1925-1966 HRO

BT   1872-1873 HRO (Mfm SLC)

Mfc   C1822-1956 M1876-1975 B1822-1993 HRO

Mfm   C1822-1876 B1822-1876 HRO, SLC

Cop   C1822-1840 B1822-1840 (Ts) SG, HRO
M1876-1883 CMI; B1822-1837 HBI; Extracts C1822-1876 IGI

BRANSGORE (Independent) Waterditch (Founded 1836)

OR   C1837-1860,1901-1919 registered at Christchurch Independent Chapel (DRO NP4/RE1,CM2)

Mfm   C1837-1860,1901-1919 SLC

BRANSGORE (Wesleyan) (Christchurch & Lymington Wesleyan Circuit, Wimborne Wesleyan Circuit from 1925, New Forest Wesleyan Mission from 1932) (Chapel erected 1844) (Records 1866,1896+ HRO)

BRANSGORE (Wesleyan) (Second Wesleyan Chapel) (Christchurch & Lymington Wesleyan Circuit) (Existed by 1895, possibly the same chapel as Thorney Hill, Christchurch)

BREAMORE St Mary (Formerly St Mary & St Michael) (600) (Fordingbridge Union)
OR   C1675-1954 M1675-1990 B1675-1905 Bn1755-1793,1860-1978 HRO
BT   1813-1837,1839-1880 HRO (Mfm SLC)
Mfc   C1675-1954 M1675-1958 B1675-1905 Bn1755-1793 HRO
Mfm   C1675-1813 M1675-1813 B1675-1813 Bn1755-1793 HRO, DRO
Cop   C1675-1840 M1675-1840 B1675-1840 (Ts,I) SG, HRO, Inc
        M1675-1837 HMI; M1675-1886 CMI; B1675-1837 HBI

BREAMORE (Wesleyan) Woodgreen (Salisbury Wesleyan Circuit) (Chapel opened 1832) (Records 1932+ WRO)

BREAMORE (Primitive Methodist) (Salisbury Primitive Methodist Circuit, Woodfalls Primitive Methodist Circuit from 1898) (Records 1846+ WRO)

BRIDGEMARY St Matthew (District of Rowner; separate parish 1982)
OR   C1968-1987 M1969-1988 PCRO; Bn1969+ Inc

BROCKENHURST St Nicholas (Original dedication unknown) (841) (Lymington Union) (Chapelry of Boldre; separate parish 1862)
OR   C1594-1940 M1629-1912 B1596-1911 Bn1757,1771-1905,1968-1984 HRO
BT   1783,1785-1791,1793-1796,1798-1862,1866-1869 HRO (Mfm SLC)
Mfc   C1594-1940 M1629-1912 B1596-1911 Bn1757,1771-1865 SG, HRO
Mfm   C1594-1812 M1629-1812 B1596-1812 Bn1757,1771-1865 HRO
Cop   M1629-1811 (possibly extracts only) (Ts,I) SG, HGS
        M1629-1836 HMI; M1629-1881 CMI; M1629-1837 Boyd; B1596-1837 HBI

BROCKENHURST St Saviour
OR   Bn1925-1938 HRO; C1940+ M1919+ Inc

BROCKENHURST (Roman Catholic) St Anne (Formed 1939 from Lyndhurst and Lymington Catholic parishes)
OR   1939+ Inc

BROCKENHURST (Baptist) Lyndhurst Road (Founded 1792, closed after 1985) (Records 1892+ Angus Library, Regent's Park College, Oxford)
OR   M1960 (one entry) HRO (69M60/1); church books 1903-1986 Angus Library

BROCKENHURST (Countess of Huntingdon's Connexion) (Founded 1849, listed in 1851 Religious Census as Independent Methodist Society; no later references)

BROCKENHURST (Wesleyan) (Christchurch & Lymington Wesleyan Circuit, New Forest Wesleyan Mission from 1925) (Founded 1901) (Records 1901+ HRO)

BROCKHAMPTON (Roman Catholic) - See HAVANT

BROCKHURST (Baptist) - See GOSPORT

BROOK (Bible Christian) Chapel - See CROOKHAM (Bible Christian) Brook

BROUGHTON St Mary (897) (Stockbridge Union)
OR   C1639-1972 M1639-1968 B1639-1933 Bn1770-1782,1823-1993 HRO
BT   1780-1783,1785-1786,1788-1845,1848-1858,1860-1866,1868-1871 HRO
   (Mfm SLC)
Mfc   C1639-1972 M1639-1968 B1639-1933 HRO
   C1639-1856 M1639-1837 B1639-1868 SG
Mfm   C1639-1876 M1639-1876 B1639-1875 Bn1770-1782,1823-1876 HRO, SLC
Cop   M1639-1837 HMI; M1639-1881 CMI; B1639-1837 HBI
   Extracts C1639-1876 M1639-1876 IGI

BROUGHTON (Baptist) High Street (Founded 1651 as a joint church with Porton,
   Wiltshire; active) (Records c1653+ Angus Library, Regent's Park College, Oxford;
   HRO holds a partial list of these records)
OR   Baptisms and membership lists occur in church record books from c1653, held
   at Angus Library; D certs 1838-1848 also at Angus Library
Mfc   B1860-2000 HRO
Mfm   Church books 1653-1684,1759-1891 HRO (Microfilm 395) (Include adult
   baptisms circa 1655, deaths 1759-1891, membership lists 1759-1891)
Cop   D1813-1837 HBI

BROUGHTON (Wesleyan) (Salisbury Wesleyan Circuit) (Erected 1819, now closed)
   (Records 1908+ WRO)
OR   C1950-1969 M1928-1969 WRO (2485/10, 1420/7a)
Pc   M1928-1969 HRO (Photocopy 307)

BROUGHTON Cemetery (Records 1950+ Parish Council)

BROWN CANDOVER St Peter (284) (Alresford Union)
OR   C1611-1889 M1612-1992 B1612-1992 Bn1824-1887,1890-1954 HRO
BT   1780,1782-1854 HRO (Mfm SLC)
Mfc   C1611-1889 M1612-1992 B1612-1992 SG, HRO
Cop   M1612-1837 HMI; M1612-1891 CMI; M1612-1837 Boyd
   B1612-1837 HBI; Extracts M1612-1837 IGI

BUCKLAND - See PORTSEA St Stephen

BULLINGTON St Michael & All Angels (189) (Andover Union) (Chapelry of
   Wherwell; separate parish 1857)
OR   C1716-1986 M1754-1984 B1715-1985 Bn1824-1986 HRO
BT   1757,1780-1781,1783-1791,1794-1801,1803,1805-1807,1809-1815,
   1817-1830,1832-1864,1866-1868,1871 HRO (Mfm SLC)
Mfc   C1716-1986 M1754-1984 B1715-1985 HRO
Mfm   C1716-1814 M1754-1812 B1715-1814 HRO
Cop   M1754-1812 Phillimore Vol 1 & 8 and Boyd; M1754-1836 HMI
   M1754-1881 CMI; M1755-1812 Pallot; B1715-1837 HBI

BURGHCLERE All Saints (802) (Kingsclere Union)
OR   C1561-1938 M1559-1981 B1561-1931 Bn1754-1812,1824-1948 HRO
BT   1780-1797,1799-1807,1809-1869,1871 HRO (Mfm SLC)
Mfc   C1561-1938 M1559-1981 B1561-1931 Bn1754-1812 HRO
Mfm   C1561-1812 M1559-1812 B1559-1812 Bn1754-1812 HRO
Cop   M1559-1812 Phillimore Vol 8 and Boyd; M1559-1837 HMI
       C1561-1654 M1563-1623 B1561-1655 (Ms,I) HRO
       M1813-1881 CMI; M1790-1812 Pallot; B1561-1837 HBI

BURGHCLERE (Primitive Methodist) (Newbury Primitive Methodist Circuit)
    (Chapel erected 1864)

BURITON St Mary (822) (Petersfield Union)
OR   C1680-1952 M1690-1989 B1678-1952 Bn1754-1776,1907-1960 HRO
       (Few C & M before 1695)
BT   1780-1804,1806-1866 HRO (Mfm SLC)
Mfc   C1680-1952 M1690-1989 B1678-1952 Bn1754-1776 HRO
Mfm   C1680-1876 M1690-1876 B1678-1875 Bn1754-1776 HRO, SLC
Cop   C1680-1812 M1690-1837 B1678-1812 (Ts) HRO; M1690-1837 HMI
       M1690-1881 CMI; B1678-1837 HBI; Extracts M1695-1876 IGI

BURITON Primitive Methodist Circuit - See PETERSFIELD Primitive Methodist
    Circuit

BURITON (Primitive Methodist) (Petersfield Primitive Methodist Circuit) (Chapel
    erected 1848, closed by 1984) (Records 1858+ HRO)

BURLEY St John the Baptist (Formed 1840 from Ringwood)
OR   C1839-1992 M1840-1989 B1843-1992 Bn1886-1927,1935-1987 HRO
Mfc   C1839-1992 M1840-1988 B1843-1992 HRO
Mfm   C1839-1877 M1840-1877 B1843-1876 HRO, DRO, SLC
Cop   M1840-1881 CMI

BURLEY (Independent, later United Reformed) Chapel Lane (Founded 1789, closed
    1998)
OR   C1833-1837 D1813,1820-1837 PRO (RG 4/715)
Mfm   C1833-1837 D1813,1820-1837 PRO, HRO, SLC
Cop   D1813,1820-1837 HBI; Extracts C1833-1837 IGI

BURNETTS LANE (Wesleyan) - See SOUTH STONEHAM

BURSLEDON St Leonard (503) (South Stoneham Union) (Chapelry of Hound; separate parish 1850)

OR   C1648-1962 M1671-1988 B1671-1992 Bn1757-1776,1843-1993 HRO
(Few C before 1657, few M before 1673, few B before 1679; gaps in C 1715-1724, M 1717-1726, B 1708-1724) (The registers of Bursledon, Hamble, and Hound intermix, and all should be consulted)

BT   1788-1794,1799-1806,1808-1813,1815-1816,1818-1873 HRO (Mfm SLC)
(See also Hound)

Mfc   C1648-1962 M1671-1980 B1671-1953 Bn1757-1776 HRO
C1760-1791 B1760-1791 (in Hamble register) SG, SCA

Mfm   C1648-1859 M1671-1836 B1671-1891 Bn1757-1776 HRO

Cop   C1648-1837 M1671-1836 B1671-1837 (Ts,I) SG, HRO, SCA, HGS
M1754-1836 (Ts) SG; M1671-1836 HMI; M1671-1882 CMI
B1671-1837 HBI

BURSLEDON (Independent) (Founded 1860)

BURTON St Luke (Formed 1877 from Christchurch)
OR   C1875-1964 M1877-1986 Bn1877-1950,1957-1980 HRO; B1878+ Inc
Mfc   C1875-1964 M1877-1986 HRO
Cop   M1877-1881 CMI

BURTON (Roman Catholic) - See CHRISTCHURCH

BURTON (Independent, now United Reformed) Burton Green (Founded 1875, active)
OR   C1901-1909 registered at Christchurch Independent Chapel (DRO NP4/CM2)
Mfm   C1901-1909 SLC

BURTON (Independent) Waterditch Chapel - See BRANSGORE

CADNAM (Independent, Primitive Methodist) - See ELING

CALMORE St Anne (Mission church to Netley Marsh)
OR   M1984-1995 Bn1984-1997 HRO; C1977+ Inc

CALSHOT - See FAWLEY St George (RAF Garrison Church)

CANADA COMMON (Primitive Methodist) - See WEST WELLOW

CANDOVER - See BROWN CANDOVER, CHILTON CANDOVER, PRESTON CANDOVER

CATHERINE'S HILL (Independent) - See CHRISTCHURCH

CATHERINGTON All Saints (944) (Catherington Union) (See also Cowplain, Denmead)

OR   C1603-1960 M1602-1989 B1602-1940 Bn1923-1994 PCRO (Volume One contains entries from 1600, but the first three pages are virtually illegible)

BT   1781-1784,1786-1792,1794-1797,1799-1802,1804-1807,1809-1863 HRO (Mfm SLC)

Mfc   C1603-1960 M1602-1961 B1602-1940 HRO, PCRO

Mfm   C1603-1875 M1602-1875 B1602-1875 PCRO, SLC

Cop   C1603-1868 M1602-1905 B1602-1900 PCI; B1602-1837 HBI
M1602-1837 HMI; Extracts M1599-1744 IGI (Claimed to be from BT)
M1608-1882 CMI; Extracts C1599-1876 M1745-1876 IGI

CATHERINGTON (Wesleyan) Horndean (Chapel purchased 1850 by Independent Methodists, associated with Boarhunt and Clanfield chapels; White's Directory 1878 lists a Wesleyan Chapel erected 1837; no later references located)

CATHERINGTON Cemetery (Records - East Hampshire District Coucil)

Mfc   B1968-1995 HRO (Includes index)

CATHERINGTON Union Workhouse

OR   No registers survive. Other records at HRO.

CHALTON St Michael & All Angels (550) (Catherington Union) (See also Idsworth)

OR   C1538-1852 M1539-1973 B1538-1882 Bn1756-1784,1824-1954 PCRO (Includes entries for Idsworth; baptism register 1852-1970 destroyed by fire)

BT   1780,1782-1871 HRO (Mfm SLC)

Mfc   C1538-1852 M1539-1973 B1538-1882 Bn1756-1784 HRO, PCRO

Mfm   C1538-1852 M1539-1939 B1538-1882 Bn1756-1784,1824-1954 HRO, PCRO
C1538-1852 M1539-1875 B1538-1875 Bn1756-1784 SLC

Cop   C1653-1684 M1658-1683 B1654-1684 (Ms) PCRO (bound with Volume One of the PR); C1538-1852 M1539-1939 B1538-1882 PCI; M1539-1837 HMI
M1700-1881 CMI; B1538-1837 HBI; Extracts C1538-1852 M1538-1883 IGI

CHALTON (Independent, now United Reformed) Providence Chapel, The Green, Rowlands Castle (Founded 1797, active)

OR   C1799-1837 PRO (RG 4/716)

Mfm   C1799-1837 PRO, HRO, PCRO, SLC

Cop   Extracts C1799-1837 IGI

CHANDLERS FORD St Boniface (Formed 1910 from North Stoneham, Ampfield, North Baddesley, Otterbourne, & Eastleigh; see also Valley Park)

OR   C1898-1976,1984-1996 M1910-1992 B1906-1993 Bn1949-1990 HRO

Mfc   C1898-1976 M1910-1974 B1906-1979 HRO

CHANDLERS FORD St Martin in the Wood (Daughter church)

OR   C1960-1986 HRO; M1971+ Bn1971+ Inc

CHANDLERS FORD (Independent, now United Reformed) King's Road (Founded 1928, active) (Records 1928+ HRO)

OR   D1931-1954 HRO (In a membership list 1928-1953 in 8M80/NC14)

CHANDLERS FORD (Primitive Methodist) Brownhill Road, Fryern Hill (Southampton Primitive Methodist Circuit) (Chapel erected 1900) (Records 1899,1935+ HRO)
OR   C1930-1931 HRO (19M73/NMC/R12) (Entries also occur in the register of Southampton Primitive Methodist Chapel, South Front - SCA D/Meth 24/4)

CHANDLERS FORD Pine Road Cemetery (Records 1906+ Eastleigh Council)

CHANDLERS FORD Ramalley Cemetery (Records 1950+ Eastleigh Council)

CHARFORD (North and South) (71 North, 67 South) (Fordingbridge Union)
A pair of decayed parishes. The portion on the east bank of the Avon was annexed to Hale and the portion on the west bank was annexed to Breamore.

CHARLTON St Thomas (Chapelry of Andover)
OR   M1968-1990 Bn1988(only) HRO
Mfc   M1968-1979 HRO

CHARLTON (Primitive Methodist) - See ANDOVER

CHARTER ALLEY (Primitive Methodist) - See WOOTTON ST LAWRENCE

CHAWTON St Nicholas (446) (Alton Union) (See also Four Marks)
OR   C1596-1959 M1620-1837 B1602-1913 Bn1757-1806,1897-1962 HRO
    (Gaps in C 1651-1662, M 1642-1662, B 1642-1662; M1837-1978 stolen)
BT   1780-1869 HRO (Mfm SLC)
Mfc   C1596-1959 M1620-1837 B1602-1913 Bn1757-1806 HRO
Mfm   C1596-1812 M1620-1812 B1602-1812 Bn1757-1806 HRO, DRO
Pc   M1837-1978 HRO (Supplied by the Registrar General to replace the stolen register. Details of professions, residences, and fathers blanked out.)
Cop   C1806-1812 M1806-1812 B1806-1812 (Ms,TsI) HRO, HGS; B1602-1837 HBI
    M1754-1806 (Ms) HRO; M1620-1837 HMI; M1620-1893 CMI

CHERITON St Michael & All Angels (722) (Alresford Union) (See also Beauworth)
OR   C1557-1910 M1558-1973 B1557-1990 Bn1754-1812,1824-1982 HRO
    (Includes Bn1967-1982 for Tichborne)
BT   1724,1780-1783,1785-1878 HRO (Mfm SLC)
Mfc   C1557-1910 M1558-1973 B1557-1990 Bn1754-1812 HRO
    C1742-1854 M1743-1837 B1742-1885 Bn1754-1812 SG
Mfm   C1557-1877 M1558-1876 B1557-1876 Bn1754-1812,1824-1876 HRO, SLC
Pc   M1754-1812 Bn1754-1812 HRO
Cop   C1557-1812 M1558-1812 B1557-1812 (Ts,I) HRO, HGS; M1558-1837 HMI
    M1558-1881 CMI; B1557-1837 HBI; Extracts C1557-1877 M1558-1876 IGI

CHERITON (Independent) (Founded 1868)

CHERITON (Wesleyan) Lane End (Winchester Wesleyan Circuit) (Existed by 1874, succeeded in 1898 by Longwood Dene, Owslebury)

CHICHESTER [Sussex] Primitive Methodist Circuit (Included Emsworth Chapel)
OR   C1874-1944 West Sussex RO (M1P/1/1/1) (Includes Emsworth C1877-1934)
Mfm   C1874-1944 West Sussex RO, SLC

CHILBOLTON St Mary the Less (375) (Andover Union)

OR   C1699-1977 M1699-1976 B1699-1938 Bn1754-1811,1824-1951 HRO

BT   1780-1796,1798-1877 HRO (Mfm SLC)

Mfc   C1699-1977 M1699-1976 B1699-1938 Bn1754-1811 HRO

Mfm   C1699-1812 M1699-1812 B1699-1812 Bn1754-1811 HRO, DRO

Cop   C1774-1812 M1754-1836 B1774-1937 Bn1754-1811 (Ts,I) HRO

       C1774-1812 B1774-1812 (Ts) SG; M1699-1836 HMI; M1699-1883 CMI

       C1813-1837 M1754-1836 Bn1754-1811 (Ts,I) HGS

       Index to C1774-1812 B1774-1812 (Ts) HGS; B1699-1837 HBI

CHILCOMB St Andrew (192) (Winchester Union) (Now within the City of
Winchester; replaced as the parish church in 1950 by Winchester All Saints)

OR   C1556-1950 M1631-1948 B1663-1987 Bn1754-1823,1935-1950 HRO
       (Gap in M 1634-1656,1706-1718)

BT   1780-1781,1783-1784,1788-1791,1796-1799,1801-1807,1810-1835,
       1837-1882 HRO (Mfm SLC)

Mfc   C1556-1950 M1631-1948 B1663-1987 Bn1754-1823 HRO

Mfm   C1556-1921 M1631-1948 B1663-1934 Bn1754-1823 HRO

Cop   M1631-1837 (Ms) HRO
       M1631-1837 HMI; M1631-1885 CMI; B1663-1837 HBI

CHILTON CANDOVER St Nicholas (130) (Alresford Union) (Demolished 1878)

OR   C1672-1847 M1681-1848 B1677-1877 Bn1825-1848 HRO

BT   1729,1780,1782-1847 HRO (Mfm SLC) (See also Brown Candover)

Mfc   C1672-1847 M1681-1848 B1677-1877 HRO
       C1672-1847 M1681-1837 B1677-1877 SG

Cop   M1681-1837 HMI; M1681-1848 CMI; B1677-1837 HBI

CHILWORTH St Denys (150) (South Stoneham Union)

OR   C1722-1956 M1721-1990 B1723-1989 Bn1756-1761,1823-1969 HRO

BT   1783-1785,1787,1789-1792,1796-1797,1799,1804-1805,1807-1808,1813,
       1815-1869 HRO (Mfm SLC)

Mfc   C1722-1956 M1721-1975 B1723-1989 Bn1756-1761 HRO

Mfm   C1722-1877 M1721-1879 B1723-1811 Bn1756-1761,1823-1875 HRO, SLC

Cop   C1722-1837 M1721-1836 B1723-1837 Bn1751-1810,1835-1837 (Ts,I) SG,
       HRO, SCA, Inc; M1721-1836 HMI; M1721-1882 CMI;
       C1722-1812 M1721-1812 B1723-1812 Bn1751-1810 (Ts,I) HGS
       B1723-1837 HBI; Extracts C1722-1877 M1721-1879 IGI

CHINEHAM Christ Church (Replaced St Joseph) (District of Old Basing; separate
parish 1991)

OR   M1987-1996 Bn1987-1996 HRO; C1987+ B1987+ Inc

Mfc   M1987-1993 HRO

CHRISTCHURCH The Priory (5,344) (Christchurch Union) (See also Bournemouth, Bransgore, Burton, Highcliffe, Hinton Admiral, St Leonards/St Ives)

OR   C1584+ M1576+ B1633+ Bn1754-1812,1834+ Inc (Gap in C 1590-1633, M 1609-1633, CMB 1643-1682; no burials recorded 1858-1869)

BT   1780,1782-1794,1796-1798,1800-1807,1810-1886 HRO (Mfm SLC)

Mfc   C1584-1643,1805-1979 M1576-1643,1754-1981 B1633-1642,1805-1921 Bn1754-1812 HRO

Mfm   C1584-1876 M1576-1876 B1633-1889 Bn1754-1812,1834-1875 HRO, DRO, SLC (M 1803-1805 missing from damaged HRO film)

Pc   C1724-1734 M1724-1734 B1724-1734 HRO

Cop   C1682-1804 (Ts,A) SG, HRO, DRO; C1682-1804 (Ts) DRO
     M1682-1762 (Ts,I) SG, DRO; M1576-1602,1605-1609 (Ts) SG, HRO
     M1576-1602,1605-1609 (Ms) Christchurch Library; M1576-1837 HMI
     Index to M1576-1602,1605-1609 (Ts) HRO; M1813-1881 CMI
     B1682-1804 (Ts) DRO, HRO (on microfilm M70)
     B1682-1805 (Ts,A) (Letters A-F only) DRO; Extracts M1754-1876 IGI
     C1780-1812 M1780-1812 B1780-1812 (BT) (Ts,I) SG; B1633-1837 HBI
     Extracts of B1682-1804 (Holdenhurst inhabitants) (Ts) HRO

CHRISTCHURCH All Saints, Mudeford

OR   C1891-1986 M1958-1995 Bn1958-1986 HRO

Mfc   C1891-1961 M1958-1972 HRO

CHRISTCHURCH St George, Stourvale

OR   C1945-1990 M1958-1982 Bn1958-1989 HRO

Mfc   M1958-1973 HRO

CHRISTCHURCH St Mary, Somerford

OR   M1979-1986 HRO

CHRISTCHURCH (Roman Catholic) Immaculate Conception & St Joseph, Purewell (Catholicism persisted at many locations in the Avon Valley from the 17th century. Worship at Springfield House, Avon, c1735, moved to Sopley in 1753, to St Augustine's Chapel Burton Green in 1911, and to Purewell in 1866)

OR   C1803+ M1810,1833+ D1787+ Inc (Entries relating to Catholics also occur in Sopley [Anglican] parish registers)

Cop   C1803-1858,1866 M1810,1833,1835 D1787-1837 (I) CRS Vol 43
     M1810,1833,1835 HMI; D1787-1837 HBI
     Extracts C1803-1866 IGI (listed as Sopley)

CHRISTCHURCH (Particular Baptist) Bargates (Chapel erected 1874, church founded 1876, active)

CHRISTCHURCH (Baptist) Parley (founded before 1851, possibly in 1813)

CHRISTCHURCH (Independent, now United Reformed) Millhams Street (Founded 1660, active) (Records 1875+ DRO)
OR   C1780-1837 B1788-1795,1817-1837 PRO (RG 4/399,717,1070)
       C1816-1918 M1875-1878,1901-1915 B1817-1882,1901-1912 DRO
       (NP4/RE1,RE2,CM1,CM2,CM5,MS2) (Includes entries for other chapels)
Mfm C1780-1837 B1788-1795,1817-1837 PRO, HRO, SLC
       C1816-1918 M1875-1878,1901-1915 B1817-1882,1901-1912 SLC
Cop C1780-1816 B1786-1794,1817-1857 (Ts,I) SG, HRO, DRO
       B1788-1795,1817-1837 HBI; Extracts C1780-1837 IGI

CHRISTCHURCH (Independent) Bockhampton
OR   C1816-1824 registered at Christchurch Independent Chapel (DRO NP4/RE1)
Mfm C1816-1824 SLC

CHRISTCHURCH (Independent) Catherine's Hill (Founded c1835; 1851 Religious Census; no other references located)
OR   C1837-1842 registered at Christchurch Independent Chapel (DRO NP4/RE1)
Mfm C1837-1842 SLC

CHRISTCHURCH (Independent) Bargates Chapel (1851 Religious Census)

CHRISTCHURCH (Independent) Ringwood Road, Walkford - See MILTON (Independent) Cranemoor

CHRISTCHURCH Wesleyan Circuit - See CHRISTCHURCH & LYMINGTON

CHRISTCHURCH (Wesleyan) Purewell (Christchurch & Lymington Wesleyan Circuit, Bournemouth Wesleyan Circuit from 1925) (Church erected 1835, moved to Mudeford Lane 1939) (Records 1910+ HRO)

CHRISTCHURCH (Wesleyan) Hill Farm, Thorney Hill (Christchurch & Lymington Wesleyan Circuit, Wimborne Wesleyan Circuit from 1925, New Forest Wesleyan Mission from 1932) (Existed by 1846; possibly the same chapel as the second Wesleyan Chapel at Bransgore)

CHRISTCHURCH (Primitive Methodist) Avon Road - See BOURNEMOUTH (Primitive Methodist) Arnewood Road, Southbourne

CHRISTCHURCH Cemetery, Jumper's Road (Established 1858)

CHRISTCHURCH Union Workhouse
OR   No registers survive. Other records at DRO.

CHRISTCHURCH & LYMINGTON Wesleyan Circuit (Formed 1834 from Poole Circuit. Known originally as Ringwood Circuit, renamed Christchurch Circuit in 1854, and Christchurch & Lymington Circuit in 1868. Became part of the New Forest Wesleyan Mission in 1925, but some chapels transferred to Wimborne Circuit. Included chapels at Bransgore, Brockenhurst, Christchurch, Holdenhurst, Lymington, Milford, Milton, Ringwood, and Sway) (Records 1846+ HRO)

OR   C1833-1837 PRO (RG 4/2111) (catalogued as Ringwood)
       C1833-1871,1885-1911 HRO (45M68/NMR1-2)
Mfc   C1885-1911 HRO
Mfm C1833-1837 PRO, HRO, SLC (catalogued as Ringwood)
Cop   Extracts C1833-1837 IGI (listed as Ringwood)

CHURCH OAKLEY St Leonard (249) (Basingstoke Union) (See also East Oakley)
OR   C1559-1985 M1565-1990 B1560-1963 Bn1754-1812,1824-1908,1970-1987 HRO
BT   1780-1781,1783-1864 HRO (Mfm SLC)
Mfc   C1559-1985 M1565-1990 B1560-1963 Bn1754-1812 HRO
Mfm C1559-1876 M1565-1876 B1560-1878 Bn1754-1812,1824-1875 HRO, SLC
Cop   M1565-1812 Phillimore Vol 3 and Boyd; M1790-1812 Pallot
       C1559-1812 B1560-1812 (Ts,I) SG, HRO (Includes index to M1565-1812)
       C1559-1812 M1565-1753 B1560-1812 (Ts) HRO; M1565-1836 HMI
       Index to C1559-1812 M1565-1753 B1560-1812 (Ms) HRO
       M1565-1893 CMI; B1560-1837 HBI; Extracts C1559-1876 M1565-1836 IGI
       Extracts C1607-1812 M1633-1812 B1677-1809 (Ms) SG (Purports to be a transcript of a register for "East Oakley within Wootton St Lawrence")

CHURCH OAKLEY (Methodist) (Basingstoke Methodist Circuit) (Records 1938+ HRO)

CLANFIELD St James (210) (Catherington Union)
OR   C1563-1964 M1567-1979 B1548-1812 Bn1824-1967 PCRO
BT   1780-1856,1861-1862 HRO (Mfm SLC)
Mfc   C1563-1964 M1567-1979 B1548-1812 HRO, PCRO
Mfm C1563-1876 M1567-1882 B1548-1881 PCRO, SLC
       C1803-1812 M1838-1939 B1803-1812 HRO
Cop   C1743-1802 M1743-1802 B1678-1802 (Ts,I) SG, HGS
       C1563-1964 M1806-1939 B1547-1802 PCI
       M1567-1837 HMI; M1701-1882 CMI; B1548-1837 HBI
       Extracts C1563-1876 M1563-1882 IGI; Extracts C1780-1812 (BT) IGI

CLANFIELD (Independent) Bethel Chapel (Chapel erected c1855, closed by 1924?)

CLANFIELD (Wesleyan) (Erected c1850 as an Independent Methodist chapel linked with Boarhunt and Catherington; listed as Wesleyan in directories from 1855)

CLANVILLE (Wesleyan, Primitive Methodist) - See WEYHILL

CLATFORD - See GOODWORTH CLATFORD, UPPER CLATFORD

CLIDDESDEN St Leonard (329) (Basingstoke Union)

OR   C1636-1948 M1636-1993 B1636-1958 HRO; Bn1942+ Inc
       (Gap in M 1642-1660, B 1643-1656) (Includes entries for Farleigh Wallop)
BT   1780-1874,1876-1886 HRO (Mfm SLC)
Mfc   C1636-1948 M1636-1993 B1636-1958 HRO
Mfm C1636-1876 M1636-1875 B1636-1879 HRO, SLC
Cop   M1636-1812 Phillimore Vol 1, Boyd, Pallot; M1636-1837 HMI
       C1636-1758 M1636-1753 B1636-1760 (Ts,A) HRO
       C1759-1812 B1760-1812 (Ts,I) HRO; M1636-1889 CMI
       C1780-1812 B1780-1812 (probably BT) (Ms) HRO; B1636-1837 HBI

CLIDDESDEN (Wesleyan) (Basingstoke Wesleyan Circuit, Surrey & North
   Hampshire Wesleyan Mission from 1900, Basingstoke Wesleyan Circuit from
   1917) (Chapel erected 1880, closed c1979) (Records 1877+ HRO)

COLBURY Christ Church (Formed 1872 from Eling)

OR   C1872-1993 M1873-1993 B1873-1993 Bn1873-1993 HRO
Mfc   C1872-1993 M1873-1993 HRO
Cop   M1873-1883 CMI

COLDEN COMMON Holy Trinity (Formed 1843 from Otterbourne, Owslebury, &
   Twyford)

OR   C1844-1977 M1844-1994 B1844-1980 Bn1845-1961 HRO
BT   1844-1857 HRO (Filed with Owslebury) (Mfm SLC)
Mfc   C1844-1977 M1844-1982 B1844-1980 HRO
Cop   M1844-1881 CMI

COLDEN COMMON (Bible Christian) (Southampton Bible Christian Circuit)
   (Chapel erected 1866) (Records 1921+ HRO)

COLMER St Peter ad Vincula (164) (Petersfield Union) (Closed 1975)

OR   C1563-1975 M1565-1967 B1563-1975 Bn1754-1812,1824-1961 HRO
BT   1714,1780-1789,1791-1841,1843-1848,1850-1879 HRO (Mfm SLC)
Mfc   C1563-1975 M1565-1967 B1563-1975 Bn1754-1812 HRO
Mfm C1563-1879 M1565-1875 B1563-1886 Bn1754-1812,1824-1876 HRO, SLC
Cop   C1563-1812 M1563-1812 B1563-1812 Bn1754-1812 Printed in "The Parish
       Registers of Priors Dean and Colmer" Ed Rev T Hervey, M.A. (1886) (I)
       M1565-1835 HMI; M1565-1883 CMI; M1790-1837 Pallot
       B1563-1837 HBI; Extracts C1563-1812 M1563-1875 IGI

COMBE St Swithin (193) (Hungerford Union) (Transferred to Berkshire in 1895)
OR   C1560-1812 M1560-1985 B1561-1812 Bn1755-1793,1827-1966 BRO
        (Gaps in C 1602-1613,1650-1675, M 1630-1639,1643-1682, B 1601-1624,
        1647-1672,1689-1697; only one marriage entry before 1574; the pages
        containing C & B prior to 1603 are badly damaged by damp)
BT   1757,1780,1782-1787,1789,1794,1796,1798,1800-1801,1803-1805,1807-1870
        HRO (Mfm SLC)
Mfc   C1560-1812 M1560-1985 B1561-1812 Bn1755-1793,1827-1966 BRO
        C1560-1812 M1560-1835 B1561-1812 Bn1755-1793 HRO
Mfm   C1560-1812 M1560-1812 B1561-1812 Bn1755-1793 HRO
Cop   M1560-1812 Phillimore Vol 2 and Boyd; B1561-1837 HBI
        C1597-1827 M1560-1835 B1562-1812 Bn1755-1793 (Ms,TsI) SG
        M1560-1835 HMI; M1560-1889 CMI; M1790-1812 Pallot

COMBE (Primitive Methodist) (Andover Primitive Methodist Circuit, Hurstbourne
    Tarrant Primitive Methodist Circuit from 1910) (Mission established 1830, active
    1909, possibly house meetings only)

COMPTON All Saints (255) (Winchester Union)
OR   C1695-1977 M1695-1971 B1678-1942 Bn1755-1812,1826-1945 HRO
BT   1775-1778,1780-1806,1808-1810,1813-1821,1823-1824,1826,1828-1845,
        1847-1879 HRO (Mfm SLC)
Mfc   C1695-1977 M1695-1971 B1678-1942 Bn1755-1812 HRO
Mfm   C1695-1812 M1695-1812 B1678-1812 Bn1755-1812 HRO
Cop   M1695-1837 (Ts) SG; M1695-1837 HMI; M1695-1913 CMI
        M1695-1837 Boyd; B1678-1837 HBI

COPNOR - See PORTSEA St Alban, St Cuthbert

COPYTHORNE St Mary (Formed 1837 from Eling)
OR   C1834-1963 M1837-1960 B1835-1951 Bn1837-1932,1944-1988 HRO
BT   1838-1872 HRO (Mfm SLC) (Listed as North Eling; some filed with Eling)
Mfc   C1834-1963 M1837-1960 B1835-1951 HRO
Cop   M1837-1881 CMI; B1835-1837 HBI

COPYTHORNE (Particular Baptist) Totton Road, Bartley - See ELING

COPYTHORNE (Independent) - See ELING (Independent) Cadnam

CORHAMPTON (Dedication unknown) (125) (Droxford Union)
OR   C1665-1984 M1677-1978 B1695-1988 Bn1754-1837,1872-1925 HRO
        (Only four baptism entries before 1678)
BT   1780-1791,1793-1854,1856-1872 HRO (Mfm SLC)
Mfc   C1665-1984 M1677-1978 B1695-1988 Bn1754-1837 HRO
Mfm   C1665-1812 M1677-1811 B1695-1812 Bn1754-1837 HRO
Cop   C1665-1812 M1677-1811 B1695-1812 Bn1754-1837 (Ts,I) HRO
        Index to C1665-c1917 M1677-1836 B1695-c1917 (Ms) HRO
        M1677-1836 HMI; M1677-1885 CMI; B1695-1837 HBI

COSHAM St Philip (Formed from Wymering, Widley, & Farlington)
OR   C1936-1973 M1938-1984 Bn1937-1985 PCRO
Mfc   C1936-1973 M1938-1971 HRO, PCRO

COSHAM (Roman Catholic) St Colman (Founded 1928)
OR   C1928+ M1928 B1958+ Inc

COSHAM (Baptist) Havant Road (Founded 1871, active)

COSHAM (Independent, now United Reformed) Mulberry Lane (Chapel erected
    c1841, existed at least until 1878; present church founded 1926, active)

COSHAM (Methodist) (Portsmouth Wesley Circuit) (Existed by 1939)

COSHAM (Hilary Free Church) Salisbury Road (Existed by 1939)

COVE St John the Baptist (District formed 1844 from Yateley; see also Minley)
OR   C1844-1952 M1845-1966 B1844-1963 Bn1845-1990 SHC
Mfc   C1844-1952 M1845-1966 B1844-1963 HRO
        C1844-1898 M1845-1900 B1844-1900 Bn1845-1875 SHC
Mfm   C1844-1898 M1845-1900 B1844-1900 Bn1845-1875 SLC
        C1844-1876 Bn1845-1875 HRO
Cop   M1845-1881 CMI; Extracts C1844-1876 M1845-1875 IGI

COVE St Christopher (Chapel to St John)
OR   C1943-1959 M1935-1967 Bn1935-1965 SHC
Mfc   C1943-1959 M1935-1967 HRO

COVE St Stephen, Southwood Camp (Garrison church)
OR   C1965-1979 RACD

COVE, RAF Farnborough
OR   C1935-1947 SHC
Mfc   C1935-1947 HRO

COVE (Particular Baptist) (Founded 1827, lapsed 1903, re-formed 1911, active)

COVE (Primitive Methodist) (Bagshot Primitive Methodist Mission, Guildford
    Primitive Methodist Circuit from 1871, Aldershot Primitive Methodist Circuit from
    1879) (Chapel erected 1867) (Records 1867+ HRO)

COWPLAIN St Wilfrid (Formed 1962 from Catherington, Waterlooville, &
    Bedhampton)
OR   C1928-1992 M1942-1984 Bn1942-1995 PCRO
Mfc   C1928-1976 M1942-1984 HRO, PCRO

COWPLAIN Hartplain Church
OR   C1968-1973 M1975-1993 Bn1975-1989 PCRO

CRANEMOOR (Independent) - See MILTON

CRAWLEY St Mary (372) (Winchester Union)
OR   C1649-1879 M1675-1836 B1665-1984 Bn1813-1945 HRO
       (C irregular before 1675; B irregular before 1695)
BT   1724,1780-1781,1783-1787,1789-1880 HRO (Mfm SLC)
Mfc   C1649-1879 M1675-1836 B1665-1984 HRO
Mfm   C1649-1812 M1675-1811 B1665-1812 HRO
Cop   M1675-1811 Phillimore Vol 11 and Boyd; M1675-1836 HMI
       C1649-1812 B1665-1812 (Ms) HRO
       M1675-1836 CMI; M1790-1812 Pallot; B1665-1837 HBI

CRAWLEY Cemetery (Records - Parish Council)
Mfc   B1894-1998 HRO

CRENDLE COMMON (Wesleyan) - See DAMERHAM

CROFTON Holy Rood (Ancient chapelry of Titchfield; separate parish 1871) (In
    1878 the ancient chapel was replaced as the parish church by Holy Rood,
    Stubbington; see also Lee on the Solent)
OR   C1838-1989 M1871-1971 B1838-1940 Bn1871-1992 PCRO
BT   1872 (only) HRO (Mfm SLC)
Mfc   C1838-1966 M1871-1971 B1838-1940 HRO, PCRO
Cop   C1838-1907 PCI; M1871-1882 CMI

CROFTON Cemetery (Records - Fareham Borough Council)
Mfc   B1864-1960 HRO

CRONDALL All Saints (2,010) (Hartley Wintney Union) (See also Crookham,
    Ewshot, Fleet)
OR   C1569-1867 M1576-1889 B1570-1859 Bn1754-1812,1823-1923 SHC
       (Gap in M 1657-1695, B 1653-1678)
BT   1780-1866 HRO (Mfm SLC)
Mfc   C1569-1867 M1576-1889 B1570-1859 Bn1754-1812 HRO
       C1569-1867 M1576-1889 B1570-1812 Bn1754-1812 SHC
Mfm   C1569-1867 M1576-1889 B1570-1812 Bn1754-1812 SLC
Cop   M1576-1812 Phillimore Vol 4 and Boyd
       C1569-1837 M1576-1970 B1570-1837 Bn1754-1811 (Ts & Ms,I) SG, HRO,
       SHC, Inc; C1836-1867 (Ms,I) SG, Inc; M1576-1837 HMI
       M1813-1889 CMI; M1790-1812 Pallot; B1570-1837 HBI

CRONDALL (Society of Friends) - See ALTON

CRONDALL (Independent) (House meetings, chapels 1798 & 1852, closed 1969)
OR   C1796-1836 (plus one birth in 1792) PRO (RG 4/718)
Mfm   C1796-1836 PRO, HRO, SLC
Cop   Extracts C1796-1836 IGI

CRONDALL (Wesleyan) (Aldershot & Farnham Wesleyan Circuit) (Founded 1918)
    (Records 1944+ HRO)
OR   C1886-1905,1935-1968 HRO (80M78/NMR8) (C1886-1905 are for Ewshot;
       some baptisms at Crondall were registered at Farnham Wesleyan Chapel)

CRONDALL Bible Christian Circuit (United Methodist Circuit from 1907) (Formed 1863 from Farnham Circuit; known as the North or North East Hampshire Mission from 1924; became part of Liphook & North Hampshire United Methodist Circuit in 1930. Included chapels at Bentley, Binsted, Crondall, and Crookham) (Records 1863+ HRO)
OR   C1863-1930 (plus C certificate stubs 1923-1941) HRO (89M72/NMR5-7)
Mfc   C1913-1930 HRO

CRONDALL (Bible Christian) Ebenezer Chapel, Dippenhall Street (Farnham Bible Christian Circuit, Crondall Bible Christian Circuit from 1863) (Chapel erected 1838; became Wesleyan)

CRONDALL Cemetery (Established 1880; records c1950s+ Parish Council)

CROOKHAM Christ Church (Formed 1842 from Crondall; see also Ewshot)
OR   C1842-1964 M1842-1980 B1842-1966 Bn1969-1989 SHC
BT   1842-1865 HRO (Mfm SLC)
Mfc   C1842-1964 M1842-1980 B1842-1966 HRO
       C1842-1901 M1842-1900 B1842-1900 SHC
Mfm   C1842-1901 M1842-1900 B1842-1900 SLC
Cop   M1842-1882 CMI; Extracts C1842-1875 M1842-1878 IGI

CROOKHAM St Luke (Garrison church)
OR   C1920-1969 M1934-1958 Bn1934-1969 RACD

CROOKHAM (Roman Catholic) Holy Trinity (Crookham Camp 1920-1945, Our Lady of Lourdes 1945, separate parish 1958, Holy Trinity 1968)
OR   C1921+ M1929+ B1958+ Inc

CROOKHAM (Baptist) Hope Chapel, Reading Road (Founded c1849, probably closed by 1900)

CROOKHAM (Primitive Methodist) Reading Road (Basingstoke Primitive Methodist Circuit) (Existed by 1895)

CROOKHAM (Bible Christian) Brook (Crondall Bible Christian Circuit) (Chapel erected 1856, probably closed by 1890)

CROWD HILL (Wesleyan) - See BISHOPSTOKE

CROWE HILL (Wesleyan) - See RINGWOOD

CRUX EASTON St Michael & All Angels (97) (Kingsclere Union)
OR   C1737-1994 M1745-1977 B1744-1993 Bn1754-1997 HRO
BT   1780-1781,1783-1787,1789,1791-1863,1867-1870 HRO (Mfm SLC)
Mfc   C1737-1992 M1745-1977 B1744-1993 Bn1754-1828 HRO
Mfm   C1737-1982 M1745-1977 B1744-1982 Bn1754-1828 HRO
Cop   M1745-1837 HMI; M1745-1881 CMI; B1744-1837 HBI

CURDRIDGE St Peter (Formed 1838 from Bishops Waltham)
OR   C1835-1946 M1838-1962 B1835-1934 Bn1841-1975 HRO
Mfc   C1835-1946 M1838-1962 B1835-1934 HRO
Cop   M1838-1885 CMI; B1835-1837 HBI

CURDRIDGE (Primitive Methodist) (Droxford Primitive Methodist Circuit)
   (Chapel erected 1925) (Records 1933+ HRO)

CURDRIDGE (Brethren) (Chapel existed by 1899)

DAMERHAM St George (716) (Fordingbridge Union) (The parish was transferred
   from Wiltshire to Hampshire in 1895; sometimes referred to as South Damerham)
OR   C1678-1968 M1678-1978 B1678-1879 Bn1746,1824-1917 HRO
      (Entries before 1699 are for 1678,1679,1691 only)
BT   1606,1622-1638,1671-1679,1696,1710-1734,1744,1748-1750,1782,1788,
      1793-1836,1839-1880 WRO (Mfm SLC)
Mfc   C1678-1968 M1678-1978 B1678-1879 Bn1746 HRO
Mfm   C1678-1812 M1678-1812 B1678-1812 Bn1746 HRO
Cop   C1753-1788 M1753-1755 B1753-1785 (Ts,I) HRO; B1678-1837 HBI
      M1813-1837 HMI; M1700-1884 CMI; M1606-1837 Nimrod Index

DAMERHAM (Baptist) Green Bank, South End Road (Founded 1828, active)

DAMERHAM (Independent) Bethel Chapel (Chapel erected c1834)

DAMERHAM (Wesleyan) Crendle Common (Salisbury Wesleyan Circuit)
   (Existed by 1880) (Records 1932+ WRO)

DAMERHAM (Primitive Methodist) (Salisbury Primitive Methodist Circuit,
   Woodfalls Primitive Methodist Circuit from 1898) (Chapel erected 1845)
   (Records 1851+ WRO)

DEAN - See EAST DEAN

DEANE All Saints (163) (Basingstoke Union)
OR   C1659-1992 M1679-1989 B1659-1991 Bn1766-1991 HRO (Gap 1720-1729)
BT   1781,1783-1789,1791,1794-1820,1822-1827,1829-1867,1869-1872 HRO
      (Mfm SLC)
Mfc   C1659-1992 M1679-1989 B1659-1991 Bn1766-1863 HRO
Mfm   C1659-1812 M1679-1834 B1659-1883 Bn1766-1863 HRO, SLC
Cop   M1679-1812 Phillimore Vol 1, Boyd, Pallot; M1679-1834 HMI
      C1659-1840 M1813-1840 B1659-1840 Bn1824-1838 (Ts,I) SG, HRO
      C1659-1892 M1679-1889 B1659-1893 (Ts & Ms) HRO
      M1679-1914 CMI; B1659-1837 HBI; Extracts C1659-1840 M1679-1813 IGI

DENMEAD All Saints (Formed 1880 from Hambledon & Catherington)
OR   C1881-1980 M1881-1990 Bn1881-1995 PCRO
Mfc   C1881-1954 M1881-1980 HRO, PCRO
Cop   M1881-1888 CMI

DENMEAD (Baptist) Anmore Road (Founded 1881, active)

DENMEAD (Primitive Methodist) World's End - See HAMBLEDON

DENMEAD Cemetery (Records - Parish Council)
Mfc   B1919-1984 HRO

DIBDEN All Saints (418) (New Forest Union)
OR   C1673-1973 M1673-1994 B1673-1992 HRO (Volumes 1 & 2, 1644-1787,
        damaged during an air raid. The legible portions have been transcribed)
BT   1701,1780-1781,1783-1784,1786-1822,1824-1859 HRO (Mfm SLC)
Mfc   C1784-1973 M1731-1986 B1784-1962 HRO
        C1784-1973 M1731-1837,1940-1988 B1784-1907 SG
Cop   C1673-1703,1731-1788 M1673-1703 B1673-1703,1731-1787 (Ts) HRO, Inc
        C1784-1812 B1784-1812 (Ms,I) HRO (HGS holds index only)
        Index to B1673-1985 (Ts) HRO; M1673-1837 HMI; B1673-1837 HBI
        M1673-1702,1754-1940 CMI

DIBDEN St Andrew (Mission Church)
OR   C1927-1970 M1955-1970 Bn1986-1997 HRO; Bn1971+ Inc
Mfc   C1927-1970 M1955-1970 HRO

DIBDEN (Wesleyan) North Road (Southampton Wesleyan Circuit, New Forest
    Wesleyan Mission from 1925) (Established 1916, chapel erected 1922, active)
    (Records 1913+ SCA)

DOGMERSFIELD All Saints (272) (Hartley Wintney Union)
OR   C1675-1911 M1677-1991 B1677-1994 Bn1755-1791,1824-1944,1965-1996
        HRO (Gap in M 1745-1755)
BT   1780-1783,1785,1787-1861,1864-1867 HRO (Mfm SLC)
Mfc   C1675-1911 M1677-1991 B1677-1994 Bn1755-1791 HRO
Mfm   C1675-1812 M1677-1812 B1677-1812 Bn1755-1791 HRO
Cop   M1695-1812 Phillimore Vol 3 and Boyd
        C1675-1693 M1677-1693 B1677-1693 (Ms) SG; M1677-1835 HMI
        M1677-1835 Bn1755-1791 (Ts,I) SG, HRO, HGS
        M1677-1883 CMI; M1790-1812 Pallot; B1677-1837 HBI

DORSET & HAMPSHIRE (Society of Friends) Quarterly Meeting (Formed 1804 by
    amalgamation of the Dorset and Hampshire Quarterly Meetings. Comprised the
    Monthly Meetings of Alton, Shaftesbury & Sherborne [Dorset], Poole & Ringwood
    [Poole & Southampton from c1824]) (Records 1804+ HRO, DRO)
OR   Z1803-1837 M1805-1837 B1804-1837 PRO (RG 6/196,624,625,1147,1148)
        (Registers 1776-1794 are for the Dorset Quarterly Meeting, and are wrongly
        shown as Dorset & Hampshire in the PRO list)
Mfm   Z1803-1837 M1805-1837 B1804-1837 HRO
Cop   Index see Hampshire Quarterly Meeting; M1805-1837 HMI; B1804-1837 HBI

DRAYTON (Wesleyan) - See FARLINGTON

DROXFORD St Mary & All Saints (1,620) (Droxford Union) (See also Shedfield, Swanmore)
OR   C1635-1976 M1633-1987 B1633-1975 Bn1754-1835,1845-1975 HRO
BT   1780-1834,1836-1846,1848-1861 HRO (Mfm SLC)
Mfc   C1635-1976 M1633-1987 B1633-1975 Bn1754-1835 HRO
Mfm C1635-1876 M1633-1875 B1633-1812 Bn1754-1835 HRO, SLC
Cop   C1635-1736 M1633-1727 B1633-1738 (Ms) HRO
       M1633-1837 HMI; M1633-1883 CMI; B1633-1837 HBI
       Extracts C1633-1876 M1633-1790,1813-1876 IGI

DROXFORD Primitive Methodist Circuit (Hambledon Branch of Winchester Circuit operated autonomously from 1885 and became Droxford Circuit in 1892. Included chapels at Bishops Waltham, Curdridge, Droxford, Hambledon, Meonstoke, Shedfield, Swanmore, Warnford, and West Meon) (Records 1885+ HRO)

DROXFORD (Primitive Methodist) (Hambledon Primitive Methodist Branch, Droxford Primitive Methodist Circuit from 1892) (Chapel erected 1886) (Records 1884+ HRO)

DROXFORD Union Workhouse
OR   No registers survive. Other records at HRO.

DUMMER All Saints (383) (Basingstoke Union)
OR   C1541-1968 M1541-1987 B1541-1924 Bn1754-1802,1824-1954 HRO
BT   1780,1782,1785,1787,1790-1792,1796,1798-1806,1808-1845,1847-1861,1864
       (plus one undated) HRO (Mfm SLC)
Mfc   C1541-1968 M1541-1987 B1541-1924 Bn1754-1802 HRO
Mfm C1541-1812 M1541-1812 B1541-1812 Bn1754-1802 HRO
Cop   M1541-1812 Phillimore Vol 1, Boyd, Pallot
       Index to C1541-1890 M1541-1890 B1541-1890 (Ms) HRO
       M1541-1836 HMI; M1541-1882 CMI; B1541-1837 HBI

DUMMER (Primitive Methodist) (Basingstoke Primitive Methodist Circuit) Chapel erected 1862) (Records 1931+ HRO)

DUNLEY (Wesleyan, Primitive Methodist) - See ST MARY BOURNE

DURLEY Holy Cross (361) (Droxford Union) (Chapelry of Upham; parish 1855)
OR   C1561-1984 M1560-1991 B1561-1914 Bn1754-1805,1825-1967 HRO
BT   1780-1785,1787-1859,1861,1863 HRO (Mfm SLC)
Mfc   C1561-1984 M1560-1991 B1561-1914 Bn1754-1805 HRO
Mfm C1561-1875 M1560-1875 B1561-1875 Bn1754-1805 HRO
Pc   C1561-1909 M1560-1956 B1561-1914 Bn1754-1805 HRO
Cop   M1560-1580 (Ts) HRO; M1560-1836 HMI; M1700-1881 CMI
       B1561-1837 HBI

DURLEY (Wesleyan) (Southampton Wesleyan Circuit, Winchester Wesleyan Circuit from 1862, Eastleigh Wesleyan Circuit from 1891, South Hampshire Wesleyan Mission from 1900) (Existed by 1828, closed 1983) (Records 1828+ HRO)
OR   C1895-1982 HRO (19M73/NMC/R13)

EAST BOLDRE St Paul (Formed 1840 from Boldre)
OR   C1840-1992 M1841-1982 B1840-1993 Bn1855-1973 HRO
BT   1840-1841,1843,1846-1854,1856-1874 HRO (Mfm SLC)
Mfc   C1840-1992 M1841-1982 B1840-1993 HRO
Cop M1841-1881 CMI

EAST BOLDRE (Baptist) Chapel Lane (Founded 1818, active)
OR   Z1822+ C1817+ reported to be at the church - unconfirmed

EAST BOLDRE (Independent) (Founded c1808)

EAST DEAN (Not dedicated) (173) (Romsey Union) (Chapelry of Mottisfont;
    separate parish 1884)
OR   C1681-1993 M1682-1992 B1681-1993 Bn1825-1993 HRO
       (Earlier entries are in the Lockerley registers)
BT   1705-1710,1780-1781,1784-1871 HRO (Mfm SLC) (1758 in Mottisfont BT)
Mfc   C1681-1993 M1682-1992 B1681-1993 HRO
Mfm C1681-1812 M1682-1835 B1681-1812 HRO, SLC
Cop C1681-1836 M1682-1835 B1681-1836 (Ts) HRO, HGS (Many errors, much
       omission of detail); M1682-1835 HMI; M1682-1885 CMI; B1681-1837 HBI

EAST END (Independent) - See LYMINGTON, WEST MEON

EAST END (Primitive Methodist) - See LYMINGTON

EASTLEIGH The Resurrection (Formed 1868 from South Stoneham; redundant
    1981; see also Chandlers Ford)
OR   C1868-1965 M1869-1978 B1868-1918,1933-1969 Bn1869-1933,1938-1979
       HRO
Mfc   C1868-1965 M1869-1978 B1868-1918,1933-1969 HRO
Cop M1869-1882 CMI

EASTLEIGH All Saints (District formed 1910; became the parish church in 1981)
OR   C1965-1994 M1954-1994 B1933-1969 Bn1954-1990 HRO
Mfc   M1954-1976 HRO

EASTLEIGH (Roman Catholic) Holy Cross (A priest was maintained at Brambridge
    House, Twyford, from the mid 17th century. Worship moved to Highbridge House,
    Otterbourne, in 1782. Chapel established 1884 at St Mary's Home, Eastleigh, Our
    Lady of Good Counsel, Leigh Road, erected 1890, present church erected 1902)
OR   C1888+ M1892+ B1889+ Inc (earlier registers missing)
Cop C1766-1869 M1769-1855 D1768-1867 (I) CRS Vol 27
       M1769-1835 HMI; Extracts C1766-1869 IGI

EASTLEIGH (Baptist) Desborough Road (Founded 1889, active)

EASTLEIGH (Baptist) Emmanuel Chapel (Active)

EASTLEIGH (Independent) Desborough Road (Founded 1910, possibly closed by
    1934) (Records 1923+ HRO, in 127M94)

EASTLEIGH (Independent, later United Reformed) Nightingale Avenue (Founded 1949, closed after 1993) (Records 1923+ HRO, in 127M94)

EASTLEIGH Wesleyan Circuit (Formed 1891 from Southampton Circuit; became part of the South Hampshire Wesleyan Mission in 1900. Included chapels at Bishopstoke, Durley, Eastleigh, and South Stoneham) (Records 1893+ HRO)

EASTLEIGH (Wesleyan) High Street (Winchester Wesleyan Circuit, Eastleigh Wesleyan Circuit from 1891, South Hampshire Wesleyan Mission from 1900) (Mission hall founded 1888, chapel erected 1893, replaced 1983 by St Andrew, Blenheim Road, active) (Records 1894+ HRO)
OR   C1891-1939 HRO (19M73/NMC/R5)
Mfc   C1891-1939 HRO

EASTLEIGH Primitive Methodist Circuit - See SOUTHAMPTON Primitive Methodist Circuit

EASTLEIGH (Primitive Methodist) Factory Road (Existed by 1893)
OR   C1893-1903 HRO (19M73/NMC/R6)
Mfc   C1893-1903 HRO

EASTLEIGH Bible Christian Circuit - See SOUTHAMPTON Bible Christian Circuit

EASTLEIGH (Bible Christian) Leigh Road (Southampton Bible Christian Circuit) (Chapel erected 1888, closed 1959 and amalgamated with High Street Wesleyan Church) (Records 1903+ HRO)
OR   M1932-1959 HRO (19M73/NMC/R7-9)
Mfc   M1932-1959 HRO

EASTLEIGH Methodist Circuit (Formed 1923 from Southampton & Eastleigh United Methodist Circuit; joined in 1946 by the Eastleigh section of the Winchester & Eastleigh Methodist Circuit) (Records 1933+ HRO)
OR   C1937-1959 HRO (19M73/NMC/R4)
Mfc   C1937-1959 HRO

EASTLEIGH (Plymouth Brethren) Meeting House (Existed by 1899)

EASTLEIGH Cemetery (Records - Eastleigh Borough Council)
Mfc   B1901-1962 HRO

EAST MEON All Saints (1,455) (Petersfield Union) (See also Langrish)
OR   C1560-1954 M1560-1995 B1560-1992 Bn1794,1824-1873,1950-1976 HRO
BT   1702,1780-1860 HRO (Mfm SLC)
Mfc   C1560-1995 M1560-1995 B1560-1995 HRO
      C1560-1742,1813-1954 M1560-1742,1754-1979 B1560-1742,1813-1874 SG
Mfm   C1560-1850 M1560-1875 B1560-1874 Bn1794 HRO, SLC
Cop   B1875-1976 (Ms) HRO; M1560-1837 HMI; M1700-1881 CMI
      B1560-1837 HBI

EAST MEON (Calvinistic Baptist) (Founded c1833, probably closed by 1900)

EAST MEON (Independent) (Chapel existed by 1855, church founded 1864)

EAST MEON (Independent) Ramsdean (Founded c1830)

EAST MEON (Primitive Methodist) (Petersfield Primitive Methodist Circuit) (Chapel erected c1867, closed by 1987) (Records 1865+ HRO)
OR   C1979-1983 HRO (89M72/NMR17)

EAST MEON (Calvinist) Halley Street (Chapel erected 1833; 1851 Religious Census; no later references located)

EASTNEY - See PORTSEA St Andrew, St Margaret

EAST OAKLEY St John (Chapelry of Church Oakley, formerly in the parish of Wootton St Lawrence)
OR   M1946-1959 Bn1962-1973 HRO
Mfc   M1946-1959 HRO

EAST OAKLEY (Primitive Methodist) - See WOOTTON ST LAWRENCE

EASTON St Mary the Virgin (494) (Winchester Union)
OR   C1692-1967 M1694-1986 B1693-1907 Bn1889-1919 HRO
BT   1780-1781,1783-1784,1786,1788-1793,1795-1799,1802-1816,1818-1819,
        1821-1849,1851-1856,1858-1874 HRO (Mfm SLC)
Mfc   C1692-1967 M1694-1986 B1693-1907 HRO
Mfm   C1692-1873 M1694-1812 B1693-1812 HRO
Cop   C1692-1754 M1694-1754 B1693-1812 (Ts,I) HRO, HGS
        M1694-1836 HMI; M1694-1882 CMI; B1693-1837 HBI

EASTON (Wesleyan) (Southampton Wesleyan Circuit) (Existed by 1855, possibly closed by 1895)

EASTON (Primitive Methodist) (Winchester Primitive Methodist Circuit) (Chapel erected 1840 in Magdalen Lane (now Chapel Lane, new chapel erected 1909 in centre of village, closed 1982) (Records 1860+ HRO)

EAST PARLEY (Baptist) - See CHRISTCHURCH

EASTROP St Mary (69) (Basingstoke Union)
OR   C1813-1941 M1759-1994 B1813-1979 Bn1759-1993 HRO (No M recorded
        1831-1840) (Volume one, containing C1750-1812, B1758-1812, was known to
        be in the church in 1931 but is now missing; transcripts exist)
BT   1780-1787,1792-1793,1796,1803-1810,1813-1878 HRO (Mfm SLC)
Mfc   C1813-1941 M1759-1994 B1813-1979 Bn1759-1807 HRO
Cop   M1759-1807 Phillimore Vol 5 and Boyd
        C1750-1840 M1759-1840 B1758-1840 (Ts,I) SG, HRO; M1759-1831 HMI
        C1750-1888 M1759-1857 B1758-1888 (Ms) HRO; M1759-1897 CMI
        Index to C1750-1888 M1759-c1888 B1758-1888 (Ms) HRO
        M1790-1807 Pallot; B1758-1837 HBI; Extracts C1750-1840 IGI

EAST STRATTON All Saints (386) (Winchester Union) (Chapelry of Micheldever; separate parish 1931)

OR   C1538-1988 M1542-1979 B1540-1738,1771-1989 Bn1724,1726,1764-1812, 1824-1970 HRO (Gaps in C 1543-1569, M 1545-1573,1735-1760, B 1546-1569; burial register 1738-1771 missing)

BT   1780-1781,1783-1793,1795-1796,1798-1864,1866-1867,1869-1872 HRO (Mfm SLC)

Mfc   C1538-1988 M1542-1979 B1540-1738,1771-1989 Bn1724,1726,1764-1812 HRO

Mfm   C1538-1809 M1542-1812 B1540-1738,1771-1806 Bn1724,1726,1764-1812 HRO, SLC

Cop   C1719-1734,1749-1809 M1718-1735,1786,1800 B1719-1737,1771-1806 Bn1724,1726 (Ts,I) HRO, HGS; M1542-1837 HMI; M1542-1884 CMI B1540-1837 HBI; Extracts C1538-1809 M1542-1812 IGI

EAST STRATTON (Primitive Methodist) (Micheldever Primitive Methodist Circuit) (Chapel erected 1886, closed 1978) (Records 1948+ HRO)

EAST TISTED St James (232) (Alton Union)

OR   C1561-1946 M1538-1978 B1561-1992 Bn1817-1865 HRO

BT   1702,1710,1780-1840,1843-1872 HRO (Mfm SLC)

Mfc   C1561-1946 M1538-1978 B1561-1987 SG, HRO

Mfm   C1561-1877 M1538-1832 B1561-1812 HRO, SLC

Cop   M1538-1832 HMI; M1538-1889 CMI; B1561-1837 HBI Extracts C1561-1877 M1538-1832 IGI

EAST TYTHERLEY St Peter (294) (Stockbridge Union)

OR   C1562-1895 M1562-1994 B1562-1993 Bn1823-1880 HRO (Gaps prior to 1680)

BT   1780-1870 HRO (Mfm SLC)

Mfc   C1562-1895 M1562-1994 B1562-1993 HRO

Mfm   C1562-1875 M1562-1875 B1562-1875 Bn1823-1875 HRO, SLC

Cop   C1813-1895 (Ts,A) HRO; M1592-1837 HMI; M1700-1886 CMI B1562-1837 HBI

EAST WELLOW (with West Wellow, Wilts) St Margaret (697) (Romsey Union)

OR   C1570-1938 M1571-1994 B1570-1977 Bn1754-1776,1779-1806,1823-1981 HRO (Gaps in M 1608-1631,1638-1645,1687-1716; several small gaps in burials; M1937-1951 damaged by water and not fit for production)

BT   1783,1786-1795,1797-1808,1810-1875 HRO (Mfm SLC)

Mfc   C1570-1938 M1571-1937,1951-1988 B1570-1977 Bn1754-1776,1779-1806 HRO; C1570-1938 M1571-1937 B1570-1940 Bn1754-1776,1779-1806 SG

Mfm   C1570-1876 M1571-1876 B1570-1876 Bn1754-1776,1779-1806,1823-1875 HRO, SLC

Pc   M1937-1951 (From registrar's duplicate; trades, residences, fathers deleted)

Cop   C1570-1887 M1571-1887 B1570-1887 (A) Printed in "Index to the Registers of the Parish of Wellow" by C.W. Empson (1889) Index to M1571-1837 (Ts) WRO; M1571-1837 HMI; M1813-1881 CMI M1571-1837 Nimrod Index; M1790-1837 Pallot; Index to B1800-1837 SG B1570-1837 HBI; Extracts C1570-1875 M1571-1876 IGI

EAST WOODHAY St Martin (1,269) (Kingsclere Union) (See also Woolton Hill)
OR   C1610-1997 M1618-1950 B1624-1909 Bn1754-1908 HRO
     (M1769-1773 missing from register)
BT   1780-1789,1791,1793-1820,1825-1868 HRO (Mfm SLC)
Mfc   C1610-1859 M1618-1950 B1624-1909 Bn1754-1804 HRO
Mfm C1610-1803 M1618-1754 B1624-1803 Bn1804 (only) HRO
Cop   M1618-1812 Phillimore Vol 9 and Boyd; M1618-1837 HMI
     M1618-1881 CMI; M1790-1812 Pallot; B1624-1837 HBI

EAST WOODHAY (Baptist) (PO Directory 1855; no other references located)

EAST WOODHAY (Independent) (Chapel erected c1803, possibly closed by 1895)

EAST WOODHAY (Wesleyan) North End (Newbury Wesleyan Circuit, Newbury &
Hungerford Wesleyan Circuit from 1908) (Existed by 1855)

EAST WOODHAY (Primitive Methodist) Gore End (Shefford Primitive Methodist
Circuit, Newbury Primitive Methodist Circuit from 1845) (Chapel erected 1838)

EAST WORLDHAM St Mary (212) (Alton Union)
OR   C1690-1964 M1692-1986 B1690-1970 HRO; Bn1942+ Inc (Volume one,
     containing CB to 1812 and M to 1754, was severely damaged by water in the
     1940s and is now mostly illegible; a transcript had previously been made)
BT   1780-1781,1784-1813,1815-1833,1835-1860 HRO (Mfm SLC)
Mfc   C1813-1964 M1755-1986 B1813-1970 HRO
Mfm C1813-1876 M1755-1875 B1813-1879 HRO, SLC
Cop   C1690-1850 M1692-1854 B1690-1844 Printed in "The Registers of East
     Worldham, West Worldham, and Hartley Mauditt", Major V Ferguson (1942)
     C1690-1840 M1692-1840 B1690-1844 (Ts) SG; M1692-1837 HMI
     C1690-1860 M1692-1840 B1690-1844 (Ts) HRO; M1692-1882 CMI
     Index to C1851-1982 M1855-1983 B1845-1983 Inc
     B1690-1837 HBI; C1690-1850 M1692-1854 IGI

EAST WORLDHAM (Wesleyan) (Alton Wesleyan Circuit, Surrey & North
Hampshire Wesleyan Mission from 1900, Alton Wesleyan Circuit from 1917)
(Founded 1878, closed by 1937) (Records 1878,1937 [only] HRO)

ECCHINSWELL St Lawrence (449) (Kingsclere Union) (Ancient Chapelry of
Kingsclere; separate parish 1852; see also Sydmonton)
OR   C1610-1673,1844-1976 M1610-1673 B1610-1673,1844-1955
     Bn1876-1971 HRO; M1844+ Inc (Includes entries for Sydmonton; for other
     periods, entries are at Kingsclere)
BT   1844-1871 HRO (Mfm SLC)
Mfc   C1610-1673,1844-1976 M1610-1673 B1610-1673,1844-1955 HRO
Cop   C1610-1673 M1610-1673 B1610-1673 (Ms,A) SG (Listed as Sydmonton)
     C1610-1673 M1610-1673 B1610-1673 (Ts,I) HRO; B1610-1673 HBI

ECCHINSWELL (Independent) (Chapel erected 1812, closed 1968)

ELDON St John the Baptist (Rectory annexed to Michelmersh & Timsbury)
OR   C1918-1953 M1919(only) HRO
Mfc C1918-1953 M1919(only) HRO

ELING St Mary (4,624) (New Forest Union) (See also Colbury, Copythorne, Marchwood, Netley Marsh, Testwood)
OR   C1538-1974 M1539-1993 B1537-1978 Bn1754-1984 HRO (Gap c1550-1563)
BT   1701-1702,1707,1780-1837,1840-1875 HRO (Mfm SLC)
Mfc C1538-1974 M1539-1983 B1537-1978 Bn1754-1783 HRO
Mfm C1538-1916,1934-1974 M1539-1901 B1537-1901 Bn1754-1783 HRO
Cop M1539-1812 Phillimore Vol 7 and Boyd; C1538-1750 (Ms,A) HRO
     M1539-1812 (Ms) HRO; M1539-1837 HMI; M1790-1812 Pallot
     C1538-1655 B1537-1660 (Ts,I) SG; M1813-1882 CMI; B1537-1837 HBI

ELING (Roman Catholic) St Theresa of the Child Jesus, Totton (Founded 1925, parish formed 1937 from Romsey & Shirley [Southampton] Catholic parishes)
OR   C1937+ Inc

ELING (Particular Baptist) Totton Road, Bartley (Meetings held at a rented chapel in Netley Marsh, chapel opened 1879)
OR   Church book 1872-1960 Gospel Standard Baptist Library

ELING (Independent) Cadnam (Founded 1790, closed 1964)
OR   D1835+ formerly at the church; present location unknown

ELING (Independent, now United Reformed) Ebenezer Chapel, Rumbridge Street, Totton (Founded 1811, united with the Methodist Church 1988, active)
OR   C1818-1837 PRO (RG 4/1885); C1811+ reported to be at the church
Mfm C1818-1837 PRO, HRO, SLC
Cop Extracts C1818-1837 IGI

ELING (Presbyterian) Rumbridge Street, Totton (Existed at least 1882-1889)

ELING (Wesleyan) Providence Chapel, Longdown (Southampton Wesleyan Circuit) (Erected 1832, burned 1940 and moved to a former school) (Records 1928+ SCA)

ELING (Primitive Methodist) Cadnam (Southampton Primitive Methodist Circuit, Romsey Primitive Methodist Circuit from 1880) (Chapel erected 1850, moved to old Independent Chapel c1965) (Records 1865+ HRO)

ELING (Primitive Methodist) Ringwood Road, Totton (Southampton Primitive Methodist Circuit, Romsey Primitive Methodist Circuit from 1880) (Chapel erected c1856) (Records 1891+ SCA)
OR   C1922-1964 SCA (D/Meth 24/20)

ELING Cemetery
OR   B1946-1982 HRO
Mfc B1946-1982 HRO

ELING Union Workhouse (New Forest Union) - See NEW FOREST

ELLINGHAM St Mary & All Saints (420) (Ringwood Union)
OR   C1602-1978 M1596-1962 B1596-1953 Bn1754-1791,1824-1967 HRO
BT   1707,1780-1782,1784-1793,1795-1798,1800-1809,1812-1813,1815-1870 HRO
      (Mfm SLC)
Mfc   C1602-1978 M1596-1962 B1596-1988 Bn1754-1791 HRO
Mfm   C1596-1811 M1596-1812 B1596-1811 Bn1754-1791 HRO
Cop   C1602-1840 M1596-1840 B1596-1840 (Ts,I) HRO, Inc
      M1596-1837 HMI; M1596-1882 CMI; B1596-1837 HBI

ELLISFIELD St Martin (245) (Basingstoke Union)
OR   C1571-1941 M1584-1987 B1540-1981 Bn1756-1952 HRO (Only 5 baptisms,
      2 marriages, and 3 burials before 1606; defective 1620-1635,1660-1667)
BT   1780-1869 HRO (Mfm SLC)
Mfc   C1571-1941 M1584-1987 B1540-1981 Bn1756-1952 HRO
      C1571-1941 M1584-1837 B1540-1812 Bn1756-1952 SG
Mfm   C1571-1812 M1584-1812 B1540-1812 Bn1756-1952 HRO
Cop   C1571-1738 M1584-1737 B1540-1605 (Ts,I) HRO, HGS (Two pages of C and
      M c1686-1690 omitted from transcript); M1584-1837 HMI; M1584-1884 CMI
      C1738-1812 M1738-1754 B1678-1812 (Ts,I) HRO, HGS; B1540-1837 HBI

ELSON (with HARDWAY) St Thomas the Apostle (Formed 1845 from Alverstoke)
OR   C1845-1977 M1846-1981 B1846-1927 Bn1846-1925,1979-1988 PCRO
BT   1845-1855,1860-1872 HRO (Filed with Alverstoke) (Mfm SLC)
Mfc   C1845-1926,1938-1977 M1846-1890,1925-1930,1939-1971 B1846-1927
      HRO, PCRO; C1845-1912 SG
Cop   M1846-1881 CMI

ELSON (Baptist) Grove Road, Hardway (Founded 1859, active)

ELSON (Independent) (Chapel established 1802; 1851 Religious Census; no other
      references located)

ELSON (Wesleyan) Hardway (Portsmouth Wesleyan Circuit, Gosport Wesleyan
      Circuit from 1831, Gosport & Fareham Wesleyan Circuit from 1908) (Chapels
      erected 1817 & 1868, closed 1987) (Records 1867+ HRO)
OR   C1918-1985 HRO (69M73/NMR21)

ELVETHAM St Mary (481) (Hartley Wintney Union) (See also Fleet,
      Hartfordbridge) (Redundant 1972)
OR   C1638-1980 M1639-1969 B1638-1902 Bn1754-1812,1824-1969 HRO
BT   1780-1781,1783-1794,1796-1799,1801-1872 HRO (Mfm SLC)
Mfc   C1638-1980 M1639-1969 B1638-1902 Bn1754-1812 HRO
Mfm   C1638-1812 M1639-1812 B1638-1813 HRO
Cop   M1639-1812 Phillimore Vol 3 and Boyd
      C1638-1837 M1639-1843 B1638-1837 (Ms,I) HRO
      M1639-1837 HMI; M1639-1882 CMI; M1790-1812 Pallot; B1638-1837 HBI

EMERY DOWN Christ Church (Formed 1864 from Lyndhurst)
OR   M1865-1991 Bn1938-1984 HRO; C1864+ B1864+ Inc
Mfc   M1865-1986 HRO
Cop   M1865-1881 CMI

EMPSHOTT Holy Rood (149) (Petersfield Union)
OR C1718-1993 M1722-1974 B1772-1992 Bn1825-1971 HRO
BT 1780,1782,1784-1872 HRO (Mfm SLC)
Mfc C1718-1993 M1722-1974 B1772-1992 HRO
Mfm C1718-1812 M1722-1875 B1772-1812 HRO, SLC
Cop M1722-1836 HMI; M1722-1882 CMI; B1772-1837 HBI

EMSWORTH St James (Formed 1841 from Warblington)
OR C1841-1991 M1841-1997 B1841-1913 Bn1841-1985 PCRO
BT 1843-1887 HRO (Mfm SLC) (Entries also occur in the Warblington BT)
Mfc C1841-1960 M1841-1964 B1841-1913 HRO, PCRO
Mfm C1841-1878 B1841-1913 Bn1841-1849 HRO
Cop C1841-1917 M1841-1911 B1841-1913 PCI; M1841-1881 CMI

EMSWORTH (Particular Baptist) Zion Chapel, North Street (Founded 1845, active)

EMSWORTH (Independent, now United Reformed) Nile Street, now at Bath Road,
    Waterside (Founded 1808, active)
OR C1817-1837 PRO (RG 4/2166)
Mfm C1817-1837 PRO, HRO, PCRO, SLC
Cop Extracts C1817-1837 IGI

EMSWORTH (Primitive Methodist) High Street (Chichester Primitive Methodist
    Circuit; possibly in Portsmouth Primitive Methodist First Circuit for a time)
    (Chapel erected 1877) (Records 1875+ West Sussex RO)
OR C1877-1934 are in the registers of Chichester Primitive Methodist Circuit
    (West Sussex RO M1P/1/1/1)

ENHAM Centre Chapel (Chapel to Smannell; see also Knights Enham)
OR C1923-1972 HRO

EVERSLEY St Mary (755) (Hartley Wintney Union)
OR C1559-1967 M1559-1961 B1559-1992 Bn1824-1859,1921-1981 HRO
    (Registers not kept 1644-1653; possibly defective 1718-1730)
BT 1703,1780-1887 HRO (Mfm SLC)
Mfc C1559-1967 M1559-1961 B1559-1992 HRO
Mfm C1559-1812 M1559-1812 B1559-1812 HRO
Cop M1559-1812 Phillimore Vol 3 and Boyd; M1790-1812 Pallot
    C1770-1851 M1754-1837 B1770-1869 (Ts,I) Inc; M1559-1837 HMI
    Index to C1559-1769 M1559-1769 Inc; M1559-1883 CMI; B1559-1837 HBI

EVERSLEY (Baptist) New Mill Chapel (Founded 1803, a village station attached to
    the Baptist Church at Woking, Surrey; 1851 Religious Census; no other references)

EVERSLEY (Baptist) Bramshill (1851 Religious Census; no other references)

EVERSLEY (Baptist) (Existed by 1907)

EVERSLEY (Wesleyan) (Sandhurst Wesleyan Circuit) (Founded 1878, closed 1938)

EVERTON (Wesleyan) - See MILFORD

EWHURST St Mary (28) (Kingsclere Union) (Redundant 1971)
OR   C1684-1960 M1682-1959 B1687-1886 HRO (No M took place 1823-1840)
BT   1781,1787,1789,1791-1792,1800,1802-1803,1807-1810,1812-1845,
        1848-1854,1857-1868 HRO (Mfm SLC)
Mfc   C1684-1960 M1682-1959 B1687-1886 HRO
Mfm   C1684-1812 M1682-1812 B1687-1886 HRO
Cop   M1682-1823 Phillimore Vol 8 and Boyd
        C1684-1838 M1682-1823 B1687-1839 (Ms,I) SG
        C1684-1836 M1682-1823 B1687-1834 (Ts) HRO; M1682-1823 HMI
        M1682-1881 CMI; M1790-1823 Pallot; B1687-1837 HBI

EWSHOT St Mary (Formed 1886 from Crondall & Crookham)
OR   C1886+ M1890+ B1886+ Bn1918+ Inc

EWSHOT (Wesleyan) (Farnham Wesleyan Circuit, Aldershot & Farnham Wesleyan
    Circuit from 1891) (Founded 1885, closed 1922) (Records 1899+ HRO)
OR   Baptisms were registered at Crondall and Farnham Wesleyan Chapels

EXBURY St Katherine (325) (New Forest Union) (Chapelry of Fawley; separate
    parish 1863)
OR   C1813-1913 M1756-1978 B1827-1992 Bn1755-1861,1899-1971 HRO
        (Early entries for Exbury appear in the Fawley registers)
BT   1707,1813-1820,1822-1825,1829-1842,1844,1847-1853,1857,1861 HRO
        (Mfm SLC) (Entries 1780-1812 occur in Fawley BT)
Mfc   C1813-1913 M1756-1978 B1827-1992 Bn1755-1861 HRO
        C1813-1913 M1756-1812 Bn1755-1861 SG
Cop   M1756-1837 HMI; M1756-1881 CMI; B1827-1837 HBI
        Extracts C1787-1812 claimed to be in IGI

EXTON St Peter & St Paul (283) (Droxford Union)
OR   C1579-1929 M1580-1975 B1579-1991 Bn1755-1799,1830-1948 HRO
        (Gap in burials 1694-1727)
BT   1780-1795,1797-1822,1824,1826-1858,1861 HRO (Mfm SLC)
Mfc   C1579-1929 M1580-1975 B1579-1991 Bn1755-1799 HRO
Mfm   C1579-1812 M1580-1811 B1579-1812 Bn1755-1799 HRO
Cop   C1579-1900 M1580-1900 B1579-1900 (Ts,I) HRO; M1580-1837 HMI
        C1579-1720 M1580-1720 B1579-1694 (Ms) HRO
        M1580-1888 CMI; M1580-1720 Boyd; B1579-1837 HBI

FACCOMBE St Barnabas (290) (Andover Union)
OR   C1580-1971 M1586-1978 B1586-1989 Bn1908-1989 HRO
        (Baptisms defective before 1585)
BT   1780-1794,1796,1798,1800,1803-1804,1808-1811,1813-1815,1818-1861,
        1866-1870 HRO (Mfm SLC)
Mfc   C1580-1971 M1586-1978 B1586-1987 HRO
Mfm   C1580-1878 M1586-1876 B1586-1812 HRO, SLC
Cop   M1586-1812 Phillimore Vol 2 and Boyd
        C1580-1812 M1813-1836 B1586-1812 (Ms,TsI) SG (Includes corrections to
        Phillimore marriage transcript); Index to M1586-1812 (Ms) HRO;
        M1586-1836 HMI; M1586-1882 CMI; M1790-1812 Pallot; B1586-1837 HBI

FACCOMBE (Wesleyan) (Newbury Wesleyan Circuit?) (Chapel erected 1812, no references located after 1855, possibly taken over by Primitive Methodists)

FACCOMBE (Primitive Methodist) (Andover Primitive Methodist Circuit, Hurstbourne Tarrant Primitive Methodist Circuit from 1910) (Mission established 1831, chapel erected 1847?, demolished c1953)

FAIR OAK St Thomas (Formed 1871 from Bishopstoke)
OR   C1871-1973 M1863-1999 B1872-1976 Bn1916-1996 HRO
Mfc   C1871-1973 M1863-1948 B1872-1976 HRO
Cop   M1863-1881 CMI

FAIR OAK (Baptist, Independent) - See BISHOPSTOKE Horton Heath

FAIR OAK Cemetery (Records 1942+ Parish Council)

FAREHAM St Peter & St Paul (4,402) (Fareham Union)
OR   C1558-1976 M1559-1988 B1558-1992 Bn1771-1772,1858-1882,1893-1987
        PCRO
BT   1780-1833,1835-1881 HRO (Mfm SLC)
Mfc   C1558-1949 M1559-1970 B1558-1992 Bn1771-1772 HRO, PCRO
        C1558-1743,1793-1812,1832-1853,1906-1949 M1559-1743,1754-1837,
        1861-1901 B1558-1743,1793-1867 Bn1771-1772 SG
Mfm   C1558-1871 M1559-1876 B1558-1867 Bn1771-1772 PCRO, SLC
        C1558-1871 M1559-1880 B1558-1842 Bn1771-1772 HRO
Pc   C1558-1743,1793-1812 M1559-1743 B1558-1743,1793-1812 PCRO
Cop   C1558-1690 M1559-1690 B1558-1690 (Ts,I) HRO, PCRO
        C1558-1853 M1559-1837 B1690-1837 PCI; B1558-1837 HBI
        M1559-1837 HMI; M1813-1882 CMI;Extracts C1558-1871 M1559-1876 IGI

FAREHAM Holy Trinity (District formed 1835)
OR   C1836-1962 M1847-1964 B1836-1896 Bn1847-1880,1899-1969 PCRO
BT   1837-1883 HRO (Mfm SLC)
Mfc   C1836-1962 M1847-1964 B1836-1896 HRO, PCRO
        C1836-1914 M1847-1908 SG
Cop   M1847-1881 CMI; B1836-1837 HBI

FAREHAM St John the Evangelist
OR   C1955-1984 M1956-1985 B1955-1985 Bn1956-1992 PCRO
Mfc   C1955-1969 M1956-1973 HRO, PCRO

FAREHAM (Roman Catholic) Sacred Heart, Hartlands Road (Founded 1873 at West Street, present site 1878)
OR   1870+ Inc

FAREHAM (Baptist) West Street, Gosport Road (Founded 1899, active)

FAREHAM (Independent, now United Reformed) West Street (Founded 1691, active) (Records 1701+ HRO)
OR   C1702-1706,1788-1890 M1841-1878 D1794-1839,1869-1911 HRO
        (in 1M93/1-5)
Cop   D1794-1834 HGBSI

FAREHAM Wesleyan Circuit (Formed 1867 from Gosport Circuit; became part of Gosport & Fareham Circuit in 1908. Included chapels at Fareham, Lee on the Solent, Portchester, Stubbington, and Wickham) (Records 1867+ HRO)
OR   C1867-1908 HRO (69M73/NMR1-2)
Mfc   C1890-1908 HRO

FAREHAM (Wesleyan) West Street, King's Road (Portsmouth Wesleyan Circuit, Gosport Wesleyan Circuit from 1831, Fareham Wesleyan Circuit from 1867, Gosport & Fareham Wesleyan Circuit from 1908) (Chapels erected in West Street 1812 & 1875, replaced 1939 by King's Road Chapel) (Records 1876+ HRO)

FAREHAM (Wesleyan) Funtley (Fareham Wesleyan Circuit) (Founded 1870, closed early 20th century)

FAREHAM (Plymouth Brethren) Meeting House, Quay Street (Existed by 1867)

FAREHAM Cemetery (Records - Fareham Borough Council)
Mfc   B1889-1953 HRO

FAREHAM Knowle Hospital Burial Ground (Existed by 1860)

FAREHAM Union Workhouse
OR   Z1914-1930 (closed until 2006) HRO; D1914-1943 (closed until 2019) HRO

FARLEIGH WALLOP St Andrew (108) (Basingstoke Union)
OR   C1840-1987 M1839-1980 B1840-1988 HRO; Bn1961+ Inc
      (Early entries for Farleigh Wallop appear at Cliddesden)
BT   1813-1840,1842-1843,1845-1857 HRO (In the Cliddesden BT) (Mfm SLC)
Mfc   C1840-1987 M1839-1980 B1840-1988 HRO
Cop   M1839-1887 CMI

FARLEY CHAMBERLAYNE St John (165) (Hursley Union)
OR   C1593-1962 M1645-1978 B1612-1992 Bn1765-1812 HRO
      (Gaps in C 1629-1643 and B 1643-1652,1737-1766)
BT   1780-1781,1785-1791,1793,1796-1797,1799-1810,1812-1815,1818-1829,
      1832-1868 (plus one undated) HRO (Mfm SLC)
Mfc   C1593-1962 M1645-1978 B1612-1992 Bn1765-1812 HRO
Mfm   C1593-1812 M1645-1812 B1612-1813 Bn1765-1812 HRO
Cop   M1645-1836 HMI; M1645-1904 CMI; B1612-1837 HBI

FARLINGTON St Andrew (778) (Havant Union; chapelry of Waterlooville in Catherington Union) (See also Cosham, Portsdown, Purbrook, Waterlooville)
OR   C1539-1960 M1654-1967 B1538-1965 Bn1949-1965,1971-1979 PCRO
      (Gap in C 1718-1766, M 1719-1750, B 1793-1808)
BT   1763,1780-1781,1783,1785-1796,1798-1850,1853-1856 HRO (Mfm SLC)
Mfc   C1539-1960 M1654-1933,1950-1967 B1538-1906 HRO, PCRO
Mfm   C1539-1875 M1654-1875 B1538-1875 PCRO, SLC
Cop   C1539-1718 M1654-1719,1750-1752,1793-1850 B1654-1793,1813-1906 PCI
      M1654-1837 HMI; M1654-1882 CMI; B1538-1837 HBI
      Extracts C1539-1876 M1654-1877 IGI

FARLINGTON The Resurrection, Drayton (Daughter church)
OR   C1935-1956 M1936-1969 PCRO; Bn1965+ Inc
Mfc   C1935-1956 M1936-1969 HRO, PCRO

FARLINGTON (Wesleyan) Drayton (Portsmouth Wesley Circuit) (Founded 1914 by
   members of Portsea Arundel Street) (Records 1914+ PCRO)

FARNBOROUGH (Dedication unknown; now referred to as St Peter) (334)
   (Farnborough Incorporation, Hartley Wintney Union from 1869)
OR   C1584-1953 M1584-1969 B1585-1945 Bn1912-1970 SHC
BT   1665,1733,1780-1809,1811,1813-1822,1824-1835,1837-1862,1869 HRO
   (Mfm SLC)
Mfc   C1584-1953 M1584-1969 B1585-1945 HRO
   C1584-1891 M1584-1895 B1585-1900 SHC
Mfm   C1584-1891 M1584-1895 B1585-1900 SLC
Pc   C1682-1727 M1683-1726 B1681-1752 HRO, SHC
Cop   M1584-1812 Phillimore Vol 3 and Boyd
   M1813-1837 (Ts,I) SG, HRO, SHC, HGS; M1584-1837 HMI
   M1584-1881 CMI; M1790-1812 Pallot; B1585-1837 HBI

FARNBOROUGH St Mark (District formed 1881; separate parish 1906; formerly
   known as South Farnborough)
OR   C1891-1981 M1906-1972 Bn1956-1985 SHC
Mfc   C1891-1981 M1906-1972 HRO

FARNBOROUGH North Camp Church - See ALDERSHOT

FARNBOROUGH (Roman Catholic) St Patrick or St Louis - See ALDERSHOT

FARNBOROUGH (Roman Catholic) Our Lady Help of Christians, Queen's Road
   (Parish formed 1901, known as St Patrick until 1903)
OR   C1901+ M1903+ Inc

FARNBOROUGH (Particular Baptist) (Founded c1825, possibly succeeded by the
   Queen's Road Chapel)

FARNBOROUGH (Baptist) Queen's Road (Founded 1922, active)

FARNBOROUGH (Wesleyan) Lynchford Road, North Camp (Aldershot Wesleyan
   Circuit, Aldershot & Farnham Wesleyan Circuit from 1891) (Founded c1881,
   active) (Records 1906+ HRO)

FARNBOROUGH (North Camp) Primitive Methodist Mission (Separated 1896 from
   Aldershot Circuit, but rejoined in 1901)

FARNBOROUGH (Primitive Methodist) Peabody Road (Aldershot Primitive
   Methodist Circuit) (Existed by 1899) (Records 1952+ HRO)
OR   C1938-1966 HRO (58M77/NMR7)

FARNBOROUGH (Primitive Methodist) Farnborough Street (Aldershot Primitive
   Methodist Circuit) (Founded 1911, closed c1984) (Records 1938+ HRO)
OR   C1938-1984 HRO (58M77/NMR5,6)

FARNBOROUGH (Methodist) Hawley Lane (Aldershot & Farnborough Methodist Circuit) (Founded 1950)

FARNBOROUGH (Unsectarian) Gospel Tabernacle (Existed by 1911)

FARNBOROUGH Victoria Road Cemetery (Records - Rushmoor Borough Council)
Mfc   B1859-1945 HRO

FARNBOROUGH Ship Lane Cemetery (Records - Rushmoor Borough Council)
Mfc   B1933-1991 HRO

FARNBOROUGH Workhouse (Farnborough Incorporation) (The Incorporation was absorbed into Hartley Wintney Union in 1869)
OR   No registers survive. Other records at HRO.

FARNHAM [Surrey] Wesleyan Circuit (Formed 1879 from Alton Circuit; became part of Aldershot & Farnham Circuit in 1891. Included chapels at Ewshot and Rowledge) (Records 1871+ HRO)

FARNHAM [Surrey] (Wesleyan)
OR   C1879-1937 HRO (80M78/NMR7) (Includes Crondall, Ewshot, Rowledge)

FARNHAM [Surrey] Bible Christian Circuit (United Methodist Circuit from 1907) (The Surrey Mission, formed in 1830, became Farnham Circuit in 1835; later known as Farnham & Liphook Mission and Crondall & Liphook Mission; became part of the Liphook & North Hampshire Circuit in 1930. Included chapels at Bentley, Binsted, Bramshott, Crondall, and Headley) (Records 1843+ HRO)
OR   C1835-1837 PRO (RG 4/2184); C1839-1874 HRO (89M72/NMR4)
       (For later entries see Bramshott)
Mfm   C1835-1837 PRO, SLC
Cop   C1835-1837 (Ts,I) SG, PRO, GL, SHC (Published on fiche by West Surrey Family History Society); Extracts C1835-1837 IGI (Surrey section)

FARNHAM [Surrey] Union Workhouse (Farnham Union included Aldershot)
OR   Baptism certificates 1908-1934 SHC (100 year closure)

FARNHAM & ALTON Methodist Circuit (Formed 1937 from Alton Circuit and part of Aldershot & Camberley Circuit) (Records 1937+ HRO)

FARRINGDON All Saints (504) (Alton Union) (See also Four Marks)
OR   C1559-1896 M1559-1837 B1559-1876 Bn1936-1966 HRO (Few entries 1635-1650; pages cut out. Gap in M 1632-1656; marriages 1837-1978 stolen)
BT   1728,1780-1784,1786-1820,1822-1824,1826-1838,1840-1877 HRO (Mfm SLC)
Mfc   C1559-1896 M1559-1837 B1559-1876 HRO
Mfm C1559-1812 M1559-1812 B1559-1812 HRO
Pc   M1837-1978 HRO (Supplied by the Registrar General to replace the stolen register. Details of professions, residences, and fathers blanked out)
Cop   M1559-1837 HMI; M1700-1881 CMI; B1559-1837 HBI

FARRINGDON (Wesleyan) (Guildford Wesleyan Circuit, Alton Wesleyan Circuit from 1860, Surrey & North Hampshire Wesleyan Mission from 1900, Alton Wesleyan Circuit from 1917) (Chapel erected 1848)

FAWLEY All Saints (1,839) (New Forest Union) (See also Holbury, Hythe, Langley)
OR   C1676-1981 M1674-1963 B1673-1980 Bn1840-1991 HRO
BT   1707,1780-1781,1783-1784,1786-1821,1826-1828,1830-1832, 1834-1874 HRO (Mfm SLC)
Mfc   C1676-1981 M1674-1963 B1673-1980 HRO
      C1676-1857 M1674-1837 B1673-1842 SG
Mfm   C1676-1876 M1674-1876 B1673-1842 HRO, SLC
Cop   C1676-1759 M1674-1754 B1673-1759 (Ms,I) HRO; M1674-1836 HMI
      M1674-1881 CMI; B1673-1837 HBI; Extracts C1678-1812 M1678-1758 IGI

FAWLEY St George, Calshot (RAF Garrison Church)
OR   C1920-1961 HRO
Mfc   C1920-1961 HRO

FAWLEY (Baptist) Hampton Lane, Blackfield Common (Founded 1828, active)

FAWLEY (Wesleyan) (Southampton Wesleyan Circuit, New Forest Wesleyan Mission from 1925) (Chapel erected 1817, active) (Records 1871+ SCA)
OR   C1951-1967 M1933-1959 SCA (D/Meth 24/19)

FAWLEY (Wesleyan) Long Lane, Hardley (New Forest Wesleyan Mission) (Established 1931, active) (Records 1931+ SCA)

FAWLEY Blackfield Cemetery
OR   B1969-1982 HRO
Mfc   B1969-1982 HRO

FINCHDEAN (Baptist, Independent) - See IDSWORTH

FLEET All Saints (Formed 1863 from Crondall, Elvetham, & Yateley)
OR   C1863-1970 M1863-1956 B1864-1972 Bn1927-1941,1957-1968 SHC
Mfc   C1863-1970 M1863-1956 B1864-1972 HRO
Cop   M1863-1883 CMI

FLEET (Roman Catholic) (Founded c1908 as the Holy Ghost, Our Lady from 1934)
OR   1910+ Inc

FLEET (Particular Baptist) (Founded 1846, used Ebenezer Chapel 1859-1868, re-established 1895, closed 1947)

FLEET (Baptist) Clarence Road (Took over Ebenezer Chapel in 1868, new chapel erected 1893, active)

FLEET (Independent, now United Reformed) Albert Street, King's Road (Founded 1912, active)
OR   M1951-1954 HRO (152M98/1/1)

FLEET (Wesleyan) (Sandhurst Wesleyan Circuit) (Founded 1888, chapel 1900)
OR   M1936-1965 HRO (58M77/NMR1-4)
Mfc   M1936-1965 HRO

FLEET (Primitive Methodist) (Basingstoke Primitive Methodist Circuit) (Chapel
    erected 1866, new chapel erected 1887)

FLEET Cemetery (Records - Hart District Council)
Mfc   B1928-1992 HRO

FORDINGBRIDGE St Mary the Virgin (2,611) (Fordingbridge Union) (See also
    Hyde)
OR   C1642-1958 M1642-1981 B1642-1963 Bn1754-1990 HRO (A contemporary
    copy of C1790-1804 M1790-1804 B1790-1803 is held, reference 24M82/PZ1)
BT   1724,1781-1784,1786-1790,1792-1870 HRO (Mfm SLC)
Mfc   C1642-1958 M1642-1981 B1642-1963 HRO
Mfm   C1642-1876 M1642-1875 B1642-1876 Bn1796-1876 HRO, SLC
    C1642-1739 M1642-1739 B1642-1739 DRO
Cop   C1642-1840 M1642-1840 B1642-1840 (Ts,MsI) SG; M1642-1837 HMI
    C1642-1840 M1642-1840 B1642-1840 (Ts) HRO, Inc; M1642-1882 CMI
    C1781-1812 M1781-1812 B1781-1812 (BT) (Ts,I) SG
    Index to M1642-1837 (Ts) HRO; B1642-1837 HBI

FORDINGBRIDGE (Roman Catholic) St Mary & St Philip (Founded 1872 as Our
    Lady of the Seven Dolours)
OR   1874+ Inc

FORDINGBRIDGE (Society of Friends) Meeting House, Round Hill
OR   B1696-1892 HRO (33M93/3-5, 24M54/267) (Other entries for Fordingbridge
    were registered at the Ringwood Monthly Meeting)

FORDINGBRIDGE (Independent, now United Reformed) Salisbury Street (Founded
    1662, active) (Records 1695+ HRO)
OR   ZC1795-1837 (plus one birth in 1782) PRO (RG 4/719)
    C1941-1978 M1911-1965 HRO (86M86/1-4)
Mfc   C1941-1978 M1911-1965 HRO
Mfm   ZC1795-1837 PRO, HRO, SLC
Cop   ZC1795-1837 (Ms,I) SG; Extracts ZC1795-1837 IGI

FORDINGBRIDGE (Independent, now Congregational) Frogham (Founded 1820,
    active)

FORDINGBRIDGE (Independent) Goreley (Chapel erected c1825; 1851 Religious
    Census; in list of registered places of worship 1882)

FORDINGBRIDGE (Independent, now Congregational) Alderholt [Dorset] (Founded
    1830, active)

FORDINGBRIDGE (Independent) Godshill (Founded 1832)

FORDINGBRIDGE (Independent, now Congregational) Stuckton (Founded 1827 at
    Hungerford, Stuckton Chapel erected c1855, active)

FORDINGBRIDGE (Wesleyan) West Street (Salisbury Wesleyan Circuit) (Chapel erected 1836) (Records 1831+ WRO)
OR   C1870-1890 WRO (1150/118)
Mfm C1870-1890 HRO, SLC
Pc   C1870-1890 HRO

FORDINGBRIDGE (Primitive Methodist) Sandleheath (Salisbury Primitive Methodist Circuit, Woodfalls Primitive Methodist Circuit from 1898) (Chapel erected 1843) (Records 1859+ WRO)

FORDINGBRIDGE Union Workhouse
OR   No registers survive. Other records at HRO.

FORTON St John the Evangelist (Formed 1841 from Alverstoke)
OR   C1840-1983 M1841-1990 B1841-1857,1870-1871 Bn1884-1895,1939-1947, 1953-1989 PCRO
BT   1843-1855,1857-1858 HRO (Filed with Alverstoke) (Mfm SLC)
Mfc C1840-1969 M1841-1990 B1841-1857,1870-1871 HRO, PCRO
       C1840-1904 M1841-1903 SG
Cop C1840-1904 M1841-1903 PCI; M1841-1883 CMI

FORTON St Francis, Melville Road (Mission Church to St John; closed)
OR   C1917-1938 PCRO
Mfc C1917-1938 HRO, PCRO

FORTON St Luke, Brockhurst (Mission Church to St John; closed)
OR   C1900-1940 PCRO
Mfc C1900-1940 HRO, PCRO

FORTON (Baptist) Victoria Street (Founded 1811 by members of Portsea Meeting House Alley, active)
OR   Z1799-1836 PRO (RG 4/400)
Mfm Z1799-1836 PRO, HRO, PCRO, SLC
Cop Extracts Z1799-1836 IGI

FORTON (Wesleyan) Lees Lane (Gosport Wesleyan Circuit, Gosport & Fareham Wesleyan Circuit from 1908) (Established c1890) (Records 1893+ HRO)

FORTON (Primitive Methodist) Bethesda Chapel, Forton Road (Portsmouth Primitive Methodist First Circuit) (Established 1864, merged with Lees Lane Wesleyan Society in 1936)

FORTON (LONGPARISH) (Primitive Methodist) - See LONGPARISH

FOUR MARKS The Good Shepherd (Chapelry of Ropley; parish formed 1973 from Ropley, Medstead, Chawton, & Farringdon)
OR   C1945-1979 M1945-1981 Bn1960-1969 HRO
Mfc C1945-1979 M1945-1981 HRO

FOXCOTT (Not dedicated) (95) (Andover Union) (Chapelry of Andover; redundant c1969)
OR   C1814-1903 B1817-1900 Bn1816-1817 HRO
BT   1814-1845,1847-1868 HRO (Mfm SLC)
Mfc   C1814-1903 B1817-1900 HRO
Cop   B1817-1837 HBI

FREEFOLK St Nicholas (73) (Whitchurch Union) (Chapelry of Whitchurch; chapelry of Laverstoke from 1859; redundant 1976)
OR   C1820-1873 M1820,1857 B1858-1872 HRO (Other entries are at Laverstoke)
Mfc   C1820-1873 M1820,1857 B1858-1872 HRO
Cop   M1820,1857 HMI

FREEMANTLE - See SOUTHAMPTON Freemantle

FRITHAM (Particular Baptist) - See BRAMSHAW

FROGHAM (Independent) - See FORDINGBRIDGE

FROXFIELD St Peter on the Green (618) (Petersfield Union) (Chapelry of East Meon; separate parish 1867) (St Peter on the Green became a chapel to the new parish church of St Peter, High Cross)
OR   C1544-1907 M1544-1979 B1545-1981 Bn1754-1812,1824-1928 HRO
        (including separate register of M1930-1976 for St Peter on the Green)
BT   1780-1787,1789-1885 HRO (Mfm SLC)
Mfc   C1544-1907 M1544-1979 B1545-1981 Bn1754-1812 HRO
Mfm   C1544-1876 M1544-1837 B1545-1875 Bn1754-1812,1824-1876 HRO, SLC
Cop   C1717-1787 M1718-1754 B1694-1787 (Ts,I) HRO, HGS; M1544-1837 HMI
        M1700-1881 CMI; B1545-1837 HBI

FROXFIELD (Wesleyan) (Guildford Wesleyan Circuit, Alton Wesleyan Circuit from 1860, Petersfield Wesleyan Circuit from 1870, Surrey & North Hampshire Wesleyan Mission from 1900) (Chapel erected 1851, closed c1900)

FROYLE Assumption of the Blessed Virgin Mary (755) (Alton Union)
OR   C1653-1922 M1654-1989 B1653-1948 Bn1754-1812,1871-1933 HRO
        (Entries prior to 1697 survive only as a nineteenth century copy)
BT   1780-1783,1786-1788,1790-1791,1793-1797,1799,1803-1809,1811-1871 HRO
        (Mfm SLC)
Mfc   C1653-1922 M1654-1973 B1653-1948 Bn1754-1812 HRO
        C1653-1846 M1654-1836 B1653-1868 Bn1754-1812 SG
Mfm   C1653-1876 M1654-1836 B1653-1868 Bn1754-1812 HRO, SLC
Cop   M1653-1836 HMI; M1653-1952 CMI; B1653-1837 HBI
        Card Index to PR (dates?) Inc

FROYLE (Wesleyan) Lower Froyle (Alton Wesleyan Circuit, Surrey & North Hampshire Wesleyan Mission from 1900, Alton Wesleyan Circuit from 1917) (Chapel erected 1862) (Records 1931+ HRO)

FROYLE (Latter-day Saints) (Records 1851 [only] in Church archives at SLC)
Mfm   Membership records 1851 SLC

FUNTLEY (Wesleyan) - See FAREHAM

FURZLEY (Primitive Methodist) - See BRAMSHAW

FYFIELD St Nicholas (211) (Andover Union)
OR   C1628-1991 M1629-1978 B1628-1996 Bn1824-1960 HRO
BT   1707,1780,1790-1810,1812-1820,1822-1837,1839-1870 HRO (Mfm SLC)
Mfc   C1628-1991 M1629-1978 B1628-1996 HRO
Mfm   C1628-1812 M1629-1810 B1628-1812 HRO
Cop   C1780-1812 M1724-1837 B1780-1812 (Ms) HRO; M1629-1837 HMI
      M1629-1881 CMI; B1628-1837 HBI

GODSHILL (Independent) - See FORDINGBRIDGE

GOODWORTH CLATFORD St Peter (414) (Andover Union)
OR   C1538-1979 M1538-1985 B1538-1906 Bn1754-1811,1823-1954,1965 HRO
      (Gap in M 1609-1623)
BT   1780-1784,1786-1819,1821-1884 HRO (Mfm SLC)
Mfc   C1538-1880 M1538-1985 B1538-1906 HRO
      C1538-1880 M1538-1837 B1538-1906 SG
Mfm   C1538-1876 M1538-1837 B1538-1876, Bn1754-1811 HRO, SLC
Cop   M1538-1837 HMI; M1700-1884 CMI; B1538-1837 HBI
      Extracts M1538-1837 IGI

GOODWORTH CLATFORD (Independent) (Founded 1845; 1851 Religious
  Census; no other references located)

GOODWORTH CLATFORD (Primitive Methodist) (Andover Primitive Methodist
  Circuit) (Chapel erected 1847, closed 1964) (Records 1847+ HRO)

GORELEY (Independent) - See FORDINGBRIDGE

GOSPORT (See also Elson, Forton)

GOSPORT Holy Trinity (Population included in Alverstoke) (Alverstoke
  Incorporation) (Ancient chapelry of Alverstoke; separate parish 1860)
OR   C1696-1983 M1696-1992 B1696-1902 Bn1754-1772,1775-1788,1823-1884,
      1904-1973 PCRO
BT   1780-1794,1796-1820,1822-1869,1873-1876 HRO (Mfm SLC)
Mfc   C1696-1957 M1696-1976 B1696-1902 Bn1754-1772,1775-1788 HRO, PCRO
      C1696-1735,1813-1908 M1696-1735,1754-1929 B1696-1735,1813-1902
      Bn1754-1772,1775-1788 SG
Mfm   C1696-1875 M1696-1875 B1696-1875 Bn1754-1772,1775-1788 PCRO, SLC
Pc   C1813-1850 Bn1823-1861 PCRO
Cop   C1708-1777,1813-1908 M1696-1754 B1696-1837 PCI; M1696-1837 HMI
      M1813-1881 CMI; B1696-1837 HBI; Extracts C1696-1875 M1696-1875 IGI

GOSPORT Christ Church (Chapelry of Alverstoke; separate parish 1913)
OR   C1881-1992 M1913-1992 Bn1913-1964 PCRO
Mfc   C1881-1939 M1913-1981 HRO, PCRO; C1881-1905 SG
Cop   C1881-1905 PCI; M1846-1881 CMI

GOSPORT St Matthew (Formed 1845 from Alverstoke; closed 1950)
OR   C1846-1950 M1846-1950 PCRO
BT   1846-1860 HRO (Mfm SLC)
Mfc   C1846-1950 M1846-1950 HRO, PCRO; C1846-1906 M1846-1902 SG
Cop   C1870-1927 M1846-1894 PCI; M1846-1882 CMI

GOSPORT St Francis, Military Road (Garrison Church) (Opened 1872, closed 1967)
OR   Reported to be at HMS Sultan, Gosport. No details available.

GOSPORT St George's Chapel, Monckton (Garrison Church)
OR   C1923-1945 RACD

GOSPORT (Roman Catholic) Our Lady of the Sacred Heart (Founded c1750 at South
    Cross Street, present site 1776)
OR   C1759+ M1775-1789,1796,1830+ B1871+ Inc
Cop   C1759-1852 M1775-1789,1796,1830-1848 (I) CRS Vol 49
       M1775-1789,1796,1830-1837 HMI; Extracts C1759-1852 IGI

GOSPORT (Roman Catholic) Hardway - See WINCHESTER French Émigré Priests

GOSPORT (Particular Baptist) Ebenezer Chapel, Roberts Lane (Founded 1853,
    probably closed by 1900)

GOSPORT (Baptist) Heaton Road, Brockhurst, now at Netherton Road (Meetings by
    1851, Church founded 1858, active)

GOSPORT (Baptist) Grove Road, Hardway - See ELSON

GOSPORT (Baptist) Stoke Road (Founded 1883, active)

GOSPORT (Independent, now United Reformed) High Street, now at Bury Road
    (Founded 1663, chapel erected c1787, active)
OR   C1691-1837 PRO (RG 4/401,805,1391)
Mfm   C1691-1837 PRO, HRO, PCRO, SLC
Cop   Extracts C1691-1837 IGI

GOSPORT (Independent) New Independent Chapel, High Street (Formerly North
    Quay Street) (Founded 1826, no references located after 1867)
OR   C1826-1837 PRO (RG 4/2108)
Mfm   C1826-1837 PRO, HRO, PCRO, SLC
Cop   Extracts C1826-1837 IGI

GOSPORT Wesleyan Circuit (Existed briefly 1818-1819; formed 1831 from
    Portsmouth Circuit; known as Portsmouth (Gosport) Circuit from 1900; became
    part of Gosport & Fareham Circuit in 1908. Included chapels at Elson, Fareham,
    Forton, Gosport, Portchester, and Stubbington) (Records 1831+ HRO)
OR   C1800-1837 PRO (RG 4/1081) (Entries to 1813 were copied from the register
       of St Peter, Daniel Street, Portsea); C1839-1939 HRO (69M73/NMR15-19)
Mfc   C1865-1939 HRO
Mfm   C1800-1837 PRO, HRO, SLC
Cop   Extracts C1800-1837 IGI

GOSPORT (Wesleyan) (Portsmouth Wesleyan Circuit, Gosport Wesleyan Circuit from 1831, Gosport & Fareham Wesleyan Circuit from 1908) (Middle Street or High Street Chapel erected 1810, Stoke Road Chapel 1910) (Records 1855+ HRO)

GOSPORT (Wesleyan) Little Church, Anglesey Road (Gosport & Fareham Wesleyan Circuit) (Existed by 1931)
OR   M1939-1984 HRO (69M73/NMR4-14)
Mfc   M1939-1984 HRO

GOSPORT (Wesleyan Methodist Association) North Street (Chapel erected c1840, probably ceased by 1856)

GOSPORT (Primitive Methodist) (PO Directory 1855; possibly refers to Forton Chapel)

GOSPORT (Methodist) Priory Road (Gosport & Fareham Methodist Circuit) (Existed by 1939)

GOSPORT (Latter-day Saints) (Records 1849+ in Church archives at SLC)
Mfm   Records 1849-1876 SLC

GOSPORT (All dissenters) Union Chapel, Stoke Road (Chapel erected 1865)

GOSPORT & FAREHAM Wesleyan Circuit (Formed 1908 by union of the Portsmouth (Gosport) Circuit and the Fareham Circuit. Included chapels at Elson, Fareham, Forton, Gosport, Lee on the Solent, Portchester, Stubbington, and Wickham) (Records 1908+ HRO)
OR   C1909-1946 HRO (69M73/NMR3)

GRATELEY St Leonard (130) (Andover Union)
OR   C1624-1957 M1647-1999 B1675-1993 Bn1754-1812 HRO (Only one M before 1654; C before 1655 are retrospective entries for two families only)
BT   1780-1802,1804-1807,1809-1811,1813-1815,1817-1818,1820-1847, 1849-1876 HRO (Mfm SLC)
Mfc   C1624-1957 M1647-1989 B1675-1993 Bn1754-1812 HRO
       C1740-1957 M1742-1855 B1741-1811 Bn1754-1812 SG
Mfm   C1624-1877 M1647-1855 B1675-1811 Bn1754-1812 HRO, SLC
Cop   M1647-1835 HMI; M1647-1890 CMI; B1675-1837 HBI

GRAYSHOTT St Luke (Chapelry formed 1901 from Headley, Churt [Surrey], & Shottermill [Surrey])
OR   C1874-1953 M1901-1948 B1905-1951 Bn1968-1978 SHC
Mfc   C1874-1953 M1901-1948 B1905-1951 HRO

GRAYSHOTT (Roman Catholic) St Joseph (Chapel founded 1891, Our Lady Immaculate from 1895, St Joseph from 1911)
OR   C1909+ M1916+ Inc

GRAYSHOTT (Wesleyan) Headley Road (Surrey & North Hampshire Wesleyan Mission, Petersfield & Haslemere Wesleyan Circuit from 1917) (Chapel erected c1901, sold 1979) (Records 1901+ HRO)

GREATHAM St John the Baptist (238) (Petersfield Union)
OR   C1558-1902 M1562-1979 B1558-1964 Bn1755-1812,1825-1993 HRO
        (Defective 1603-1615,1639-1657)
BT   1782-1874 HRO (Mfm SLC)
Mfc   C1558-1902 M1562-1978 B1558-1964 Bn1755-1812 HRO
Mfm   C1558-1812 M1562-1812 B1558-1812 Bn1755-1812 HRO
Cop   C1558-1603 M1562-1603 B1558-1603 (Ts) HRO
        M1562-1836 HMI; M1700-1883 CMI; B1558-1837 HBI

GREATHAM St Martin, Longmoor (Garrison Church) (Closed 1977, demolished)
OR   C1926-1977 Bn1933-1960 RACD

GREATHAM (Wesleyan) (Petersfield Wesleyan Circuit, Surrey & North Hampshire
    Wesleyan Mission from 1900, Petersfield & Haslemere Wesleyan Circuit from
    1917) (Chapel erected 1887, closed 1965, demolished) (Records 1908+ HRO)
OR   C1906-1963 HRO (89M72/NMR8)
Mfc   C1906-1963 HRO

GREYWELL St Mary the Virgin (287) (Hartley Wintney Union) (Chapelry of
    Odiham; separate parish 1901)
OR   C1604-1965 M1605-1753,1799-1806,1826-1992 B1604-1979 Bn1828-1983
        HRO (Gap in M 1642-1672 and B 1640-1672) (During the periods 1753-1799
        and 1806-1826 Greywell couples married at Odiham)
BT   1785,1789-1792,1798-1855,1857-1883 HRO (Mfm SLC)
Mfc   C1604-1965 M1605-1753,1799-1806,1826-1992 B1604-1979 HRO
        C1604-1908 M1605-1753,1799-1806,1826-1837 B1604-1979 SG
Mfm   C1604-1812 M1605-1753 B1604-1812 HRO
Cop   C1604-1837 M1605-1753,1799-1806,1826-1837 B1604-1837 (Ms,I) HRO
        M1799-1806,1826-1837 (Ts,I) SG, HRO, HGS; B1604-1837 HBI
        M1605-1753,1799-1806,1826-1837 HMI
        M1605-1753,1799-1806,1826-1893 CMI

GREYWELL (Independent) (Chapel opened 1817; 1851 Religious Census; no other
    references located; building still stands)

GREYWELL (Wesleyan) (Basingstoke Wesleyan Circuit, Surrey & North Hampshire
    Wesleyan Mission from 1900, Basingstoke Wesleyan Circuit from 1917) (Existed
    by 1895)

GUILDFORD [Surrey] Wesleyan Circuit (Formed 1835; became part of the Surrey &
    North Hampshire Wesleyan Mission in 1900. Included chapels at Alton,
    Farringdon, Froxfield, Liss, and Petersfield)
OR   C1828-1840 PRO (RG 4/2716,2208) (Titled "Methodist Chapel, Petersfield")
Mfm   C1828-1840 PRO, HRO, SLC
Cop   C1828-1840 (Ts,I) SG, PRO, GL, SHC (Published on fiche by West Surrey
        Family History Society)
        Extracts C1828-1840 IGI (Listed as Petersfield Wesleyan)

GUILDFORD [Surrey] Primitive Methodist Circuit - See ALDERSHOT Primitive
    Methodist Circuit

HALE St Mary (203) (Fordingbridge Union)

OR   C1626-1951 M1626-1993 B1626-1950 Bn1755-1813,1929-1982 HRO

BT   1813-1829,1831-1863 HRO (Mfm SLC)

Mfc   C1626-1951 M1626-1837 B1626-1950 Bn1755-1813 HRO
       C1626-1862 M1626-1837 B1626-1950 Bn1755-1813 SG

Mfm   C1626-1951 M1626-1837 B1626-1950 Bn1755-1813 HRO

Cop   C1618-1619,1626-1896 M1626-1895 B1619,1626-1896 (Ts,I) HRO (On
       microfilm M449 with Hale Estate Papers; includes C & B 1618-1619 which are
       no longer in the register; index gives the first and last year for each name)
       M1626-1837 HMI; M1626-1900 CMI; B1626-1837 HBI

HAMBLE St Andrew the Apostle (318) (South Stoneham Union)

OR   C1674-1973 M1730-1978 B1679-1979 Bn1759-1783,1815-1979 HRO
       (Gap in M 1801-1814) (The registers of Bursledon, Hamble, and Hound
       intermix, and all should be consulted)

BT   1788-1794,1799,1801-1822,1824-1871 HRO (Mfm SLC) (See also Hound BT)

Mfc   C1674-1973 M1730-1978 B1679-1920 Bn1759-1783 HRO
       C1674-1717,1760-1873 M1759-1835 B1679-1714,1760-1920 Bn1759-1783
       SG; C1760-1791 B1760-1791 SCA

Cop   C1674-1841 M1730-1835 B1679-1841 Bn1825-1841 (Ts,I) SG, HRO, SCA,
       HGS; M1730-1835 HMI; M1730-1881 CMI; B1679-1837 HBI

HAMBLEDON St Peter & St Paul (2,026) (Droxford Union) (See also Denmead,
    Newtown [Soberton])

OR   C1596-1937 M1596-1960 B1596-1910 Bn1754-1798,1838-1980 HRO
       (1596 only, then C and M from 1601, B from 1603; defective 1613-1621)

BT   1704,1738-1739,1741-1742,1780-1811,1813-1868,1870,1872 HRO
       (Mfm SLC)

Mfc   C1596-1937 M1596-1960 B1596-1910 Bn1754-1798 HRO

Mfm   C1596-1876 M1596-1876 B1596-1876 Bn1754-1798 HRO, SLC

Cop   C1596-1998 M1596-1998 B1596-1998 (Ts,I) HRO, PCRO
       C1596-1778 M1596-1753 B1596-1779 (Ms,I) HRO
       Index to C1778-1938 M1754-1945 B1779-1951 (Ms) HRO
       Index to Bn1838-1920 HRO (46M69/PR17); M1596-1837 HMI
       M1657-1882 CMI; B1596-1837 HBI; Extracts C1596-1876 M1596-1876 IGI

HAMBLEDON (Particular Baptist) Anmore Chapel (See also Denmead) (Founded
    c1828, closed by 1867)

OR   Z1820-1837 PRO (RG 4/2109)

Mfm   Z1820-1837 PRO, HRO, SLC

Cop   Z1820-1837 (Ms,I) SG; Extracts Z1820-1837 IGI

HAMBLEDON Primitive Methodist Branch - See DROXFORD Primitive Methodist
    Circuit

HAMBLEDON (Primitive Methodist) Ebenezer Chapel (Hambledon Primitive
    Methodist Branch from 1885, Droxford Primitive Methodist Circuit from 1892)
    (Chapel erected 1864) (Records 1864+ HRO)

HAMBLEDON (Primitive Methodist) Bethel Chapel, World's End (Hambledon Primitive Methodist Branch from 1885, Droxford Primitive Methodist Circuit from 1892) (Chapel erected 1862, sold c1900)

HAMPSHIRE (Society of Friends) Quarterly Meeting (Founded 1668; became part of the Dorset & Hampshire Quarterly Meeting in 1804. Included the Meetings of Alton, Ringwood, Southampton 1668-1756, Andover 1691-1737, Portsmouth & Isle of Wight 1681-1687, Isle of Wight 1695-1752) (Records 1675+ HRO)
OR   Z1654-1729,1772-1803 M1663-1733,1776-1803 B1657-1729,1776-1803 (plus a few C and B entries 1729-1776) PRO (RG 6/195,469,1027,1377)
Mfm   Z1654-1729,1772-1803 M1663-1733,1776-1803 B1657-1729,1776-1803 HRO
Cop   Digests of Z1638-1837 M1658-1837 B1657-1837 HRO (24M54/25,26) (These index the registers of all meetings in Dorset and Hampshire; arranged by the first letter of the surname) (Another set is held at Friends' House, Euston, and a third set, possibly less complete, is held at DRO ref N10/Q2-Q4; also on microfilm at SG); M1663-1733,1776-1803 HMI; B1657-1729,1776-1803 HBI

HANNINGTON All Saints (287) (Kingsclere Union)
OR   C1771-1994 M1768-1993 B1771-1962 Bn1768-1805,1823-1997 HRO
BT   1780-1794,1796-1834,1836-1871,1873 HRO (Mfm SLC)
Mfc   C1813-1994 M1768-1993 B1813-1962 Bn1768-1773 SG, HRO
Mfm   C1771-1812 M1768-1812 B1771-1812 HRO
Cop   M1768-1837 Phillimore Vol 11 and Boyd; M1790-1837 Pallot
        C1771-1837 M1768-1837 B1771-1837 Bn1770-1812 (Ms,I) SG
        M1768-1837 HMI; M1768-1883 CMI; B1771-1837 HBI

HANNINGTON (Primitive Methodist) (Silchester Primitive Methodist Circuit) (Society formed 1866, chapel erected 1871, active) (Records 1866+ BRO)

HARBRIDGE All Saints (322) (Ringwood Union)
OR   C1679-1907 M1616-1993 B1572-1992 Bn1754-1823 HRO
        (Gaps in C 1698-1712, M 1657-1712, B 1636-1654,1685-1690)
BT   1701,1705,1780-1867 HRO (Mfm SLC)
Mfc   C1679-1988 M1616-1993 B1572-1988 Bn1754-1823 HRO
Mfm   C1679-1812 M1616-1812 B1572-1812 Bn1754-1823 HRO
Cop   C1679-1837 M1616-1837 B1572-1840 (Ts,MsI) SG
        C1679-1837 M1616-1837 B1572-1840 (Ts) HRO, Inc
        M1616-1837 HMI; M1616-1889 CMI; B1572-1837 HBI

HARDLEY (Wesleyan) - See FAWLEY

HARDWAY (Church of England, Baptist, Wesleyan) - See ELSON

HARDWAY (Roman Catholic) - See WINCHESTER French Émigré Priests

HARTFORDBRIDGE All Souls (Chapelry of Elvetham)
OR   B1902+ Inc of Hartley Wintney

HARTLEY MAUDITT St Leonard (69) (Alton Union)

OR   C1672-1993 M1673-1939,1961-1979 B1679-1992 Bn1761-1804,1824-1992
HRO (M1939-1961 entered at West Worldham; Bn1939+ include Worldham)

BT   1780-1781,1783-1814,1817-1865 HRO (Mfm SLC)

Mfc   C1672-1993 M1673-1939,1961-1979 B1679-1992 Bn1761-1804 HRO

Mfm   C1672-1876 M1673-1761,1804-1876 B1679-1879 HRO, SLC

Cop   C1672-1812 M1673-1811 B1679-1812 Printed in "The Registers of East
Worldham, West Worldham, and Hartley Mauditt", Major V Ferguson (1942)
C1672-1761 M1673-1761 B1679-1761 (Ts,I) HRO; M1673-1833 HMI
Index to C1814-1978 M1827-1972 B1813-1983 Inc; M1673-1914 CMI
B1679-1837 HBI; Extracts C1672-1812 M1673-1811 IGI

HARTLEY WESPALL St Mary the Blessed Virgin (283) (Basingstoke Union)

OR   C1540-1938 M1558-1986 B1558-1992 Bn1755-1819,1824-1938 HRO
(Only three baptisms before 1558) (The register for the period 1678-1733 was
found in an empty house in Pentonville in 1852, and restored to the parish)

BT   1703,1780,1782-1877 HRO (Mfm SLC)

Mfc   C1540-1938 M1558-1986 B1558-1992 Bn1755-1819 HRO

Mfm   C1540-1877 M1558-1876 B1558-1877 Bn1755-1819 HRO, SLC

Cop   M1558-1812 Phillimore Vol 9 and Boyd; M1790-1812 Pallot
C1540-1812 M1558-1758 B1558-1812 (Ts) HRO; M1558-1837 HMI
C1813-1837 M1813-1837 B1813-1837 (Ts,I) SG, HRO, HGS
Index to M1558-1812 (Ts) HRO; M1558-1883 CMI; B1558-1837 HBI

HARTLEY WINTNEY St Mary (1,139) (Hartley Wintney Union) (In 1870 St Mary
became a chapel to the new St John the Evangelist; St Mary redundant 1974)

OR   C1658-1995 M1658-1994 B1658-1971 Bn1754-1792,1952-1997 HRO

BT   1702,1780-1812,1814-1837,1839-1845,1847-1849,1854-1869 HRO
(Mfm SLC)

Mfc   C1658-1969 M1658-1967,1974-1994 B1658-1942 Bn1754-1792 HRO

Mfm   C1658-1812 M1658-1812 B1658-1812 Bn1754-1792 HRO

Cop   M1658-1812 Phillimore Vol 3 and Boyd; M1658-1837 HMI
M1658-1852 CMI; M1790-1812 Pallot; B1658-1837 HBI

HARTLEY WINTNEY (Particular Baptist) Hartley Row (Erected 1807, active)

HARTLEY WINTNEY (Baptist) (Established c1842; 1851 Religious Census)

HARTLEY WINTNEY (Wesleyan) Hartley Row (Sandhurst Wesleyan Circuit)
(Chapel erected c1876)

HARTLEY WINTNEY (Primitive Methodist) West Green (Basingstoke Primitive
Methodist Circuit) (Existed by 1880, possibly closed by 1939)

HARTLEY WINTNEY Union Workhouse (The workhouse was demolished in 1871
and replaced by a new one at Winchfield)

OR   No registers survive. Other records at HRO.

HARTPLAIN - See COWPLAIN

HATCH BOTTOM (Bible Christian) - See SOUTHAMPTON

HATHERDEN Christ Church (District formed 1858 from Andover; parish formed with Smannell 1870; separate parish 1874)
OR   C1857-1988 M1861-1977 Bn1877-1990 HRO; B1857+ Inc
BT   1860-1871 HRO (Mfm SLC) (Includes Smannell)
Mfc   C1857-1988 M1861-1977 HRO
Cop   M1861-1883 CMI

HAUGHURST HILL (Primitive Methodist) - See BAUGHURST

HAVANT St Faith (2,083) (Havant Union) (See also Leigh Park, Rowlands Castle, West Leigh)
OR   C1653-1966 M1654-1971 B1654-1936 Bn1794-1951,1956-1984 PCRO
BT   1663,1780-1784,1786-1861 HRO (Mfm SLC)
Mfc   C1653-1731,1813-1845,1877-1902,1916-1966 M1654-1729,1754-1971
      B1654-1936 HRO, PCRO
Mfm   C1653-1877 M1654-1875 B1654-1875 Bn1794-1812 PCRO, SLC
Cop   C1653-1845 M1654-1837 B1654-1854 Bn1754-1856 (Ts,I) SG, HRO
      C1653-1877 M1654-1893 B1654-1854 PCI; M1654-1837 HMI
      M1654-1881 CMI; B1654-1837 HBI; Extracts C1653-1875 M1654-1876 IGI

HAVANT (Roman Catholic) St Joseph, West Street (Chaplains at Warblington, Farlington, and Catherington served Catholics until a mission was established at Langstone in 1711. Moved to Brockhampton c1750 and to West Street in 1875)
OR   C1733-1855 M1744-1750,1788-1824 D1758-1817 Portsmouth (Catholic)
      Diocesan Archives; C1855+ M1855+ B1855+ Inc
      (No registers of M 1824-1855 or B 1817-1855)
Cop   C1733-1855 M1744-1750,1788-1824 D1758-1817 (I) CRS Vol 44
      M1744-1750,1788-1824 HMI; D1758-1793 HBI; Extracts C1733-1855 IGI

HAVANT (Independent, now United Reformed) The Pallant, later North Street (Founded 1710, chapel erected 1718, North Street erected 1891, active)
OR   C1779-1837 PRO (RG 4/720)
Mfm   C1779-1837 PRO, HRO, PCRO, SLC
Cop   Extracts C1779-1837 IGI

HAVANT (Wesleyan) West Street (Portsmouth Wesley Circuit) (North Street Chapel erected 1833, probably closed by 1867; West Street Chapel erected 1889 by members of Portsea Arundel Street) (Records 1899+ PCRO)

HAVANT (Primitive Methodist) (Portsmouth Primitive Methodist First Circuit) (Existed by 1889, probably closed by 1931)

HAVANT Cemetery (Records - Havant Borough Council)
Mfc   B1896-1968 (plus B1832,1854-1970 in Dissenters' Cemetery) HRO

HAVANT Union Workhouse
OR   No registers survive. Other records at HRO, PCRO.

HAWKLEY St Peter & St Paul (277) (Petersfield Union) (Chapelry of Newton
   Valence; separate parish 1860)
OR   C1640-1981 M1640-1978 B1640-1981 Bn1759-1812,1824-1909 HRO
BT   1679,1780-1782,1784-1796,1798-1799,1801-1802,1806-1809,1812,
      1815-1816,1818-1875 HRO (Mfm SLC)
Mfc   C1640-1981 M1640-1978 B1640-1981 Bn1759-1812 HRO
Mfm   C1640-1876 M1640-1837 B1640-1876 Bn1759-1812 HRO, SLC
Cop   C1640-1797 M1640-1757 B1640-1797 (Ts,I) HRO, HGS
      M1640-1837 HMI; M1640-1881 CMI; B1640-1837 HBI

HAWLEY Holy Trinity (Formed 1838 from Yateley; see also Minley)
OR   C1838-1962 M1839-1991 B1838-1945 Bn1901-1939,1952-1969 SHC
Mfc   C1838-1962 M1839-1991 B1838-1945 HRO
      C1838-1876 M1839-1877 B1838-1877 SHC
Mfm   C1838-1876 M1839-1877 B1838-1877 SLC
Cop   M1839-1883 CMI; Extracts C1838-1875 M1839-1877 IGI

HAWLEY All Saints (Chapel to Holy Trinity)
OR   C1932-1971 SHC; M1964+ Inc
Mfc   C1932-1971 HRO

HAYLING - See NORTH HAYLING, SOUTH HAYLING

HAZELEY (Baptist) - See HECKFIELD

HEADBOURNE WORTHY St Swithun (190) (Winchester Union)
OR   C1615-1951 M1637-1984 B1637-1988 Bn1824-1932 HRO (Gap 1647-1660)
BT   1780-1786,1788,1794,1796,1799,1801,1803-1810,1812-1871 HRO
      (Mfm SLC)
Mfc   C1615-1951 M1637-1984 B1637-1988 HRO
Mfm   C1615-1812 M1637-1812 B1637-1812 HRO
Cop   M1637-1836 HMI; M1637-1882 CMI; B1637-1837 HBI

HEADBOURNE WORTHY (Wesleyan) - See KINGSWORTHY (Wes)

HEADLEY All Saints (1,228) (Headley Incorporation, Alton Union from 1869)
   (See also Grayshott)
OR   C1540-1963 M1539-1967 B1539-1962 Bn1658-1659,1754-1812,1823-1964
      SHC
BT   1780-1810,1812-1871 HRO (Mfm SLC)
Mfc   C1540-1963 M1539-1967 B1539-1962 Bn1658-1659,1754-1812 HRO
Mfm   C1540-1875 M1539-1876 B1539-1889 Bn1658-1659,1754-1812 SHC, SLC
Cop   C1540-1895 M1539-1897 B1539-1915 (Ms) SG; Index to C1961-1983 Inc
      C1540-1962 M1539-c1901 B1539-c1902 (A) Inc; M1539-1837 HMI
      M1539-1881 CMI; B1539-1837 HBI; Extracts C1540-1875 M1539-1876 IGI

HEADLEY St George, Bordon (Garrison Church) (Established 1921)
OR   No information

HEADLEY (Roman Catholic) Sacred Heart, Bordon (Founded 1919, military until parish formed in 1949)

OR   C1908-1949 M1925-1987 B1914-1972,1984-1987 (military) RCRO (1908 register marked "Volume 2"); M1935-1989 HRO; C1914+ B1914+ Inc

HEADLEY (Society of Friends) - See BRAMSHOTT

HEADLEY (Independent) (Founded 1867 as a branch of Alton, closed 1952)

HEADLEY (Bible Christian) Lindford Chapel, Lindford Chase (Farnham Bible Christian Circuit, Liphook Bible Christian Circuit from 1863) (Chapel erected c1833, active) (Records 1870+ HRO; some baptisms registered at Bramshott)

HEADLEY (Bible Christian) Standford Hill (Farnham Bible Christian Circuit, Liphook Bible Christian Circuit from 1863) (Existed by 1861, active) (Records 1927+ HRO; some baptisms registered at Bramshott)

OR   M1895,1969-1979 HRO (89M72/NMR16) (M1895 in 89M72/NMR18)

HEADLEY (Brethren) Standford (Chapel existed by 1899)

HEADLEY Bordon Military Cemetery (Records 1910+ Bordon Garrison)

HEADLEY Workhouse (Headley Incorporation) (The Incorporation was absorbed into Alton and Petersfield Unions in 1869)

OR   No registers survive.

HEADLEY (KINGSCLERE) St Peter (Chapelry of Kingsclere Woodlands)

OR   M1945-1967 HRO

Mfc   M1945-1967 HRO

HEADLEY (KINGSCLERE) (Baptist) - See KINGSCLERE

HECKFIELD St Michael (1,202) (Hartley Wintney Union) (See also Mattingley)

OR   C1538-1921 M1538-1968 B1538-1939 Bn1823-1999 HRO (Gap in M 1637-1664)

BT   1724,1780-1792,1794-1796,1798,1800-1860,1863-1865 HRO (Mfm SLC)

Mfc   C1538-1921 M1538-1968 B1538-1939 HRO
       C1538-1812 M1538-1968 B1538-1939 SG

Mfm   C1538-1812 M1538-1812 B1538-1812 HRO, SLC

Cop   M1538-1812 Phillimore Vol 6 and Boyd
       C1538-1812 M1538-1812 B1538-1812 (Ts) HRO, Inc
       M1538-1837 HMI; M1538-1881 CMI; M1790-1812 Pallot
       B1538-1837 HBI; Extracts C1538-1664 M1538-1637 IGI

HECKFIELD (Particular Baptist) Hazeley (Founded 1844, a village station attached to the chapel at Hartley Row; 1851 Religious Census; no other references located)

HECKFIELD Cemetery (Records 1920?+ Parish Council)

HEDGE END St John the Evangelist (Formed 1876 from Botley & Southampton West End)
OR   C1874-1994 M1876-1993 B1875-1985 Bn1876-1994 HRO
Mfc   C1874-1973 M1876-1986 B1875-1985 HRO
Cop   M1876-1881 CMI

HEDGE END (Baptist) (Chapel erected 1811, active)

HEDGE END (Independent, now United Reformed) Lower Northam Road (Founded 1909, moved to St John's Road after 1985, active)

HEDGE END (Bible Christian) St John's Road (Southampton Bible Christian Circuit) (Society existed by 1840, chapel erected 1857, active) (Records 1969+ SCA)

HEDGE END Cemetery (Records - Parish Council)
Mfc   B1931-1977 HRO

HERRIARD St Mary (426) (Basingstoke Union)
OR   C1666-1875 M1701-1963 B1668-1947 Bn1754-1830,1840-1926 HRO
BT   1780-1867,1873-1875 HRO (Mfm SLC)
Mfc   C1666-1875 M1701-1963 B1668-1947 Bn1754-1830 HRO
Mfm C1666-1875 M1701-1876 B1668-1878 Bn1754-1830 HRO, SLC
Cop   M1701-1812 Phillimore Vol 8 and Boyd; M1701-1837 HMI; B1668-1837 HBI
       C1666-1812 M1701-1812 B1668-1812 Bn1826-1830 (Ts) HRO
       M1813-1837 (Ts) SG; M1701-1881 CMI; M1790-1812 Pallot

HIGHBRIDGE (Roman Catholic) - See EASTLEIGH

HIGHCLERE St Michael & All Angels (444) (Kingsclere Union)
OR   C1652-1957 M1656-1985 B1655-1947 Bn1825-1994 HRO
       (Few baptisms before 1656)
BT   1780-1871 HRO (Mfm SLC)
Mfc   C1652-1957 M1656-1985 B1655-1779,1813-1947 HRO
Mfm C1652-1812 M1656-1812 B1655-1813 HRO
Cop   M1656-1813 Phillimore Vol 8 and Boyd; B1655 -1837 HBI
       C1652-1812 M1656-1754 B1655-1779 (Ms) HRO
       M1656-1837 HMI; M1656-1882 CMI; M1790-1812 Pallot

HIGHCLIFFE St Mark (Formed 1843 from Christchurch & Milton)
OR   C1843-1970 M1856-1985 B1844-1980 Bn1880-1988 HRO
Mfc   C1843-1970 M1856-1985 B1844-1980 HRO
Mfm C1843-1876 M1856-1876 B1844-1877 HRO, DRO, SLC
Cop   M1856-1882 CMI

HIGHCLIFFE (Primitive Methodist) (Bournemouth Primitive Methodist First Circuit) (Chapel erected 1908, new church erected 1963) (Records 1907+ HRO)

HIGHFIELD - See SOUTHAMPTON Highfield

HIGHTOWN (Bible Christian) - See SOUTHAMPTON

HILLBROW (Presbyterian) - See LISS

HILL FARM (Wesleyan) - See CHRISTCHURCH

HINTON ADMIRAL St Michael & All Angels (Chapelry of Christchurch; separate parish 1867)
OR   C1810-1920 M1863-1990 Bn1912-1973 HRO; B1866+ Inc (The Christchurch registers include a register of C1813-1828 for Hinton Admiral)
Mfc   C1810-1920 M1863-1990 HRO
Mfm   C1810-1879 M1863-1876 B1866-1878 HRO, DRO, SLC
Cop   M1863-1881 CMI

HINTON ADMIRAL (Independent) - See MILTON (Independent) Cranemoor

HINTON AMPNER All Saints (389) (Alresford Union)
OR   C1561-1903 M1561-1982 B1561-1990 Bn1755-1812,1823-1995 HRO (Gap in M 1639-1651)
BT   1724,1780-1791,1793-1794,1797-1801,1804-1811,1813-1833, 1835-1875 HRO (Mfm SLC)
Mfc   C1561-1903 M1561-1955 B1561-1990 Bn1755-1812 HRO
Mfm   C1561-1876 M1561-1876 B1561-1877 Bn1755-1812,1823-1876 HRO, SLC
Pc   C1561-1813 M1561-1812 B1561-1813 (negative copies) HRO (1M61/1-3)
Cop   C1774-1903 M1755-1955 B1774-1877 Bn1823-1932 (Ts,I) HRO, HGS
        M1561-1837 HMI; M1561-1881 CMI; M1790-1812 Pallot
        B1561-1837 HBI; Extracts C1561-1876 M1561-1876 IGI

HINTON AMPNER (Wesleyan) (Winchester Wesleyan Circuit, South Hampshire Wesleyan Mission from 1900) (Chapel erected 1894, closed c1903) (Records 1894+ HRO)

HOLBURY The Good Shepherd (Chapelry of Fawley)
OR   C1975-1978 HRO
Mfc   C1975-1978 HRO

HOLBURY (Roman Catholic) St Bernard (Founded 1939)
OR   C1939-1960 Inc of Totton Roman Catholic Church; C1960-1965 Inc of Hythe Roman Catholic Church; C1965+ M1966+ B1966+ Inc

HOLDENHURST St John the Evangelist (733) (Christchurch Union) (Chapelry of Christchurch; separate parish 1876; see also Bournemouth, St Leonards & St Ives)
OR   C1679-1985 M1680-1796,1813-1985 B1679-1789,1834-1991 Bn1754-1796, 1826-1989 HRO; M1797-1812 Inc of Christchurch (Burials 1789-1834 were registered at Christchurch)
BT   1780-1783,1785-1813,1815-1858,1862-1879 HRO (Mfm SLC)
Mfc   C1679-1866 M1680-1796,1813-1973 B1679-1789,1834-1991 Bn1754-1796 HRO
Mfm   C1679-1866 M1680-1956 B1679-1789 Bn1754-1796 HRO, DRO (M1789-1812 are on the microfilm of Christchurch PR)
Cop   M1680-1796,1813-1837 (Ts,I) SG; M1680-1837 HMI; M1680-1881 CMI
        B1679-1789,1834-1837 HBI

HOLDENHURST St Barnabas, Queen's Park (Daughter church)
OR   M1968-1978 HRO; C1960+ Bn1975+ Inc

HOLDENHURST (Independent, now United Reformed) Muscliffe Lane, Throop (Founded 1828, active)

HOLDENHURST (Wesleyan) (Christchurch & Lymington Wesleyan Circuit) (Existed by 1846, probably short-lived)

HOLYBOURNE Holy Rood (594) (Alton Union) (Chapelry of Alton; parish 1862)
OR   C1690-1948 M1692-1743,1823-1988 B1694-1970 Bn1928-1957 HRO
     (During the period 1743-1823 Holybourne couples married at Alton)
BT   1780-1783,1786-1831,1833-1863 HRO (Mfm SLC) (See also Alton)
Mfc C1690-1948 M1692-1743,1823-1977 B1694-1970 HRO
     C1690-1854 M1692-1743,1823-1837 B1694-1885 SG
Mfm C1690-1876 M1692-1743,1823-1876 B1694-1876 HRO, SLC
Cop C1692-1812 B1694-1812 (Ts,A) HRO (possibly defective)
     M1692-1743,1823-1837 HMI; M1823-1887 CMI; B1694-1837 HBI
     Extracts C1690-1876 M1692-1743,1823-1876 IGI

HOLYBOURNE (Presbyterian) (Established by 1878 in a chapel erected in 1864)
OR   M1893-1960 HRO (2M99/1/1)

HOLYBOURNE (Wesleyan) (Alton Wesleyan Circuit, Surrey & North Hampshire Wesleyan Mission from 1900, Alton Wesleyan Circuit from 1917) (Chapel erected 1867) (Records 1865+ HRO)

HOOK St John the Evangelist (Formed from Newnham, Odiham, Nately Scures, & Up Nately)
OR   C1945-1984 M1939-1987 Bn1939-1989 HRO; B1943+ Inc
Mfc C1945-1984 M1939-1987 HRO

HOOK (Independent) (Foundation date given as 1816 but possibly founded 1837, linked with Odiham 1847-1956, closed) (Records 1918+ HRO, in 127M94)
OR   C1920-1955 M1918-1955 B1919-1952 HRO (127M94/72, 150M98/1/1)

HOOK with WARSASH St Mary (Formed 1872 from Titchfield; see also Locks Heath)
OR   C1871-1973 M1872-1977 B1872-1978 Bn1872-1984 PCRO
BT   1871-1884 HRO (Mfm SLC)
Mfc C1871-1973 M1872-1977 B1872-1978 HRO, PCRO
Cop M1872-1883 CMI

HOOK with WARSASH (Independent, now United Reformed) Warsash (Founded 1811, active)

HORDLE All Saints (699) (Lymington Union) (Chapelry of Milford; parish 1860)
OR C1772-1942 M1754-1993 B1772-1961 Bn1754-1796,1820,1824-1971 HRO
BT 1780-1807,1809-1874 HRO (Mfm SLC)
Mfc C1772-1942 M1754-1993 B1772-1961 Bn1754-1796,1820 HRO
Mfm C1772-1812 M1754-1813 B1772-1812 Bn1754-1796,1820 HRO
Cop C1772-1859 M1754-1837 B1771-1837 Bn1754-1796,1820 (Ms & Ts,I) HRO
      M1754-1813 Bn1754-1796,1820 (Ms & Ts,I) HGS; Extracts M1754-1812 IGI
      Index to C1772-1837 M1813-1837 B1771-1837 HGS; M1754-1837 HMI
      M1754-1881 CMI; M1754-1812 Boyd; B1772-1837 HBI

HORDLE (Baptist) Mount Jireh Chapel, Arnewood (Chapel erected c1824; 1851
      Religious Census and White's Directory 1878; no other references located)

HORDLE (Baptist) Tiptoe (Chapel erected 1906, active)

HORNDEAN (Wesleyan) - See CATHERINGTON

HORTON HEATH (Baptist, Independent) - See BISHOPSTOKE

HOUGHTON All Saints (435) (Stockbridge Union)
OR C1669-1992 M1670-1982 B1669-1991 Bn1755-1930 HRO
BT 1735,1780-1832,1835-1870 HRO (Mfm SLC)
Mfc C1669-1992 M1670-1982 B1669-1991 HRO
      C1669-1889 M1670-1835 B1669-1930 SG
Mfm C1669-1875 M1670-1875 B1669-1812 HRO
Cop M1670-1835 HMI; M1679-1885 CMI; B1669-1837 HBI

HOUGHTON (Wesleyan, Wesleyan Methodist Association) (Southampton Wesleyan
      Circuit, Winchester United Methodist Free Church Circuit from 1835) (House
      registered 1822, chapel erected 1833, closed 1972) (Records 1867+ HRO)
OR C1894-1968 HRO (79M72/NMR6) (Includes other places in the circuit)
Mfc C1894-1968 HRO

HOUND St Mary the Virgin (417) (South Stoneham Union) (St Mary became a chapel
      to the new parish church of St Edward the Confessor, Netley, established 1886; see
      also the Southampton parishes of Sholing and Woolston) (The registers of
      Bursledon, Hamble, and Hound intermix, and all should be consulted)
OR C1660-1961 M1667-1972 B1667-1941 Bn1759-1791,1866-1955,1971-1989
      HRO (Includes C1880-1888 for St Augustine, Netley Abbey)
BT 1780-1814,1816-1873 HRO (Mfm SLC)
Mfc C1660-1716,1760-1961 M1667-1715,1759-1972 B1667-1716,1760-1941
      Bn1759-1791 HRO; C1760-1791 M1759-1812 B1760-1791 Bn1759-1791 SG
      (with Hamble); C1760-1961 M1759-1972 B1760-1941 Bn1759-1791 SCA
Mfm C1792-1812 B1792-1812 HRO
Cop C1660-1837 M1667-1837 B1667-1837 (Ts,I) SG, HRO, SCA
      C1792-1837 M1813-1837 B1792-1837 (Ts,I) SG, HGS
      M1667-1836 HMI; M1667-1881 CMI; B1667-1837 HBI

HOUND Royal Chapel, Royal Victoria Hospital, Netley (Cemetery attached)
OR   M1934-1943,1948-1978 Bn1933-1976 RACD
       B1864+ Ministry of Defence, Marchwood
Pc   B1864-1976 Royal Victoria Country Park, Netley

HOUND (Roman Catholic) St Joseph, Royal Victoria Hospital, Netley
OR   C1864-1971 RCRO
Cop C1864-1918 (Ts,I) SG

HOUND (Independent) Netley Chapel (Meeting House registered 1795, 1818, 1819;
    1851 Religious Census; no later references located)

HOUND (Wesleyan) New Road, Netley (Southampton Wesleyan Circuit) (Chapel
    purchased from Independents 1912, active) (Records 1960+ SCA)

HOUND Roman Catholic Burial Ground, Netley
OR   B1880+ Inc of Netley Roman Catholic church

HOUNSDOWN (Primitive Methodist) - See ELING

HUNGERFORD [Berkshire] Union Workhouse (The Union included Combe)
OR   Z1866-1914 D1866-1914 BRO
Mfm Z1866-1914 D1866-1914 BRO; Z1866-1914 SLC

HUNTON St James (114) (Winchester Union) (Chapelry of Crawley; parish 1909)
OR   C1564-1995 M1575-1936 B1564-1993 Bn1755-1810,1825-1936 HRO (Gap in
       C & B 1758-1769; gap in M 1744-1755. M1936+ took place at Stoke Charity)
BT   1780-1782,1785-1792,1794-1833,1835-1892 HRO (Mfm SLC)
Mfc C1564-1995 M1575-1936 B1564-1993 Bn1755-1810 HRO
Mfm C1564-1812 M1575-1885 B1564-1812 Bn1755-1810 HRO
Cop M1575-1810 Phillimore Vol 9 and Boyd; M1575-1836 HMI
       M1575-1885 CMI; B1564-1837 HBI

HURSLEY All Saints (1,418) (Hursley Union) (See also Ampfield, Braishfield, Pitt)
OR   C1600-1940 M1600-1991 B1600-1971 Bn1654-1662,1767-1821,1905-1965
       HRO
BT   1701,1723-1724,1780-1868 HRO (Mfm SLC)
Mfc C1600-1940 M1600-1987 B1600-1971 Bn1654-1662,1767-1821 HRO
       C1600-1666,1706-1852 M1600-1666,1706-1838 B1600-1666,1706-1888
       Bn1654-1662 SG
Mfm C1600-1876 M1600-1876 B1600-1876 Bn1654-1662,1767-1821 HRO, SLC
Cop C1665-1705 M1666-1705 B1665-1705 (Ts,I) HRO (HGS holds index only)
       C1755-1774 M1754-1767 B1755-1774 (Ts,I) HRO
       Index to 1754-1767 (Ts,I) HGS; M1600-1838 (Ts) SG, HGS
       M1600-1837 HMI; M1600-1883 CMI; M1600-1837 Boyd; B1600-1837 HBI

HURSLEY Union Workhouse
OR   No registers survive.

HURSTBOURNE PRIORS St Andrew (490) (Whitchurch Union)
OR   C1621-1986 M1604-1985 B1604-1955 Bn1755-1816,1824-1974 HRO
BT   1780,1782-1798,1800-1801,1803-1807,1809-1859 HRO (Mfm SLC)
Mfc   C1621-1986 M1604-1985 B1604-1955 Bn1755-1816 HRO
Mfm   C1621-1812 M1604-1813 B1604-1812 Bn1755-1816 HRO
Cop   M1604-1812 Phillimore Vol 1, Boyd, Pallot
      C1621-1838 M1604-1837 B1604-1837 (Ts,A) SG, HRO, Guildhall Library
      M1604-1837 HMI; M1604-1886 CMI; B1604-1837 HBI

HURSTBOURNE PRIORS (Wesleyan) (Andover Wesleyan Circuit) (Erected 1822,
   possibly lapsed but re-established by 1889, closed 1968) (Records 1955+ HRO)

HURSTBOURNE TARRANT St Peter (786) (Andover Union)
OR   C1546-1992 M1546-1998 B1546-1937 Bn1824-1961 HRO
BT   1780-1802,1805,1807-1841,1844-1877 HRO (Mfm SLC)
Mfc   C1546-1992 M1546-1991 B1546-1937 HRO
Mfm   C1546-1876 M1546-1837 B1546-1877 Bn1824-1875 HRO, SLC
Cop   M1546-1812 Phillimore Vol 1, Boyd, Pallot
      M1546-1837 HMI; M1813-1837 CMI; B1546-1837 HBI

HURSTBOURNE TARRANT (Independent) (Founded 1840, closed)

HURSTBOURNE TARRANT (Independent) Upton - See VERNHAM DEAN

HURSTBOURNE TARRANT Primitive Methodist Circuit (Formed 1910 from
   Andover Circuit; became part of Andover and Hurstbourne Methodist Circuit in
   1937. Included chapels at Ashmansworth, Combe, Faccombe, Hurstbourne Tarrant,
   Kings Somborne, Leckford, Longstock, St Mary Bourne, Stockbridge, Vernham
   Dean, and Wherwell) (Records 1908+ HRO)
OR   C1908-1959 HRO (96M72/NMC/R6)
Mfc   C1908-1959 HRO

HURSTBOURNE TARRANT (Primitive Methodist) (Andover Primitive Methodist
   Circuit, Hurstbourne Tarrant Primitive Methodist Circuit from 1910) (Mission at
   Ibthorpe from 1831, chapel erected 1864) (Records 1864+ HRO)

HURSTBOURNE TARRANT (Primitive Methodist) Upton - See VERNHAM
   DEAN

HYDE Holy Ascension (Formed 1855 from Fordingbridge)
OR   C1856-1896 M1856-1993 B1856-1952 Bn1938-1974 HRO
BT   1856-1878 HRO (Mfm SLC)
Mfc   C1856-1896 M1856-1993 B1856-1952 HRO
Mfm   C1856-1876 M1856-1876 B1856-1877 HRO, SLC
Cop   M1856-1881 CMI

HYDE (Independent) - See FORDINGBRIDGE (Independent) Frogham

HYTHE St John the Baptist (Formed 1841 from Fawley)
OR   C1823-1989 M1844-1991 B1823-1993 Bn1862-1990 HRO
BT   1823,1831 HRO (Mfm SLC) (Entries also occur in Fawley BT)
Mfc   C1823-1989 M1844-1991 B1823-1993 HRO
Cop   C1823-1837 (Ts) SG, HGS; M1844-1890 CMI; B1823-1837 HBI

HYTHE (Independent, now United Reformed) Ebenezer Chapel, New Road (Founded 1839, active)

IBSLEY St Martin (316) (Ringwood Union) (Chapelry of Fordingbridge)
OR   C1654-1989 M1654-1988 B1654-1993 Bn1751-1817,1824-1928,1982-1988 HRO
BT   1780-1782,1784-1794,1796-1797,1800-1816,1818-1858,1860-1870 HRO (Mfm SLC)
Mfc   C1654-1988 M1654-1988 B1654-1987 Bn1751-1817 HRO
Mfm C1654-1812 M1654-1812 B1654-1812 Bn1751-1817 HRO
Cop   C1654-1839 M1654-1840 B1654-1840 (Ts,MsI) SG
       C1654-1839 M1654-1840 B1654-1840 (Ts) HRO
       M1654-1837 HMI; M1706-1889 CMI; B1654-1837 HBI

IBSLEY (Independent) Cross Lane (Chapel erected 1851, possibly founded earlier)

IDSWORTH St Hubert (Formerly St Peter) (Chapelry of Chalton; see also Rowlands Castle)
OR   M1838-1956 Bn1824-1922 PCRO (For other periods, see Chalton)
Mfc   M1838-1939 HRO
Cop   M1838-1886 CMI

IDSWORTH (Baptist) Finchdean (White's Directory 1878; possibly refers to the Independent Chapel)

IDSWORTH (Independent, now United Reformed) Ashcroft Lane, Finchdean (Founded 1830, active)

ITCHEN ABBAS St John the Baptist (243) (Winchester Union)
OR   C1586-1942 M1586-1989 B1586-1812 Bn1754-1812,1828-1982 HRO (Entries prior to 1702 are an eighteenth century copy) (Gap in B 1600-1702)
BT   1736,1758,1784-1795,1798-1801,1803-1837,1839-1873 HRO (Mfm SLC)
Mfc   C1586-1942 M1586-1989 B1586-1812 Bn1754-1812 HRO
Mfm C1586-1812 M1586-1812 B1586-1812 Bn1754-1812 HRO
Cop   C1699-1812 M1708-1754 B1703-1812 Bn1735 (Ms,I) HRO
       M1586-1835 HMI; M1586-1882 CMI; B1586-1837 HBI

ITCHEN STOKE St Mary the Virgin (267) (Alresford Union) (Redundant 1975)
OR   C1719-1969 M1723-1970 B1721-1991 Bn1828-1970 HRO
BT   1780-1781,1783-1784,1786-1792,1796-1797,1799-1804,1807-1812, 1814-1841,1843,1846-1880 HRO (Mfm SLC)
Mfc   C1719-1969 M1723-1970 B1721-1986 HRO
       C1719-1920 M1723-1836 B1721-1986 SG
Mfm C1719-1812 M1723-1812 B1721-1812 HRO
Cop   M1723-1836 HMI; M1723-1881 CMI; B1721-1837 HBI

KEMPSHOTT (Wesleyan) - See BASINGSTOKE

KILMESTON St Andrew (255) (Alresford Union) (Chapelry of Cheriton; separate parish 1879)
OR   C1661-1960 M1703-1973 B1700-1992 Bn1754-1794,1809-1810,1824-1991 HRO
BT   1780-1788,1790-1793,1797-1874 HRO (Mfm SLC)
Mfc   C1661-1960 M1703-1973 B1700-1992 Bn1754-1794,1809-1810 HRO
Mfm C1661-1877 M1703-1876 B1700-1876 Bn1754-1794,1809-1810 HRO, SLC
Cop   M1703-1836 HMI; M1703-1882 CMI; B1700-1837 HBI
       Extracts C1661-1877 M1704-1876 IGI

KIMPTON St Peter & St Paul (383) (Andover Union)
OR   C1589-1996 M1593-1978 B1593-1991 Bn1824-1911 HRO
       (Gap in M 1656-1671 and B 1652-1670)
BT   1708,1733-1734,1780-1788,1790-1836,1838-1856,1858-1868,1870 HRO
       (Mfm SLC)
Mfc   C1589-1996 M1593-1978 B1593-1991 HRO
Mfm C1589-1812 M1593-1845 B1593-1812 HRO
Cop   M1593-1836 HMI; M1593-1883 CMI; B1593-1837 HBI

KINGSCLERE St Mary (2,532) (Kingsclere Union) (See also Ecchinswell, Kingsclere Woodlands, Sydmonton)
OR   C1543-1967 M1538-1961 B1538-1959 Bn1754-1803,1809,1812,1827-1989 HRO
BT   1780-1889 HRO (Mfm SLC)
Mfc   C1543-1967 M1538-1961 B1538-1959 Bn1754-1803,1809,1812,1827-1885 SG, HRO
Mfm C1543-1876 M1538-1876 B1538-1876 Bn1754-1803,1809,1812,1827-1885 HRO, SLC
Cop   C1543-1812 M1538-1754 B1538-1678 (Ts,I) HRO
       C1543-1665 M1538-1664,1695-1701 B1538-1665,1678-1767 (Ms) HRO
       C1653-1682 M1653-1681 B1653-1678 (Ts,I) HGS; M1538-1837 HMI
       Index to C1543-1655 M1538-1655 B1538-1655 (Ts) HGS
       C1780-1837 M1780-1837 B1780-1837 (BT) (Ts,I) SG, HRO
       B1538-1837 HBI; Extracts C1780-1837 M1780-1837 (BT) IGI
       M1813-1881 CMI; Extracts C1837-1876 M1837-1876 IGI

KINGSCLERE (Baptist) Swan Street (PO Directory 1867; no other references)

KINGSCLERE (Baptist) Headley Common (Chapel erected c1838)

KINGSCLERE (Wesleyan) George Street (Newbury Wesleyan Circuit, Newbury & Hungerford Wesleyan Circuit from 1908) (Erected c1807) (Records 1891+ BRO)

KINGSCLERE (Methodist, possibly Wesleyan) Ashford Hill (Chapel erected 1831; 1851 Religious Census; no later references located)

KINGSCLERE (Primitive Methodist) Ashford Hill (Shefford Primitive Methodist Circuit, Newbury Primitive Methodist Circuit from 1845) (Chapel erected 1838, closed c1968)

OR   M1912-1968 HRO (5M82/NMR1) (For C1835-1837 see Shefford)

Mfc   M1912-1968 HRO

KINGSCLERE (Primitive Methodist) Plaistow Green (Newbury Primitive Methodist Circuit) (Existed by 1878) (Records 1922+ BRO)

KINGSCLERE (Primitive Methodist) Wolverton End (Newbury Primitive Methodist Circuit?) (Existed by 1867)

KINGSCLERE Cemetery (Records 1924+ Parish Council)

KINGSCLERE Union Workhouse

OR   Z1866-1914 D1866-1913 HRO (PL5/7/52,54)

        Z1915-1930 (closed until 2020) D1914-1956 (closed until 2032) HRO

KINGSCLERE WOODLANDS St Paul (Formed 1845 from Kingsclere, now known as Ashford Hill; see also Headley [Kingsclere])

OR   C1846-1917 M1846-1986 B1846-1975 HRO; Bn1928+ Inc (Includes entries for Headley [Kingsclere])

BT   1846-1896 HRO (Mfm SLC)

Mfc   C1846-1917 M1846-1986 B1846-1975 HRO

Cop   M1846-1881 CMI

KINGSLEY St Nicholas (345) (Headley Incorporation, Alton Union from 1869) (Chapelry of Alton; separate parish 1853) (St Nicholas was replaced as the parish church by All Saints, established 1876; St Nicholas declared redundant 1926)

OR   C1568-1959 M1568-1762,1845-1989 B1618-1949 Bn1915-1976 HRO (Gap in M 1703-1723. In the period 1762-1845 Kingsley couples married at Binsted)

BT   1780-1783,1785-1874 HRO (Mfm SLC)

Mfc   C1568-1959 M1568-1762,1845-1977 B1618-1949 HRO

        C1568-1871 M1568-1762 B1618-1949 SG

Mfm   C1568-1871 M1568-1762,1845-1877 B1618-1878 HRO, SLC

Cop   C1719-1812 M1723-1762 B1719-1755,1770 (Ms,I) HRO (HGS holds index)

        B1683-1812 (Ts,I) HRO (HGS holds index only)

        M1568-1762 HMI; M1568-1762,1845-1881 CMI; B1618-1837 HBI

KINGSLEY (Independent) (Founded 1862)

KINGSLEY (Independent) Shortheath, Oakhanger (In the ecclesiastical parish of Kingsley and the civil parish of Selborne) (Founded 1820, closed)

OR   The chapel does not appear to have kept registers. Some baptisms were registered at Normandy Street, Alton

KINGSLEY (Bible Christian) (PO Directory 1867; no other references located)

KINGS SOMBORNE St Peter & St Paul (1,046) (Stockbridge Union)
OR   C1567-1961 M1567-1971 B1567-1951 Bn1754-1766,1883-1969 HRO
       (Gap 1632-1672)
BT   1707,1780-1860 HRO (Mfm SLC)
Mfc   C1567-1961 M1567-1971 B1567-1951 Bn1754-1766 HRO
       C1672-1858 M1672-1837 B1672-1888 Bn1754-1766 SG
Mfm C1567-1812 M1567-1812 B1567-1812 Bn1754-1766 HRO
Cop   M1567-1837 HMI; M1700-1881 CMI; B1567-1837 HBI

KINGS SOMBORNE (Independent & Baptist) (Founded c1830, originally Baptist & Independent mixed communion, later Independent, probably closed by 1930)

KINGS SOMBORNE (Wesleyan, Wesleyan Methodist Association from 1835, United Methodist Free Church from 1857) (Southampton Wesleyan Circuit, Winchester United Methodist Free Church Circuit from 1835) (Chapel erected 1826, moved to the Primitive Methodist Chapel in 1919)

KINGS SOMBORNE (United Methodist Free Church) Up Somborne (Winchester United Methodist Free Church Circuit) (Chapel opened 1843, new chapel opened 1902, closed 1981) (Records 1903+ HRO)
OR   C1928-1981 HRO (79M72/NMR19)
Mfc   C1928-1981 HRO

KINGS SOMBORNE (Primitive Methodist) (Andover Primitive Methodist Circuit, Hurstbourne Primitive Methodist Circuit from 1910) (Society formed 1841, chapel erected 1871, lapsed 1919 and joined the United Methodist Free Church, which transferred to this chapel) (Records 1843+ HRO)

KINGS SOMBORNE Cemetery (Records 1910+ Parish Council)

KINGSTON (Independent) -See RINGWOOD

KINGSWORTHY St Mary (345) (Winchester Union)
OR   C1541-1988 M1538-1989 B1538-1967 Bn1754-1812,1823-1986 HRO
BT   1780-1782,1784,1786,1793,1801-1802,1804-1810,1812-1856,1862-1863,
       1865-1867 HRO (Mfm SLC)
Mfc   C1541-1988 M1538-1989 B1538-1967 Bn1754-1812 HRO
Mfm C1541-1812 M1538-1812 B1538-1812 Bn1754-1812 HRO
Cop   M1538-1812 Phillimore Vol 11 and Boyd; M1538-1836 HMI
       M1538-1883 CMI; M1790-1812 Pallot; B1538-1837 HBI

KINGSWORTHY (United Methodist Free Church) St Faith's Chapel (Winchester United Methodist Free Church Circuit) (Chapel erected 1841, new chapel 1885 in Basingstoke Road, demolished 1935, chapel erected at Nations Hill 1936) (Records 1887+ HRO)

KNIGHTS ENHAM St Michael & All Angels (123) (Andover Union)
OR   C1683-1994 M1697-1999 B1684-1992 Bn1825-1978 HRO
BT   1780-1812,1816-1854,1857-1866,1868-1870 HRO (Mfm SLC)
Mfc   C1683-1974 M1697-1989 B1684-1992 HRO
Mfm   C1683-1812 M1697-1836 B1684-1812 HRO, SLC
Cop   M1697-1805 Phillimore Vol 1, Boyd, Pallot; M1697-1836 HMI
        M1697-1899 CMI; B1684-1837 HBI; Extracts C1683-1812 M1697-1805 IGI

KNIGHTS ENHAM St Paul's Church Centre
OR   Bn1978-1995 HRO; C1981+ M1982+ Inc

LAINSTON St Peter (40) (Winchester Union) (Redundant 1980)
    The parish registers of Sparsholt include a volume labelled "Marriage Register, Lainston" containing two entries in 1778 and 1789. A note at the front indicates that the parish register of Lainston was taken to London for the trial of Elizabeth Chudleigh in 1776 and never recovered. (See Victoria County History of Hampshire Volume 3 page 446). Subsequent entries were at Sparsholt.

LANDPORT - See PORTSEA All Saints, Circus Church, St Agatha, St Martin, St Michael & All Angels

LANE END (Wesleyan) - See CHERITON

LANGLEY St Francis (Chapelry of Fawley)
OR   Bn1965-1983 HRO

LANGRISH St John the Evangelist (Formed 1871 from East Meon)
OR   C1871-1934 M1872-1976 B1872-1992 Bn1872-1947 HRO
Mfc   C1871-1934 M1872-1976 HRO
Cop   M1872-1882 CMI

LANGRISH (Independent) Ramsdean - See EAST MEON

LASHAM St Mary (236) (Alton Union)
OR   C1560-1949 M1560-1978 B1561-1978 Bn1755-1812,1824,1924-1983 HRO
        (Gap in marriages 1732-1755)
BT   1761,1780-1784,1786-1851,1853-1865,1868 HRO (Mfm SLC)
Mfc   C1560-1949 M1560-1978 B1561-1978 Bn1755-1812,1824 HRO
Mfm   C1560-1812 M1560-1812 B1561-1812 Bn1755-1812,1824 HRO
Pc   C1560-1784 M1560-1732 B1561-1790 HRO
Cop   M1560-1837 HMI; M1700-1886 CMI; B1561-1837 HBI

LAVERSTOKE St Mary (117) (Whitchurch Union) (See also Freefolk)
OR   C1657-1935 M1657-1990 B1656-1989 Bn1762-1787,1826-1907 HRO
       (Gap in marriages 1754-1760)
BT   1780-1809,1811-1836,1838-1858,1862-1863 HRO (Mfm SLC)
Mfc   C1657-1935 M1657-1978 B1656-1989 Bn1762-1787 HRO
Mfm C1657-1812 M1657-1811 B1656-1812 Bn1762-1787 HRO
Cop   M1657-1811 Phillimore Vol 9; M1657-1834 HMI; M1657-1882 CMI
       C1657-1838 M1657-1834 B1656-1837 (Ms,A) SG, HRO
       C1657-1812 M1657-1811 B1656-1812 (Ts) HRO
       M1657-1834 Boyd; M1790-1812 Pallot; B1656-1837 HBI

LECKFORD St Nicholas (221) (Stockbridge Union)
OR   C1760-1984 M1757-1975 B1784-1992 Bn1757-1786,1824-1929 HRO
       (The early registers were destroyed by fire in 1769. Baptisms prior to 1783 are
       retrospective entries for a few families only)
BT   1780-1797,1799-1817,1819-1863 HRO (Mfm SLC)
Mfc   C1760-1984 M1757-1975 B1784-1992 Bn1757-1786 HRO
Mfm C1760-1812 M1757-1811 B1784-1812 Bn1757-1786 HRO
Cop   M1757-1837 HMI; M1757-1882 CMI; B1784-1837 HBI

LECKFORD (Primitive Methodist) (Andover Primitive Methodist Circuit,
    Hurstbourne Tarrant Primitive Methodist Circuit from 1910, but later returned to
    Andover Circuit) (Erected 1846 & 1872, closed 1971) (Records 1872+ HRO)

LEE Chapel (Chapel to Romsey, erected 1862; transferred to Nursling in 1929)
OR   C1942-1958 HRO
Mfc   C1942-1958 HRO

LEE ON THE SOLENT St Faith (District formed 1930 from Crofton; now a parish)
OR   C1930-1981 M1933-1975 Bn1974-1981 PCRO
Mfc   C1930-1981 M1933-1975 HRO, PCRO

LEE ON THE SOLENT (Roman Catholic) St John the Evangelist (Founded 1918)
OR   C1919+ M1945+ B1946+ Inc

LEE ON THE SOLENT (Wesleyan) (Fareham Wesleyan Circuit, Gosport &
    Fareham Wesleyan Circuit from 1908) (Founded c1896) (Records 1896+ HRO)

LEIGH - See WEST LEIGH

LEIGH PARK St Francis (District formed 1952 from Havant, Bedhampton, &
    Rowlands Castle; separate parish 1968; see also Warren Park)
OR   C1954-1987 M1955-1987 Bn1955-1991 PCRO
Mfc   M1955-1979 HRO, PCRO

LINDFORD (Bible Christian) - See HEADLEY

LINKENHOLT St Peter (87) (Andover Union)
OR   C1586-1741,1801-1988 M1579-1738,1803-1972 B1577-1741,1801-1989
      Bn1803-1810,1887-1896,1948-1955 HRO (A register containing C, M, B
      1741-1799 is listed by Fearon & Williams but is now missing; several gaps
      prior to 1700, including M 1662-1695)
BT   1780-1799,1802-1812,1814-1818,1820-1823,1825-1868 HRO (Mfm SLC)
Mfc   C1586-1741,1801-1985 M1579-1738,1803-1972 B1577-1741,1801-1986
      Bn1803-1810,1887-1896,1948-1955 HRO
Mfm   C1586-1741,1801-1812 M1579-1738,1813-1876 B1577-1741,1801-1812
      Bn1803-1810 HRO, SLC
Cop   M1579-1810 Phillimore Vol 9 and Boyd (Includes M1741-1799 from the
      register which is now missing); M1579-1837 HMI; M1579-1905 CMI
      M1790-1816 Pallot; B1577-1741,1801-1837 HBI

LIPHOOK (Roman Catholic, Wesleyan, Bible Christian) - See BRAMSHOTT

LIPHOOK Bible Christian Circuit (United Methodist Circuit from 1907) (Formed
      1863 from Farnham & Liphook Mission [Farnham Circuit]; became part of Liphook
      & North Hampshire United Methodist Circuit in 1930. Included chapels at
      Bramshott and Headley) (Records 1863+ HRO)

LIPHOOK & NORTH HAMPSHIRE United Methodist Circuit (Formed 1930 by
      union of the Crondall and Liphook United Methodist [former Bible Christian]
      Circuits) (Records 1930+ HRO)

LISS St Peter (663) (Petersfield Union) (Chapelry of Odiham; separate parish 1867)
      (St Peter became a chapel to the new parish church of St Mary, established 1892)
OR   C1599-1974 M1599-1981 B1599-1964 Bn1754-1766,1902-1988 HRO
      (Includes separate registers of M1898-1984 for St Peter)
BT   1780,1782-1810,1812-1818,1820-1888 HRO (Mfm SLC)
Mfc   C1599-1974 M1599-1981 B1599-1964 Bn1754-1766 HRO
Mfm   C1599-1974 M1599-1976 B1599-1964 Bn1754-1766,1902-1953 HRO
      Bn1953-1974 DRO
Cop   C1599-1837 M1599-1837 B1599-1837 (Ts,I) HRO
      M1599-1837 HMI; M1599-1881 CMI; B1599-1837 HBI

LISS (Presbyterian, now United Reformed) St Paul, Hillbrow (Founded 1911, active)

LISS (Wesleyan) (Guildford Wesleyan Circuit, Alton Wesleyan Circuit from 1860,
      Petersfield Wesleyan Circuit from 1870, Surrey & North Hampshire Wesleyan
      Mission from 1900, Petersfield & Haslemere Wesleyan Circuit from 1917) (Chapels
      erected c1832 & 1874, closed c1968) (Records 1874+ HRO)
OR   C1906-1958 HRO (89M72/NMR12) (Some baptisms were entered at Alton)
Mfc   C1906-1958 HRO

LISS Cemetery (Records - East Hampshire District Council)
Mfc   B1954-1992 HRO (Includes index)

LITCHFIELD St James the Less (82) (Kingsclere Union)
OR   C1624-1992 M1627-1968 B1629-1992 Bn1754-1817,1894-1989 HRO
      (Gap in M 1717-1738 and B 1717-1731)
BT   1780-1781,1783-1799,1801,1803,1805,1807-1811,1813-1863 HRO
      (Mfm SLC)
Mfc   C1624-1992 M1627-1968 B1629-1992 Bn1754-1817 HRO
Mfm C1624-1877 M1627-1883 B1629-1880 Bn1754-1817 HRO, SLC
Cop   M1627-1812 Phillimore Vol 8
      C1624-1838 M1627-1837 B1629-1837 (Ms,A) SG, HRO
      M1627-1837 HMI; M1627-1883 CMI; M1627-1837 Boyd
      M1790-1812 Pallot; B1629-1837 HBI; Extracts M1815-1883 IGI

LITTLEDOWN (Primitive Methodist) - See VERNHAM DEAN

LITTLE LONDON (Primitive Methodist) - See PAMBER

LITTLE SOMBORNE All Saints (84) (Stockbridge Union) (Ancient chapelry of
   Kings Somborne; redundant 1974)
OR   M1852-1952 Bn1852-1935 HRO
Mfc   M1852-1952 HRO
Cop   M1852-1915 CMI

LITTLETON St Catherine of Alexandria (120) (Winchester Union)
OR   C1736-1966 M1752-1989 B1738-1997 Bn1759-1790,1825-1925,1935-1995
      HRO
BT   1780-1784,1786-1795,1803-1805,1807-1808,1810,1812-1815,1819,
      1822-1829,1831-1870 HRO (Mfm SLC)
Mfc   C1736-1966 M1752-1989 B1738-1997 HRO
Mfm C1736-1812 M1752-1812 B1738-1812 HRO
Cop   C1736-1812 M1752-1809 B1738-1812 Bn1759-1790 (Ms) HRO
      M1752-1835 HMI; M1752-1852 CMI; B1738-1837 HBI

LOCKERLEY St John the Evangelist (560) (Romsey Union) (Chapelry of
   Mottisfont; separate parish 1884)
OR   C1583-1866 M1583-1981 B1583-1920 Bn1754-1812,1932-1965 HRO
      (The register 1583-1780 also contains entries for East Dean)
BT   1705-1710,1780-1861,1863-1866 HRO (Mfm SLC) (1758 in Mottisfont BT)
Mfc   C1583-1866 M1583-1981 B1583-1920 Bn1754-1812 HRO
Mfm C1583-1876 M1583-1876 B1583-1876 Bn1754-1812 HRO, SLC
Cop   C1583-1680 M1583-1678 B1583-1680 (Ts) HRO, HGS (Many errors and
      much omission of detail); C1583-1706 M1583-1703 B1583-1706 (Ms) HRO
      C1681-1800 M1681-1753 B1681-1800 (Ts,I) HRO, HGS; M1583-1837 HMI
      Index to PR c1638-1696 (A-K only) HRO (Ms); M1583-1882 CMI
      B1583-1837 HBI; Extracts C1583-1876 M1583-1876 IGI

LOCKERLEY (Baptist) Ebenezer (Founded 1752, active)

LOCKERLEY (Primitive Methodist) Newtown (Southampton Primitive Methodist
   Circuit, Romsey Primitive Methodist Circuit from 1880) (Erected 1844; a lease at
   HRO refers to a movable chapel on cast iron wheels) (Records 1967+ HRO)

LOCKS HEATH St John the Baptist (Formed 1893 from Hook with Warsash, Sarisbury, & Titchfield)
OR   C1893-1968 M1896-1992 Bn1919-1997 PCRO
Mfc   C1893-1968 M1896-1979 HRO, PCRO

LOCKS HEATH (Baptist) Hunts Pond Road (Probably modern, active)

LOCKS HEATH (Independent, later United Reformed) Hunts Pond Road (Founded 1903, amalgamated with the Baptist Church in 1981)

LOCKS HEATH Cemetery (Records 1925+ Fareham Borough Council)

LONGDOWN (Wesleyan) - See ELING

LONGMOOR St Martin (Garrison Church) - See GREATHAM

LONGPARISH St Nicholas (775) (Andover Union)
OR   C1654-1953 M1654-1980 B1654-1994 Bn1754-1783,1802-1812,1914-1992 HRO
BT   1678,1780-1841,1843-1862,1864-1865,1867-1868 HRO (Mfm SLC)
Mfc   C1654-1953 M1654-1952 B1654-1994 Bn1754-1783,1802-1812 HRO
Mfm   C1654-1812 M1654-1812 B1654-1812 Bn1754-1783,1802-1812 HRO
Cop   C1654-1838 M1654-1837 B1654-1837 (Ts,A) SG, HRO
      M1654-1837 HMI; M1754-1881 CMI; B1654-1837 HBI

LONGPARISH (Particular Baptist) (Chapel erected 1818; closed)
OR   Church book 1818-1914 Gospel Standard Baptist Library

LONGPARISH (Wesleyan) (Andover Wesleyan Circuit) (Meetings by 1844, chapel erected 1866, closed c1974) (Records 1918+ HRO)

LONGPARISH (Primitive Methodist) Forton (Micheldever Primitive Methodist Circuit) (Chapel erected 1869, closed by 1947) (Records 1869+ HRO)

LONGPARISH Cemetery (Records 1884?+ Parish Council)

LONGSTOCK St Mary (428) (Stockbridge Union)
OR   C1718-1985 M1718-1987 B1718-1988 Bn1755-1812,1843-1996 HRO
BT   1780-1791,1793-1797,1799-1859,1861 HRO (Mfm SLC)
Mfc   C1718-1985 M1718-1987 B1718-1988 Bn1755-1812 HRO
Mfm   C1718-1812 M1718-1812 B1718-1812 Bn1755-1812 HRO
Cop   C1718-1864 M1718-1836 B1718-1921 Bn1760-1769 (Ts,I) HRO, HGS
      M1718-1836 HMI; M1718-1881 CMI; B1718-1837 HBI

LONGSTOCK (Primitive Methodist) (Andover Primitive Methodist Circuit, Hurstbourne Tarrant Primitive Methodist Circuit from 1910, but later returned to Andover Circuit) (Erected 1846 & 1878, closed 1965) (Records 1878+ HRO)

LONG SUTTON All Saints (326) (Ash Incorporation, Hartley Wintney Union from 1869) (Chapelry of Crondall; separate parish by 1828)
OR   C1561-1891 M1561-1985 B1561-1995 Bn1823-1994 HRO
        (Largely illegible 1693-1720; gap 1721-1733)
BT   1780-1794,1796-1871 HRO (Mfm SLC)
Mfc   C1561-1891 M1561-1985 B1561-1995 HRO
Mfm   C1561-1812 M1561-1812 B1561-1812 HRO
Cop   M1561-1812 Phillimore Vol 5 and Boyd; M1813-1836 (Ts) SG, HGS
        M1561-1836 HMI; M1561-1881 CMI; M1790-1812 Pallot; B1561-1837 HBI

LONG SUTTON (Independent, linked to Countess of Huntingdon's Connexion) (Church founded 1815, chapel erected 1816, closed early 20th century)

LONGWOOD DENE (Wesleyan) - See OWSLEBURY

LOWER SWANWICK (Particular Baptist) - See SARISBURY

LYMINGTON St Thomas the Apostle (3,361) (Lymington Union)
OR   C1658-1888 M1662-1963 B1662-1916 Bn1754-1812,1823-1898,1913-1990
        HRO
BT   1780-1783,1786-1874 HRO (Mfm SLC)
Mfc   C1658-1888 M1662-1963 B1662-1916 Bn1754-1784 HRO
Cop   C1658-1812 M1665-1812 B1662-1886 (Ts) SG; M1662-1837 (Ms,I) HGS
        C1755-1812 B1755-1812 (Ts,I) HRO; Index to B1755-1812 HGS
        M1662-1837 HMI; M1662-1881 CMI; B1662-1837 HBI

LYMINGTON All Saints (Chapel to St Thomas)
OR   M1911-1982 Bn1911-1966 HRO; C1910+ Inc (B are entered at St Thomas)
Mfc   M1911-1982 HRO

LYMINGTON (Roman Catholic) Our Lady of Mercy & St Joseph (Founded 1805 at Pylewell House; chapel of Our Lady Immaculate established 1852; Walhampton from 1856, present site from 1859. See also Milford Rook Cliff House)
OR   C1805-1840 M1805-1808,1832-1837 PRO (RG 4/2303)
        C1840+ M1840?+ B1856+ Inc
Mfm   C1805-1840 M1805-1808,1832-1837 PRO, HRO, SLC
Cop   C1805-1840 M1805-1808,1832-1837 (I) CRS Vol 14
        M1805-1808,1832-1837 HMI; Extracts C1805-1840 IGI

LYMINGTON (Roman Catholic) French Émigré Priests
OR   1806-1815 Centre des Archives Diplomatiques, Nantes (The entries are indexed with other Émigré registers in a separate index volume held at Nantes. A microfilm copy of the index volume is held at PCRO)

LYMINGTON (Particular Baptist) New Lane (now New Street) (Founded 1688, chapels erected 1767 & 1834, active) (Records 1693+ HRO)
OR   Adult baptisms 1771-1934 Z1783-1837,1853-1855 D1784-1966
        B1794-1854 HRO (58M71/1,12-14) (The baptism and death entries occur in minutes 1771-1831 and membership lists 1771-1961 in 58M71/1,2,15,19,20)
Mfc   Z1783-1837,1853-1855 HRO
Cop   B1813-1836 HBI

LYMINGTON (Independent, now United Reformed) High Street (Founded 1700, active) (Records 1812+ HRO)
OR C1753-1837 PRO (RG 4/721,2300,2301)
  C1843-1921,1953-1955 M1848-1885,1900-1971 B1847-1885,1903,1954-1955
  D1848-1859,1929-1937 (plus D certs 1828-1921) HRO (12M83/1,2,37,65-69)
  (Deaths occur in membership lists 1821-1861, 1848-1937 in 12M83/1,2,11)
Mfm C1753-1837 PRO, HRO, SLC
Cop Extracts C1753-1837 IGI

LYMINGTON (Independent, now United Reformed) Main Road, East End (Founded 1810 as a branch church to High Street, joint church with Pilley [Boldre] formed 1913, active) (Records 1913+ HRO, with High Street records)

LYMINGTON (Countess of Huntingdon's Connexion) Ashley's Lane (In a former Baptist chapel; 1851 Religious Census; no later references located)

LYMINGTON Wesleyan Circuit - See CHRISTCHURCH Wesleyan Circuit

LYMINGTON (Wesleyan) Gosport Street (Christchurch & Lymington Wesleyan Circuit, New Forest Wesleyan Mission from 1925) (Society existed by 1846) (Records 1921+ HRO)

LYMINGTON (Primitive Methodist) East End (Southampton Primitive Methodist Circuit, Romsey Primitive Methodist Circuit from 1880) (Existed by 1855, possibly closed by 1890) (Records 1859+ HRO)

LYMINGTON (Catholic Apostolic Church) Southampton Buildings (Chapel erected 1838, probably closed by 1890)

LYMINGTON Cemetery
OR B1890-1982 HRO
Mfc B1890-1982 HRO
Cop Index to burial register (unspecified dates) HRO

LYMINGTON Union Workhouse
OR No registers survive. Other records at HRO.

LYNDHURST St Michael & All Angels (1,236) (New Forest Union) (Chapelry of Minstead; separate parish 1828; see also Emery Down)
OR C1737-1928 M1737-1992 B1737-1813 Bn1772-1817,1823-1962 HRO
BT 1782-1836,1838-1872 HRO (Mfm SLC)
Mfc C1737-1928 M1737-1962 B1737-1813 Bn1772-1817 HRO
Mfm C1737-1876 M1737-1875 B1737-1876 Bn1772-1817,1823-1882 HRO, SLC
Cop C1737-1789 M1737-1754 B1737-1798 (Ts,I) HRO
  M1737-1837 HMI; M1772-1881 CMI; B1737-1837 HBI

LYNDHURST (Roman Catholic) Our Lady of the Assumption & St Edward the Confessor (Chapel founded 1886, present church erected 1896)
OR C1897+ M1903+ B1911+ Inc

LYNDHURST (General Baptist) Ebenezer Chapel, Chapel Lane (Founded 1700, chapels erected 1745 & 1848, active)
OR   Adult baptisms 1783-1810 Z1813-1837 B1786-1837 PRO (RG 4/2302)
Mfm   C1783-1810 Z1813-1837 B1786-1837 PRO, HRO, SLC
Cop   B1813-1837 HBI; Extracts C1783-1810 Z1813-1837 IGI

LYNDHURST Cemetery (Records - Parish Council)
Mfc   B1885-1980 HRO

MAPLEDURWELL St Mary (211) (Basingstoke Union) (Chapelry of Newnham; separate parish 1918)
OR   C1618-1987 M1629-1988 B1618-1987 Bn1867-1979 HRO
        (Only one marriage entry before 1668; gap in M 1744-1754)
BT   1780-1784,1787-1792,1794-1863,1873-1874 HRO (Mfm SLC)
Mfc   C1618-1987 M1629-1988 B1618-1987 HRO
Mfm   C1618-1676 M1629-1676,1754-1812 B1618-1676 HRO
Cop   M1629-1837 Phillimore Vol 9 and Boyd
        C1618-1905 M1629-1837 B1618-1905 (Ts) HRO; M1629-1837 HMI
        M1629-1882 CMI; M1790-1837 Pallot; B1618-1837 HBI

MAPLEDURWELL (Independent) (Founded 1864)

MARCHWOOD St John the Apostle (Formed 1843 from Eling)
OR   C1843-1972 M1846-1997 B1843-1954 Bn1874-1969 HRO
BT   1843-1853 HRO (Mfm SLC)
Mfc   C1843-1972 M1846-1970 B1843-1954 HRO
Cop   C1906-1959 M1846-1959 B1870-1959 (Ts,I) HRO, SCA; M1846-1881 CMI

MARCHWOOD (Independent) (Founded c1836)

MARTIN All Saints (599) (Fordingbridge Union) (Chapelry of Damerham; separate parish 1866; the parish was transferred from Wiltshire to Hampshire in 1895)
OR   C1590-1880 M1589-1978 B1589-1898 Bn1754-1790,1824-1889 HRO
BT   1623-1637,1662,1667-1676,1696,1711-1741,1769-1770,1789,1794-1838, 1840-1880 WRO
Mfc   C1590-1880 M1589-1978 B1589-1898 Bn1754-1790 HRO
Cop   B1592-1715 (Ts) HRO; M1813-1837 (Ts) WRO; M1813-1837 HMI
        M1700-1881 CMI; M1622-1837 Nimrod Index; B1589-1837 HBI

MARTIN (Independent) (Existed by 1889, probably closed by 1930)

MARTIN (Primitive Methodist) (Salisbury Primitive Methodist Circuit, Wilton Primitive Methodist Circuit from 1898) (Erected 1829) (Records 1829+ WRO)

MARTYR WORTHY St Swithun (219) (Winchester Union)
OR   C1542-1946 M1550-1981 B1539-1990 Bn1754-1812,1824-1974 HRO
        (Gaps in C 1589-1598, M 1584-1597, B 1580-1594)
BT   1780-1787,1789-1819,1821-1880 HRO (Mfm SLC)
Mfc   C1542-1946 M1550-1981 B1539-1990 Bn1754-1812 HRO
Cop   "The most illegible entries" (brief extracts of CMB 1539-1630) (Ms) SG
        M1550-1837 HMI; M1700-1882 CMI; B1539-1837 HBI

MATTINGLEY (Dedication unknown) (Ancient chapelry of Heckfield; separate parish 1863)
OR   C1863-1910 M1863-1989 B1863-1979 Bn1887-1923 HRO
BT   1863-1865 HRO (Mfm SLC) (Filed with Heckfield)
Mfc   C1863-1910 M1863-1989 B1863-1979 HRO, SG
Cop   M1863-1882 CMI

MEDSTEAD St Andrew (418) (Alton Union) (Chapelry of Old Alresford; separate parish 1850; see also Four Marks)
OR   C1561-1947 M1560-1995 B1560-1917 Bn1824-1987 HRO
      (Gap in burials 1702-1738) (For B1917+ see Medstead Cemetery)
BT   1780-1866 HRO (Mfm SLC)
Mfc   C1561-1947 M1560-1991 B1560-1917 HRO
Mfm C1561-1876 M1560-1876 B1560-1876 Bn1824-1875 HRO, SLC
Cop   C1561-1812 M1560-1812 B1560-1812 (Ts) SG, HRO; M1560-1836 HMI
      M1560-1881 CMI; B1560-1837 HBI; Extracts C1561-1876 M1560-1876 IGI

MEDSTEAD (Independent, now United Reformed) Southtown Road (Founded 1850, associated with Alton from c1865, lapsed c1873 but re-established in a new chapel 1896, active)

MEDSTEAD Cemetery (Records - Parish Council)
Mfc   B1917-1986 (plus register of private graves 1884-1961) HRO

MEON - See EAST MEON, WEST MEON

MEONSTOKE St Andrew (382) (Droxford Union)
OR   C1599-1966 M1599-1989 B1599-1928 Bn1754-1812,1824-1959 HRO
BT   1780-1835,1837-1872 HRO (Mfm SLC)
Mfc   C1599-1966 M1599-1989 B1599-1928 Bn1754-1812 HRO
Cop   C1599-1900 M1599-1900 B1599-1900 (Ts,I) HRO
      M1599-1836 HMI; M1599-1900 CMI; B1599-1837 HBI

MEONSTOKE (Primitive Methodist) (Hambledon Primitive Methodist Branch from 1885, Droxford Primitive Methodist Circuit from 1892) (Chapel erected 1864, closed 1962) (Records 1864+ HRO)

MICHELDEVER St Mary the Virgin (936) (Winchester Union)
OR   C1538-1978 M1539-1979 B1538-1923 Bn1823-1961 HRO
      (Gaps in C 1650-1662, M 1648-1691, B 1650-1662,1669-1678,1735-1791; M deficient 1735-1754)
BT   1780-1781,1783-1788,1790-1794,1797-1864 HRO (Mfm SLC)
Mfc   C1538-1978 M1539-1979 B1538-1923 HRO
Mfm C1538-1875 M1539-1875 B1538-1875 Bn1823-1875 HRO, SLC
Cop   C1538-1577 M1539-1567 B1538-1576 (from PR vol 1) (Ts,I) HRO, HGS
      C1538-1690 M1539-1648 B1538-1683 (from PR vol 2) (Ts,I) HRO, HGS
      C1691-1810 M1691-1809 B1684-1810 (Ts,I) HRO (Omits many entries in the periods C1766-1812, M1754-1812, B1791-1812); M1539-1837 HMI
      M1691-1883 CMI; B1538-1837 HBI; Extracts C1538-1875 M1539-1875 IGI

MICHELDEVER Primitive Methodist Circuit (Formed 1835 from Shefford Circuit; became part of Andover Trinity Methodist Circuit in 1948. Included chapels at Barton Stacey, East Stratton, Longparish, Micheldever, North Waltham, Preston Candover, Steventon, Swarraton, Whitchurch, Wield, and Wonston) (Records 1835+ HRO)
OR   C1833-1837 PRO (RG 4/2547); C1835-1898 HRO (96M72/NMC/R5)
Mfc   C1835-1898 HRO
Mfm   C1833-1837 PRO, HRO, SLC
Cop   Extracts C1833-1837 IGI

MICHELDEVER (Primitive Methodist) (Micheldever Primitive Methodist Circuit) (Chapel erected 1867, closed by 1981) (Records 1863,1981 [only] HRO)

MICHELDEVER (Primitive Methodist) Micheldever Station (Micheldever Primitive Methodist Circuit) (Chapel existed by 1876, closed by 1947)

MICHELMERSH St Mary (962) (Romsey Union) (See also Awbridge, Braishfield, Eldon)
OR   C1558-1943 M1559-1996 B1558-1869 Bn1754-1803,1823-1942 HRO
        (Gaps 1563-1579,1653-1660; gaps in C 1710-1718, M 1680-1718,
        B 1685-1718; entries prior to 1606 were copied from an earlier register)
BT   1780-1873 HRO (Mfm SLC)
Mfc   C1558-1943 M1559-1996 B1558-1869 Bn1754-1803 HRO
Cop   M1559-1836 HMI; M1559-1851 CMI; B1558-1837 HBI

MICHELMERSH (Wesleyan) (PO Directory 1855, conveyances 1844 & 1864, no later references located)

MIDDLE WALLOP (Baptist, Presbyterian, Methodist) - See OVER WALLOP

MILFORD All Saints (1,533) (Lymington Union) (See also Pennington)
OR   C1594-1972 M1594-1968 B1594-1942 Bn1754-1827,1918-1971 HRO
BT   1780-1794,1796-1870,1872 HRO (Mfm SLC)
Mfc   C1594-1972 M1594-1968 B1594-1942 Bn1754-1827 HRO
Mfm   C1594-1812 M1594-1759 B1594-1812 HRO
Cop   C1691-1784 M1693-1760 B1693-1784 (Ts,MsI) HRO
        M1594-1837 HMI; M1813-1882 CMI; B1594-1837 HBI

MILFORD (Roman Catholic) Rook Cliff House (Became a refugee centre for French Catholics; a chapel had been established by 1798)
OR   C1813-1815 D1813 PRO (with Lymington, RG 4/2303) (plus baptism
        certificates 1806-1817; one refers to a marriage in 1814)
Mfm   C1813-1815 D1813 PRO, HRO
Cop   C1813-1815 D1813 (I) CRS Vol 14; M1814 HMI; D1813 HBI

MILFORD (Particular Baptist) Barnes Lane (Founded 1816, active)

MILFORD (Baptist Free Church, Evangelical Free Church) (Founded 1911, chapel sold to Methodists c1959) (Records 1908+ HRO, in 45M68)

MILFORD (Wesleyan) Everton (Christchurch & Lymington Wesleyan Circuit, New Forest Wesleyan Mission from 1925) (Chapel erected 1881, closed 1957)

MILLBROOK St Nicholas (2,735) (South Stoneham Union) (St Nicholas was replaced as the parish church by Holy Trinity, established 1874. St Nicholas closed 1889-1916 and 1920+, demolished 1939. Millbrook is now within the City of Southampton; see also the Southampton parishes of Freemantle, Maybush, Redbridge, Shirley, Shirley Warren)

OR   C1633-1965 M1633-1981 B1633-1918 Bn1754-1964,1984-1988 SCA

BT   1780-1886 (plus Quaker burials 1865-1869) HRO (Mfm SLC)

Mfc   C1633-1965 M1633-1961 B1633-1918 HRO, SCA

Mfm   C1633-1885 M1633-1903 B1633-1895 SCA, SLC

Cop   C1633-1837 M1633-1837 B1633-1837 Bn1759-1812 (Ts,I) SG, HRO, SCA, HGS; C1780-1812 M1780-1812 B1780-1812 (BT) (Ts,I) SG, (Ts) SCA
C1838-1885 M1838-1871 B1838-1895 SCI; M1633-1837 HMI
M1813-1881 CMI; B1633-1837 HBI
Extracts C1780-1812 M1780-1812 (BT) IGI

MILLBROOK (Society of Friends) Burial Ground

OR   B1865-1869 HRO (24M54/268)

MILLBROOK (Baptist) Union Church, Testwood Road (Founded 1931, active)

MILLBROOK (Independent) Redbridge Lane (Chapel erected c1838; 1851 Religious Census; no other references located)

MILLBROOK (Wesleyan) Wimpson (Southampton Wesleyan Circuit) (Established c1859, active) (Records 1962+ SCA)

MILLBROOK Cemetery, Millbrook Road

OR   B1909+ Bereavement Services Unit, 6 Bugle Street, Southampton

MILTON St Mary Magdalen (956) (Lymington Union) (Chapelry of Milford; separate parish 1867; see also Ashley [Milton], Highcliffe)

OR   C1654-1983 M1659-1977 B1658-1961 Bn1754-1790,1879-1952,1966-1993 HRO

BT   1755,1780-1805,1807-1811,1813-1872,1874 HRO (Mfm SLC)

Mfc   C1654-1983 M1659-1969 B1658-1961 Bn1754-1790 HRO

Cop   C1654-1812 M1659-1812 B1658-1810 (Ts,I) HRO; M1659-1837 HMI
Index to M1754-1812 HGS; M1659-1882 CMI; B1658-1837 HBI
Index to C1654-1739 M1659-1739 B1658-1739 (Ms) HRO

MILTON (Roman Catholic) Our Lady of Lourdes (Opened 1927, parish 1928)

OR   1928+ Inc

MILTON (Baptist) Lower Ashley Road, Ashley (Founded 1817, active)

MILTON (Baptist) Old Milton Road (Mission Hall erected 1910, Church founded 1940, active)

MILTON (Independent, now United Reformed) Cranemoor, or Ringwood Road Walkford (Founded 1829, active)
OR   C1836-1852,1861-1883,1901-1916 M1901,1907,1909 registered at Christchurch Independent Chapel (DRO NP4/RE1,CM1,CM2,CM5) (C1836-1852 are for Hinton Chapel, which is probably the same chapel) M1971-1987 HRO (149M98/1/1-2)
Mfm   C1836-1852,1861-1883,1901-1916 M1901,1907,1909 SLC

MILTON (Wesleyan) Barton on Sea (Bournemouth Wesleyan Circuit, Christchurch & Lymington Wesleyan Circuit from 1966) (Chapel erected 1932, new church erected 1970) (Records 1934+ HRO)

MILTON (Primitive Methodist) Wootton (Southampton Primitive Methodist Circuit, Romsey Primitive Methodist Circuit from 1880) (Chapel erected c1844)

MILTON Cemetery
OR   B1957-1982 HRO
Mfc   B1957-1982 HRO

MILTON (PORTSEA) - See PORTSEA St James, St Patrick, St Mary's Hospital

MINLEY St Andrew (Chapelry formed 1874 from Cove & Hawley)
OR   M1871-1988 SHC; C1873+ B1881+ Bn1871+ Inc
Mfc   M1871-1988 HRO
Cop   M1871-1918 CMI

MINSTEAD All Saints (1,074) (New Forest Union)
OR   C1682-1859 M1682-1957 B1682-1914 Bn1755-1812,1823-1964 HRO
BT   1687,1781-1867 HRO (Mfm SLC)
Mfc   C1682-1859 M1682-1957 B1682-1914 Bn1755-1812 HRO
Pc   C1764-1812 M1773 B1764-1812 HRO
Cop   C1682-1837 (Ts,A) M1688-1812 (Ts,I) M1813-1837 (Ts,A) SG
      C1764-1812 B1764-1812 (plus one M 1773) (Ts,I) HRO, HGS
      C1682-1837 HGS; Card index to C1682-1837 M1688-1812 Inc
      M1688-1812 Boyd; M1682-1837 HMI; M1682-1881 CMI
      B1682-1837 HBI; Extracts M1688-1812 IGI

MONK SHERBORNE All Saints (522) (Basingstoke Union) (See also Ramsdell)
OR   C1620-1986 M1618-1982 B1619-1980 Bn1823-1868,1953-1976 HRO
      (Includes M1837-1849 for Pamber)
BT   1728,1780-1783,1785-1876 HRO (Mfm SLC)
Mfc   C1620-1986 M1618-1971 B1619-1980 HRO
Cop   M1618-1811 (Ts,I) & (Ts,A) SG; M1618-1811 Boyd; M1618-1837 HMI
      C1620-1812 M1618-1811 B1619-1812 (Ts) HRO, Inc
      M1618-1888 CMI; B1619-1837 HBI; Extracts M1618-1811 IGI

MONXTON St Mary (276) (Andover Union)

OR   C1717-1931 M1716-1971 B1716-1994 Bn1730-1744,1755-1990 HRO

BT   1780-1784,1786-1882 HRO (Mfm SLC)

Mfc   C1717-1931 M1716-1971 B1716-1994 Bn1730-1744,1755-1843 HRO

Mfm   C1717-1877 M1716-1877 B1716-1812 Bn1730-1744,1755-1843 HRO, SLC

Cop   M1716-1811 Phillimore Vol 1, Boyd, Pallot

      C1717-1812 M1716-1753 B1716-1811 Bn1730-1744 (Ts,I) HRO (HGS holds index only) ; M1716-1837 HMI; M1716-1881 CMI; B1716-1837 HBI Extracts C1813-1877 M1813-1877 IGI

MOORDOWN - See BOURNEMOUTH St John the Baptist, Moordown

MOORGREEN (Wesleyan) - See SOUTH STONEHAM

MORESTEAD (Dedication unknown) (90) (Winchester Union)

OR   C1549-1992 M1550-1925 B1553-1989 Bn1760-1811,1825-1990 HRO (Gaps in C 1657-1668, M 1646-1668, B 1651-1667. Includes M1740-1754 for the chapel of Wolvesey Palace, Winchester)

BT   1724,1780-1784,1787-1789,1793-1798,1800,1802-1814,1818-1832,1836-1843,1845-1855,1857-1858,1864 HRO (Mfm SLC)

Mfc   C1549-1992 M1550-1925 B1553-1989 Bn1760-1811 HRO

      C1549-1811 M1550-1851 B1553-1811 Bn1760-1811 SG

Mfm   C1549-1811 M1550-1753 B1553-1811 HRO

Cop   C1549-1980 M1550-1925 B1553-1978 Bn1825-1978 (Ts,I) SG, HRO, HGS M1550-1837 HMI; M1550-1881 CMI; B1553-1837 HBI

MORTIMER WEST END St Saviour (Formed 1870 from the Hampshire portion of Stratfield Mortimer)

OR   M1870-1981 B1869-1982 Bn1873-1969 BRO; C1860+ Inc

BT   1864-1898 Oxfordshire Record Office

Mfc   M1870-1981 B1869-1982 BRO, HRO

Cop   M1870-1882 CMI

MORTIMER WEST END (Independent, Countess of Huntingdon's Connexion) (Chapel erected 1798, Countess of Huntingdon's Connexion from 1826)

OR   C1806-1837 PRO (RG 4/235); C1806+ B1803+ Inc (entries prior to 1858 are arranged alphabetically)

Mfm   C1806-1837 PRO, HRO, BRO, SLC

Cop   B1803-1836 HBI; Extracts C1806-1837 IGI (Berkshire section)

MORTIMER WEST END (Primitive Methodist) Drury Lane (Silchester Primitive Methodist Circuit) (Chapel erected 1866, later moved to West End Road) (Records 1869+ BRO)

MOTTISFONT St Andrew (515) (Romsey Union)
OR   C1701-1915 M1701-1983 B1701-1950 Bn1754-1772,1824-1955 HRO
BT   1758,1780-1808,1810-1859,1861 HRO (Mfm SLC) (The 1758 BT includes entries for Lockerley and East Dean)
Mfc   C1701-1915 M1701-1983 B1701-1950 Bn1754-1772 HRO, SG
Mfm   C1701-1876 M1701-1877 B1701-1876 Bn1754-1772,1824-1875 HRO, SLC
Cop   M1701-1837 HMI; M1701-1882 CMI; B1701-1837 HBI
       Extracts C1701-1812 M1701-1733 IGI

MOTTISFONT (Baptist) Spearywell (Founded 1752, active)

MUDEFORD (Wesleyan) - See CHRISTCHURCH

NATELY - See NATELY SCURES, UP NATELY

NATELY SCURES St Swithun (245) (Basingstoke Union) (See also Hook)
OR   C1666-1987 M1684-1988 B1679-1987 Bn1754-1812,1951-1978 HRO (Only three marriage entries before 1721)
BT   1780-1794,1796-1812,1814-1823,1825-1865 HRO (Mfm SLC)
Mfc   C1666-1987 M1684-1988 B1679-1987 Bn1754-1812 HRO
Mfm   C1666-1928 M1684-1836 B1679-1812 Bn1754-1812 HRO
Cop   M1684-1812 Phillimore Vol 11 and Boyd; M1684-1836 HMI
       C1666-1812 M1684-1754 B1679-1786 (Ts) HRO; M1684-1889 CMI
       C1813-1837 B1780-1837 (Ms,I) HRO; M1790-1812 Pallot
       M1684-1836 Bn1754-1812 (Ts,I) SG, HRO, HGS
       Index to C1666-1812 B1679-1812 (Ms) HRO; B1679-1837 HBI

NETHER WALLOP St Andrew (900) (Stockbridge Union)
OR   C1629-1892 M1631-1988 B1631-1678,1776-1955 Bn1754-1835 HRO (No burial register 1678-1776)
BT   1780,1782-1795,1798-1799,1801-1810,1813-1866 HRO (Mfm SLC)
Mfc   C1629-1892 M1631-1988 B1631-1678.1776-1955 Bn1754-1835 HRO
       C1629-1851 M1631-1837 B1631-1678,1776-1864 Bn1754-1835 SG
Pc   C1629-1892 M1631-1970 B1631-1678,1776-1955 Bn1754-1835 HRO
Cop   M1631-1837 HMI; M1754-1881 CMI; B1631-1678,1776-1837 HBI

NETHER WALLOP (Wesleyan) (Andover Wesleyan Circuit) (Chapel erected c1818, closed 1976) (Records 1819+ HRO)
OR   M1949-1967 HRO (96M72/NMC/R12)
Mfc   M1949-1967 HRO

NETLEY Royal Chapel, Royal Victoria Hospital - See HOUND

NETLEY St Edward the Confessor - See HOUND

NETLEY (Roman Catholic, Independent, Wesleyan) - See HOUND

NETLEY MARSH St Matthew (Formed 1855 from Eling; see also Calmore)
OR   C1854-1993 M1855-1996 B1854-1924 Bn1855-1975 HRO
Mfc   C1854-1940 M1855-1945 B1854-1924 HRO
Cop   C1854-1950 M1855-1949 B1854-1950 (Ts,I) HRO; M1855-1882 CMI

NETLEY MARSH (Particular Baptist) - See ELING (Particular Baptist) Bartley

NETLEY MARSH (Independent) (White's Directory 1878; no later references located)

NEW ALRESFORD St John the Baptist (1,437) (Alresford Union) (Chapelry of Old Alresford; separate parish 1850)
OR   C1714-1971 M1724-1991 B1678-1949 Bn1823-1930,1970-1991 HRO (Few baptisms before 1724. PR1, PR2, and the copy register PR4 overlap, and all should be checked. Many entries survive only as abbreviated copies)
BT   1780-1878 HRO (Mfm SLC)
Mfc   C1714-1971 M1724-1991 B1678-1949 HRO
Cop   C1719-1812 M1724-1754 B1678-1812 (Ts,I) HRO (From the copy register, PR4); M1724-1837 HMI; M1724-1882 CMI; B1678-1837 HBI

NEW ALRESFORD (Roman Catholic) - See TICHBORNE

NEW ALRESFORD (Society of Friends) - See ALTON

NEW ALRESFORD (Independent) Pound Hill (Founded 1825, chapel sold to Methodists 1964) (Records c1840+ HRO, in 127M94)
OR   C1832-1837 PRO (RG 4/1072); C1832-1837,1852-1903 M1853-1855, 1863-1880,1884-1899 B1885-1900 D1854-1889 plus D certs 1885-1900 HRO (127M94/66-68) (The death entries occur in membership lists)
Mfm   C1832-1837 PRO, HRO, SLC
Cop   Extracts C1832-1837 IGI

NEW ALRESFORD (Wesleyan) Jacklyns Lane (Winchester Wesleyan Circuit, South Hampshire Wesleyan Mission from 1900) (Chapel opened 1894, closed 1935 and joined the Primitive Methodist congregation) (Records 1893+ HRO)
OR   C1918-1931 HRO (79M72/NMR3)
Mfc   C1918-1931 HRO

NEW ALRESFORD (Primitive Methodist) The Dean (Winchester Primitive Methodist Circuit) (Society founded 1875, chapel opened 1896 at The Dean, transferred 1964 to the old Independent Chapel at Pound Hill, then in 1980 to a new church in Jacklyn's Lane) (Records 1874+ HRO)
OR   M1970-1978 HRO (79M72/NMR18)
Mfc   M1970-1978 HRO

NEW ALRESFORD Union Workhouse (Alresford Union)
OR   No registers survive. Other records at HRO.

NEWBURY [Berkshire] Wesleyan Circuit (Formed 1795 from Oxfordshire Circuit; became part of Newbury & Hungerford Circuit in 1908. Included chapels at Baughurst, East Woodhay, Kingsclere, possibly Faccombe) (Records 1836+ BRO)
OR   C1795-1837 PRO (RG 4/300,2691) (Covers Tadley, Kingsclere, Combe area) C1838-1852,1908-1977 BRO (D/MC7/7A/1-3, D/MC9/7A/1)
Mfm   C1795-1837 PRO, BRO, SLC
Cop   Extracts C1795-1837 IGI (Berkshire section)

NEWBURY [Berkshire] Primitive Methodist Circuit (Known as Shefford Circuit until 1845. Included chapels at Burghclere, East Woodhay, and Kingsclere)
OR   C1831-1952 BRO (D/MC8/7A/1-4)
Mfm C1831-1952 BRO

NEWBURY [Berkshire] Union Workhouse (Union included Newtown until 1895)
OR   Z1835-1909,1914-1947 D1868-1909,1914-1943 BRO
Mfm Z1835-1909 D1868-1909,1914-1943 BRO, SLC; Z1914-1947 BRO

NEWBURY & HUNGERFORD [Berkshire] Wesleyan Circuit (Formed 1908 by union of the Newbury and Hungerford Circuits. Included chapels at East Woodhay and Kingsclere)

NEW FOREST Wesleyan Mission (Formed 1925 from Christchurch & Lymington Circuit and part of Southampton Circuit; ceased 1966. Included chapels at Bransgore, Brockenhurst, Christchurch, Dibden, Fawley, Lymington, Milford, and Ringwood) (Records 1925+ HRO)

NEW FOREST Union Workhouse (situated in the parish of Eling)
OR   No registers survive. Other records at HRO.

NEWFOUND (Wesleyan) - See WOOTTON ST LAWRENCE

NEWNHAM St Nicholas (329) (Basingstoke Union) (See also Hook)
OR   C1725-1972 M1753-1988 B1755-1932 Bn1754-1812,1866-1954 HRO (The few baptism entries before 1752 appear to have been entered retrospectively)
BT   1780-1783,1786-1788,1790-1863,1868,1873-1874 HRO (Mfm SLC)
Mfc C1725-1972 M1753-1988 B1755-1932 Bn1754-1812 HRO
Cop M1754-1812 Phillimore Vol 8 and Boyd; M1753-1836 HMI
      C1725-1812 M1753-1812 B1755-1812 (Ts) HRO, Inc; M1753-1881 CMI
      C1813-1837 B1813-1837 (Ms,I) HRO; M1790-1812 Pallot
      M1753-1836 (Ts,I) SG, HRO, HGS; B1755-1837 HBI

NEWNHAM (Primitive Methodist) (Basingstoke Primitive Methodist Circuit) (Chapel erected 1846)

NEWTON VALENCE St Mary (289) (Alton Union)
OR   C1538-1896 M1541-1979 B1562-1992 Bn1754-1811,1947-1957 HRO (Gap in baptisms 1796-1813, but the register 1813-1896 contains an extract made in 1849 of baptisms from the BT 1798-1802,1806,1808-1810,1812-1813)
BT   1780-1797,1810,1815-1874 HRO (Mfm SLC)
Mfc C1538-1896 M1541-1979 B1562-1992 Bn1754-1811,1947-1957 HRO
Mfm C1538-1896 M1541-1837 B1562-1811 Bn1754-1811,1947-1957 HRO
Cop M1541-1837 HMI; M1700-1882 CMI; B1562-1837 HBI

NEWTOWN St Mary the Virgin & St John the Baptist (269) (Newbury Union, Kingsclere Union from 1895) (Chapelry of Burghclere)
OR   C1666-1890 M1679-1978 B1738-1966 Bn1756-1811 HRO
        (Gap in M 1683-1729; B entries before 1750 are for 1738 only)
BT   1780-1782,1784-1790,1792-1795,1798-1800,1802-1803,1806,1815-1876 HRO
        (Mfm SLC)
Mfc   C1666-1890 M1679-1978 B1738-1966 HRO
Cop   M1679-1811 Phillimore Vol 8 and Boyd; M1679-1837 HMI
        C1666-1812 M1679-1811 B1738-1812 Inc
        M1679-1886 CMI; M1790-1812 Pallot; B1738-1837 HBI

NEWTOWN (Baptist) (Existed by 1851, no references located after 1883)

NEWTOWN (LOCKERLEY) (Primitive Methodist) - See LOCKERLEY

NEWTOWN (SOBERTON) Holy Trinity (Formed 1851 from Soberton & Hambledon)
OR   C1850-1904 M1850-1981 B1850-1950 Bn1856-1892,1911-1976 HRO
Mfc   C1850-1904 M1850-1981 B1850-1950 HRO
Cop   M1850-1883 CMI

NEWTOWN (SOBERTON) Cemetery (Established 1920)

NEWTOWN (SOUTHAMPTON) - See SOUTHAMPTON Newtown

NORTHAM - See SOUTHAMPTON Northam

NORTH BADDESLEY St John the Baptist & All Saints (297) (Hursley Union) (See also Chandlers Ford, Rownhams, Valley Park)
OR   C1682-1982 M1682-1990 B1682-1967 Bn1754-1810,1826-1837,1872-1997
        HRO
BT   1813-1815,1819,1821-1826,1828,1831-1833,1838-1873 HRO (Mfm SLC)
Mfc   C1682-1967 M1682-1974 B1682-1967 Bn1754-1810 HRO
        C1682-1926 M1682-1837 B1682-1967 Bn1754-1810 SG
Mfm   C1682-1876 M1682-1837 B1682-1816 Bn1754-1810 HRO, SLC
Cop   M1682-1837 HMI; M1682-1886 CMI; B1682-1837 HBI
        Extracts C1682-1876 M1682-1837 IGI

NORTH BADDESLEY (Baptist) Nutburn Road (Founded 1830, active)

NORTH CHARFORD - See CHARFORD

NORTH ELING - See COPYTHORNE

NORTH END - See PORTSEA Ascension, St Francis, St Mark, St Nicholas, St Saviour

NORTH HAYLING St Peter (294) (Havant Union) (Chapelry of South Hayling)
OR   C1571-1980 M1571-1984 B1571-1975 Bn1824-1988 PCRO
BT   1780-1817,1819-1831,1833-1835,1837-1877,1879 HRO (Mfm SLC)
Mfc   C1571-1980 M1571-1984 B1571-1975 HRO, PCRO
Mfm   C1571-1875 M1571-1875 B1571-1875 PCRO, SLC
Pc   C1813-1920 B1813-1974 PCRO
Cop   C1571-1653 M1571-1649 B1571-1649 (Ts) HRO; M1571-1812 (Ts,I) SG
      C1571-1920 M1571-1837 B1571-1975 PCI
      M1571-1812 Boyd; M1571-1837 HMI; M1571-1883 CMI
      B1571-1837 HBI; Extracts C1734-1876 M1571-1879 IGI

NORTH HAYLING (Independent, now United Reformed) Havant Road, Stoke
    (Founded 1875, closed after 1990)

NORTHINGTON St John the Evangelist (291) (Alresford Union) (Chapelry of
    Micheldever; chapelry of Swarraton from 1847)
OR   C1579-1906 M1618-1836 B1607-1993 Bn1754-1812,1824-1875,1953 HRO
      (Several gaps, notably C1642-1695 M1647-1667 B1659-1678,1705-1715)
BT   1780,1782-1784,1786-1792,1795-1858 HRO (Mfm SLC)
Mfc   C1579-1906 M1618-1993 B1607-1993 Bn1754-1812 SG, HRO
Cop   M1618-1836 HMI; M1618-1902 CMI; B1607-1837 HBI
      Extracts C1630-1726 M1579-1584,1618-1724 IGI

NORTH STONEHAM St Nicholas (766) (South Stoneham Union) (See also Bassett,
    Chandlers Ford, Southampton St Alban, Valley Park)
OR   C1640-1974 M1640-1988 B1640-1980 Bn1754-1824,1872-1895,1940-1983
      HRO
BT   1780-1784,1786-1793,1795-1855,1857-1873 HRO (Mfm SLC)
Mfc   C1640-1974 M1640-1988 B1640-1980 Bn1754-1824 HRO
      (Omits draft register of C & B 1832-1839,1851-1856)
      C1640-1974 M1640-1975 B1640-1875 Bn1754-1824 SCA
Cop   C1640-1837 M1640-1837 B1640-1837 (Ts,I) SG, HRO, HGS, SCA
      M1640-1837 HMI; M1640-1881 CMI; B1640-1837 HBI

NORTH TADLEY St Mary (Formerly Heath End Chapel; district formed 1957 from
    Aldermaston [Berks], Baughurst, & Tadley; separate parish 1973)
OR   C1896-1906,1957-1967 M1961-1976 Bn1961-1988 HRO
Mfc   C1896-1906,1957-1967 M1961-1976 HRO
Cop   C1896-1906 (Ts) HRO

NORTH WALTHAM St Michael (458) (Basingstoke Union)
OR   C1654-1978 M1654-1996 B1654-1914 Bn1754-1805,1823-1985 HRO
BT   1781-1793,1795-1799,1801-1864,1866 HRO (Mfm SLC)
Mfc   C1654-1978 M1654-1996 B1654-1914 Bn1754-1805 HRO
Mfm   C1654-1876 M1654-1765 B1654-1877 Bn1754-1765 HRO, SLC
Cop   M1654-1811 Phillimore Vol 3 and Boyd; M1654-1836 HMI
      C1654-1812 B1654-1812 Bn1765-1805 (Ts) HRO; M1654-1881 CMI
      M1790-1812 Pallot; B1654-1837 HBI; Extracts C1654-1876 M1654-1765 IGI

NORTH WALTHAM (Primitive Methodist) (Micheldever Primitive Methodist Circuit) (Preaching in a converted malthouse from 1837, new chapel erected 1864, active) (Records 1864+ HRO)

NORTH WARNBOROUGH (Wesleyan) - See ODIHAM

NURSLING St Boniface (884) (Romsey Union) (See also Lee, Rownhams)
OR   C1617-1930 M1630-1968 B1630-1943 Bn1754-1824,1924-1974 HRO
BT   1687,1780-1871 HRO (Mfm SLC)
Mfc   C1617-1930 M1630-1968 B1630-1943 Bn1754-1824 HRO
      C1617-1930 M1630-1942 B1630-1943 Bn1754-1824 SG
Mfm C1736-1876 M1736-1876 B1736-1876 Bn1754-1824 HRO, SLC
Cop C1617-1878 M1630-1837 B1630-1943 Bn1754-1824 (Ts & Ms,I) HRO
      C1736-1878 M1736-1812 B1736-1943 Bn1754-1824 (Ts & Ms) HGS
      M1630-1837 HMI; M1630-1882 CMI; B1630-1837 HBI
      Extracts M1736-1876 IGI

NURSLING (Wesleyan) (Southampton Wesleyan Circuit) (Chapel erected 1815, closed 1977) (Records 1932+ SCA)

NUTLEY St Mary (138) (Basingstoke Union) (Closed 1951, demolished 1956)
OR   C1813-1950 M1758-1941 B1801-1945 HRO (Plus single baptisms in
      1766,1768, and one burial in 1765; other entries appear at Preston Candover)
BT   1780-1796,1799-1806,1808-1809,1811,1813-1816,1818-1836,1846-1869 HRO
      (Mfm SLC) (Entries also occur in the Preston Candover BT)
Mfc   C1813-1950 M1758-1941 B1801-1945 HRO
Cop M1758-1813 (Ts) SG; M1758-1836 HMI; M1758-1890 CMI
      B1801-1837 HBI

OAKHANGER (Independent) - See KINGSLEY

OAKLEY - See CHURCH OAKLEY, EAST OAKLEY

ODIHAM All Saints (2,647) (Hartley Wintney Union) (See also Hook)
OR   C1538-1953 M1538-1993 B1538-1943 Bn1653-1659,1754-1988 HRO
BT   1701,1780-1781,1783-1873 HRO (Mfm SLC)
Mfc   C1538-1953 M1538-1979 B1538-1943 Bn1653-1659,1754-1771 HRO
Mfm C1538-1812 M1538-1812 B1538-1812 Bn1653-1659,1754-1771 HRO
Cop M1538-1812 Phillimore Vol 6 and Boyd; B1740-1837 HBI
      M1538-1837 HMI; M1813-1881 CMI; M1790-1812 Pallot

ODIHAM (Baptist) (Chapel erected 1877)

ODIHAM (Independent) High Street (Founded 1662, closed 1958)
    (Records 1827+ HRO, in 127M94)
OR   C1795-1837 B1832-1837 PRO (RG 4/723); C1795-1891 M1837-1883,
      1951-1955 B1832-1839,1889-1893 D1828-1886, 1896-1904 HRO
      (127M94/74, 151M98/1/1) (The death entries occur in membership lists)
Mfm C1795-1837 B1832-1837 PRO, HRO, SLC
Cop B1832-1837 HBI; Extracts C1795-1837 IGI

ODIHAM (Wesleyan) North Warnborough (Basingstoke Wesleyan Circuit, Surrey & North Hampshire Wesleyan Mission from 1900, Basingstoke Wesleyan Circuit from 1917) (Chapel erected 1861, active)

ODIHAM (Primitive Methodist) (Basingstoke Primitive Methodist Circuit) (Existed by 1880, probably closed by 1939)

ODIHAM Cemetery (Records - Parish Council)
Mfc   B1860-1958 (plus register of graves 1915-1970) HRO (Includes index)

OLD ALRESFORD St Mary (459) (Alresford Union)
OR   C1556-1866 M1539-1979 B1562-1903 Bn1754-1812,1824-1897 HRO
       (Gap in M 1553-1564)
BT   1780-1876 HRO (Mfm SLC)
Mfc   C1556-1866 M1539-1979 B1562-1903 Bn1754-1812 HRO, SG
Mfm   C1556-1866 M1539-1837 B1562-1875 Bn1754-1812,1824-1876 HRO, SLC
Cop   M1539-1837 HMI; M1700-1837 CMI; B1562-1837 HBI
       Extracts M1540-1837 IGI

OLD BASING St Mary (1,103) (Basingstoke Union) (Chapelry of Basingstoke; separate parish 1864) (See also Chineham)
OR   C1668-1911 M1655-1940 B1655-1923 Bn1824-1995 HRO
       (Some gaps, notably B1680-1695)
BT   1780-1866 HRO (Mfm SLC)
Mfc   C1668-1911 M1655-1940 B1655-1923 HRO
Mfm   C1668-1876 M1655-1876 B1655-1875 HRO, SLC
Cop   M1655-1812 Phillimore Vol 3 and Boyd; M1655-1837 HMI
       C1671-1812 M1655-1837 B1655-1875 (Ts) HRO; M1655-1881 CMI
       C1671-1750 M1655-1750 B1655-1750 (Ts) Inc; C1671-1676 (Ts,I) SG
       Index to B1655-1750 (Ms) HRO; M1790-1812 Pallot
       B1655-1837 HBI; Extracts M1837-1876 IGI

OLD BASING (Independent) Pyotts Hill (Erected 1868, Church founded 1872)

OLD BASING (Primitive Methodist) (Basingstoke Primitive Methodist Circuit) (Chapel erected 1867, active) (Records 1922+ HRO)

OLD BASING Union Workhouse (Basingstoke Union) - See BASINGSTOKE

OTTERBOURNE St Matthew (583) (Hursley Union) (Chapelry of Hursley; separate parish 1876; see also Bursledon, Chandlers Ford, Colden Common)
OR   C1642-1956 M1647-1988 B1648-1942 Bn1786-1992 HRO (The register
       1747-1805, missing for many years, was left outside the Vicarage in 1999;
       only two baptisms before 1648; gap in M 1653-1663)
BT   1780-1790,1792-1869 HRO (Mfm SLC)
Mfc   C1642-1956 M1647-1981 B1648-1942 HRO
Cop   C1642-1747,1806-1840 M1647-1747,1752-1840 B1648-1747,1806-1840 (Ts,I)
       HRO; B1648-1747,1806-1840 HGS; M1647-1836 HMI
       M1647-1883 CMI; B1648-1837 HBI

OTTERBOURNE (Roman Catholic) Highbridge House - See EASTLEIGH

OTTERBOURNE (Primitive Methodist) Otterbourne Hill (Chapel erected 1859, probably closed by 1900)

OVERTON St Mary (1,507) (Whitchurch Union)
OR   C1621-1972 M1621-1972 B1617-1977 Bn1754-1812,1966-1991 HRO (Many gaps before 1680; entries 1617-1633 are extracts only, from an earlier register)
BT   1780-1875 HRO (Mfm SLC)
Mfc   C1621-1972 M1621-1972 B1617-1977 Bn1754-1812 HRO
Cop   M1640-1812 Phillimore Vol 2 & Boyd; M1621-1837 HMI; M1640-1881 CMI
    C1621-1765 M1628-1750 B1669-1765 (Ts) HRO; M1790-1812 Pallot
    C1766-1904 M1813-1837 B1766-1901 (Ts,I) HRO; B1617-1837 HBI

OVERTON (Independent) Winchester Street (Chapel opened 1827, Church founded 1837, chapel sold to Methodists c1961) (Records 1895+ HRO)
OR   C1927-1957 M1929-1949 B1927-1947 HRO (159M85/3)
Mfc   C1927-1957 M1929-1949 B1927-1947 HRO

OVERTON (Wesleyan) High Street, Winchester Street (Southampton Wesleyan Circuit, Winchester Wesleyan Circuit from 1816, Andover Wesleyan Circuit from 1818) (Society possibly existed by 1814, High Street Chapel erected 1842, moved to former Independent Chapel in 1966, active) (Records 1891+ HRO)

OVER WALLOP St Peter (478) (Stockbridge Union)
OR   C1684-1967 M1540-1988 B1538-1892 Bn1754-1775,1942-1977 HRO
    (Gaps in C 1719-1730, M 1703-1753, B 1625-1664, and a few smaller gaps)
BT   1783-1807,1809-1815,1817-1861 HRO (Mfm SLC)
Mfc   C1684-1967 M1540-1988 B1538-1892 Bn1754-1775 HRO, SG
Cop   M1540-1836 HMI; M1700-1881 CMI; B1538-1837 HBI

OVER WALLOP (Baptist) Middle Wallop (Chapel erected 1841, Church founded 1848, now united with Broughton) (Records 1935+ HRO)

OVER WALLOP (Presbyterian, Methodist, United Board) RAF Middle Wallop
OR   C1954-1963 RACD

OVINGTON St Peter (179) (Alresford Union)
OR   C1591-1991 M1591-1980 B1591-1990 Bn1755-1812 HRO
BT   1780-1792,1794,1796-1807,1809-1840,1842-1858,1860-1870 HRO
    (1866-67 are in 32M69/PI6) (Mfm SLC)
Mfc   C1591-1985 M1591-1980 B1591-1969 Bn1755-1812 HRO
Cop   C1738-1785 M1738-1751 B1739-1785 (Ms,I) HRO; M1591-1836 HMI
    Index to C1783-1785 (Ms) HGS; M1700-1884 CMI; B1591-1837 HBI

OWSLEBURY St Andrew (664) (Winchester Union) (See also Colden Common)
OR   C1696-1900 M1696-1990 B1678-1887 Bn1754-1823,1918-1968 HRO
    (Few marriage entries before 1722; gap in M 1723-1747)
BT   1708,1780-1858,1862-1863 HRO (Mfm SLC)
Mfc   C1696-1900 M1696-1967 B1678-1887 Bn1754-1823,1918-1919 HRO
Mfm   C1696-1812 M1696-1751 B1678-1812 HRO
Cop   M1696-1837 HMI; M1696-1881 CMI; B1678-1837 HBI

OWSLEBURY (Wesleyan) Longwood Dene (Winchester Wesleyan Circuit, South Hampshire Wesleyan Mission from 1900) (Founded 1898 to succeed Lane End, Cheriton; chapel erected 1904, closed 1946)

OWSLEBURY (Primitive Methodist) Baybridge (Winchester Primitive Methodist Circuit) (Chapel opened 1862, closed 1962)

PAMBER Priory of St Mary & St John the Baptist (473) (Basingstoke Union)
OR   C1659-1935 M1661-1980 B1661-1997 Bn1852-1920 HRO
        (Gap in burials 1757-1774; only one baptism before 1661; some marriages
        1837-1849 are entered at Monk Sherborne)
BT   1780-1832 HRO (Mfm SLC)
Mfc   C1659-1935 M1661-1980 B1661-1909 HRO
Cop   C1659-1812 M1661-1812 B1661-1812 (Ts) HRO, Inc
        Index to C1661-1837 (partly from BT) (Ts) HRO
        M1661-1812 (Ts,I) SG; M1661-1837 HMI; M1661-1881 CMI
        M1661-1812 Boyd; B1661-1837 HBI; Extracts M1661-1812 IGI

PAMBER (Primitive Methodist) Little London (Silchester Primitive Methodist Circuit) (Existed by 1872, closed) (Records 1943+ BRO)

PAMBER HEATH St Luke (Mission church to Pamber; annexed to Tadley in 1972)
OR   M1947-1985 HRO; C1972+ Bn1981+ Inc
Mfc   M1947-1985 HRO

PARLEY (Baptist) - See CHRISTCHURCH

PASSFIELD COMMON (Bible Christian) - See BRAMSHOTT

PAULSGROVE St Michael & All Angels (Formed from Portchester)
OR   C1948-1966 M1955-1984 Bn1955-1984 PCRO
Mfc   C1948-1966 M1955-1984 HRO, PCRO

PEARTREE - See SOUTHAMPTON St Mary Extra

PENNINGTON St Mark (Chapelry of Milford, established 1839; parish 1843)
OR   C1839-1988 M1839-1996 B1839-1992 Bn1839-1988 HRO
BT   1849-1850,1852-1873 HRO (Mfm SLC) (1863,1865,1867 filed with Milford)
Mfc   C1839-1957 M1839-1970 B1839-1980 HRO
Cop   M1839-1882 CMI

PENNINGTON (Baptist) Stotes (Founded c1850; 1851 Religious Census; no other references located)

PENTON GRAFTON - Alternative name for WEYHILL

PENTON MEWSEY Holy Trinity (254) (Andover Union)
OR   C1648-1926 M1649-1977 B1647-1995 Bn1828-1939 HRO (Gap 1664-1674)
BT   1758,1780-1797,1799-1801,1803-1877 HRO (Mfm SLC)
Mfc   C1648-1926 M1649-1977 B1647-1995 HRO
Cop   M1649-1812 Phillimore Vol 1, Boyd, Pallot
        M1649-1837 HMI; M1649-1882 CMI; B1647-1837 HBI

PETERSFIELD St Peter (1,803) (Petersfield Union) (Chapelry of Buriton; separate parish 1886; see also Sheet)

OR	C1558-1996 M1558-1996 B1558-1875,1889 Bn1761-1770,1823-1987 HRO B1963+ Inc
BT	1700-1702,1726,1729,1741,1780-1782,1784,1786-1851,1855-1860, 1862,1864-1868 HRO (Mfm SLC)
Mfc	C1558-1965 M1558-1976 B1558-1875,1889 Bn1761-1770 HRO
Mfm	C1558-1965 M1558-1964 B1558-1875,1889 Bn1761-1770,1823-1877 HRO
Pc	C1558-1667 M1558-1667 B1558-1667 HRO
Cop	C1558-1842 M1558-1837 B1558-1866 (Ts) HRO M1558-1837 HMI; M1558-1882 CMI; B1558-1837 HBI

PETERSFIELD (Roman Catholic) St Laurence (Founded 1890)

OR	C1890+ M1896+ B1890+ Inc

PETERSFIELD (Independent, now United Reformed) College Street (Founded 1722, active)

OR	C1799-1837 B1810,1825 PRO (RG724,2855)
Mfm	C1799-1837 B1810,1825 PRO, HRO, SLC
Cop	B1810,1825 HBI; Extracts C1799-1837 IGI

PETERSFIELD Wesleyan Circuit (Formed 1826 from Portsmouth Circuit; known as Petersfield & Godalming Circuit from 1827; became part of Guildford Circuit in 1834, but re-established as Petersfield Circuit in 1870; became part of the Surrey & North Hampshire Wesleyan Mission in 1900. Included chapels at Froxfield, Greatham, Liss, and Petersfield) (Records 1870+ HRO)

OR	C1871-1899 HRO (89M72/NMR1) (For later entries see Station Road)
Mfc	C1871-1899 HRO

PETERSFIELD (Wesleyan) (Petersfield Wesleyan Circuit, Guildford Wesleyan Circuit from 1834, Petersfield Wesleyan Circuit from 1870, Surrey & North Hampshire Wesleyan Mission from 1900, Petersfield & Haslemere Wesleyan Circuit from 1917) (Chapel in Dragon Street existed by 1828, New Way Chapel erected c1868, Station Road Chapel erected 1903) (Records 1894+ HRO)

OR	C1902-1965 M1918-1938 HRO (89M72/NMR13-14) (Includes baptisms at other chapels in the circuit; for C1828-1840 see Guildford Wesleyan Circuit)
Mfc	M1918-1938 HRO

PETERSFIELD Primitive Methodist Circuit (Petersfield Mission was formed 1843 within Shefford Circuit, and transferred to Newbury Circuit in 1846. Known as Buriton Mission from 1852, Buriton Circuit from c1864, and Petersfield Windsor Road Circuit from 1902. Included chapels at Buriton, East Meon, Petersfield, and Steep) (Records 1844+ HRO)

OR	C1852-1901,1909-1968 HRO (89M72/NMR2-3) (Entries after 1940 are for Petersfield & Haslemere Methodist Circuit)
Mfc	C1852-1901 HRO

PETERSFIELD (Primitive Methodist) Windsor Road (Petersfield Primitive
  Methodist Circuit) (Chapel erected c1902, closed by 1964) (Records 1899+ HRO)
OR   M1940-1941 HRO (89M72/NMR15)
Mfc   M1940-1941 HRO

PETERSFIELD & HASLEMERE Wesleyan Circuit (Formed 1917 from the Surrey
  & North Hampshire Wesleyan Mission. Included chapels at Grayshott, Greatham,
  Liss, and Petersfield) (Records 1916+ HRO)
OR   See Petersfield Wesleyan Circuit

PETERSFIELD Cemetery, Ramshill (Records - East Hampshire District Council)
Mfc   B1857-1995 HRO (Includes index)

PETERSFIELD Union Workhouse
OR   No registers survive. Other records at HRO.

PICKET PIECE (Independent) - See ANDOVER

PILLEY (Independent) - See BOLDRE

PITT The Good Shepherd (Chapelry of Hursley, established 1858, closed 1983)
OR   M1967-1981 HRO
Mfc   M1967-1981 HRO

PLAISTOW GREEN (Primitive Methodist) - See KINGSCLERE

PLAITFORD St Peter (263) (Romsey Union) (Chapelry of West Grimstead,
  Wiltshire; separate parish 1866; the parish was transferred from Wiltshire to
  Hampshire in 1895)
OR   C1715-1933 M1717-1985 B1710-1992 Bn1773-1810,1824-1994 HRO
       (Gap c1733-1749)
BT   1622-1637,1665-1679,1712-1713,1717-1841,1843-1880 WRO (Mfm SLC)
Mfc   C1715-1933 M1717-1985 B1710-1992 Bn1773-1810 HRO
Cop   M1764-1836 (Ts) WRO; M1717-1836 HMI; M1622-1886 CMI
       M1622-1836 Nimrod Index; B1710-1837 HBI

PLAITFORD (Primitive Methodist) (Salisbury Primitive Methodist Circuit)
  (Registered 1842; possibly house meetings only) (Records 1842 [only] WRO)

POKESDOWN (Independent) - See BOURNEMOUTH

POOLE [Dorset] Wesleyan Circuit (Included chapels at Bournemouth c1865-1873)
OR   C1810-1840 PRO (RG 4/1230,1231,2412); C1841-1935 DRO

POOLE & RINGWOOD (Society of Friends) Monthly Meeting (Formed 1804 from
Poole and Ringwood Monthly Meetings; known as Poole & Southampton from
c1824; became part of Alton, Southampton, & Poole Monthly Meeting in 1870.
Included meetings at Ringwood, Southampton, Fordingbridge, Portsmouth,
Romsey, Isle of Wight, Channel Islands) (Records 1804+ HRO)

OR   Z1805-1837 M1805-1836 B1805-1837 PRO (RG 6/198,398,399)
      (Listed with the registers of Poole Monthly Meeting)
      Z1839-1869 M1837-1871 B1837-1910 HRO (24M54/120-134,251,269-271)

Mfm Z1805-1837 M1805-1836 B1805-1837 HRO

Cop Index see Hampshire Quarterly Meeting; M1805-1836 HMI; B1805-1837 HBI

POPHAM St Catherine (104) (Basingstoke Union) (Chapelry of Micheldever;
separate parish 1847; closed c1945)

OR   C1628-1945 M1630-1942 B1637-1789,1881-1979 Bn1775-1809 HRO
      (Gap c1732-1775; no B register 1789-1881; no M registered 1809-1839)

BT   1849,1851,1854,1859-1861 HRO (Mfm SLC) (Filed with Woodmancote)

Mfc C1628-1945 M1630-1942 B1637-1789,1881-1979 Bn1775-1809 HRO

Cop M1630-1809 Phillimore Vol 9 and Boyd; M1630-1809 HMI
      C1628-1795 M1630-1809 B1637-1789 (Ms) HRO
      M1630-1895 CMI; M1790-1812 Pallot; B1637-1789 HBI

PORTCHESTER St Mary (739) (Fareham Union) (See also Paulsgrove)

OR   C1608-1988 M1620-1994 B1619-1959 Bn1846-1987 PCRO (Gaps in C
      1640-1653, M 1629-1653, B 1627-1653; C defective 1608-1619,1626-1640)

BT   1780-1804,1806-1815,1818-1881 HRO (Mfm SLC)

Mfc C1608-1979 M1620-1988 B1619-1959 HRO, PCRO

Mfm C1608-1873 M1620-1875 B1619-1875 PCRO, SLC

Cop C1813-1837 M1620-1837 B1813-1837 (Ts) PCRO (CHU27/5/12)
      Index to B 1894-1931 (Ts) PCRO (CHU27/5/12); M1620-1837 HMI
      C1608-1813 M1620-1810 B1619-1812 (Ms) PCRO (CHU27/5/3)
      C1653-1813 M1653-1837 B1696-1837 PCI; M1620-1882 CMI
      B1619-1837 HBI; Extracts C1608-1873 M1620-1877 IGI

PORTCHESTER Ascension (Closed)

OR   C1937-1968 PCRO

PORTCHESTER (Wesleyan) (Portsmouth Wesleyan Circuit, Gosport Wesleyan
Circuit from 1831, Fareham Wesleyan Circuit from 1867, Gosport & Fareham
Wesleyan Circuit from 1908) (Society existed by 1843, chapels erected 1867 &
1933) (Records 1843+ HRO)

PORTSDOWN Christ Church (Formed 1870 from Farlington, Widley, & Wymering)

OR   C1871-1995 M1875-1985 B1874-1992 Bn1916-1992 PCRO

BT   1881-1901,1903-1905,1907-1914 HRO (Mfm SLC)

Mfc C1871-1975 M1875-1954,1964-1975 B1874-1935 HRO, PCRO

Cop M1875-1889 CMI

PORTSEA

Most parishes within the present City of Portsmouth were formed from the ancient parish of Portsea. See also Portsmouth, Southsea.

PORTSEA St Mary (42,306) (Portsea Island Union)
OR   C1654-1996 M1654-1992 B1654-1913 Bn1824-1841,1875-1966 PCRO (Gap in C 1665-1674, B 1665-1675) (Burials 1856+ were in Kingston Cemetery)
BT   1740,1746-1747,1752,1755,1758,1762,1780-1807,1809-1811,1813-1835 HRO (Mfm SLC)
Mfc   C1654-1825,1827-1972 M1654-1914,1927-1972 B1654-1913 HRO, PCRO
        C1654-1831,1833-1834,1836-1837,1846-1853,1855-1858,1873-1881, 1884-1890 M1654-1830,1832-1845 B1654-1902 SG
Mfm   C1674-1873 M1666-1875 B1674-1873 PCRO, SLC
Pc   C1813-1814 M1764-1773,1802-1806,1814-1815,1832,1834-1836 B1855-1857 PCRO
Cop   C1654-1710,1773-1800,1813-1881 M1654-1710,1832-1834 B1654-1710, 1789-1837 PCI; M1654-1837 HMI; M1666-1875 CMI
        Index to M1819-1958 (1949-1958 incomplete) (Ms) PCRO (CHU3/1F/1-6)
        C1837 only (Ts) HGS; M1780 only (BT) (Ts,A by groom) SG
        B1654-1837 HBI; Extracts C1674-1873 M1666-1875 IGI

PORTSEA All Saints, Landport (Established 1828; district formed 1835)
OR   C1828-1975 M1839-1958 Bn1925-1956 PCRO
Mfc   C1828-1937 M1839-1869,1882-1941 HRO, PCRO
Cop   C1828-1838 (Ts,I) SG, HGS, PCRO (CHU9/4/17)
        C1828-1897 M1839-1903 PCI; M1839-1881 CMI

PORTSEA Ascension, North End (Mission church to St Mark; separate parish 1926)
OR   C1923-1967 M1926-1992 Bn1959-1975 PCRO
Mfc   C1923-1967 M1926-1973 HRO, PCRO

PORTSEA Circus Church, Landport (Mission church established 1857; closed 1951)
OR   C1918-1950 M1922-1947 Bn1922-1936 PCRO
Mfc   C1918-1950 M1922-1947 HRO (Filed under Southsea), PCRO

PORTSEA Holy Trinity (Established 1841; separate parish 1844; destroyed)
OR   C1841-1906 M1845-1905 PCRO
Mfc   C1841-1906 M1845-1905 HRO, PCRO
Cop   C1841-1906 M1845-1905 PCI

PORTSEA St Agatha, Landport (Established 1882; separate parish 1898; closed 1955)
OR   C1892-1950 M1898-1955 Bn1933-1964 PCRO
Mfc   C1892-1950 M1898-1955 HRO, PCRO
Cop   C1892-1927 M1898-1911 PCI

PORTSEA St Alban, Copnor (Formed 1914 from St Stephen Buckland & St Mark North End)
OR   C1907-1954 M1914-1961 PCRO; Bn1966+ Inc
Mfc   C1907-1954 M1914-1961 HRO, PCRO

PORTSEA St Andrew, Eastney (Royal Marine Artillery Church) (Erected 1866 in St George's Road; present church in Henderson Road erected 1905; closed. The adjacent St Andrew's Church Centre is now a chapel to St James Milton) (See also Portsmouth Royal Marines)

OR   C1866-1921 PRO (ADM 6/437); C1921-1973 Chaplain's Office, Portsmouth Naval Base

PORTSEA St Ann, Portsmouth Dockyard (Established 1704)

OR   C1887+ M1935+ at the church (Present location of earlier registers, if any, unknown; many baptisms were performed on board ship)

Cop   C1887-1948 (Ts,I) PCRO (1409A/8/1,2)

C1949-1978 (Ms,I) PCRO (1409A/9) (References in the index refer not to this transcript, but to a typed transcript held by the chaplain)

M1935-1987 (Ms,I) PCRO (1409A/11) (Entries abbreviated)

PORTSEA St Barbara, HMS Excellent, Whale Island (Garrison Church) (Established 1934)

OR   No information. Licensed for marriages

PORTSEA St Barbara, Hilsea (Garrison Church) - See WYMERING

PORTSEA St Barnabas (Mission church to St Mary; destroyed)

OR   C1896-1941 PCRO

Mfc   C1896-1941 HRO, PCRO

PORTSEA St Boniface (Mission church to St Mary; closed)

OR   C1928-1961 PCRO

Mfc   C1928-1961 HRO, PCRO

PORTSEA St Cuthbert, Copnor (District formed 1913 from St James Milton; separate parish 1916)

OR   C1910-1986 M1916-1986 Bn1916-1973 PCRO

Mfc   C1910-1986 M1916-1986 HRO, PCRO

PORTSEA St Faith (Mission church to St Mary)

OR   C1904-1943 PCRO

Mfc   C1904-1943 HRO, PCRO

PORTSEA St Francis, North End (Mission church to St Mark)

OR   C1940-1967 M1962-1984 PCRO; Bn1962+ Inc

Mfc   C1940-1967 HRO, PCRO

PORTSEA St George (Established 1754; separate parish 1875)

OR   C1876-1968 M1876-1941,1961-1986 Bn1917-1921,1928-1941,1961-1993 PCRO (No marriages took place 1941-1961)

Mfc   C1876-1968 M1876-1941,1961-1986 HRO, PCRO

C1876-1909 M1876-1904 SG

Cop   C1876-1912 M1876-1904 PCI; M1876-1881 CMI

PORTSEA St James, Milton (Established 1841; separate parish 1844)
OR   C1844-1980 M1845-1989 B1845-1936 Bn1893-1896,1971-1991 PCRO
Mfc   C1844-1953 M1845-1868,1873-1960 B1845-1936 HRO, PCRO
Cop   C1844-1890 M1845-1879 B1845-1936 PCI

PORTSEA St John the Baptist, Rudmore (Formed 1917 from St Mark North End &
    All Saints Landport; closed)
OR   C1909-1978 M1917-1977 Bn1932-1961,1968-1978 PCRO
Mfc   C1909-1978 M1917-1977 HRO, PCRO

PORTSEA St John the Evangelist (Established 1788; district formed 1835; separate
    parish 1865; destroyed during World War Two)
OR   C1789-1951 M1865-1940 Bn1865-1883,1912-1940 PCRO
Mfc   C1789-1916,1945-1951 M1865-1940 HRO, PCRO
       C1789-1813,1820-1848 SG
Mfm C1789-1875 PCRO, SLC
Pc   C1813-1820 PCRO
Cop   C1789-1916 M1865-1897 PCI; M1865-1882 CMI; Extracts C1789-1875 IGI

PORTSEA St Margaret of Scotland, Eastney (Established 1899; parish formed 1910
    from St James Milton)
OR   C1901-1991 M1910-1982 B1958-1982 Bn1935-1986 PCRO
Mfc   C1901-1962 M1910-1966 B1958-1968 HRO, PCRO

PORTSEA St Mark, North End (Established 1874; district formed 1875)
OR   C1874-1983 M1875-1977 B1910-1930 Bn1951-1976,1982-1988 PCRO
Mfc   C1874-1968 M1875-1977 B1910-1930 HRO, PCRO
Cop   C1874-1895 PCI; M1875-1881 CMI

PORTSEA St Martin, Landport (Mission church to All Saints; closed)
OR   C1908-1920 PCRO
Mfc   C1908-1920 HRO, PCRO

PORTSEA St Mary's Mission (Mission church to St Mary; closed)
OR   C1925-1961 PCRO
Mfc   C1925-1961 HRO, PCRO

PORTSEA St Michael & All Angels, Landport (District formed 1882 from Southsea
    St Paul; demolished)
OR   C1872-1946 M1882-1944 PCRO
Mfc   C1872-1946 M1882-1944 HRO, PCRO
Cop   C1872-1885 PCI

PORTSEA St Nicholas, North End (Mission church to St Mark)
OR   C1930-1972 M1960-1979 Bn1960-1982 PCRO
Mfc   C1930-1972 M1960-1979 HRO, PCRO

PORTSEA St Patrick, Milton (Mission church to St James)
OR   C1906-1979 M1972-1992 Bn1972-1992 PCRO
Mfc   C1906-1979 HRO, PCRO

PORTSEA St Peter (Chapel to St Mary; closed)
OR   C1788-1794 PCRO
Mfc   C1788-1794 HRO, PCRO
Cop   C1788-1794 PCI

PORTSEA St Saviour (Chapel to St Mark North End; separate parish 1929)
OR   C1913-1989 M1926-1990 Bn1950-1978 PCRO
Mfc   C1913-1966 M1926-1972 HRO, PCRO

PORTSEA St Stephen, Buckland (Mission church to St Mark North End; separate parish 1926; closed)
OR   C1902-1961 M1906-1961 Bn1941-1958 PCRO
Mfc   C1902-1961 M1906-1961 HRO, PCRO

PORTSEA St Wilfrid (Mission church to St Mary)
OR   C1902-1982 M1962-1977 PCRO
Mfc   C1902-1963 M1962-1977 HRO, PCRO

PORTSEA St Mary's Hospital Chapel, Milton
OR   C1948-1967 PCRO
Mfc   C1948-1967 HRO, PCRO

PORTSEA (Roman Catholic) St John the Evangelist, Edinburgh Road (Founded 1792 at Unicorn Row, Prince George Street 1796, present site 1882)
OR   C1794-1923 M1828-1910 B1865-1885 Bn1902-1930,1939-1960 PCRO
      C1909-1950 (Army register) RCRO
Cop   C1794-1846 M1828-1847 (I) CRS Vol 49; Card index to C1846-1923 PCRO
      M1828-1837 HMI; Extracts C1794-1846 IGI

PORTSEA (Roman Catholic) St Swithun, Waverley Road, Southsea (Founded 1884)
OR   1891+ Inc; Bn1886-1908,1911-1913,1917-1919,1937-1940,1944-1947, 1949-1952 PCRO

PORTSEA (Roman Catholic) Corpus Christi, Gladys Avenue, North End (Founded 1893)
OR   C1893+ M1895+ B1894+ Inc

PORTSEA (Roman Catholic) St Joseph, Copnor (Founded 1908)
OR   C1908+ M1909+ Inc

PORTSEA (Roman Catholic) St Mary's Hospital
OR   C1919-1936 PCRO (CHU90/1)

PORTSEA (Particular Baptist) Meeting House Alley, later known as Kent Street (Erected 1704; succeeded 1956 by Kent Street Memorial Church, Paulsgrove)
OR   Z1729-1837 PRO (RG 4/403,1806)
Mfm Z1729-1837 PRO, HRO, PCRO, SLC
Cop   Extracts Z1729-1837 IGI

PORTSEA (Particular Baptist) White's Row (Founded c1782, sold to Independents, moved to St Paul's Square Southsea 1852)
OR   Z1811-1837 PRO (RG 4/562)
Mfm Z1811-1837 PRO, HRO, PCRO, SLC
Cop   Extracts Z1811-1837 IGI

PORTSEA (Particular Baptist) Marlborough Road (Founded c1790)

PORTSEA (General Baptist) Clarence Street, Landport; Commercial Road, Landport; Tangier Road, Copnor (Chapel erected 1798, Church founded 1802, moved to Commercial Road by 1888, then to Tangier Road in 1919, active) (Records 1821+ PCRO)
OR   M1937-1952 PCRO (CHU85/1/1,2)

PORTSEA (Particular Baptist) Green Row, Marylebone (Chapel erected 1808 by members of Meeting House Alley, Church formed 1828, united with Lake Lane 1831) (Records 1820+ PCRO)
OR   Adult baptisms 1828-1849 D1830-1851 (plus notes of five marriages 1846-1850) PCRO (The entries are in membership lists 1828-1849 in CHU86/2/1)
Cop   D1830-1837 HBI

PORTSEA (Particular Baptist) Ebenezer Chapel, Park Lane, Southsea (Established c1808, Church founded 1812, probably closed by 1890)
OR   Z1808-1836 PRO (RG 4/407)
Mfm Z1808-1836 PRO, HRO, PCRO, SLC
Cop   Extracts Z1808-1836 IGI

PORTSEA (Particular Baptist) Salem Chapel, Salem Street, Landport (Chapel erected c1813)

PORTSEA (Particular Baptist) Landport Chapel, Lake Lane, Landport (later known as Lake Road) (Founded 1820, chapel erected 1822, moved to Powerscourt Road after war damage, active) (Records 1819+ PCRO)
OR   Adult baptisms 1820-1870 D1821-1870 PCRO (in membership lists 1820-1870 in CHU86/2/2,3)
Cop   D1821-1837 HBI

PORTSEA (Scotch Sandemanian Baptist) Dock Row (Existed by 1834, short-lived)

PORTSEA (Particular Baptist) Providence Chapel, Southsea (Founded c1846; 1851 Religious Census; no other references located)

PORTSEA (Baptist) Park View Chapel (Founded c1850; 1851 Religious Census; no other references located)

PORTSEA (Baptist) Ivy Street, Southsea (PO Directory 1855; possibly the same as Park View Chapel)

PORTSEA (Baptist) Zoar Chapel, Wellington Street, Southsea (Existed by 1851; possibly closed by 1867)

PORTSEA (Particular Baptist) St Paul's Square, Southsea; Elm Grove, Southsea (White's Row moved here in 1852 but closed; new Church founded 1853, moved to Elm Grove 1878)

PORTSEA (Baptist) Herbert Street, Landport (Chapel erected 1863, probably closed by 1890)

PORTSEA (Baptist) Immanuel, Castle Road, Victoria Road North, Southsea (Founded 1892, active)

PORTSEA (Baptist) Rehoboth, Terwick Street (Existed by 1903)

PORTSEA (Baptist) London Road, Landport (Founded 1904, active)

PORTSEA (Baptist) Devonshire Avenue, Southsea (Founded 1913, active)

PORTSEA (Independent) Bethel Chapel, White's Row (Purchased from Baptists; became a school by 1878)

PORTSEA (Independent) Orange Street (Founded 1754, served from King Street after 1813; closed 1936) (Records 1769+ PCRO)
OR   C1785-1837 PRO (RG 4/867); C1785-1893 D1774-1863 PCRO (CHU91/2) (The deaths occur in membership lists 1769-1834 in CHU91/1)
Mfm C1785-1837 PRO, HRO, SLC
Cop   C1785-1838 (Ts,A) SG, PCRO (CHU91/3); Extracts C1785-1837 IGI

PORTSEA (Independent) King Street (Chapel erected 1813 to replace Orange Street Chapel; replaced 1896 by Edinburgh Road Chapel) (Records 1805+ PCRO)
OR   C1865-1869 M1865-1872 B1866-1872 D1838-1882 PCRO (CHU92/6) (The death entries occur in membership lists 1835-1889 in CHU92/4)

PORTSEA (Independent, now United Reformed) Kingston Road, Buckland (Chapel erected 1822, Church founded 1835, active) (Records 1835+ PCRO)
OR   C1878-1925 M1879-1923 B1878-1884,1905-1924 D1838-1871 PCRO (CHU94/1A/2-5) (A few deaths 1877-1893 occur in membership lists 1835-1894 in CHU94/1A/2,3 and CHU94/1B/2)

PORTSEA (Independent, now United Reformed) Milton (Established 1842 as an outstation to King Street Chapel, Church founded 1861, now known as Kendall Memorial Church, active)

PORTSEA (Independent) Stafford Road, Southsea (Chapel erected c1844)

PORTSEA (Independent) Zion Chapel, Abercrombie Street, later Unicorn Road, Landport (Founded 1846; the 1851 Religious Census gives a date of 1812)

PORTSEA (Independent) Allen's Fields (Founded 1846, served from King Street, noted in 1929 as temporarily closed)

PORTSEA (Independent) Victoria Street (Founded 1852, served from King Street)

PORTSEA (Independent) Zoar Chapel (PO Directory 1867; possibly an incorrect reference to Zoar Baptist Chapel)

PORTSEA (Independent, now United Reformed) Christ Church, Kent Road & Asburton Road, Southsea (Founded 1868, active)

PORTSEA (Independent) Buckland Street (Founded 1882, served from Buckland)

PORTSEA (Independent, now United Reformed) Victoria Road, Southsea (Founded 1884, amalgamated with St Andrew's Presbyterian Church in 1978, active) (Records 1883+ PCRO)
OR   C1895,1902-1926 M1905-1927 B1902-1925 D1889-1937 PCRO (CHU95/1A/1-3) (The deaths occur in membership lists in CHU95/1A/1-3)

PORTSEA (Independent) Edinburgh Road (Chapel erected 1896 to replace Orange Street and King Street Chapels) (Records 1903+ PCRO, 1933+ HRO in 127M94)
OR   C1896-1940 M1897-1926 PCRO (CHU93/3,4)

PORTSEA (Presbyterian, now United Reformed) St Andrew, St Michael's Road, Landport (Founded 1859, amalgamated with Victoria Road Church in 1978) (Records 1856+ PCRO)
OR   C1856-1946 PCRO (Includes military C1883-1939) PCRO (CHU92/2A/1,2)

PORTSEA (Presbyterian, now United Reformed) Stamshaw Road, North End (Founded 1932, active)

PORTSEA (Wesleyan) St Peter, Daniel Street, later at Queen Street (Salisbury Wesleyan Circuit, Portsmouth Wesleyan Circuit from 1790, Portsmouth Green Row Wesleyan Circuit from 1874, Southsea Wesleyan Circuit from 1883, Portsmouth Garrison & Naval Port Mission from 1898) (Founded 1768 in Bishop Street, moved in 1800 to the former Anglican Chapel of St Peter, Daniel Street, moved 1913 to Queen Street) (Records 1798+ PCRO)
OR   C1798-1837 PRO (RG 4/404,563)
        C1798-1839,1842-1964 M1921-1963 PCRO (CHU81/W13/1A/1-5 & 1B/1,2) (Includes C1921-1928 for Alfred Street Hall)
Mfm C1798-1837 PRO, HRO, SLC
Cop   Extracts C1798-1837 IGI

PORTSEA (Wesleyan) Green Row, later Pembroke Road (Salisbury Wesleyan Circuit, Portsmouth Wesleyan Circuit from 1790, Portsmouth Green Row Wesleyan Circuit from 1874) (Room in Warblington Street used from 1767, Oyster Street Chapel erected 1788, Green Row Church erected 1811, later known as Pembroke Road, sold 1919) (Records 1811+ PCRO)
OR   C1814-1837 PRO (RG 4/408); C1814-1919 PCRO (CHU81/W10/1A/1-3) (Includes C1888-1896 at Grigg Street, Southsea; C1814-1843 are in a register of St Peter's Chapel, Daniel Street - CHU81/W13/1A/1)
Mfm C1814-1837 PRO, HRO, SLC
Cop   Extracts C1814-1831 IGI

PORTSEA (Wesleyan) Wesley Chapel, Arundel Street, Landport (Portsmouth Wesleyan Circuit, Portsmouth Wesley Circuit from 1874) (Chapel erected c1844, destroyed in World War Two) (Records 1844+ PCRO)

PORTSEA (Wesleyan) Bethesda Chapel, Little Southsea Street, Southsea (Former Bible Christian Chapel taken over by Wesleyans by 1851; no references located after 1867)

PORTSEA (Wesleyan) Chester Road, later Victoria Road, Southsea (Portsmouth Green Row Wesleyan Circuit, Southsea Wesleyan Circuit from 1883) (Meetings 1865, church opened 1878, formed from Pembroke Road) (Records 1865+ PCRO)
OR   C1870-1971 M1921-1971 PCRO (CHU81/W15/1A/1,2 & 1B/1-8)

PORTSEA (Wesleyan) Eastney Central Hall & Soldiers' Home, Highland Road, Southsea (Portsmouth Green Row Wesleyan Circuit, Portsmouth Wesley Circuit from 1891, Portsmouth Garrison & Naval Port Mission from 1898) (Founded 1867) (Records 1877+ PCRO)
OR   C1867-1951 PCRO (CHU81/W16/1A/1-3)

PORTSEA (Wesleyan) Kingston Road, Landport (Founded c1875, probably closed by 1925)

PORTSEA (Wesleyan) Buckland (Portsmouth Wesley Circuit) (Opened 1875, founded by members of Arundel Street) (Records 1861+ PCRO)
OR   C1888-1970 M1900-1965 PCRO(CHU81/W8/1A/1,2 & 1B/1-7)

PORTSEA (Wesleyan) Eastney (Portsmouth Green Row Wesleyan Circuit) (Founded by members of Pembroke Road, existed 1877-1886)

PORTSEA (Wesleyan) Wingfield Street (Portsmouth Wesley Circuit) (Founded 1878 by members of Arundel Street) (Records 1878+ PCRO)
OR   C1897-1941 PCRO (CHU81/W12/1A/1)

PORTSEA (Wesleyan) Grigg Street, Southsea (Portsmouth Green Row Wesleyan Circuit) (Founded 1878 as South Street Mission by members of Pembroke Road, Grigg Street opened 1888)
OR   C1888-1896 PCRO (in a register of Pembroke Road - CHU81/W10/1A/3)

PORTSEA (Wesleyan) Stamshaw Road (Portsmouth Wesley Circuit) (Founded by 1882)

PORTSEA (Wesleyan) Twyford Avenue (Portsmouth Wesley Circuit) (Founded 1884 by members of Arundel Street) (Records 1874+ PCRO)
OR   C1884-1965 M1916-1948 PCRO (CHU81/W14/1A/1-4 & 1B/1-5)

PORTSEA (Wesleyan) Rivers Street, Southsea (Portsmouth Green Row Circuit) (Mission formed 1886 from Green Row (Pembroke Road), separate society 1887, closed 1919) (Records 1896+ PCRO)
OR   C1886-1917 PCRO (CHU81/W11/1A/1)

PORTSEA (Wesleyan) Wesley Central Hall, Penhale Road, Fratton (Portsmouth Wesley Circuit) (Founded 1889) (Records 1886+ PCRO)
OR   C1889-1936,1941 PCRO (CHU81/W17/1A/1-3) (includes entries for Duchess of Albany Hall in Edinburgh Road, Albany Church, and Albany Home)

PORTSEA (Wesleyan) Trinity Church, Albert Road, Southsea (Southsea Wesleyan Circuit) (Founded 1901 by members of Daniel Street) (Records 1892+ PCRO)
OR   C1893-1949 PCRO (CHU81/W6/1A/1,2)

PORTSEA (Wesleyan) Copnor (Portsmouth Wesley Circuit) (Founded 1911 by members of Arundel Street) (Records 1903+ PCRO)
OR   C1911-1952 PCRO (CHU81/W9/1A/1)

PORTSEA (Wesleyan) Alfred Street Hall (Served from Queen Street)
OR   C1921-1928 PCRO (In registers of Queen Street CHU81/W13/1A/5 and Wesley Central Hall CHU81/W17/1A/3)

PORTSEA (Wesleyan) Woodlands Home, Albany Road, Southsea
OR   C1922-1939 PCRO (1219A/4/8/1)

PORTSEA (Wesleyan Methodist Association) South Street (Founded c1845; PRO Chancery Rolls 1846.68.12)

PORTSEA (Primitive Methodist) Green Row, Landport (1851 Religious Census; no other reference located)

PORTSEA (Primitive Methodist) Jubilee Chapel, Somers Road (Portsmouth Primitive Methodist First Circuit) (Opened 1861)
OR   C1900-1941 M1915-1940 PCRO (Baptisms are in a register of Albert Road Church CHU81/P1/1A/1, marriages are in CHU81/P5/1,2)

PORTSEA (Primitive Methodist) Ebenezer Chapel, Twyford Avenue (Portsmouth Primitive Methodist First Circuit) (Opened 1873, new church erected 1913)
OR   C1913-1944 M1915-1963 PCRO (CHU81/P2/1A/1 & 1B/1)

PORTSEA (Primitive Methodist) Albert Road, Southsea (Portsmouth Primitive Methodist Second Circuit) (Purchased from Bible Christians in 1875, replaced 1901 by a new Central Hall on the same site, closed 1935) (Records 1901+ PCRO)
OR   C1900-1941 PCRO (CHU81/P1/1A/1) (Includes baptisms for Somers Road)

PORTSEA (Primitive Methodist) Stamshaw Road (Established by 1878, probably closed by 1900) (Portsmouth Primitive Methodist Circuit)

PORTSEA (Primitive Methodist) Eastney (1904-1919 only)

PORTSEA Bible Christian Circuit - See PORTSMOUTH Bible Christian Circuit

PORTSEA (Bible Christian) Bethesda Chapel, Little Southsea Street; later at Grosvenor Street, then Brougham Road, Southsea (Portsmouth Bible Christian Circuit) (Probably erected 1822, Grosvenor Street 1847, Brougham Road 1876) (Records 1848+ PCRO)
OR   C1909-1935 M1935-1939 PCRO (CHU81/U3/1A/1 & 1B/1)

PORTSEA (Bible Christian) Emmanuel Chapel, York Place, Landport; later at Stamford Street, Landport (Portsmouth Bible Christian Circuit) (Founded 1825 as Messiah Chapel, York Place, in a building erected in 1820, known as Emmanuel from 1827; Stamford Street, Landport, opened 1861 and replaced Emmanuel by 1863) (Records 1903+ PCRO)
OR   C1910-1940 M1930-1940 PCRO (CHU81/U5/1A/1,2 & 1B/1)

PORTSEA (Bible Christian) Albert Road, Southsea (Portsmouth Bible Christian Circuit) (Preaching in schoolroom from 1863, chapel erected 1867, sold to Primitive Methodists 1875)

PORTSEA (Bible Christian) Fawcett Road, Southsea (Portsmouth Bible Christian Circuit) (Opened 1893) (Records 1890+ PCRO)
OR   C1907-1947 M1949-1983 PCRO (CHU81/U4/1A/1 & 1B/1-3)

PORTSEA (Bible Christian) Powerscourt Road (Portsmouth Bible Christian Circuit) (Opened 1903) (Records 1900+ PCRO)
OR   C1926-1949 M1921-1949 PCRO (CHU81/U6/1A/1,2 & 1B/1-4)

PORTSEA (Latter-day Saints) Southsea (Records 1848+ in Church archives at SLC)
Mfm   Membership records 1848-1865 SLC

PORTSEA (Catholic Apostolic Church) St Ronan's Road, Southsea (Existed by 1907, closed in 1960s)

PORTSEA (Christian Scientist) Pembroke Road (Existed by 1923)

PORTSEA (Elim Pentecostal Church) Arundel Street (Established 1930)

PORTSEA (Spiritualist) Victoria Road South, Southsea (Established 1901)

PORTSEA (Christian Spiritualist) Buckingham Place, Landport (Existed by 1939)

PORTSEA (Progressive Spiritualist) Francis Avenue, Southsea (Existed by 1939)

PORTSEA (Seventh Day Adventist) Margate Road, Southsea (Existed by 1939)

PORTSEA (Nonconformist) St Mary's Hospital
OR   C1919-1954 PCRO (CHU90/2)

PORTSEA (No denomination) Seamen's Bethel, White's Row (Listed in PO Directory 1855 & 1867)

PORTSEA (Jewish) Synagogue (Community established by 1749, Synagogue in White's Row erected 1780, Synagogue at The Thicket, Southsea erected 1936; cemetery in Fawcett Road acquired 1749; also use cemeteries at New Road Kingston and at Catherington)
Cop   Circumcisions 1762-1807 Transactions of the Jewish Historical Society Vol XVII p 251 (1951) (Few surnames given)

PORTSEA Mile End Cemetery (Portsea Island General Cemetery Company)
OR   B1831-1955 PCRO
Mfm   B1831-1918 PCRO, SLC
Cop   Index to B1831-1955 PCRO; B1831-1837 HBI

PORTSEA Kingston Cemetery
OR   B1856-1902 PCRO
Mfm   B1856-1902 PCRO, SLC

PORTSEA Milton Cemetery
OR   B1912-1946 PCRO

PORTSEA Union Workhouse (Portsea Island Union)
OR   Z1898-1922 PCRO

PORTSMOUTH

Most parishes within the present City of Portsmouth were formed from the ancient parish of Portsea, and are listed under Portsea or Southsea. The city now also includes Cosham, Farlington, Widley, and Wymering, which are listed separately.

PORTSMOUTH St Thomas of Canterbury (8,083) (Portsea Island Union)
(The church became Portsmouth Cathedral in 1927)
OR   C1654-1926 M1654-1980 B1654-1855 Bn1863-1993 PCRO (Gap in B 1678-1695) (From 1854, burials took place at Highland Road Cemetery, Southsea)
BT   1682,1702-1704,1720-1721,1724-1725,1740,1781-1791,1794-1809, 1811-1858 HRO (Mfm SLC)
Mfc   C1697-1820,1840-1882,1900-1925 M1697-1872,1877-1936 B1695-1855 HRO, PCRO; C1697-1812,1852-1882 M1697-1778,1785-1795,1806-1828, 1835-1872,1877-1900 B1695-1823,1833-1855,1858-1859,1864-1874,1883, 1885,1906 SG
Mfm   C1654-1873 M1654-1872 B1654-1854 PCRO, SLC
Pc   C1654-1694,1770-1787 M1654-1695,1855-1859 B1654-1678,1770-1787 PCRO
Cop   M1654-1775 Phillimore Vol 10 & 15; M1776-1812 Printed, Ed A.H. Coltart C1654-1694,1770-1787,1813-1820,1840-1862 M1654-1695,1837-1847, 1855-1859,1883-1889 B1654-1678,1770-1787,1823-1906 PCI
M1654-1700 (Ts & Ms,I) PCRO (CHU2/6/2) (Reference numbers in the index do not relate to the typescript); M1654-1837 HMI; B1563,1654-1837 HBI
C1770-1776 M1813-1838 (Ts) SG; Index to M1654-1700 (Ts) SG
Index to C1748-1900 M1748-1870 B1748-1855 (Ms) PCRO (CHU2/1E/1-4)
B Mar-Oct 1563 (Ms) (Copied from British Library Add Mss 8153 folio 106)
HGS, PCRO (CHU2/6/1, CHU2/3/4); M1654-1775,1813-1837 Boyd
M & B May-Aug 1698 (Ms) PCRO (CHU2/3/132); M1790-1812 Pallot
M1776-1812 (Ms) HGS; M1813-1837 CMI
Extracts C1654-1873 M1653-1757,1795-1872 IGI

PORTSMOUTH St John the Baptist & St Nicholas (Royal Garrison Church) (Closed)

OR   C1849-1970 Bn1933-1968 RACD; B1741-1863 PCRO
      (Some baptisms 1849-1887 are entered in the registers of St Thomas)

Mfc   B1741-1863 HRO (Filed under Southsea), PCRO

Cop   B1741-1842,1874 (Ms,I) SG; B1741-1863 PCI; B1741-1837 HBI

PORTSMOUTH Royal Marines (See also Portsea St Andrew Eastney)

OR   C1807-1858 M1801-1853 (Royal Marine Artillery) PRO (ADM 193/9)
      M1869-1881 (Royal Marines) PRO (ADM 185/69) (These registers record
      baptisms and marriages in other churches and register offices)

PORTSMOUTH (General Baptist) St Thomas Street (Founded 1693, chapel erected
    1715, destroyed 1941, united with the Unitarian Church) (Records 1797+ PCRO)

OR   Z1765,1785-1837 B1788-1832 PRO (RG 4/2304)

Mfm Z1765,1785-1837 B1788-1832 PRO, HRO, PCRO, SLC

Cop   Z1765,1785-1836 B1788-1832 (Ts) SG; B1813-1832 HBI
      Extracts Z1765,1785-1837 IGI

PORTSMOUTH (Independent) Highbury (Chapel erected 1842, closed by 1900)

PORTSMOUTH (Presbyterian, Unitarian) High Street (Meeting possibly existed
    1662, chapel erected 1718, became Unitarian by 1819; destroyed 1941, rebuilt 1955
    as John Pounds Memorial Church, active) (Records 1697+ PCRO)

OR   C1676-1857 B1787-1853 PRO (RG 4/405,406,564)
      C1837-1936 M1844-1940 B1837-1853,1884-1886 PCRO (CHU82/1/1,
      CHU82/7/1,2) (Baptisms 1906-1922 possibly deficient)

Mfm C1676-1857 B1787-1853 PRO, SLC; C1676-1837 B1787-1837 PCRO
      C1676-1857 B1837-1853 HRO (Omits folios 58-68 of RG 4/564)

Cop   Extracts C1676-1837 IGI

PORTSMOUTH Wesleyan Circuit (Formed 1790 from Salisbury Circuit; divided
    1874 into Portsmouth Green Row Circuit and Portsmouth Wesley Circuit. Included
    chapels at Fareham, Gosport, Hardway, Portchester, and Portsea)

PORTSMOUTH Green Row Wesleyan Circuit, later Pembroke Road Circuit (Formed
    1874 from Portsmouth Circuit. Divided 1883 into Pembroke Road [Green Row]
    Circuit and Southsea [Victoria Road] Circuit. The two circuits reunited in 1900 as
    Southsea & Pembroke Road Circuit. Included chapels at Portsea) (Records 1845+
    PCRO)

PORTSMOUTH Wesley Circuit (Formed 1874 from Portsmouth Circuit. Included
    chapels at Farlington, Havant, Portsea, and Wymering) (Records 1896+ PCRO)

PORTSMOUTH Garrison & Naval Port Wesleyan Mission (Established 1898.
    Comprised two Portsea chapels: St Peter Daniel Street and Eastney Central Hall)
    (Records 1891+ PCRO)

PORTSMOUTH (Wesleyan) Bethel, Bath Square (School erected 1824, rented to
    Wesleyans, probably closed by 1890)

PORTSMOUTH Primitive Methodist Mission (Formed c1836 as a mission of the Hull [Yorkshire] Circuit; later divided into the Portsmouth Primitive Methodist First and Second Circuits) (Records 1836-1841 IWRO AC 80/1/248)

PORTSMOUTH Primitive Methodist First Circuit (Included chapels at Bedhampton, Forton, Havant, Portsea, and Purbrook)

PORTSMOUTH Primitive Methodist Second Circuit (Included chapels at Emsworth and Portsea)

PORTSMOUTH Bible Christian Circuit (United Methodist Circuit from 1907) (Formed 1825 as Portsea Mission, renamed Portsmouth Mission in 1862, and later became Portsmouth Circuit. Included chapels at Portsea) (Records 1825+ PCRO)
OR   C1830-1837 PRO (RG 4/2110); C1840-1921 PCRO (CHU81/U1/1A/1,2)
Mfm   C1830-1837 PRO, HRO, PCRO, SLC
Cop   Extracts C1830-1837 IGI

PORTSMOUTH (Latter-day Saints) (Records 1851+ in Church archives at SLC)
Mfm   Records 1851-1874 SLC (Catalogued with Gosport)

PORTSMOUTH (GOSPORT) Wesleyan Circuit - See GOSPORT Wesleyan Circuit

PORTSMOUTH Highland Road Cemetery - See SOUTHSEA

PORTSWOOD - See SOUTHAMPTON St Denys

POULNER St John the Baptist (Chapelry of Ringwood)
OR   C1917+ M1973+ Bn1975+ Inc

POULNER (Baptist) - See RINGWOOD

PRESTON CANDOVER St Mary the Virgin (442) (Basingstoke Union)
OR   C1688-1867 M1584-1992 B1724-1919 Bn1853-1947 HRO (Includes entries for Nutley. Several gaps prior to 1760; M deficient 1639-1663,1667-1696. The section containing M1624-1639 was found in 1978)
BT   1780-1793,1795-1797,1799-1822,1824-1869 HRO (Mfm SLC) (Includes Nutley)
Mfc   C1688-1867 M1584-1992 B1724-1919 HRO
Cop   M1584-1812 Phillimore Vol 9 and Boyd (Omits M1624-1639)
      C1688-1812 M1696-1752 B1724-1812 (Ts) HRO; M1584-1837 HMI
      M1584-1882 CMI; M1790-1812 Pallot; B1724-1837 HBI

PRESTON CANDOVER (Primitive Methodist) (Micheldever Primitive Methodist Circuit) (Meetings by 1851, chapel 1865, sold 1934) (Records 1865+ HRO)

PRIORS DEAN (Dedication unknown) (166) (Petersfield Union) (Chapelry of Colmer; chapelry of Hawkley from 1949)
OR   C1538-1978 M1547-1977 B1539-1978 Bn1755-1812,1824-1938 HRO
BT   1780-1795,1799-1844,1846-1879 HRO (Mfm SLC)
Mfc   C1538-1978 M1547-1877 B1539-1978 HRO
Mfm C1538-1876 M1547-1837 B1539-1880 Bn1755-1812 HRO, SLC
Cop   C1538-1811 M1547-1812 B1538-1812 Bn1754-1812 Printed in "The Parish Registers of Priors Dean and Colmer" Ed Rev T Hervey, M.A. (1886) (I)
      M1547-1837 HMI; M1547-1923 CMI; M1790-1837 Pallot
      B1539-1837 HBI; Extracts C1538-1876 M1547-1837 IGI

PRIVETT Holy Trinity (225) (Petersfield Union) (Chapelry of West Meon; separate parish 1874; redundant 1975)
OR   C1538-1980 M1545-1966 B1552-1979 Bn1824-1977 HRO
      (Gap 1628-1653; gap in M 1607-1621)
BT   1741-1742,1758,1780-1784,1786-1812,1814-1823,1825-1838, 1840-1863 HRO (Mfm SLC)
Mfc   C1538-1980 M1545-1966 B1552-1979 HRO
Cop   M1545-1835 HMI; M1700-1883 CMI; B1552-1837 HBI

PUCKNALL (Wesleyan, Wesleyan Methodist Association) - See BRAISHFIELD

PURBROOK St John the Baptist (Formed 1858 from Farlington)
OR   C1858-1977 M1858-1983 B1859-1985 Bn1858-1983 PCRO
Mfc   C1950-1977 M1858-1983 B1859-1974 HRO, PCRO
Cop   M1858-1881 CMI

PURBROOK (Roman Catholic) St Richard of Chichester (Opened 1975)
OR   M1980-1986 Portsmouth (Catholic) Diocesan Archives

PURBROOK (Primitive Methodist) (Portsmouth Primitive Methodist First Circuit) (Chapel erected 1878, active) (Records 1878+ PCRO)
OR   C1913-1955 PCRO (CHU81/P3/1A/1)

PUREWELL (Wesleyan) - See CHRISTCHURCH

QUARLEY St Michael & All Angels (201) (Andover Union)
OR   C1559-1993 M1560-1978 B1559-1993 Bn1755-1798,1816-1819,1827-1992 HRO
BT   1780-1784,1786-1792,1794-1802,1805-1822,1824,1826-1868 HRO (Mfm SLC)
Mfc   C1559-1993 M1560-1978 B1559-1993 Bn1755-1798,1816-1819 HRO
Mfm C1559-1812 M1560-1851 B1559-1812 Bn1755-1798,1816-1819 HRO, SLC
Cop   M1560-1837 HMI; M1700-1886 CMI; B1559-1837 HBI
      Extracts C1559-1812 M1560-1851 IGI

RAMSDEAN (Independent) - See EAST MEON

RAMSDELL Christ Church (Formed 1868 from Monk Sherborne, Tadley, & Wootton St Lawrence)
OR   C1868-1982 M1869-1994 HRO; B1868+ Bn1970+ Inc
Mfc C1868-1982 HRO

RAMSDELL (Independent) Bethel Chapel (Founded c1834, probably closed by 1915)

READING [Berkshire] Wesleyan Circuit (Formed 1811. The circuit did not include Hampshire chapels, but the registers of Reading Church Street Chapel include entries for residents of Hampshire)

READING [Berkshire] (Wesleyan) Church Street (Reading Wesleyan Circuit)
OR   C1813-1837 PRO (RG 4/314) (Includes entries for Baughurst, Hartley Wintney, Pamber, Silchester)
Mfm C1813-1837 PRO, BRO, SLC
Cop Extracts C1813-1837 IGI (Berkshire section)

READING [Berkshire] Primitive Methodist Circuit (Formed 1837 from Shefford Circuit. Included chapels at Baughurst, Silchester, and Wootton St Lawrence) (Records 1837+ BRO)
OR   C1831-1837 PRO (RG 4/270) (Includes Silchester, Mortimer West End)
Mfm C1831-1837 PRO, BRO, SLC
Cop Extracts C1831-1837 IGI (Berkshire section)

REDHILL - See ROWLANDS CASTLE

RINGWOOD St Peter & St Paul (3,449) (Ringwood Union) (See also Bisterne, Burley, Poulner, St Leonards & St Ives)
OR   C1561-1897 M1561-1930 B1561-1894 Bn1754-1824,1900-1909,1921-1992 HRO
BT   1700,1710,1780-1865 HRO (Mfm SLC)
Mfc C1561-1897 M1561-1930 B1561-1894 Bn1754-1824 HRO
Cop C1561-1839 (Ts,I) M1561-1840 (Ts) B1561-1839 (Ts,I) SG
     C1561-1839 (Ts,I) C1840-1898 (Ts) M1561-1897,1907-1920 (Ts)
     B1561-1894 (Ts) HRO; M1561-1837 HMI; M1813-1881 CMI
     B1561-1837 HBI; Extracts M1561-1840 IGI

RINGWOOD (Roman Catholic) Sacred Heart & St Theresa of Lisieux (Formed 1936 from Fordingbridge Catholic parish)
OR   1936+ Inc

RINGWOOD (Society of Friends) Monthly Meeting, Christchurch Road (Established 1668; became part of Poole & Ringwood Monthly Meeting in 1804; Meeting House erected 1692, demolished c1965) (Records 1687+ HRO)
OR   Z1654-1804 M1677-1773,1779-1794,1802-1804 B1669-1804 PRO (RG 6/199,342,400,401,430,431,1416)
Mfm Z1654-1804 M1677-1773,1779-1794,1802-1804 B1669-1804 HRO
Cop For index, see Hampshire Quarterly Meeting
     M1677-1773,1779-1794,1802-1804 HMI; B1669-1804 HBI

RINGWOOD (Baptist) Poulner (Chapel erected 1840, became a branch of Ringwood Particular Baptist Church in 1862, but became General Baptist by 1874, active)

RINGWOOD (Particular Baptist) (Founded 1862, closed by 1900)

RINGWOOD (Presbyterian, later Unitarian) Upper Meeting House Lane (Founded 1676, chapel erected 1727, united with Bournemouth Unitarian Church in 1976) (Records 1725+ HRO)

OR   C1748-1837 B1815-1837 PRO (RG 4/655)
      C1748-1974 M1933-1969 D&B1815-1976 HRO (11M89/1-2) (entries to 1837 are copies)
Mfm C1748-1837 B1815-1837 PRO, HRO, SLC
Cop   C1748-1974 M1933-1969 B1815-1895 (Ts,I) HRO; B1815-1837 HBI
      C1748-1838 B1815-1839 (Ts) SG, HRO; Extracts C1748-1837 IGI

RINGWOOD (Independent, now United Reformed) Lower Meeting House, Christchurch Street (Established 1740 by members of the Presbyterian congregation; chapel erected 1766, lapsed c1772, re-established 1781, active) (Records 1858+ HRO)

OR   C1808-1837 PRO (RG 4/725); C1790-1964 M1856-1876,1916-1929,
      1940-1973 B1820-1871 D1864-1878,1936-1975 HRO (57M83/1,25,26,88)
      (The deaths are in membership lists in 57M83/1,27)
Mfc   C1790-1862,1875-1940 M1874-1876 B1820-1862 HRO
Mfm C1808-1837 PRO, HRO, SLC
Cop   C1790-1835 B1820-1839 (Ts) SG, HRO; B1820-1837 HBI
      Extracts C1808-1837 IGI

RINGWOOD (Independent) Burley - See BURLEY

RINGWOOD (Independent) Kingston (Founded 1841, closed by 1966)

RINGWOOD (Independent) Ebenezer Chapel, Old Hall Lane (Seceded from the Lower Meeting in 1850 and rejoined in 1864)

RINGWOOD Wesleyan Circuit - See CHRISTCHURCH & LYMINGTON Wesleyan Circuit

RINGWOOD (Wesleyan) Christchurch Road (formerly Christchurch Street) (Christchurch & Lymington Wesleyan Circuit, Wimborne Wesleyan Circuit from 1925, New Forest Wesleyan Mission from 1932) (Existed by 1846) (Records 1891+ DRO, records 1870 [only] HRO)

RINGWOOD (Wesleyan) Crowe Hill (Christchurch & Lymington Wesleyan Circuit, Wimborne Wesleyan Circuit from 1925, New Forest Wesleyan Mission from 1932) (Chapel erected 1833) (Records 1897+ DRO, records 1878,1911+ HRO)

RINGWOOD (Wesleyan) St Ives (Christchurch & Lymington Wesleyan Circuit) (Established 1902, closed 1915) (Records 1902+ DRO)

RINGWOOD Cemetery (Records - Town Council)
BT   B1864-1869 HRO
Mfc   B1864-1966 HRO

RINGWOOD Union Workhouse
OR   No registers survive. Other records at HRO.

RIPLEY (Independent) - See SOPLEY

ROCKBOURNE St Andrew (517) (Fordingbridge Union)
OR   C1561-1878 M1561-1978 B1561-1924 Bn1779-1786,1790-1801,1806-1812,
       1824-1983 HRO (Gap 1748-1771; few entries 1771-1779)
BT   1677,1813-1829,1838-1888,1891-1892 HRO (Mfm SLC - omits 1677)
       (For 1677 see HRO document Q9/2/5)
Mfc   C1561-1878 M1561-1978 B1561-1924 Bn1779-1786,1790-1801,1806-1812
       HRO
Mfm   C1561-1876 M1561-1837 B1561-1877 Bn1779-1786,1790-1801,1806-1812
       HRO, SLC
Cop   M1561-1837 HMI; M1561-1884 CMI; B1561-1837 HBI
       Extracts M1561-1837 IGI

ROCKBOURNE (Baptist) (Probably founded c1801)

ROCKBOURNE (Independent) (White's Directory 1878; no other references located)

ROMSEY St Mary & St Ethelflaeda (5,432) (Romsey Union) (See also Awbridge,
    Braishfield, Lee, Rownhams)
OR   C1569-1974 M1569-1979 B1569-1943,1952-1983 Bn1823-1905,1945-1986
       HRO (Defective 1689-1729)
BT   1780-1783,1785-1794,1797-1808,1810-1811,1813-1897 HRO (Mfm SLC)
Mfc   C1569-1974 M1569-1979 B1569-1943,1952-1983 HRO
       C1569-1852 M1569-1837 B1569-1856 SG
Mfm   C1569-1876 M1569-1876 B1569-1875 HRO, SLC
Cop   C1569-1629 M1569-1629 B1569-1629 (Ts) HRO, (Ts,I) HGS
       M1569-1837 HMI; M1813-1881 CMI
       B1570-1837 HBI; Extracts M1569-1621 IGI

ROMSEY (Roman Catholic) St Joseph (Founded 1892)
OR   C1892+ M1965+ Inc

ROMSEY (Roman Catholic) - See WINCHESTER French Émigré Priests

ROMSEY (Society of Friends) - See SOUTHAMPTON, ALTON

ROMSEY (Particular Baptist) Bell Street (Founded 1750, present chapel erected 1811,
    active)
OR   Z1804-1837 B1809-1836 PRO (RG 4/609,1397)
Mfm   Z1804-1837 B1809-1836 PRO, HRO, SLC
Cop   B1813-1836 HBI; Extracts Z1804-1837 IGI

ROMSEY (Baptist) Toothill (Chapel erected c1825; 1851 Religious Census; no later
    references located)

ROMSEY (Independent, now United Reformed) Abbey Chapel (Founded 1662, active)
OR   C1768-1837 B1784-1834 D1783-1818 PRO (RG 4/1364,1365) (plus Z1758-1763 for one family); C1772-1778 PRO (in a register of Queen Street Meeting House, Ratcliff, Stepney - RG 4/4168); M1946-1966 HRO (148M98/1/1-3)
Mfm   C1768-1837 B1784-1834 D1783-1818 PRO, HRO, SLC (includes RG 4/4168)
Cop   B1814-1834 HBI; Extracts C1758-1837 IGI
        Extracts C1772-1778 IGI (from RG 4/4168, listed as Romsey Independent)

ROMSEY (Unitarian) Newton Lane (Possibly existed by 1800; 1851 Religious Census; PO Directory 1855 lists a Sandemanian Chapel in Newton Lane; no other references)

ROMSEY Wesleyan Circuit (Formed 1873 from Winchester Circuit; became part of the South Hampshire Wesleyan Mission in 1900; re-established as Romsey Methodist Circuit in 1933. Included chapels at Bramshaw, Copythorne, Romsey, Timsbury, and West Wellow) (Records 1873+ HRO)

ROMSEY (Wesleyan) (Southampton Wesleyan Circuit, Winchester Wesleyan Circuit from 1862, Romsey Wesleyan Circuit from 1873, South Hampshire Wesleyan Mission from 1900) (Banning Street Chapel erected 1813, chapel at The Hundred erected 1881, active) (Records 1854+ HRO)
OR   C1809-1837 PRO (RG 4/1398); C1841-1899 HRO (69M77/NMR1) (Includes entries for other chapels in the Romsey area)
Mfc   C1841-1899 HRO
Mfm   C1809-1837 PRO, HRO, SLC
Cop   Extracts C1847-1898 (Bramshaw, Plaitford, West Wellow entries) WRO, SLC
        Extracts C1809-1837 IGI

ROMSEY Primitive Methodist Circuit (Romsey Mission, formed 1835 within Micheldever Circuit, became part of Andover Circuit, and later Southampton Circuit; a separate Romsey Circuit was formed in 1880. Included chapels at Ampfield, Boldre, Copythorne, Eling, Lockerley, Milton, Romsey, Sway, and West Wellow) (Records 1880+ HRO)

ROMSEY (Primitive Methodist) (Southampton Primitive Methodist Circuit, Romsey Primitive Methodist Circuit from 1880) (Chapel at The Hundred erected 1845, Middlebridge Street Chapel erected 1895, closed and amalgamated with the Wesleyan Chapel 1932) (Records 1871+ HRO)

ROMSEY (Elim Foursquare Church) Middlebridge Street (In former Primitive Methodist Chapel) (Existed by 1935)

ROMSEY Cemetery (Records - Test Valley Borough Council)
OR   B1857+ Test Valley Borough Council
        B1872+ (one volume) HRO (Damaged and not fit for production)
Mfc   B1857-1980s HRO (Includes index)

ROMSEY New Cemetery (Records - Test Valley Borough Council)
Mfc   B1980s-1990s HRO (Includes index)

ROMSEY Union Workhouse
OR   Z1925-1931 (closed until 2007) HRO
      D1835-1925 HRO

ROPLEY St Peter (779) (Alresford Union) (Chapelry of Bishops Sutton; separate parish 1882; see also Four Marks)
OR   C1539-1965 M1539-1977 B1539-1989 Bn1888-1987 HRO
      (Gap in C & B 1631-1653; gaps in M 1625-1653,1702-1755);
BT   1707-1708,1724,1728,1780-1781,1783-1804,1806-1807,1809-1870 HRO
      (Mfm SLC)
Mfc   C1539-1965 M1539-1977 B1539-1989 HRO
Mfm C1539-1876 M1539-1876 B1539-1875 HRO, SLC
Cop C1704-1783 M1704-1753 B1704-1783 (Ts) HRO
      C1704-1986 M1704-1986 B1702-1986 (Ts, alphabetical by first letter) HRO
      M1539-1837 HMI; M1676-1881 CMI; B1539-1837 HBI

ROPLEY (Baptist) Bethel Chapel (Meetings established 1825, Bethel Chapel erected 1891; met at Alton for part of the nineteenth century)

ROPLEY (Primitive Methodist) (Winchester Primitive Methodist Circuit) (Chapel erected 1869, new chapel erected 1909, closed 1968) (Records 1867+ HRO)

ROTHERWICK (Dedication unknown) (436) (Hartley Wintney Union) (Chapelry of Odiham; separate parish 1867)
OR   C1582-1950 M1560-1991 B1561-1936 Bn1754-1812,1832-1897 HRO
BT   1780-1783,1785-1822,1824-1849,1851-1864 HRO (Mfm SLC)
Mfc   C1582-1950 M1560-1991 B1561-1936 Bn1754-1812 HRO
Mfm C1582-1876 M1560-1837 M1561-1875 Bn1754-1812 HRO, SLC
Cop M1560-1812 Phillimore Vol 11 and Boyd; M1560-1837 HMI
      C1582-1812 M1560-1812 B1561-1812 (Ts) HRO; M1790-1812 Pallot
      M1560-1885 CMI; B1561-1837 HBI; Extracts C1582-1876 M1560-1837 IGI

ROTHERWICK (Primitive Methodist) (Basingstoke Primitive Methodist Circuit) (Chapel erected 1882)

ROWLANDS CASTLE St John the Baptist (Formerly Redhill) (District formed 1840 from Havant & Warblington; absorbed part of Idsworth; see also Leigh Park)
OR   C1841-1954 M1841-1966 B1842-1934 Bn1841-1949 PCRO
BT   1851-1853 HRO (Mfm SLC) (filed with Havant)
Mfc   C1841-1954 M1841-1966 B1842-1934 HRO, PCRO
Cop M1841-1886 CMI

ROWLANDS CASTLE (Independent) Providence Chapel - See CHALTON

ROWLEDGE St James (Formed 1871 from Farnham [Surrey], Frensham [Surrey], & Binsted [Hampshire])
OR   C1871-1955 M1871-1987 B1871-1940 Bn1974-1994 SHC
Cop M1871-1882 CMI

ROWLEDGE (Wesleyan) (Farnham Wesleyan Circuit, Aldershot & Farnham
  Wesleyan Circuit from 1891) (Existed by 1879, active) (Records 1880+ HRO)
OR   Some baptisms at Rowledge were registered at Farnham Wesleyan Chapel

ROWNER St Mary the Virgin (140) (Fareham Union) (See also Bridgemary)
OR   C1583-1995 M1591-1965,1976-1988 B1590-1995 Bn1754-1822,1838-
  1973,1977-1996 PCRO (No marriages took place in the period 1818-1838;
  marriage register 1965-1976 missing)
BT   1780-1804,1806-1868,1870-1872,1874 HRO (Mfm SLC)
Mfc   C1583-1977 M1591-1965,1976-1988 B1590-1952 HRO, PCRO
Mfm   C1583-1885 M1591-1875 B1590-1875 Bn1754-1822 PCRO, SLC
Cop   M1591-1810 Phillimore Vol 8 and Boyd; Index to PR 1590-1922 (Ms) SG
  C1583-1812 M1591-1812 B1590-1812 (Ms) PCRO (CHU46/1E/1,3,4,5)
  C1590-1700 M1591-1700 B1593-1701 (Ts) SG, HRO; M1591-1817 HMI
  C1780-1812 M1780-1812 B1780-1812 (BT?) (Ts) SG; M1591-1886 CMI
  C1583-1951 M1591-1954 B1590-1952 PCI; M1790-1812 Pallot
  B1590-1837 HBI; Extracts C1752-1875 M1754-1878 IGI

ROWNER Church Centre, Rowner Naval Base
OR   C1971-1982 PCRO

ROWNER Gospel Hall, Copse Lane
OR   M1965-1991 PCRO

ROWNHAMS St John the Evangelist (Formed 1856 from Romsey, Nursling, & North
  Baddesley)
OR   C1855-1986 M1856-1991 B1855-1963 Bn1856-1988 HRO
BT   1855-1862 HRO (Mfm SLC)
Mfc   C1855-1969 M1856-1978 B1855-1963 HRO
Mfm   C1855-1875 M1856-1876 B1855-1876 HRO, SLC
Cop   B1855-1978 (Ms) HGS; M1856-1885 CMI

RUDMORE - See PORTSEA St John the Baptist

ST DENYS - See SOUTHAMPTON St Denys

ST IVES (Wesleyan) - See RINGWOOD

ST LEONARDS & ST IVES All Saints (Chapelry of Ringwood; parish formed 1969
  from Ringwood, Christchurch, & Holdenhurst)
OR   M1934-1966 Bn1934-1967 HRO; C1927+ Inc
Mfc   M1934-1966 HRO

ST MARY BOURNE St Peter (1,125) (Whitchurch Union) (Chapelry of Hurstbourne
  Priors; separate parish 1928)
OR   C1661-1960 M1662-1959 B1661-1897 Bn1754-1817,1824-1856,1896-1962
        HRO
BT   1758,1780-1814,1816-1861,1863 HRO (Mfm SLC)
Mfc   C1661-1960 M1662-1959 B1661-1897 Bn1754-1817 HRO
Cop   M1662-1812 Phillimore Vol 1 and Pallot; M1662-1837 Boyd
        C1661-1838 M1662-1837 B1661-1837 (Ts,A) SG, HRO, Inc
        C1662-1799 M1662-1749 B1661-1799 (Ts) HRO; M1662-1837 HMI
        M1662-1882 CMI; B1661-1837 HBI

ST MARY BOURNE (Baptist) Swampton (Erected c1842, probably closed by 1930)

ST MARY BOURNE (Wesleyan) (Andover Wesleyan Circuit) (Society existed by
  1829, chapels erected 1833 & 1886, closed 1942 and amalgamated with the
  Primitive Methodist Chapel) (Records 1829+ HRO)

ST MARY BOURNE (Wesleyan) Dunley (Existed by 1889, probably became
  Primitive Methodist by 1911)

ST MARY BOURNE (Primitive Methodist) (Andover Primitive Methodist Circuit,
  Hurstbourne Tarrant Primitive Methodist Circuit from 1910) (Chapel erected 1838)
  (Records 1887+ HRO)

ST MARY BOURNE (Primitive Methodist) Stoke (Andover Primitive Methodist
  Circuit, Hurstbourne Tarrant Primitive Methodist Circuit from 1910) (Chapel
  erected 1864, closed 1975) (Records 1864+ HRO)

ST MARY BOURNE (Primitive Methodist) Dunley (Existed by 1911, probably in the
  former Wesleyan Chapel, short-lived)

SALISBURY [Wiltshire] Wesleyan Circuit (Formed 1768; known as Wiltshire South
  Circuit until 1780. Included chapels at Breamore, Broughton, Damerham,
  Fordingbridge, Portsea, and West Tytherley) (Records 1816+ WRO)
OR   C1819-1837 PRO (RG 4/3046); C1841-1972 WRO (1150/1-12)
Mfm   C1819-1837 PRO, SLC; C1841-1949 SLC (Excludes the separate series of
        entries from 1902 in 1150/10-12)

SALISBURY [Wiltshire] Primitive Methodist Circuit (Included chapels at Breamore,
  Damerham, Fordingbridge, Martin, Plaitford, and Sherfield English)
OR   C1832-1942 WRO (1150/269-270)
Mfm   C1832-1942 SLC

SANDHURST [Berkshire] Wesleyan Circuit (Formed 1870; became part of Aldershot
  & Camberley Methodist Circuit in 1933. Included chapels at Eversley, Fleet, and
  Hartley Wintney) (Records 1892+ HRO)

SANDLEHEATH (Primitive Methodist) - See FORDINGBRIDGE

SARISBURY (with SWANWICK) St Paul (Formed 1837 from Titchfield; see also
  Locks Heath)
OR   C1836-1979 M1852-1978 B1836-1961 Bn1912-1980 PCRO
BT   1851-1852,1855-1856,1859-1883 HRO (Mfm SLC)
Mfc   C1836-1979 M1852-1978 B1836-1961 HRO, PCRO
Cop   M1852-1882 CMI; B1836-1837 HBI

SARISBURY (Particular Baptist) Lower Swanwick (Meetings in a boathouse from
  1833, chapel erected 1844)

SARISBURY (Baptist) Sarisbury Green (Existed by 1882)

SARISBURY (Independent) Providence Chapel, Swanwick Lane (Chapel erected
  c1803, Church founded 1871)

SARISBURY (Independent, Free Church, now United Reformed) Bridge Road,
  Sarisbury Green (Chapel erected c1844 but possibly closed, Free Church founded
  1878, later became Independent, active)

SARISBURY St Paul's Cemetery (Records - Fareham Borough Council)
Mfc   B1872-1951 HRO

SCRUBB HILL (Independent) - See EAST BOLDRE

SELBORNE St Mary (924) (Alton Union) (See also Blackmoor)
OR   C1563-1975 M1557-1976 B1556-1953 Bn1823-1961 HRO
      (Gaps in M 1640-1648,1656-1663 and B 1641-1649)
BT   1677,1780-1803,1805-1831,1834-1837,1839-1842,1844-1866 HRO (Mfm SLC
      - omits 1677) (For 1677 see HRO document Q9/2/6)
Mfc   C1563-1975 M1557-1976 B1556-1953 HRO
Cop   Transcriber's notes referring to PR1556-1678 (but no transcript) HRO
      M1557-1837 HMI; M1557-1882 CMI; B1556-1837 HBI
      Extracts C1562-1663 M1557-1672 IGI

SELBORNE (Independent) (Founded 1860, closed)

SELBORNE (Independent) Shortheath, Oakhanger - See KINGSLEY

SHALDEN St Peter & St Paul (167) (Alton Union)
OR   C1686-1812 M1687-1979 B1687-1812 Bn1754-1811,1824-1976 HRO
BT   1780-1784,1787,1790,1792-1802,1804-1861,1863 HRO (Mfm SLC)
Mfc   C1686-1812 M1687-1979 B1687-1812 HRO
Mfm C1686-1790 M1687-1754 B1687-1790 HRO
Cop   M1687-1836 HMI; M1687-1881 CMI; M1687-1836 Boyd
      B1687-1837 HBI; Extracts M1687-1836 IGI

SHEDFIELD St John the Baptist (Formed 1843 from Droxford)
OR   C1829-1994 M1843-1980 B1830-1993 Bn1950-1984 HRO
BT   1829-1831,1848-1858 HRO (Mfm SLC)
Mfc   C1829-1994 M1843-1980 B1830-1993 HRO
Mfm C1829-1876 M1843-1876 B1830-1877 HRO, SLC
Cop   M1843-1881 CMI; B1830-1837 HBI

SHEDFIELD (Primitive Methodist) Zion Chapel, Shirrell Heath (Hambledon Primitive Methodist Branch from 1885, Droxford Primitive Methodist Circuit from 1892) (Chapel erected 1864) (Records 1864+ HRO)

SHEET St Mary Magdalen (District formed 1869 from Petersfield; parish 1886)
OR   C1868-1969 M1869-1996 B1872-1883 Bn1868-1979 HRO
Mfm C1868-1969 M1869-1968 B1872-1883 Bn1920-1964 HRO
Cop M1869-1881 CMI

SHEFFORD [Berkshire] Primitive Methodist Circuit - See NEWBURY Primitive Methodist Circuit

SHEFFORD [Berkshire] (Primitive Methodist) (Shefford Primitive Methodist Circuit, Newbury Primitive Methodist Circuit from 1845)
OR   C1831-1837 PRO (RG 4/2146) (Includes three baptisms at Kingsclere)
Mfm C1831-1837 PRO, BRO, SLC

SHERBORNE ST JOHN St Andrew (702) (Basingstoke Union)
OR   C1652-1969 M1653-1980 B1652-1989 Bn1869-1980 HRO
      (Gap in B 1705-1736)
BT   1780,1785-1786,1789-1863,1869-1870 HRO (Mfm SLC)
Mfc C1652-1969 M1653-1980 B1652-1989 HRO
Cop M1653-1812 Phillimore Vol 3 and Boyd; M1790-1812 Pallot
      C1652-1837 M1653-1837 B1652-1837 (Ts,I) SG, Inc (Omits M1810-1812;
      HRO holds the index only); M1653-1837 HMI; M1653-1881 CMI
      B1652-1837 HBI; Extracts C1652-1852 M1653-1852 IGI

SHERFIELD ENGLISH St Leonard (338) (Romsey Union)
OR   C1640-1964 M1645-1980 B1640-1963 Bn1824-1965 HRO
BT   1764-1765,1780-1856,1858-1871 HRO (Mfm SLC)
Mfc C1640-1964 M1645-1980 B1640-1963 HRO
Mfm C1640-1877 M1645-1878 B1640-1877 HRO, SLC
Cop M1645-1837 HMI; M1645-1885 CMI; B1640-1837 HBI
      Extracts C1640-1877 M1645-1878 IGI

SHERFIELD ENGLISH (Primitive Methodist) Wellow Wood (Salisbury Primitive Methodist Circuit, Woodfalls Primitive Methodist Circuit, from 1898) (Records 1910+ WRO)

SHERFIELD ON LODDON St Leonard (599) (Basingstoke Union)
OR   C1574-1857 M1574-1998 B1574-1977 Bn1754-1812,1823-1869 HRO
BT   1781-1791,1793-1862 HRO (Mfm SLC)
Mfc C1574-1857 M1574-1990 B1574-1977 Bn1754-1812 HRO
Mfm C1574-1876 M1574-1875 B1574-1876 Bn1754-1812 HRO, SLC
Cop M1574-1812 Phillimore Vol 9 and Boyd; M1790-1812 Pallot
      C1574-1767 M1574-1812 B1574-1771 (Ts & Ms) HRO; M1574-1837 HMI
      C1574-1813 M1574-1978 B1574-1977 Inc; M1574-1882 CMI;
      Index to C1574-1651 B1574-1631 (Ts) HGS; B1574-1837 HBI

SHERFIELD ON LODDON (Baptist) (Existed by 1889, active)

SHERFIELD ON LODDON (Independent) (Erected c1831, probably closed by 1890)

SHERFIELD ON LODDON (Primitive Methodist) (Basingstoke Primitive Methodist Circuit) (Chapel erected 1810)

SHERFIELD ON LODDON (Plymouth Brethren) (Meetings by 1878, chapel 1899)

SHIPTON BELLINGER St Peter (287) (Andover Union)
OR   C1562-1913 M1546-1722,1812-1978 B1565-1972 Bn1824-1908 HRO
      (Gaps in C 1722-1749 and B 1723-1756; M register 1722-1812 missing)
BT   1780-1872 HRO (Mfm SLC)
Mfc C1562-1913 M1546-1722,1812-1978 B1565-1972 HRO
Cop M1546-1722,1780-1837 HMI; M1780-1889 CMI; B1565-1837 HBI

SHIPTON BELLINGER (Particular Baptist) Rehoboth Chapel (Chapel erected 1849, no references located after 1878)

SHIRLEY - See SOUTHAMPTON Shirley

SHIRLEY WARREN - See SOUTHAMPTON Shirley Warren

SHIRRELL HEATH (Primitive Methodist) - See SHEDFIELD

SHOLING - See SOUTHAMPTON Sholing

SHORTHEATH (Independent) - See KINGSLEY

SILCHESTER St Mary (414) (Basingstoke Union)
OR   C1653-1886 M1654-1836 B1653-1930 Bn1754-1812,1824-1833 HRO
BT   1780-1810,1812-1823,1825-1858,1860 HRO (Mfm SLC)
Mfc C1653-1886 M1654-1997 B1653-1930 Bn1754-1812 HRO
Cop M1654-1812 Phillimore Vol 7 and Boyd
      C1653-1812 M1654-1812 B1653-1812 (Ts) HRO, Inc; M1654-1836 HMI
      M1654-1886 CMI; M1790-1812 Pallot; B1653-1837 HBI

SILCHESTER Primitive Methodist Circuit (The Silchester Branch of Reading Circuit became a separate circuit in 1865. Included chapels at Baughurst, Hannington, Mortimer West End, Pamber, Silchester, Tadley, Wolverton, and Wootton St Lawrence) (Records 1858+ BRO)
OR   C1844-1889 BRO
Mfc C1844-1889 HRO
Mfm C1844-1889 BRO
Cop C1844-1889 (Ts,I) BRO

SILCHESTER (Primitive Methodist) Silchester Common (Reading Primitive Methodist Circuit, Silchester Primitive Methodist Circuit) (Chapel erected 1839, new church erected 1927, active) (Records 1839+ BRO)

SILKSTEAD (United Methodist Free Church) - See HURSLEY

SMANNELL Christ Church (District formed 1858 from Andover; parish 1870) (See also Enham)
OR   C1857-1965 Bn1876-1970 HRO; M1858+ B1857+ Inc
BT   1857-1871 HRO (Mfm SLC) (In Andover BT and Hatherden BT)
Cop   M1858-1882 CMI

SMANNELL (Baptist) - See ANDOVER

SOBERTON St Peter & St Paul (931) (Droxford Union) (Chapelry of Meonstoke; separate parish 1897; see also Newtown [Soberton])
OR   C1546-1879 M1540-1987 B1538-1957 Bn1754-1812,1823-1885,1907-1960 HRO (Gap in M 1621-1654; C defective 1760-1767)
BT   1780-1858,1866 HRO (Mfm SLC)
Mfc   C1546-1879 M1540-1987 B1538-1957 Bn1754-1812 HRO
Cop   C1546-1700 M1540-1700 B1539-1700 (Ms) HRO
      M1540-1837 HMI; M1540-1881 CMI; B1538-1837 HBI

SOBERTON (United Methodist Free Church) Forest Chapel (Winchester United Methodist Free Church Circuit) (Chapel erected 1868) (Records 1905+ HRO)
OR   C1922-1951 HRO (58M75/NMR1)

SOBERTON (Christian Catholic) Soberton Heath (Established c1850; 1851 Religious Census; no later references located)

SOMBORNE - See KINGS SOMBORNE, LITTLE SOMBORNE

SOPLEY St Michael & All Angels (1,012) (Christchurch Union) (See also Bransgore)
OR   C1682-1988 M1682-1987 B1678-1941 Bn1754-1817 HRO
      (Plus C1661-1674 for one family only)
BT   1773-1774,1776,1780,1782,1785-1812,1814-1871,1873-1880 HRO (Mfm SLC)
Mfc   C1682-1988 M1682-1987 B1678-1941 HRO
Mfm   C1682-1812 M1682-1812 B1678-1812 HRO
Cop   M1682-1812 Phillimore Vol 7 and Boyd; C1682-1812 B1690-1812 (Ts) HRO
      C1682-1732 M1682-1728 B1678-1732 (Ms) HRO; M1682-1837 HMI
      M1682-1881 CMI; M1790-1812 Pallot; B1678-1837 HBI

SOPLEY (Roman Catholic) - See CHRISTCHURCH

SOPLEY (Baptist) - See SOPLEY (Independent) Ripley

SOPLEY (Independent) Ripley (Founded 1829, closed 1942)
OR   Z1818-1837 C1829-1837 B1829-1837 PRO (RG 4/656,657) (The birth entries relate to Baptists; one baptism in 1823 is entered at Christchurch Independent Chapel - DRO NP4/RE1)
Mfm   Z1818-1837 C1829-1837 B1829-1837 PRO, HRO, SLC
Cop   B1829-1837 HBI; Extracts Z1818-1837 C1829-1837 IGI

SOPLEY Cemetery (Records 1881+ Parish Council)

SOUTHAMPTON

The present City of Southampton includes the ancient parishes of Millbrook and South Stoneham, and the chapelry of Bassett, which are listed separately.

SOUTHAMPTON All Saints (5,560) (Southampton Incorporation) (Destroyed 1940)

OR   C1653-1664,1723-1940 M1653-1664,1723-1801,1813-1831,1837-1926 B1653-1664,1723-1812,1855-1876 Bn1785-1804,1913-1923 SCA (Registers damaged by bombing in 1940. The following are at SCA but are not fit for production: M1801-1812,1831-1837,1927-1938 B1813-1855 Bn1754-1785,1804-1847,1860s,1923-1932)

BT   1780-1787,1789-1867 HRO (Mfm SLC)

Mfc   C1723-1915 M1754-1801,1813-1831,1837-1876 B1775-1812,1855-1876 Bn1785-1804 HRO, SCA

Mfm   C1653-1664, 1723-1878 M1653-1664,1723-1785,1813-1831,1837-1862 B1653-1664,1723-1812 SCA, SLC

Pc   1780-1867 (BT) SCA

Cop   C1723-1837 M1723-1837 B1723-1837 Bn1785-1812 (Ts,I) (Gaps filled from BT) HRO, SCA, HGS; C1838-1899 M1838-1878 B1838-1876 SCI C1723-1812 M1723-1812 B1723-1812 Bn1785-1812 (Ts,I) SG C1653-1664 M1653-1664 B1653-1663 (plus a few entries 1666-1704) (Ts,I) SCA, HGS; B1861-1865 (BT) (Ms,I) SG; M1653-1664,1723-1837 HMI M1663-1664,1723-1881 CMI; B1653-1664,1723-1837 HBI

SOUTHAMPTON Holy Rood (1,772) (Southampton Incorporation) (Destroyed 1940)

OR   C1653-1812 M1653-1812 B1653-1813 Bn1653-1696,1713,1718-1719,1753-1807 SCA (All later registers were destroyed in 1940)

BT   1780-1842,1844-1858 HRO (Mfm SLC)

Mfc   C1653-1812 M1653-1812 B1653-1813 Bn1653-1696,1713,1718-1719,1753-1807 HRO, SCA

Mfm   C1653-1812 M1653-1812 B1653-1813 SCA, SLC

Pc   1794-1795,1813-1858 (BT) SCA

Cop   C1653-1812 M1653-1812 B1653-1813 Bn1653-1660,1684-1697,1713-1719, 1754-1806 (Ts,I) SG, HRO, SCA, HGS; M1780-1812 (BT) (Ts,I) SG, HRO C1813-1837 M1813-1837 B1813-1837 (BT) (Ts,I) SG, HRO, SCA C1838-1855,1858 B1838-1855,1858 (BT) (Ms,I) SG; M1653-1837 HMI C1838-1858 B1838-1850 (BT) SCI; M1813-1837 CMI; B1653-1837 HBI

SOUTHAMPTON St John (Demolished 1708 and united with St Lawrence)

OR   No registers survive

SOUTHAMPTON St Lawrence & St John (1,066) (Southampton Incorporation)
   (St Lawrence demolished 1924 and united with Holy Rood)
OR   C1768-1813 M1754-1811 B1768-1813 Bn1754-1811 SCA (All later registers
        destroyed in 1940; entries also occur in the registers of Holy Rood)
BT   1781-1836,1838-1875 HRO (Mfm SLC)
Mfc   C1768-1813 M1754-1811 B1768-1813 Bn1754-1811 HRO, SCA
        C1768-1813 B1768-1813 SG
Mfm C1768-1813 M1754-1811 B1768-1813 Bn1754-1811 SCA, SLC
Pc   1813-1836,1838-1875 (BT) SCA (M from 1811)
Cop   C1768-1812 M1754-1812 B1768-1812 (Ts,I) SG, HRO, SCA, HGS
        C1813-1836 M1813-1836 B1813-1836 (BT) (Ts,I) SG, HRO, SCA
        C1838-1875 B1838-1875 (BT) SCI
        M1813-1836 HMI; M1754-1836 CMI; B1768-1836 HBI

SOUTHAMPTON St Mary (8,520) (Southampton Incorporation)
OR   C1675-1966 M1675-1976 B1675-1882 Bn1754-1829 SCA
        (Earlier register destroyed by fire in 1706; entries prior to 1706 are
        retrospective from notes made by parish officials)
BT   1780-1810,1812-1836,1838-1850,1856-1857 HRO (Mfm SLC)
Mfc   C1675-1879,1929-1966 M1675-1976 B1675-1871 Bn1754-1795 HRO, SCA
Mfm C1675-1879 M1675-1876 B1675-1893 Bn1754-1829 SCA, SLC
        C1675-1812 M1675-1812 B1675-1810 Bn1754-1829 HRO
Cop   C1675-1837 M1675-1837 B1675-1837 plus burials of soldiers who died in
        hospitals 1741-1748 (Ts,I) SG, HRO, SCA, HGS
        C1838-1878 M1838-1876 B1838-1871 SCI
        M1675-1837 HMI; M1813-1881 CMI; B1675-1837 HBI

SOUTHAMPTON St Mary Extra (1,068) (South Stoneham Union) (Chapel to
   St Mary; separate parish 1881)
OR   C1681-1986 M1687-1752,1843-1981 B1671-1950 Bn1948-1993 SCA
        (Gap circa 1707-1733; in the period 1752-1843, couples married at St Mary)
BT   1785-1789,1791-1792,1802-1855 HRO (Mfm SLC)
Mfc   C1681-1972 M1687-1752,1843-1978 B1671-1950 HRO, SCA
Cop   C1681-1837 M1687-1752 B1671-1837 (Ts,I) SG, HRO, SCA, HGS
        Index to C1681-1915 M1687-1752,1843-1915 B1671-1915 SCA (in register
        PR6/1/34) (Also on microfiche at HRO); M1687-1752 HMI; B1671-1837 HBI
        C1838-1885 M1838-1904 B1838-1870 SCI; M1843-1883 CMI

SOUTHAMPTON St Michael (1,752) (Southampton Incorporation)
OR   C1552-1927 M1552-1985 B1552-1878 Bn1754-1890,1914-1967 SCA
        (Gaps 1575-1589,1604-1618,1652-1664)
BT   1780-1860 HRO (Mfm SLC)
Mfc   C1552-1927 M1552-1956 B1552-1878 Bn1754-1821 HRO, SCA
        C1552-1927 M1552-1943 B1552-1878 Bn1754-1821 SG
Mfm C1552-1879 M1552-1900 B1552-1878 Bn1754-1804 SCA, SLC
Cop   C1552-1837 M1552-1837 B1552-1837 Bn1757-1812 (Ts,I) SG, HRO, SCA,
        HGS; C1838-1879 M1838-1866 B1838-1878 SCI
        M1552-1837 HMI; M1813-1900 CMI; B1552-1837 HBI

SOUTHAMPTON Bitterne, Holy Saviour (Formed 1853 from South Stoneham)
OR   C1852-1936 M1853-1951 B1853-1901 Bn1958-1964,1968-1986 SCA
Mfc   C1852-1913 M1853-1906 B1853-1881 HRO, SCA
Cop   C1852-1913 M1853-1906 B1853-1881 SCI; M1853-1881 CMI

SOUTHAMPTON Bitterne Park, Ascension (Formed 1899 from South Stoneham & Bitterne)
OR   C1899-1991 M1926-1984 B1960-1993 Bn1969-1986 SCA
Mfc   C1899-1913 M1926-1946 HRO, SCA

SOUTHAMPTON Freemantle, Christ Church (Formed 1866 from Millbrook)
OR   C1856-1950 M1866-1974 B1875-1929 Bn1903-1907,1911-1916,1929-1989 SCA
BT   1865-1879,1881-1888,1890 HRO (Mfm SLC)
Mfc   C1856-1950 M1866-1906,1916-1974 B1875-1929 HRO, SCA
Mfm C1856-1877 M1866-1884 SCA, SLC
Cop   C1856-1890 M1866-1884 B1875-1929 SCI; M1866-1884

SOUTHAMPTON Highfield, Christ Church (Formed 1847 from South Stoneham)
OR   C1847-1983 M1848-1996 B1850-1881,1894-1899 Bn1848-1939,1945-1995 SCA
Mfc   C1847-1954 M1848-1977 B1850-1881,1894-1899 HRO, SCA
Cop   C1847-1881 M1848-1891 B1850-1899 SCI; M1848-1881 CMI

SOUTHAMPTON Holy Trinity (Formed 1848 from St Mary; destroyed 1940 and reabsorbed into St Mary)
OR   C1848-1940 M1848-1940 B1848-1877 SCA
BT   1855-1857 HRO (Mfm SLC)
Mfc   M1848-1940 B1848-1877 HRO, SCA
Mfm C1848-1878 M1848-1880 B1848-1877 SCA, SLC
Cop   C1848-1878 M1848-1880 B1848-1877 SCI; M1848-1881 CMI

SOUTHAMPTON Maybush, St Peter (Formed 1932 from Millbrook & Shirley)
OR   C1932-1989 M1945-1996 Bn1957-1995 SCA
Mfc   C1932-1972 HRO, SCA

SOUTHAMPTON Maybush, St Hugh, Aldermoor (Mission church)
OR   C1951-1960 SCA
Mfc   C1951-1960 HRO, SCA

SOUTHAMPTON Newtown, St Luke (Formed 1853 from St Mary & South Stoneham; redundant 1982)
OR   C1853-1980 M1853-1979 B1854-1878 Bn1891-1922,1925-1977 SCA
Mfc   C1853-1980 M1853-1979 B1854-1878 HRO, SCA
Mfm C1853-1885 M1853-1878 SCA, SLC
Cop   C1853-1875 M1853-1881 B1854-1878 SCI; M1853-1882 CMI

SOUTHAMPTON Northam, St Augustine (Formed 1854 from St Mary; originally
Christ Church; replaced by St Augustine in 1884; St Augustine closed 1977)
OR   C1856-1977 M1856-1977 B1856-1900 Bn 1929-1976 SCA
Mfc   C1856-1977 M1856-1977 B1856-1900 HRO, SCA
Mfm   C1856-1893 M1856-1894 B1856-1900 SCA, SLC
Cop   C1856-1893 M1856-1894 B1856-1900 SCI; M1856-1894 CMI

SOUTHAMPTON Redbridge, All Saints (Formed 1954 from Millbrook)
OR   C1956-1986 M1964-1993 B1966-1972 Bn1965-1994 SCA
Mfc   C1956-1960 M1964-1967 HRO, SCA

SOUTHAMPTON St Alban (District formed 1905 from North & South Stoneham;
originally St Agnes; parish of St Alban formed 1933)
OR   C1905-1973 M1933-1984 B1905-1921,1968-1976 Bn1960-1977 SCA

SOUTHAMPTON St Barnabas (District formed 1892 from Newtown & Highfield;
separate parish 1903)
OR   C1892-1925 M1893-1962 Bn1955-1982 SCA; B1955+ Inc (Bn1945-1955 for
St Barnabas are entered at Highfield)

SOUTHAMPTON St Denys (Formed 1867 from Highfield)
OR   C1867-1964 M1870-1985 B1867-1888 Bn1924-1987 SCA
Mfc   C1867-1884 B1867-1888 HRO, SCA
Mfm   C1867-1884 M1870-1880 B1867-1888 SCA, SLC
Cop   C1867-1885 B1867-1888 SCI; M1870-1882 CMI

SOUTHAMPTON St James (Docks) (Formed 1858 from St Mary; redundant 1966)
OR   C1858-1967 M1858-1967 B1933-1955 Bn1940-1970 SCA
Mfc   C1858-1967 M1858-1967 B1933-1955 HRO, SCA
Mfm   C1858-1886 M1858-1877 SCA, SLC
Cop   C1858-1886 M1858-1872 SCI; M1858-1882 CMI

SOUTHAMPTON St Mark (Formed 1892 from Shirley)
OR   C1889-1982 M1892-1963 Bn1916-1994 SCA
Mfc   C1889-1982 M1892-1963 HRO, SCA

SOUTHAMPTON St Matthew (Formed 1866 from St Mary & Holy Trinity;
redundant 1981)
OR   C1870-1976 M1870-1962 B1868-1873 Bn1870-1911,1940-1964 SCA
Mfc   C1870-1976 M1870-1962 B1868-1873 HRO, SCA
Mfm   C1870-1896 M1870-1892 SCA, SLC
Cop   C1870-1896 B1868-1873 SCI; M1870-1881 CMI

SOUTHAMPTON St Paul (Formed 1863 from All Saints; destroyed 1940 and united
with St Peter)
OR   No registers survive

SOUTHAMPTON St Peter (Formed 1861 from All Saints; redundant 1981)
OR   C1861-1976 M1861-1977 Bn1861-1955 SCA
BT   1862-1869 HRO (Mfm SLC)
Mfc   C1861-1976 M1861-1977 HRO, SCA
Mfm   C1861-1900 M1861-1913 SCA, SLC
Cop   C1861-1900 M1861-1913 SCI; M1861-1881 CMI

SOUTHAMPTON Shirley, St James (Formed 1836 from Millbrook)
OR   C1836-1986 M1837-1993 B1836-1911 Bn1931-1958,1976-1992 SCA
BT   1836-1840,1848 HRO (Mfm SLC)
Mfc   C1836-1903 M1837-1905 B1836-1911 HRO, SCA
Mfm   C1836-1876 M1837-1882 B1836-1885 SCA, SLC
Cop   C1836-1899 M1837-1882 B1836-1865 SCI; M1837-1881 CMI
      B1836-1837 HBI

SOUTHAMPTON Shirley, St John (Mission church)
OR   C1912+ Inc

SOUTHAMPTON Shirley Warren, St Jude (District formed 1952 from Shirley &
    Millbrook; separate parish 1956)
OR   C1952-1965 M1956-1973 Bn1956-1986 SCA

SOUTHAMPTON Sholing, St Mary (Formed 1866 from Hound & St Mary Extra)
OR   C1866-1971 M1867-1983 B1866-1924 Bn1954-1960,1968-1985 SCA
Mfc   C1866-1964 M1867-1970 B1866-1924 HRO, SCA
Mfm   C1866-1886 M1867-1907 B1866-1893 SCA, SLC
Cop   C1866-1886 M1867-1907 B1866-1893 SCI; M1867-1882 CMI

SOUTHAMPTON Sholing, St Francis of Assisi
OR   C1950-1974 SCA; M1974+ Bn1974+ Inc

SOUTHAMPTON Thornhill, St Christopher (District formed c1960 from West End;
    separate parish 1971)
OR   Bn1961-1982 SCA; C1960+ M1961+ Inc

SOUTHAMPTON West End, St James (District formed 1834 from South Stoneham;
    separate parish 1843; see also Hedge End)
OR   C1840-1973 M1840-1981 B1840-1972 Bn1840-1981 SCA
Mfc   C1840-1973 M1840-1981 B1840-1972 HRO, SCA
Mfm   C1840-1891 M1840-1881 B1840-1887 SCA, SLC
Cop   C1840-1891 M1840-1881 B1840-1887 SCI; M1840-1882 CMI

SOUTHAMPTON Weston, Holy Trinity (Formed 1866 from St Mary Extra)
OR   C1865-1975 M1865-1977 Bn1866-1986 SCA; B1865+ Inc
Mfc   C1865-1975 M1865-1957 HRO, SCA
Mfm   C1865-1880 M1866-1880 SCA, SLC
Cop   C1865-1931 SCI; M1865-1883 CMI

SOUTHAMPTON Woolston, St Mark (Formed 1864 from Hound & St Mary Extra)
OR   C1864-1978 M1864-1975 Bn1903-1968,1972-1983 SCA; B1979+ Inc
Mfc   C1864-1898 M1864-1911 HRO, SCA
Mfm C1864-1898 M1864-1911 SCA, SLC
Cop   C1864-1898 M1864-1911 SCI; M1864-1881 CMI

SOUTHAMPTON (Roman Catholic) St Joseph, Bugle Street (French Chapel, High
    Street, from 1792; Hanover Buildings 1805, Pepper Alley 1822, Bugle Street 1830)
OR   C1792-1804 M1803 Centre des Archives Diplomatiques, Nantes; 1805+ Inc
    (Entries 1792-1804 are indexed with other Émigré registers in a separate index
    volume held at Nantes. A microfilm of the index volume is held at PCRO)
Cop   C1792-1804 M1803 (Ts) SG, HRO, SCA
    C1805-1848 M1805-1823,1837-1849 plus a few Z from 1773 (Ts,I) SG, HRO
    C1805-1837 M1805-1823 (Ts,I) HRO, SCA, HGS; M1803-1823 HMI

SOUTHAMPTON (Roman Catholic) St Edmund, The Avenue (Founded 1884)
OR   C1884+ M1885+ B1884+ Inc

SOUTHAMPTON (Roman Catholic) St Patrick, Portsmouth Road, Woolston
    (Founded 1879 at Obelisk Road, various sites in Portsmouth Road from 1909)
OR   C1879+ M1882+ B1880+ Inc

SOUTHAMPTON (Roman Catholic) Christ the King, Bitterne (Convent Chapel
    founded 1904, parish formed 1944 from St Patrick Woolston, present church 1960)
OR   C1906+ M1947+ B1907+ Inc

SOUTHAMPTON (Roman Catholic) Immaculate Conception, Portswood (Founded
    1910, served from St Edmund until 1931)
OR   C1931+ Inc

SOUTHAMPTON (Roman Catholic) St Boniface, Shirley (Founded c1902 at
    Foundry Lane, present church erected 1927)
OR   C1913+ M1920+ B1914+ Inc

SOUTHAMPTON (Walloon, French Protestant) St Julien, Winkle Street
    (Closed 1939) (Records 1702+ SCA)
OR   C1567-1779 M1567-1753 D1567-1722 PRO (RG 4/4600) (No later registers
    kept; events were probably registered at Holy Rood)
Mfm C1567-1779 M1567-1753 D1567-1722 PRO
Cop   C1567-1779 M1567-1753 D1567-1722 (I) Huguenot Society Vol 4 (1890)
    M1567-1753 HMI; D1567-1722 HBI; Extracts C1567-1779 IGI

SOUTHAMPTON (Society of Friends) Monthly Meeting (Established 1668; became
    part of Ringwood Monthly Meeting in 1756) (Records 1734+ HRO)
OR   Z1622,1664-1695 M1665-1715 B1678-1699 PRO (RG 6/1273) (listed as
    Romsey & Southampton Monthly Meeting)
Mfm Z1622,1664-1695 M1665-1715 B1678-1699 HRO
Cop   Index see Hampshire Quarterly Meeting; M1665-1715 HMI; B1678-1699 HBI

SOUTHAMPTON (Baptist) East Street (Erected 1797, probably closed by 1915)

SOUTHAMPTON (Baptist) Portland Chapel, Portland Terrace (Chapel erected 1840, destroyed c1940)
OR   M1917-1940 SCA (D/BRA 1/2/1-2)

SOUTHAMPTON (Baptist) Church Street, Shirley (Founded 1852, active)

SOUTHAMPTON (Particular Baptist) Carlton Chapel, corner of London Road & Bellevue Road (Chapel erected 1865, war damaged, demolished 1968)
OR   M1922-1941 SCA (D/BRA 1/1/1,2)

SOUTHAMPTON (Baptist) Bedford Place (PO Directory 1867; no other references)

SOUTHAMPTON (Particular Baptist) Ebenezer Chapel, Cardigan Terrace (Existed by 1878, probably short-lived)

SOUTHAMPTON (Baptist) Ascupart Chapel - See SOUTHAMPTON (Plymouth Brethen)

SOUTHAMPTON (Baptist) Middle Road, Sholing (Erected c1879, active 1975)

SOUTHAMPTON (Particular Baptist) New Road (Existed by 1889)

SOUTHAMPTON (Baptist) Oaktree Road, Bitterne Park, now at Wellington Avenue (Founded 1900, active)

SOUTHAMPTON (Baptist) Polygon Chapel (now Central Church), Devonshire Road (Chapel erected 1910, active)

SOUTHAMPTON (Baptist) Fleming Road, Swaythling (Founded 1925, active)

SOUTHAMPTON (Independent) Above Bar (Founded 1662, destroyed 1940, united with St Andrew 1942 to form the United Presbyterian-Congregational Church) (Records 1688+ SCA)
OR   C1674-1693,1726-1783,1838-1895 D1726-1809,1831 B1837-1851 SCA (D/ABC 1/1-6); C1895-1915 M1896-1915 B1896-1913 SCA (D/ABC 1/7 - not fit for production); C1783-1837 B1821-1837 PRO (RG 4/610,624,658)
Mfm   C1783-1837 B1821-1837 PRO, HRO, SLC
Cop   C1674-1837 D1726-1809 B1821-1837 (Ts,I) SG, SCA, HGS
       C1838-1868 B1837-1851 SCI; B1821-1837 HBI; Extracts C1783-1837 IGI

SOUTHAMPTON (Independent, now United Reformed) Pear Tree Green, Bridge Road (Founded 1808, active)
OR   M1988-1989 SCA (D/URC 5/1)

SOUTHAMPTON (Independent) Albion Chapel, St Mary Street (Founded 1844, closed 1935)
OR   M1918-1934 SCA (D/URC 1/1-2)

SOUTHAMPTON (Independent) Oxford Street, Shirley (Chapel erected 1858, no references located after 1883)

SOUTHAMPTON (Independent) Kingsfield, Havelock Road, West Marlands (Chapel erected 1861, probably closed by 1930)

SOUTHAMPTON (Independent, now United Reformed) Bitterne (Founded 1863, active)

SOUTHAMPTON (Independent) Belvidere Terrace, Northam (Founded 1863, destroyed 1940)
OR   M1913-1940 SCA (D/URC 2/1-2)

SOUTHAMPTON (Independent) Highfield (PO Directory 1867; no other references)

SOUTHAMPTON (Independent, now United Reformed) Roberts Road or Shirley Road, Freemantle (Founded 1885, active)

SOUTHAMPTON (Independent, now United Reformed) The Avenue (Founded 1893, amalgamated with St Andrew 1986 to form Avenue St Andrew, active)

SOUTHAMPTON (Independent, now United Reformed) Cobden Avenue, Bitterne Park (Founded 1902, active)

SOUTHAMPTON (Independent, now United Reformed) Isaac Watts Memorial, Winchester Road (Founded 1932, active)

SOUTHAMPTON (Presbyterian, later United Reformed) St Andrew, Brunswick Place (Founded 1849, church erected 1853, amalgamated with The Avenue 1986) (Records 1849+ SCA)
OR   M1906-1986 SCA (D/URC 3/1-11); Communicants' Roll Books 1851-1864, 1881-c1900,1904-1908,1917-1960 SCA (D/APC 3/1-7)

SOUTHAMPTON (Presbyterian) St Mary, Portsmouth Road, Woolston (Founded 1874, church erected 1876, demolished)
OR   C1881(two only) M1878-1911,1915,1920-1956 SCA (D/URC 4/1-2)

SOUTHAMPTON (Unitarian) Bellevue Road, London Road (Founded 1846 at St Michael's Square, new church erected 1860, active) (Records 1859+ SCA)
OR   C1883-1944 M1884-1939 B1883-1940 SCA (D/UC 3)

SOUTHAMPTON Wesleyan Circuit (Formed 1798 from Portsmouth Circuit. Included chapels at Bishopstoke, Braishfield, Copythorne, Dibden, Durley, Easton, Eling, Fawley, Houghton, Hound, Kings Somborne, Millbrook, Nursling, Overton, Romsey, Southampton, South Stoneham, Timsbury, Twyford, West Wellow, Whitchurch, and Winchester) (Records 1801+ SCA)
OR   C1798-1837 PRO (RG 4/659,1395,1396); C1883-1930 SCA (D/Meth 24/3)
Mfm   C1798-1837 PRO, HRO, SLC
Cop   C1798-1812 (Ts,I) SG; C1798-1837 (Ts,I) HRO, SCA, HGS
        Extracts C1798-1837 IGI

SOUTHAMPTON (Wesleyan)
OR   C1806-1813 HRO (in a register of Andover Circuit, 96M72/NMC/R1)

SOUTHAMPTON (Wesleyan) Union Terrace, formerly Canal Walk (Southampton Wesleyan Circuit) (Established 1798, reopened 1823, probably the forerunner of East Street. The chapel was possibly used later by the Reformed Wesleyans) (Records from 1798 - see East Street)

SOUTHAMPTON (Wesleyan) Bitterne (Southampton Wesleyan Circuit) (Meetings from 1806, chapel erected 1823 in Chapel Road [now Dean Road], moved to Pound Street 1906 and White's Road 1969, active) (Records 1903+ SCA)

SOUTHAMPTON (Wesleyan) Moorgreen, West End - See SOUTH STONEHAM Burnetts Lane

SOUTHAMPTON (Wesleyan) Church Street, Shirley (Southampton Wesleyan Circuit) (Chapel erected 1843, amalgamated 1928 with Howard Road to form St James Road Church) (Records 1877+ SCA)
OR   C1851-1927 SCA (D/Meth 24/9)
Cop   C1851-1927 SCI

SOUTHAMPTON (Wesleyan) East Street; later at Central Hall, St Mary Street (Southampton Wesleyan Circuit) (Chapel erected 1850, probably to succeed Canal Walk Chapel, replaced by Central Hall 1925, closed 1965) (Records 1798+ SCA)
OR   C1837-1965 M1880-1965 SCA (D/Meth 24/1-2, 25/3-6) (Includes other chapels in Southampton Wesleyan Circuit, plus baptisms on board ship)
Cop   C1837-1861 SCI; M1880-1881 CMI

SOUTHAMPTON (Wesleyan) Newtown (Former Wesleyan chapel purchased for temporary Anglican use in 1850; listed as Wesleyan in PO Directory 1855)

SOUTHAMPTON (Wesleyan) Broad Street (Listed as Wesleyan in PO Directory 1855, Independent Methodist in PO Directory 1867; no later references located)

SOUTHAMPTON (Wesleyan) Bevois Valley Road (Southampton Wesleyan Circuit) (Erected 1858, closed 1948, became a Sikh Temple 1971) (Records 1875+ SCA)
OR   C1858-1948 M1882-1948 SCA (D/Meth 24/5-7, 25/1-2)
Cop   C1858-1866 SCI

SOUTHAMPTON (Wesleyan) Obelisk Road, Woolston (Southampton Wesleyan Circuit) (Chapel erected 1866, closed c1933 and amalgamated with Manor Road United Methodist Church)

SOUTHAMPTON (Wesleyan) Park Road, later Howard Road, Freemantle (Southampton Wesleyan Circuit) (Established 1866 in Park Road as an offshoot of East Street, moved to Howard Road 1907, amalgamated with Church Street 1928) (Records 1864+ SCA)
OR   C1866-1928 M1909-1920 SCA (D/Meth 24/12-13, 25/8)

SOUTHAMPTON (Wesleyan) Cobden Avenue, Bitterne Park (Southampton Wesleyan Circuit) (Established c1901, closed 1932) (Records 1901+ SCA)
OR   C1903-1930 M1905-1932 SCA (D/Meth 24/14, 25/7)

SOUTHAMPTON (Wesleyan) Portswood Road (Southampton Wesleyan Circuit) (Established 1905 in a former Bible Christian Chapel, closed 1932 and transferred to Swaythling Methodist Church) (Records 1905+ SCA)
OR   C1905-1932 SCA (D/Meth 24/16)

SOUTHAMPTON (Wesleyan) St James Road, Shirley (Erected 1928 to replace Church Street and Howard Road Chapels, active) (Records 1926+ SCA)
OR   C1928-1950 SCA (D/Meth 24/11)

SOUTHAMPTON (Wesleyan) Burgess Road, Swaythling (Southampton Methodist Circuit) (Founded 1932 to replace Portswood Road, active) (Records 1930+ SCA)

SOUTHAMPTON (Reformed Wesleyan) Lower Canal Walk (Opened 1855, probably short-lived)

SOUTHAMPTON (Wesleyan Methodist Association) St Mary Street (Established by 1836, chapel erected 1838, sold to Primitive Methodists 1841)

SOUTHAMPTON Primitive Methodist Circuit (A Southampton Mission of Hull [Yorkshire] Circuit existed c1836-1841; a new Southampton Mission, formed 1842 from Andover Circuit, became Southampton Circuit in 1852; later divided into the Primitive Methodist First and Second Circuits. Included chapels at Boldre, Bramshaw, Chandlers Ford, Copythorne, Eling, Lockerley, Lymington, Milton, Romsey, Southampton, Sway, and West Wellow) (Records 1836-1841 IWRO AC 80/1/248, records 1852+ SCA, records 1860+ HRO)

SOUTHAMPTON (Primitive Methodist) St Mary Street (Southampton Primitive Methodist Circuit) (Chapel purchased 1841 from Wesleyan Methodist Association, closed by 1887)

SOUTHAMPTON (Primitive Methodist) Pound Street, Shirley, later known as Oriental Street (Southampton Primitive Methodist First Circuit) (Chapel in Shirley 1851, Pound Street Chapel erected 1860, closed 1960) (Records 1864+ SCA)
OR   C1924-1958 SCA (D/Meth 24/10)

SOUTHAMPTON (Primitive Methodist) South East Road, Sholing (Southampton Primitive Methodist Circuit) (Established 1855, amalgamated 1969 with Hightown Bible Christian to form St Andrew South East Road, active) (Records 1856+ SCA)

SOUTHAMPTON (Primitive Methodist) Priory Road, St Denys; Ivy Road, St Denys (Southampton Primitive Methodist First Circuit) (Chapel erected 1860 in Priory Road, Ivy Road Chapel erected 1883, closed 1969, became the New Testament Church of God) (Records 1965+ SCA)
OR   M1922-1969 SCA (D/Meth 25/9-12)

SOUTHAMPTON (Primitive Methodist) Ebenezer Chapel, Bevois Town (Southampton Primitive Methodist Circuit) (Erected 1864, probably closed c1900)

SOUTHAMPTON (Primitive Methodist) Upper Liverpool Street (Southampton Primitive Methodist First Circuit) (Existed by 1867, probably closed by 1940)

SOUTHAMPTON (Primitive Methodist) Weston Common, Sholing (Established 1880, probably short-lived)

SOUTHAMPTON (Primitive Methodist) Firgrove Road, Freemantle; Shirley Road, Freemantle (Southampton Primitive Methodist First Circuit) (Chapel established c1869, Shirley Road Chapel erected c1906, destroyed 1940) (Records 1906+ SCA)

SOUTHAMPTON (Primitive Methodist) South Front (Southampton Primitive Methodist Second Circuit) (Established 1885, closed by 1932)
OR   C1890-1927 SCA (D/Meth 24/4) (Fragile, restricted access) (Includes entries for South Stoneham and Chandlers Ford)

SOUTHAMPTON (Primitive Methodist) Union Road, Northam (Southampton Primitive Methodist First Circuit) (Established 1873, demolished 1942) (Records 1902+ SCA)

SOUTHAMPTON Bible Christian Circuit (United Methodist Circuit from 1907) (A mission formed 1825 lapsed; re-formed 1840 as the Botley Mission, soon renamed Southampton Circuit, later Southampton & Eastleigh Circuit. Included chapels at Bishopstoke, Colden Common, Eastleigh, Hedge End, Southampton, Sway, and Upham) (Records 1867+ HRO)
OR   C1840-1935 HRO (19M73/NMC/R1-3) (Entries from 1917 relate to Eastleigh Section; for continuation see Eastleigh Methodist Circuit)
       C1916-1948 SCA (D/Meth 24/15) (Southampton & Eastleigh Circuit)
Mfc   C1876-1935 HRO

SOUTHAMPTON (Bible Christian) Ebenezer Chapel, Chapel Road, West End (Southampton Bible Christian Circuit) (Existed by 1840, sold 1964) (Records 1902+ SCA)
OR   C1956(only) SCA (D/Meth 24/17)

SOUTHAMPTON (Bible Christian) Jubilee Chapel, Princess Street (Southampton Bible Christian Circuit) (Established c1863, replaced 1874 by St Mary's Road, but not closed and sold until 1882)

SOUTHAMPTON (Bible Christian) Melbourne Street (Southampton Bible Christian Circuit) (Chapel erected 1864, probably closed c1882)

SOUTHAMPTON (Bible Christian) Portswood Road (Southampton Bible Christian Circuit) (Established c1867 in a converted laundry, new chapel erected c1898, possibly ceased 1906 when old chapel sold to Wesleyans)

SOUTHAMPTON (Bible Christian) Stratton Road, Shirley (Southampton Bible Christian Circuit) (Chapel erected 1867, closed 1949 and amalgamated with St James Road Wesleyan) (Records 1867+ HRO)

SOUTHAMPTON (Bible Christian) St Mary's Road (Southampton Bible Christian Circuit) (Purchased 1874 to replace Jubilee; sold 1943) (Records 1931+ SCA)

SOUTHAMPTON (Bible Christian) Peartree Green (Southampton Bible Christian Circuit) (Existed 1899-1909)

SOUTHAMPTON (Bible Christian) Hightown, Bursledon Road & Botley Road (Southampton Bible Christian Circuit) (Existed by 1905, amalgamated 1969 with South East Road Primitive Methodist) (Records 1908+ SCA)
OR   C1935-1957 SCA (D/Meth 24/18)

SOUTHAMPTON (United Methodist) Manor Road, Itchen (Southampton Bible Christian / United Methodist Circuit) (Existed by 1927, active) (Records 1927+ SCA)

SOUTHAMPTON (Methodist) Stratton Road (Southampton Methodist Circuit) (Existed by 1939)

SOUTHAMPTON (Methodist) Bevois Town, Liverpool Street
OR   C1956-1960 SCA (D/Meth 24/8)

SOUTHAMPTON (Catholic Apostolic Church) Southampton Street (Founded c1833)

SOUTHAMPTON (Latter-day Saints) (Records 1849+ in Church archives at SLC)
Mfm   Membership records 1849-1903 (Southampton District) and 1845 (Southampton Branch) SLC

SOUTHAMPTON (Church of Christ) Above Bar (Chapel erected 1883, active 1975)

SOUTHAMPTON (Evangelical) Woolston (Chapel listed in Kelly's Directory 1899)

SOUTHAMPTON (Plymouth Brethren) Woolston (Chapel listed in White's Directory 1878)

SOUTHAMPTON (Plymouth Brethren) Shirley (Chapel in White's Directory 1878)

SOUTHAMPTON (Plymouth Brethren) Ascupart Chapel (Listed in White's Directory 1878, formerly a Baptist Chapel)

SOUTHAMPTON (Plymouth Brethren) Sholing (Chapel in Kelly's Directory 1899)

SOUTHAMPTON (Christadelphian) St James Road, Shirley (Existed by 1939)

SOUTHAMPTON (Christian Scientist) Alma Road (Existed by 1939, active 1975)

SOUTHAMPTON (Spiritualist) Cavendish Grove, The Avenue (Existed by 1939)

SOUTHAMPTON (Evangelic Church) Sholing, Spring Road
OR   M1982-1984 SCA (D/OPCS 1/1) (Two entries only)

SOUTHAMPTON (Community Church) West End, Quob Lane
OR   M1982-1990 SCA (D/OPCS 2/1)

SOUTHAMPTON (Jewish) (Synagogue in East Street founded 1833; Synagogue in Albion Place erected 1864, demolished 1963; Synagogue in Mordaunt Road erected 1963; there is a Jewish section in Hollybrook Cemetery)

SOUTHAMPTON Cemetery, Southampton Common (Hill Lane)
OR   B1846+ Bereavement Services Unit, 6 Bugle Street, Southampton

SOUTHAMPTON St Mary Extra Cemetery, Portsmouth Road, Sholing
OR   B1879+ Bereavement Services Unit, 6 Bugle Street, Southampton

SOUTHAMPTON Hollybrook Cemetery, Tremona Road, Shirley
OR   B1913+ Bereavement Services Unit, 6 Bugle Street, Southampton

SOUTHAMPTON Workhouse (Southampton Incorporation)
OR   Z1848-1909 SCA
Cop   Z1848-1881 SCI

SOUTHAMPTON & EASTLEIGH Bible Christian (later United Methodist) Circuit
  - See SOUTHAMPTON Bible Christian Circuit

SOUTH BADDESLEY St Mary (Formed 1859 from Boldre)
OR   C1858-1928 M1860-1978 B1859-1992 Bn1859-1930 HRO
Mfc   C1858-1928 M1860-1978 HRO
Cop   M1860-1884 CMI

SOUTH BADDESLEY (Baptist) Beaulieu Rails (Chapel erected 1810, rebuilt 1844;
  1851 Religious Census; no other references located)

SOUTHBOURNE - See BOURNEMOUTH St Katharine, Southbourne

SOUTH CHARFORD - See CHARFORD

SOUTH DAMERHAM - See DAMERHAM

SOUTH FARNBOROUGH - See FARNBOROUGH St Mark

SOUTH HAMPSHIRE Wesleyan Mission (Formed 1900 by union of the Eastleigh,
  Romsey, and Winchester Circuits. Romsey Circuit was re-established in 1933, and
  Winchester & Eastleigh Methodist Circuit formed in 1936. Included chapels at
  Bishopstoke, Bramshaw, Durley, Eastleigh, Fawley, Hinton Ampner, New
  Alresford, Owslebury, Romsey, South Stoneham, Timsbury, Weeke, West Wellow,
  and Winchester) (Records 1930+ HRO)

SOUTH HAYLING St Mary (588) (Havant Union)
OR   C1672-1967 M1676-1979 B1672-1980 Bn1824-1893,1899-1928,1960-1986
       PCRO
BT   1780-1796,1798-1807,1809-1879 HRO (Mfm SLC)
Mfc   C1672-1957 M1676-1979 B1672-1980 HRO, PCRO
Mfm   C1672-1875 M1676-1875 B1672-1875 PCRO, SLC
Cop   Index to B c1780-1950 (Ms) PCRO (CHU28/5/1) (Many entries undated;
       reference numbers appear to refer to graves rather than than register entries)
       M1676-1812 (Ts,I) SG; C1672-1813 M1676-1923 B1672-1915 PCI
       M1676-1837 HMI; M1676-1882 CMI; B1672-1837 HBI
       M1676-1812 Boyd; Extracts C1734-1876 1676-1875 IGI

SOUTH HAYLING (Roman Catholic) St Patrick (Founded 1925, parish 1927)
OR   C1927+ M1929+ Inc

SOUTH HAYLING (Independent, now United Reformed) Hollow Lane
  (Founded 1811, active)

SOUTHSEA

Southsea parishes were formed from the ancient parish of Portsea.

SOUTHSEA Holy Spirit (Formed 1948 by amalgamation of St Bartholomew & St Matthew; church erected 1958)
OR   C1958-1970 M1958-1973 Bn1954-1969,1973-1978 PCRO
Mfc   C1958-1970 M1958-1973 HRO, PCRO

SOUTHSEA St Bartholomew (Established 1864; separate parish 1865; closed 1958; demolished)
OR   C1864-1958 M1865-1958 PCRO
Mfc   C1864-1958 M1865-1958 HRO, PCRO
Cop   M1865-1881 CMI

SOUTHSEA St Jude (Established 1851; separate parish 1879)
OR   C1851-1961 M1851-1989 Bn1933-1945,1955-1974 PCRO
Mfc   C1851-1961 M1851-1989 HRO, PCRO
Cop   C1851-1887 M1851-1889 PCI; M1851-1859 CMI

SOUTHSEA St Luke (Established 1861; separate parish 1864)
OR   C1864-1960 M1864-1962 Bn1928-1974 PCRO
Mfc   C1864-1960 M1864-1962 HRO, PCRO
Cop   M1864-1881 CMI

SOUTHSEA St Matthew (Formed 1904; destroyed 1941; rebuilt 1958 as Holy Spirit)
OR   C1899-1941 M1904-1941 PCRO
Mfc   C1899-1941 M1904-1941 HRO, PCRO

SOUTHSEA St Paul (Established 1822; district formed 1835; destroyed)
OR   C1931-1942 Bn1932-1942 PCRO (Other registers lost in blitz)
Mfc   C1931-1942 HRO, PCRO

SOUTHSEA St Peter (Formed 1883 from St Jude & St Paul)
OR   C1883-1986 M1883-1970 Bn1883-1969 PCRO
Mfc   C1883-1986 M1883-1970 HRO, PCRO

SOUTHSEA St Simon (District formed 1868)
OR   C1868-1966 M1868-1980 Bn1923-1985 PCRO
Mfc   C1868-1966 M1868-1980 HRO, PCRO
Cop   M1868-1882 CMI

SOUTHSEA

For ease of reference, Portsea and Southsea nonconformist chapels are listed together under Portsea.

SOUTHSEA (Victoria Road) Wesleyan Circuit (Formed 1883 from Portsmouth Green Row Circuit; the two circuits reunited in 1900 as Southsea and Pembroke Road Circuit. Included chapels at Portsea) (Records 1883+ PCRO)

SOUTHSEA Highland Road Cemetery (Portsmouth Burial Board)
OR   B1854-1901 PCRO
Mfm B1854-1901 PCRO, SLC

SOUTH STONEHAM St Mary (2,083) (South Stoneham Union) (Now within the City of Southampton; see also Eastleigh, and the Southampton parishes of Bitterne, Bitterne Park, Highfield, Newtown, St Alban, St Barnabas, St Denys, West End)
OR   C1659-1951 M1663-1954 B1663-1930,1960-1982 Bn1754-1985 SCA (Only two baptism entries before 1663)
BT   1780-1792,1794-1822,1824-1871 HRO (Mfm SLC)
Mfc   C1659-1951 M1663-1903 B1663-1860 Bn1754-1794 HRO, SCA
Mfm   C1659-1897 M1663-1903 B1663-1860 Bn1754-1812 SCA, SLC
Cop   C1659-1837 M1663-1837 B1663-1837 (Ts,I) SG, HRO, SCA, HGS
       C1838-1913 M1838-1903 B1838-1860 SCI
       M1663-1837 HMI; M1663-1881 CMI; B1663-1837 HBI

SOUTH STONEHAM (Wesleyan) Burnetts Lane, Moorgreen (Southampton Wesleyan Circuit, Winchester Wesleyan Circuit from 1862, Eastleigh Wesleyan Circuit from 1891, South Hampshire Wesleyan Mission from 1900) (Chapels erected 1826 & 1845, closed 1977, demolished) (Records 1898+ HRO)
OR   C1895-1969 HRO (19M73/NMC/R10)

SOUTH STONEHAM (Primitive Methodist) - See SOUTHAMPTON (Primitive Methodist) South Front

SOUTH STONEHAM (Bible Christian) Ebenezer (Chapel erected 1847; 1851 Religious Census; no later references located)

SOUTH STONEHAM Cemetery, Mansbridge Road, Swaythling
OR   B1905+ Bereavement Services Unit, 6 Bugle Street, Southampton

SOUTH STONEHAM Union Workhouse
OR   No registers survive. Other records at SCA.

SOUTH TIDWORTH St Mary (217) (Andover Union) (Redundant 1972)
OR   C1627-1970 M1600-1970 B1599-1992 Bn1762-1811,1825-1970 HRO (Few entries of C1643-1684 M1635-1718 B1644-1690; gap in M 1752-1761)
BT   1758,1780,1782-1783,1786-1789,1791-1796,1799-1813,1815-1832, 1834-1835,1837-1842,1844-1845,1847-1858,1861-1875 HRO (Mfm SLC)
Mfc   C1627-1970 M1600-1970 B1599-1992 Bn1762-1811 HRO
Cop   M1600-1837 HMI; M1600-1893 CMI; B1599-1837 HBI

SOUTH TIDWORTH St Michael (Garrison Church)
OR   No information

SOUTH TIDWORTH (Roman Catholic) St Patrick & St George (Garrison Church)
OR   C1911-1963 M1911-1971 B1920-1971 RCRO (Earlier entries were at St Osmund, Salibury)

SOUTH TIDWORTH (Methodist) St Mark, Tidworth Barracks
OR   C1931-1986 RACD (From 1964, entries are for the Methodist, Church of Scotland, & United Board Churches)
       M1937-1965 HRO (96M72/NMC/R10-11)
Mfc   M1937-1965 HRO

SOUTH TIDWORTH (Church of Scotland) St Andrew (Garrison Church)
OR   C1950-1964 M1951-1962 Bn1950-1954 RACD (The marriage register is not a statutory register; from 1964, baptisms were entered in the Methodist register)

SOUTH TIDWORTH (Church of Scotland, Methodist, United Board) St Andrew & St Mark (Established c1964 by amalgamation of St Andrew and St Mark)
OR   M1966-1985 HRO

SOUTH WARNBOROUGH St Andrew (374) (Hartley Wintney Union)
OR   C1539-1963 M1539-1989 B1539-1867 Bn1814,1824-1902 HRO
BT   1780-1839,1841-1883 HRO (Mfm SLC)
Mfc   C1539-1963 M1539-1989 B1539-1867 HRO
Cop   M1539-1811 Phillimore Vol 6 and Boyd; Index to PR 1539-1812 (Ms) HRO
        M1539-1837 HMI; M1539-1881 CMI; M1790-1812 Pallot; B1539-1837 HBI

SOUTH WARNBOROUGH (Independent) (Opened 1832; 1851 Religious Census; no other references located)

SOUTHWICK St James (723) (Fareham Union)
OR   C1586-1979 M1612-1994 B1588-1926 Bn1755-1808,1824-1905,1917-1974 HRO (Fragmentary before 1628; gap in burials 1724-1752; Southwick baptisms and burials 1803-1812 are entered at Boarhunt, and vice versa)
BT   1813-1827,1830-1833,1835-1838,1841,1844-1852,1855,1857-1874 HRO (Mfm SLC) (For 1853-1854,1856 see Boarhunt BT)
Mfc   C1586-1979 M1612-1975 B1588-1926 Bn1755-1808 HRO, PCRO
Mfm   C1586-1876 M1612-1837 B1588-1876 Bn1755-1808 HRO, SLC
Cop   C1581-1998 M1612-1999 B1588-1998 (Ts,I) HRO, PCRO; M1612-1837 HMI Index to M1628-1812 (Ts) HRO; M1628-1881 CMI; B1628-1837 HBI

SPARSHOLT St Stephen (357) (Winchester Union) (See also Lainston)
OR   C1607-1963 M1630-1995 B1628-1919 Bn1823-1965 HRO
BT   1780-1867,1875-1877 HRO (Mfm SLC)
Mfc   C1607-1963 M1630-1995 B1628-1919 HRO
Cop   M1630-1837 HMI; M1630-1882 CMI; B1628-1837 HBI

SPARSHOLT (United Methodist Free Church) (Winchester United Methodist Free Church Circuit) (Chapel erected 1893, closed 1956)

SPEARYWELL (Baptist) - See MOTTISFONT

STAMSHAW - See PORTSEA St Saviour

STANDFORD (Brethren) - See HEADLEY

STANDFORD HILL (Bible Christian) - See HEADLEY

STEEP All Saints (531) (Petersfield Union) (Until 1844, the parish of Steep included Ambersham, a strip of land adjacent to Fernhurst and Easebourne in Sussex)
OR   C1610-1960 M1611-1974 B1610-1891 Bn1754-1812,1823-1941 HRO
       (Gaps in CB 1644-1655,1673-1695, gaps in M 1644-1668,1673-1696)
BT   1780-1836,1838,1840-1862 HRO (Mfm SLC)
Mfc   C1610-1960 M1611-1974 B1610-1891 Bn1754-1812 HRO
Cop   C1610-1840 M1611-1837 B1610-1840 (Ts,I) SG; M1611-1837 HMI
       M1780-1812 (probably BT) (Ts,A by grooms) SG; M1611-1881 CMI
       C1610-1974 M1611-1974 B1610-1974 (Ts) HRO; B1610-1837 HBI

STEEP (Primitive Methodist) Stroud Common (Petersfield Primitive Methodist Circuit) (Chapel erected 1852, closed by 1958) (Records 1853+ HRO)

STEEP (Primitive Methodist) Bowyers (Petersfield Primitive Methodist Circuit) (Chapel erected 1869, closed 1977) (Records 1880+ HRO)

STEVENTON St Nicholas (197) (Basingstoke Union)
OR   C1604-1988 M1604-1989 B1607-1988 Bn1755-1812,1824-1959 HRO
       (Gaps in C 1725-1738, M 1727-1738, B 1695-1738)
BT   1780-1791,1796,1799-1802,1805-1847,1849-1872 HRO (Mfm SLC)
Mfc   C1604-1988 M1604-1989 B1607-1988 Bn1755-1812 HRO
Mfm   C1604-1812 M1604-1837 B1607-1812 Bn1755-1812 HRO, SLC
Cop   M1604-1812 Phillimore Vol 1, Boyd, Pallot
       C1604-1840 M1814-1840 B1607-1840 Bn1824-1838 (Ts,I) SG, HRO
       C1604-1888 M1604-1888 B1607-1888 Bn1755-1812,1824-1888 (Ts) HRO
       C1840-1886 M1839-1874 B1840-1891 (Ts,I) SG; M1604-1837 HMI
       M1604-1888 CMI; B1607-1837 HBI; Extracts C1604-1840 IGI

STEVENTON (Primitive Methodist) (Micheldever Primitive Methodist Circuit) (Chapel erected 1903, closed 1973) (Records 1947+ HRO)

STOCKBRIDGE St Peter (851) (Stockbridge Union) (Chapelry of Kings Somborne; separate parish 1842)
OR   C1663-1935 M1670-1973 B1669-1918 Bn1810-1915,1950-1977 HRO
BT   1707,1780-1784,1787,1789,1791,1793-1809,1811-1819, 1821,1823-1826,
       1828-1831,1841,1843-1859 HRO (Mfm SLC)
Mfc   C1663-1935 M1670-1973 B1669-1918 HRO
Mfm   C1663-1876 M1670-1876 B1669-1876 HRO, SLC
Cop   C1663-1768 M1670-1754 B1669-1768 (Ms) HRO
       M1670-1837 HMI; M1670-1883 CMI; B1669-1837 HBI

STOCKBRIDGE (Baptist) (Chapel by 1889, Church founded 1905, active)
OR   No information
Mfm   A membership list 1886-1890 occurs in the church book 1759-1891 of
       Broughton Baptist Church (HRO microfilm 395)

STOCKBRIDGE (Independent) Salem Chapel (Founded c1814, closed by 1925?)
OR   C1815-1836 PRO (RG 4/625)
Mfm   C1815-1836 PRO, HRO, SLC
Cop   Extracts C1815-1836 IGI

STOCKBRIDGE (Primitive Methodist) (Andover Primitive Methodist Circuit, Hurstbourne Tarrant Primitive Methodist Circuit from 1910) (Chapel erected 1864, possibly ceased by 1924) (Records 1844,1865 [only] HRO)

STOCKBRIDGE Romsey Road Cemetery (Records 1891+ Parish Council)
Mfc   Register of public graves 1921-1998 HRO (Includes Winton Hill)

STOCKBRIDGE Winton Hill Cemetery (Records 1935+ Parish Council)

STOCKBRIDGE Union Workhouse
OR   D1914-1939 (closed until 2015) HRO

STOKE (Independent) - See NORTH HAYLING

STOKE (Primitive Methodist) - See ST MARY BOURNE

STOKE CHARITY St Michael (135) (Winchester Union)
OR   C1540-1995 M1542-1975 B1540-1991 Bn1759-1812,1826-1994 HRO
     (Gap in B 1771-1778)
BT   1780-1784,1786-1788,1791-1795,1797-1799,1802-1805,1808,1810-1820,
     1822-1823,1825-1872 HRO (Mfm SLC)
Mfc   C1540-1995 M1542-1975 B1540-1991 Bn1759-1812 HRO
Mfm   C1540-1812 M1542-1873 B1540-1812 Bn1759-1812 HRO, SLC
Cop   M1542-1812 Phillimore Vol 9 and Boyd; M1790-1812 Pallot
     C1551-1837 M1553-1836 B1551-1837 (Ts) HRO; Extracts M1542-1836 IGI
     M1542-1836 HMI; M1542-1884 CMI; B1540-1837 HBI

STOKE COMMON (Bible Christian) - See BISHOPSTOKE

STONEHAM - See NORTH STONEHAM, SOUTH STONEHAM

STRATFIELD MORTIMER St Mary the Virgin (860 in Berkshire, 348 in Hampshire) (Bradfield Union; Hampshire portion transferred to Basingstoke Union by 1880) (See also Mortimer West End)
OR   C1681-1968 M1681-1989 B1681-1977 Bn1864-1987 BRO
     (plus a few baptisms 1629-1680; previous volume destroyed by fire)
BT   1615-1623,1628,1631,1635,1637,1668-1703,1707,1713-1739,1742-1835
     WRO; 1836-1874 Oxfordshire Record Office
Mfc   C1681-1968 M1681-1989 B1681-1977 BRO, HRO
Cop   CMB1615-1623,1628,1631,1635,1637,1668-1680 (BT) (Ts) SG, BRO
     C1681-1753 M1681-1753 B1681-1753 (Ts,I) SG, BRO
     C1752-1840 M1753-1837 B1753-1840 (Ts) SG, BRO; M1837-1882 CMI
     M1813-1837 (Ts,I) BRO; M1615-1837 Berks Marriage Index

STRATFIELD MORTIMER St John the Evangelist (Chapel to St Mary)
OR   C1896-1913 M1965-1976 BRO
Mfc   C1896-1913 M1965-1976 BRO, HRO

STRATFIELD SAYE St Mary the Virgin (559 in Hampshire, 249 in Berkshire)
(Basingstoke Union) (See also Beech Hill)
OR   C1539-1962 M1539-1981 B1539-1871 Bn1754-1799,1823-1987 HRO
(Gap in M & B 1642-1653)
BT   1702,1709,1780-1782,1784-1870 HRO (Mfm SLC)
Mfc   C1539-1879 M1539-1966 B1539-1871 Bn1754-1799 HRO
Mfm   C1539-1876 M1539-1876 B1539-1875 Bn1754-1799 HRO, SLC
Cop   M1539-1812 Phillimore Vol 5 and Boyd; M1790-1812 Pallot
B1813-1837 (Ts,I) SG, HRO, HGS; M1539-1836 HMI
Index to M1539-1812 (Ts) HRO; M1539-1881 CMI
C1539-1672 M1539-1672 B1539-1673 (I) Inc; B1539-1837 HBI
Index to C1673-1883 M1673-1883 B1673-1883 Inc

STRATFIELD TURGIS All Saints (232) (Basingstoke Union) (Redundant 1973)
OR   C1672-1971 M1672-1971 B1674-1974 Bn1754-1809,1823-1971 HRO
(Gap in M 1692-1697,1709-1716)
BT   1709,1782,1784,1786-1787,1789-1829,1831-1832,1834-1856,1858-1871 HRO
(Mfm SLC)
Mfc   C1672-1971 M1672-1971 B1674-1974 Bn1754-1809 HRO
Mfm   C1672-1876 M1672-1876 B1674-1877 Bn1754-1809 HRO, SLC
Cop   M1672-1809 Phillimore Vol 6 and Boyd; M1790-1812 Pallot
C1672-1812 M1672-1809 B1674-1812 (Ts) HRO, Inc; M1672-1837 HMI
C1813-1837 M1814-1837 B1813-1837 (Ts,I) SG, HRO, HGS
Index to M1672-1809 (Ts) HRO; M1672-1884 CMI
B1674-1837 HBI; Extracts C1672-1812 M1672-1809 IGI

STRATTON - See EAST STRATTON

STROUD COMMON (Primitive Methodist) - See STEEP

STUBBINGTON Holy Rood - See CROFTON

STUBBINGTON (Wesleyan) (Gosport Wesleyan Circuit, Fareham Wesleyan Circuit
from 1867, Gosport & Fareham Wesleyan Circuit from 1908) (Society existed by
1833, chapel erected c1860) (Records 1891+ HRO)

STUCKTON (Independent) - See FORDINGBRIDGE

SURREY Bible Christian Mission - See FARNHAM Bible Christian Circuit

SURREY & NORTH HAMPSHIRE Wesleyan Mission (Formed 1900 by union of
the Alton, Basingstoke, Petersfield, and Guildford Circuits; divided 1917 into the
Alton, Basingstoke, and Petersfield & Haslemere Circuits. Included chapels at
Alton, Basingstoke, Binsted, Cliddesden, East Worldham, Farringdon, Froxfield,
Froyle, Grayshott, Greatham, Greywell, Holybourne, Liss, Odiham, Petersfield, and
Wootton St Lawrence) (Records 1900+ HRO, records 1900+ SHC)

SUTTON - See BISHOPS SUTTON, LONG SUTTON

SUTTON SCOTNEY (Wesleyan, Primitive Methodist) - See WONSTON

SWAMPTON (Baptist) - See ST MARY BOURNE

SWANMORE St Barnabas (District formed 1846 from Droxford & Bishops Waltham)
OR   C1845-1978 M1846-1991 B1846-1993 Bn1899-1990 HRO
Mfc   C1845-1978 M1846-1991 B1846-1993 HRO
Mfm   C1845-1876 M1846-1875 B1846-1875 HRO, SLC
Cop   M1846-1882 CMI; Extracts C1845-1876 M1846-1875 IGI

SWANMORE (Society of Friends) Burial Ground (In use 1657-1703)

SWANMORE (Primitive Methodist) (Hambledon Primitive Methodist Branch from 1885, Droxford Primitive Methodist Circuit from 1892) (Chapel erected 1862) (Records 1900+ HRO)

SWANWICK (Church of England, Baptist, Independent) - See SARISBURY

SWARRATON St Andrew (120) (Alresford Union) (Demolished 1851, churchyard closed 1886)
OR   C1584-1705,1754-1850 M1606-1618,1754-1845 B1754-1885
       Bn1756-1809,1823-1930 HRO (The volume containing C1584-1705 and
       M1606-1618 was found in 1975. Gaps in C 1759-1769 and B 1756-1769)
BT   1781-1787,1789-1796,1798-1805,1808-1837,1839-1847,1858 HRO
       (Mfm SLC)
Mfc   C1584-1705,1754-1850 M1606-1618,1754-1845 B1754-1885
       Bn1756-1809 HRO
Cop   C1584-1694, extracts M1606-1616 (Ts,I) SG, HRO, HGS
       M1606-1618,1754-1837 HMI; M1754-1845 CMI; B1754-1837 HBI

SWARRATON (Primitive Methodist) Zion Chapel (Micheldever Primitive Methodist Circuit) (Chapel erected 1831, closed by 1958) (Records 1889+ HRO)

SWAY St Luke (Formed 1841 from Boldre)
OR   C1839-1958 M1843-1982 B1839-1981 Bn1923-1990 HRO
BT   1839,1843,1868-1876 HRO (Mfm SLC)
Mfc   C1839-1958 M1843-1982 B1839-1981 HRO
Cop   M1843-1882 CMI

SWAY (Baptist) (Chapel erected c1827)

SWAY (Wesleyan) (Christchurch & Lymington Wesleyan Circuit) (1883-1902 only)

SWAY (Primitive Methodist) (Southampton Primitive Methodist Circuit, Romsey Primitive Methodist Circuit from 1880) (Erected c1845) (Records 1852+ HRO)

SWAY (Bible Christian) (Southampton Bible Christian Circuit) (1864-1882 only)

SWAY Cemetery
OR   B1956-1982 HRO
Mfc   B1956-1982 HRO

SYDMONTON St Mary the Virgin (170) (Kingsclere Union) (Ancient chapelry of
    Kingsclere, annexed to Ecchinswell in 1852; redundant 1981)
OR   M1854-1980 HRO (For other periods see Kingsclere, Ecchinswell)
Mfc   M1854-1980 HRO
Cop   M1854-1980 CMI

TADLEY St Peter (683) (Kingsclere Union) (Chapelry of Overton; separate parish
    1878; see also North Tadley, Pamber Heath, Ramsdell)
OR   C1683-1976 M1691-1992 B1695-1968 Bn1754-1811,1824-1868,1872-
        1983,1989-1990 HRO
BT   1780-1825,1827-1869 HRO (Mfm SLC) (1811 filed with Whitchurch)
Mfc   C1683-1976 M1691-1985 B1695-1968 Bn1754-1811 HRO
Mfm   C1683-1812 M1691-1837 B1695-1812 Bn1754-1811 HRO, SLC
Cop   M1691-1812 Phillimore Vol 6 and Boyd; M1790-1812 Pallot
        C1683-1812 B1695-1812 (Ts,I) SG; M1691-1837 HMI; M1691-1885 CMI
        C1683-1854 M1691-1754 B1695-1886 (Ms & Ts) HGS; B1695-1837 HBI

TADLEY St Paul (Erected 1966 on the site of St Saviour's chapel)
OR   C1966-1979 M1966-1997 Bn1966-1994 HRO
Mfc   C1966-1979 M1966-1983 HRO

TADLEY (Independent, now United Reformed) Malthouse Lane (Founded 1662,
    active)
OR   C1788-1835 PRO (RG 4/2305); C1787+ M1880+ B1879+ Inc
Mfm   C1788-1835 PRO, HRO, SLC
Cop   C1787-1981 M1880-1976 B1879-1948 Members 1811-1944 (from records
        held at the church) HGS
        C1930(only) B1916-1930,1948-1980 (Ts) HRO; Extracts C1788-1835 IGI

TADLEY (Primitive Methodist) (Silchester Primitive Methodist Circuit) (Chapel
    existed by 1867, active) (Records 1892+ BRO)

TANGLEY St Thomas of Canterbury (283) (Andover Union) (Chapelry of Faccombe;
    separate parish 1898)
OR   C1704-1920 M1703-1990 B1679-1995 HRO (Gap in M 1753-1781)
        Bn1865+ Inc
BT   1707,1780-1863 HRO (Mfm SLC)
Mfc   C1704-1920 M1703-1990 B1679-1995 HRO
Cop   M1703-1812 Phillimore Vol 2 and Boyd; PR c1679-1780 (Ts) Inc
        M1703-1835 HMI; M1703-1883 CMI; M1790-1812 Pallot; B1679-1837 HBI

TESTWOOD St Winfrid (Formed 1938 from Eling)
OR   C1938-1964 M1939-1959 B1946-1979 Bn1968-1992 HRO
Mfc   C1938-1964 M1939-1959 B1946-1979 HRO

TESTWOOD (Baptist) Salisbury Road (Founded 1938, active)

THORNEY HILL (Wesleyan) Hill Farm - See CHRISTCHURCH

THROOP - See BOURNEMOUTH St Paul

THROOP (Independent) - See HOLDENHURST

THRUXTON St Peter & St Paul (269) (Andover Union)
OR   C1600-1921 M1603-1978 B1607-1992 Bn1754-1771,1802,1823-1978 HRO
       (Gap in C 1693-1702, M 1667-1708, B 1666-1703,1716-1721)
BT   1780-1821,1823-1833,1835-1875 HRO (Mfm SLC)
Mfc   C1600-1921 M1603-1978 B1607-1992 Bn1754-1771,1802,1823-1881 HRO
Cop   C1702-1840 M1721-1847 B1721-1812 Bn1754-1881 (Ms,TsI) SG, HRO
       M1603-1837 HMI; M1608-1884 CMI; B1607-1837 HBI

THRUXTON (Wesleyan) (Winchester Wesleyan Circuit, Andover Wesleyan Circuit
     from 1818) (Chapel erected 1817, converted to Village Hall c1945, Society
     remained active) (Records 1818+ HRO)

TICHBORNE St Andrew (363) (Alresford Union) (Chapelry of Cheriton; separate
     parish 1974)
OR   C1667-1948 M1716-1981 B1713-1992 Bn1755-1812,1823-1944 HRO
       (Only three baptism entries before 1713; gap in C 1748-1773, M 1745-1755, B
       1743-1774; Bn1967-1982 are entered at Cheriton)
BT   1780-1793,1795-1859 HRO (Mfm SLC)
Mfc   C1667-1948 M1716-1981 B1713-1992 Bn1755-1812 HRO
Mfm   C1667-1875 M1716-1883 B1713-1876 Bn1755-1812,1823-1875 HRO, SLC
Cop   M1716-1812 (Ts) HRO, HGS; M1716-1836 HMI; M1716-1883 CMI
       B1713-1837 HBI; Extracts C1667-1875 M1716-1883 IGI

TICHBORNE (Roman Catholic) St Margaret of Scotland (In the Catholic parish of
     Alresford from 1968) (A mission was maintained at Tichborne House from 1633)
OR   C1837-1862 M1844-1857 D1846-1863 HRO
       C1864+ M1866+ B1859+ Inc of Alresford Roman Catholic
       (Register of C1785-1837 D1743-1835 missing)
Mfc   C1837-1862 M1844-1857 D1846-1863 HRO
Cop   C1785-1837 D1700-1835 (I) CRS Vol 43 (includes Z&C1779-1816 M1778,
       1806 for Tichborne family; few D before 1777); Extracts C1785-1837 IGI
       M1778,1806 HMI; D1700-1835 HBI

TIDWORTH - See SOUTH TIDWORTH

TIMSBURY St Andrew (165) (Romsey Union) (See also Eldon)
OR   C1564-1964 M1564-1980 B1564-1997 Bn1760-1825 HRO
       (Gaps in C 1790-1815, M 1754-1760, B1790-1813)
BT   1780-1781,1783-1795,1797-1799,1801-1804,1813-1815,1817-1834,
       1836-1837,1841-1872 HRO (Mfm SLC)
Mfc   C1564-1964 M1564-1980 B1564-1997 Bn1760-1825 HRO
Mfm   C1564-1790 M1564-1754 B1564-1790 HRO
Cop   M1564-1812 (Ts,I) SG, HGS; M1564-1812 (Ms) Guildhall Library
       M1564-1837 HMI; M1564-1888 CMI; M1564-1812 Boyd; B1564-1837 HBI

TIMSBURY (Wesleyan) (Southampton Wesleyan Circuit, Winchester Wesleyan
     Circuit from 1862, Romsey Wesleyan Circuit from 1872, South Hampshire
     Wesleyan Mission from 1900) (Society founded 1777, chapel erected 1867)
     (Records 1859+ HRO)

TIPTOE (Baptist) - See HORDLE

TISTED - See EAST TISTED, WEST TISTED

TITCHFIELD St Peter (3,712) (Fareham Union) (See also Crofton, Hook with Warsash, Locks Heath, Sarisbury)
OR C1590-1982 M1590-1984 B1590-1919 Bn1754-1782,1823-1985 HRO
BT 1780-1788,1790,1792-1850,1852-1886 HRO (Mfm SLC)
Mfc C1590-1982 M1590-1984 B1590-1919 Bn1754-1782 HRO
      C1634-1947 M1634-1920,1949-1962 B1634-1919 Bn1754-1782 PCRO
Mfm C1590-1812 M1590-1812 B1590-1812 Bn1754-1782 HRO
Cop C1590-1634 M1590-1634 B1590-1634 (Ptd,I) Titchfield History Society
      C1763-1812 B1763-1812 (Ms,I) SG
      M1590-1837 HMI; M1678-1883 CMI; B1590-1837 HBI

TITCHFIELD (Independent, now Evangelical) High Street (Founded 1799 [possibly 1789], active)
OR C1803-1837 PRO (RG 4/870); C1854+ B1854+ (plus membership lists 1854-1939) Inc (A list is held at HRO under reference 194M86)
Mfm C1803-1837 PRO, HRO, SLC
Cop Extracts C1803-1837 IGI

TITCHFIELD (Brethren) (Chapel existed by 1899)

TITCHFIELD Cemetery (Records - Fareham Borough Council)
Mfc B1861-1971 HRO

TITCHFIELD Claypits Cemetery (Records - Fareham Borough Council)
Mfc B1918-1950 HRO

TOOTHILL (Baptist) - See ROMSEY

TOTTON (Roman Catholic, Independent, Presbyterian, Primitive Methodist) - See ELING

TOTTON (Baptist) - See TESTWOOD

TUFTON St Mary (197) (Whitchurch Union) (Chapelry of Wherwell; parish 1857)
OR C1716-1992 M1762-1985 B1714-1992 Bn1824-1968 HRO (The register containing C1716-1784 M1714-1761 B1714-1784 is missing, but the baptism and burial entries were copied in 1893 into the register of C and B 1784-1810)
BT 1758,1780-1782,1784-1791,1794-1800,1803,1810-1837,1840-1870 HRO (Mfm SLC)
Mfc C1716-1992 M1762-1985 B1714-1992 HRO
Mfm C1716-1879 M1762-1875 B1714-1878 HRO, SLC
Cop M1754-1812 Phillimore Vol 1 & 8, Boyd, Pallot (With Bullington) (Includes four marriages 1754-1758 which are now missing from the register)
      C1716-1838 M1754-1837 B1714-1837 (Ms,A) SG, HRO; M1754-1836 HMI
      M1754-1985 CMI; B1714-1837 HBI; Extracts M1762-1875 IGI

TUNWORTH All Saints (122) (Basingstoke Union)
OR   C1749-1967 M1754-1971 B1756-1997 Bn1754-1845 HRO
BT   1780,1783,1786-1790,1792-1799,1801-1833,1835-1870 HRO (Mfm SLC)
Mfc   C1749-1967 M1754-1971 B1756-1997 Bn1754-1845 HRO
Mfm   C1749-1878 M1754-1877 B1756-1877 Bn1754-1845 HRO, SLC
Cop   C1749-1967 M1754-1971 B1756-1812 Bn1754-1812 (Ms,I) HRO
      C1749-1967 M1754-1837 B1756-1812 Bn1754-1812 (Ms,I) HGS
      M1754-1833 HMI; M1754-1892 CMI; B1756-1837 HBI
      Extracts M1814-1877 IGI

TWYFORD St Mary the Virgin (1,177) (Winchester Union) (See also Colden
    Common)
OR   C1626-1962 M1627-1987 B1626-1950 Bn1754-1898,1934-1980 HRO
BT   1708,1781-1880 HRO (Mfm SLC)
Mfc   C1626-1962 M1627-1975 B1626-1950 Bn1754-1823 HRO
Cop   C1626-1837 M1627-1837 B1626-1837 Bn1754-1786,1815-1823 (Ts,I) SG,
      HRO, HGS; C1838-1855 B1828-1840 (Ms) HGS
      M1627-1837 HMI; M1627-1881 CMI; B1626-1837 HBI

TWYFORD (Roman Catholic) Brambridge House - See EASTLEIGH

TWYFORD (Wesleyan, United Methodist Free Church) Providence Chapel
    (Southampton Wesleyan Circuit, Winchester United Methodist Free Church Circuit
    from 1835) (Chapel opened 1851, active) (Records 1850+ HRO)

TYTHERLEY - See EAST TYTHERLEY, WEST TYTHERLEY

UPHAM Blessed Mary (511) (Droxford Union) (Dedication was discovered in 1957)
OR   C1598-1862 M1622-1993 B1598-1892 Bn1758-1770,1773-1810,1934-1986
      HRO
BT   1704,1780-1784,1786-1826,1828-1855,1857,1859-1879 HRO (Mfm SLC)
Mfc   C1598-1862 M1622-1993 B1598-1892 Bn1758-1770,1773-1810 HRO
Pc   C1598-1862 M1622-1953 B1598-1892 Bn1758-1770 HRO
Cop   C1658-1816 M1655-1814 B1658-1816 (Ms) HRO
      M1622-1837 HMI; M1655-1885 CMI; B1538-1837 HBI

UPHAM (Bible Christian) Bethel Chapel, Scivier's Lane (Southampton Bible
    Christian Circuit) (Existed by 1855, closed by 1963) (Records 1864+ HRO)

UP NATELY St Stephen (153) (Basingstoke Union) (Chapelry of Old Basing;
    chapelry of Greywell from 1934 and of Mapledurwell from 1955; see also Hook)
OR   C1695-1987 M1695-1988 B1695-1988 Bn1756-1796,1831-1982 HRO
      (Gap in M 1750-1756)
BT   1782-1783,1785-1786,1789,1791-1799,1801-1866 HRO (Mfm SLC)
Mfc   C1695-1987 M1695-1988 B1695-1988 Bn1756-1796 HRO
Cop   M1695-1750 Phillimore Vol 2 and Boyd; M1695-1837 HMI
      C1695-1812 M1695-1750 B1695-1812 (Ts) HRO; M1695-1881 CMI
      M1695-1837 Bn1756-1796 (Ts,I) SG, HRO, HGS; B1695-1837 HBI

UPPER CLATFORD All Saints (487) (Andover Union)
OR   C1571-1978 M1571-1990 B1570-1897 Bn1755-1810,1815,1824-1965 HRO
      (Many gaps prior to 1725, notably C 1679-1690, M 1606-1634,1673-1697,
      B 1610-1632,1677-1695)
BT   1780-1781,1783-1880 HRO (Mfm SLC)
Mfc   C1571-1978 M1571-1986 B1570-1897 HRO
Mfm C1571-1876 M1571-1835 B1570-1876 Bn1755-1810 HRO, SLC
Cop   M1571-1835 HMI; M1571-1884 CMI; B1570-1837 HBI
      Extracts M1755-1836 IGI

UPPER CLATFORD (Primitive Methodist) (Andover Primitive Methodist Circuit)
   (Chapels erected 1846, 1883, 1903) (Records 1887+ HRO)

UP SOMBORNE (Wesleyan Methodist Association) - See KINGS SOMBORNE

UPTON (Independent, Primitive Methodist) - See VERNHAM DEAN

UPTON GREY St Mary (452) (Basingstoke Union)
OR   C1558-1875 M1558-1990 B1558-1943 Bn1754-1812 HRO
BT   1780-1783,1785-1791,1793,1795-1801,1803-1873 HRO (Mfm SLC)
Mfc   C1558-1875 M1558-1990 B1558-1943 Bn1754-1812 HRO
Mfm C1558-1875 M1558-1836 B1558-1876 Bn1754-1812 HRO, SLC
Cop   M1558-1836 HMI; M1680-1881 CMI; B1558-1837 HBI

UPTON GREY (Independent) (Chapel opened 1842; 1851 Religious Census; no other
   references located)

VALLEY PARK (District formed from Chandlers Ford, North Baddesley, & North
   Stoneham)
OR   M1991-1997 HRO; C1988+ Bn1988+ Inc

VERNHAM DEAN St Mary (694) (Andover Union) (Chapelry of Hurstbourne
   Tarrant; separate parish 1871)
OR   C1598-1701,1800-1991 M1607-1700,1754-1991 B1598-1701,1813-1971
      Bn1754-1812,1822-1969 HRO (C1701-1800, M1700-1754, B1701-1813
      missing; gaps in M 1621-1628,1645-1652,1672-1695 B 1628-1654,1677-1695)
BT   1780-1798,1800,1805-1841,1844-1864,1867 HRO (Mfm SLC)
Mfc   C1598-1701,1800-1991 M1607-1700,1754-1991 B1598-1701,1813-1971
      Bn1754-1812,1822,1829-1830 HRO
Mfm C1598-1701,1800-1877 M1607-1700,1754-1875 B1598-1701,1813-1877
      Bn1754-1812,1822-1875 HRO, SLC
Cop   M1607-1672,1754-1812 Phillimore Vol 2 and Boyd (Omits M1695-1700)
      C1642-1661 M1607-1652 B1598-1629 (Ms,TsI) SG, Guildhall Library
      C1598-1653 (Ms) HRO; M1607-1700,1754-1836 HMI
      M1607-1700,1754-1881 CMI; B1598-1701,1780-1837 HBI
      M1790-1812 Pallot; Extracts C1598-1701,1800-1839 M1607-1700 IGI

VERNHAM DEAN (Independent) Upton (part in Vernham Dean and part in
   Hurstbourne Tarrant) (Erected c1839, sold to Primitive Methodists by 1909)

VERNHAM DEAN (Wesleyan) (Andover Wesleyan Circuit) (Chapel erected 1816) (Records 1819+ HRO)

VERNHAM DEAN (Primitive Methodist) (Andover Primitive Methodist Circuit, Hurstbourne Tarrant Primitive Methodist Circuit from 1910) (Erected 1845)

VERNHAM DEAN (Primitive Methodist) Littledown (Andover Primitive Methodist Circuit, Hurstbourne Tarrant Primitive Methodist Circuit from 1910) (Chapel erected 1845)

VERNHAM DEAN (Primitive Methodist) Upton (Andover Primitive Methodist Circuit, Hurstbourne Tarrant Primitive Methodist Circuit from 1910) (Existed by 1909 in the former Independent Chapel; closed 1966) (Records 1940,1965+ HRO)

WALKFORD (Independent) - See MILTON

WALLOP - See FARLEIGH WALLOP, NETHER WALLOP, OVER WALLOP

WALTHAM - See BISHOPS WALTHAM, NORTH WALTHAM

WALTHAM CHASE (Primitive Methodist) - See BISHOPS WALTHAM

WARBLINGTON St Thomas of Canterbury (2,118) (Havant Union) (See also Emsworth, Rowlands Castle)
OR   C1631-1965 M1644-1964 B1648-1966 Bn1793-1994 PCRO
BT   1780-1883 HRO (Mfm SLC)
Mfc   C1631-1965 M1644-1964 B1648-1966 HRO, PCRO
Mfm C1631-1878 M1644-1837 B1648-1913 Bn1793-1869 HRO
      C1631-1875 M1644-1875 B1648-1875 PCRO, SLC
Pc   Bn1793-1869 PCRO
Cop C1631-1890 M1644-1927 B1648-1891 PCI; Extracts M1701-1837 Boyd
      M1644-1837 HMI; M1700-1882 CMI; M1791-1837 Pallot; B1648-1837 HBI
      Extracts C1635-1787,1813-1875 M1644-1877 IGI

WARBLINGTON Old Cemetery (Records - Havant Borough Council)
Mfc   B1894-1952 HRO

WARBLINGTON New Cemetery (Records - Havant Borough Council)
Mfc   B1914-1981 HRO

WARNBOROUGH - See SOUTH WARNBOROUGH

WARNFORD Our Lady (418) (Droxford Union)
OR   C1541-1996 M1604-1978 B1617-1997 Bn1754-1775,1811-1972 HRO
BT   1780-1783,1785-1801,1803-1842,1844-1851,1853-1856,1858 HRO
      (Mfm SLC)
Mfc   C1541-1872 M1604-1836 B1617-1812 Bn1754-1775,1811-1823 HRO
Cop M1604-1836 HMI; M1604-1886 CMI; B1617-1837 HBI

WARNFORD (Primitive Methodist) (Hambledon Primitive Methodist Branch from 1885, Droxford Primitive Methodist Circuit from 1892) (Erected 1872, sold 1924)

WARREN PARK St Clare (District formed 1975 from Leigh Park)
OR   M1971-1976 PCRO; C1968+ Bn1971+ Inc

WARSASH (Church of England, Independent) - See HOOK with WARSASH

WATERDITCH (Independent) - See BRANSGORE

WATERLOOVILLE St George the Martyr (Chapelry of Farlington; separate parish 1910; see also Cowplain)
OR   C1832-1976 M1858-1950 B1831-1908 Bn1863-1918,1924-1984 PCRO
BT   1831-1861 HRO (Mfm SLC)
Mfc   C1832-1976 M1858-1950 B1831-1908 HRO, PCRO
Cop   M1858-1886 CMI; B1831-1837 HBI

WATERLOOVILLE (Roman Catholic) The Sacred Heart (Founded 1886)
OR   1900+ Inc

WATERLOOVILLE (Baptist) Ebenezer Chapel, London Road (Founded 1856, new chapel erected 1885, active; originally used by Baptists and Independents) (Records 1868+ PCRO)

WATERLOOVILLE Cemetery (Records - Havant Borough Council)
Mfc   B1934-1985 HRO

WEEKE St Matthew (182) (Winchester Union) (Now within the City of Winchester)
OR   C1573-1968 M1573-1974 B1573-1863 Bn1756-1812,1926-1963 HRO
       (Gap circa 1646-1675; several earlier gaps)
BT   1780-1808,1810,1818-1819,1821-1868 HRO (Mfm SLC)
Mfc   C1573-1968 M1573-1974 B1573-1863 Bn1756-1812 HRO
Mfm C1573-1876 M1573-1876 B1573-1863 Bn1756-1812 HRO, SLC
Cop   C1573-1812 M1573-1753 B1573-1810 (Ts) HRO; M1573-1835 (Ts,I) SG
       M1573-1835 HMI; M1573-1882 CMI; M1573-1835 Boyd
       B1573-1837 HBI; Extracts C1813-1876 M1756-1876 IGI

WEEKE St Barnabas (Daughter church; separate parish 1989)
OR   C1956-1991 M1967-1988 Bn1867-1997HRO
Mfc   C1956-1991 M1967-1988 HRO

WEEKE St Paul (Chapel to St Matthew)
OR   M1929-1974 Bn1929-1991 HRO; C1968+ Inc
Mfc   M1929-1974 HRO

WEEKE (Wesleyan) (South Hampshire Wesleyan Mission) (Society existed by 1928, proposed chapel at Winchester Stanmore succeeded by chapel at Weeke erected 1956, active) (Records 1928+ HRO)

WEEKE Union Workhouse (Winchester Union) - See WINCHESTER

WELLOW - See EAST WELLOW

WELLOW WOOD (Primitive Methodist) - See SHERFIELD ENGLISH

WEST END - See SOUTHAMPTON West End

WEST LEIGH St Alban (Formed from Havant)
OR   C1959-1975 M1964-1974 Bn1963-1977 PCRO
Mfc   C1959-1975 M1964-1974 HRO, PCRO

WEST MEON St John the Evangelist (711) (Droxford Union)
OR   C1543-1972 M1538-1973 B1536-1924 Bn1754-1800,1823-1997 HRO
BT   1758,1780-1787,1789-1863 HRO (Mfm SLC)
Mfc   C1543-1972 M1538-1973 B1536-1924 Bn1754-1800 HRO
Cop   M1538-1800 Phillimore Vol 7 and Boyd; M1790-1800 Pallot
        C1543-1640 M1538-1639 B1536-1640 (Ms) HRO (67M81/PR2)
        M1538-1837 HMI; M1538-1881 CMI; B1536-1837 HBI

WEST MEON (Independent) East End (Chapel erected c1821, became
  Undenominational by 1910)

WEST MEON (Primitive Methodist) (Droxford Primitive Methodist Circuit) (Chapel
  erected 1872 short-lived, new chapel erected 1922, closed 1974)
  (Records 1871+ HRO, some listed under Bowyers Chapel, Steep)

WESTON - See SOUTHAMPTON Weston

WESTON PATRICK St Lawrence (210) (Basingstoke Union) (Chapelry of Odiham;
  separate parish 1866)
OR   C1596-1996 M1574-1834 B1575-1996 Bn1755-1809,1830-1996 HRO
        (Gap in M 1643-1705,1725-1755)
BT   1780-1791,1793-1795,1797,1799-1812,1814-1865 HRO (Mfm SLC)
Mfc   C1596-1996 M1574-1834 B1575-1996 Bn1755-1809 HRO
Mfm   C1596-1876 M1574-1875 B1575-1878 Bn1755-1809 HRO, SLC
Cop   C1780-1820 M1780-1820 B1780-1820 (BT) (Ts) SG, HGS (SG copy includes
        a photocopy of the original BT); M1574-1834 HMI
        M1813-1875 CMI; B1575-1837 HBI; Extracts C1597-1876 M1574-1875 IGI

WEST SHEFFORD [Berkshire] (Primitive Methodist) - See SHEFFORD

WEST TISTED St Mary Magdalen (264) (Alresford Union)
OR   C1560-1934 M1538-1976 B1538-1981 Bn1754-1812,1824-1976 HRO
BT   1728,1780-1781,1783,1785-1858,1860-1862 HRO (Mfm SLC)
Mfc   C1560-1934 M1538-1976 B1538-1981 Bn1754-1812 HRO
Mfm   M1837-1878 B1813-1876 HRO, SLC
Cop   M1538-1837 HMI; M1700-1881 CMI; B1538-1837 HBI

WEST TYTHERLEY St Peter (Original dedication unknown) (489) (Stockbridge
  Union)
OR   C1654-1863 M1662-1987 B1662-1899 Bn1873-1960 HRO (Gap in C
        1655-1662,1708-1729, and M 1681-1702,1708-1739 [except odd years])
BT   1738-1745,1780-1809,1811,1813-1819,1821-1829,1831-1870 HRO
        (Mfm SLC)
Mfc   C1654-1863 M1662-1966 B1662-1899 HRO
Mfm   C1654-1875 M1662-1875 B1662-1875 HRO, SLC
Cop   M1662-1837 HMI; M1662-1882 CMI; B1662-1837 HBI

WEST TYTHERLEY (Baptist) (1851 Religious Census; no other references located)

WEST TYTHERLEY (Wesleyan) (Salisbury Wesleyan Circuit) (Existed by 1911)

WEST WELLOW (Wesleyan) (Southampton Wesleyan Circuit, Winchester
Wesleyan Circuit from 1862, Romsey Wesleyan Circuit from 1873, South
Hampshire Wesleyan Mission from 1900) (Erected c1820) (Records 1907+ HRO)

WEST WELLOW (Primitive Methodist) (later known as Canada Common)
(Southampton Primitive Methodist Circuit, Romsey Primitive Methodist Circuit
from 1880) (Chapels erected c1815 & 1866) (Records 1867+ HRO)

WEST WORLDHAM St Nicholas (96) (Alton Union)
OR   C1653-1994 M1654-1972 B1653-1994 HRO (No M recorded 1806-1832; no B
       recorded 1789-1815; some banns were registered at Hartley Mauditt)
BT   1780-1784,1786-1798,1800-1802,1804-1809,1811-1828,1830-1831,
       1833-1834,1836,1838-1841,1843-1858 HRO (Mfm SLC)
Mfc   C1653-1994 M1654-1945 B1653-1812 HRO
Mfm   C1653-1872 M1654-1872 B1653-1878 HRO, SLC
Cop   C1649-1840 M1654-1845 B1653-1844 Printed in "The Registers of East
       Worldham, West Worldham, and Hartley Mauditt", Major V Ferguson (1942)
       C1649-1812 M1654-1806 B1653-1789 (Ts) SG, HRO; M1654-1836 HMI
       C1762-1812 M1761-1796 B1763-1812 (Ms) HRO; M1654-1935 CMI
       Index to C1840-1976 M1846-1972 B1845-1978 Inc; B1653-1837 HBI
       Extracts C1649-1840 IGI

WEYHILL St Michael & All Angels (429) (Andover Union)
OR   C1564-1966 M1564-1988 B1564-1915 Bn1754-1812,1819,1824-1920 HRO
BT   1780-1793,1795-1810,1812-1819,1821-1868 HRO (Mfm SLC)
Mfc   C1564-1966 M1564-1988 B1564-1915 Bn1754-1812,1819 HRO
Pc   C1564-1780,1813-1880 M1564-1799,1813-1839 B1564-1780
       Bn1754-1819 HRO
Cop   M1564-1812 Phillimore Vol 11 and Boyd; M1790-1812 Pallot
       C1564-1812 M1564-1754 B1564-1812 (Ts) HRO
       C1564-1780 M1564-1754 B1564-1780 (Ts) Inc
       M1564-1837 HMI; M1564-1881 CMI; B1564-1837 HBI

WEYHILL (Wesleyan) Clanville (Listed in White's Directory 1878; may refer to the
Primitive Methodist Chapel)

WEYHILL (Primitive Methodist) Clanville (Andover Primitive Methodist Circuit)
(Existed by 1889, closed by 1954, demolished) (Records 1923+ HRO)

WEYHILL Cemetery (Records 1893+ Penton Grafton Parish Council)

WHERWELL St Peter & Holy Cross (686) (Andover Union)
OR   C1634-1984 M1634-1986 B1634-1984 Bn1755-1823,1896-1972 HRO
BT   1757,1780-1781,1783-1787,1789-1885 HRO (Mfm SLC)
Mfc   C1634-1984 M1634-1986 B1634-1984 Bn1755-1823 SG, HRO
Cop   C1720-1837 (Ts) HGS; M1634-1836 HMI; M1700-1885 CMI
       B1634-1837 HBI

WHERWELL (Wesleyan) (Andover Wesleyan Circuit) (Chapel erected 1846, closed by 1983) (Records 1871+ HRO)

WHERWELL (Primitive Methodist) (Andover Primitive Methodist Circuit, Hurstbourne Tarrant Primitive Methodist Circuit from 1910, but later returned to Andover Circuit) (Chapel erected 1835 but probably ceased after 1851; new chapel erected 1887, sold 1959) (Records 1904+ HRO)

WHITCHURCH All Hallows (1,673) (Whitchurch Union)

OR   C1607-1962 M1605-1984 B1605-1918 Bn1754-1818,1823-1845,1948-1988 HRO (Gaps in C prior to 1623; gap in B 1630-1635)

BT   1807,1811-1858 HRO (Mfm SLC) (1811 relates to Tadley)

Mfc   C1607-1962 M1605-1984 B1605-1918 Bn1754-1818 HRO

Mfm   C1607-1876 M1605-1876 B1605-1876 Bn1754-1818,1823-1845 HRO, SLC

Cop   M1605-1812 Phillimore Vol 8; M1790-1812 Pallot; M1605-1837 HMI
C1607-1838 M1605-1837 B1605-1837 (Ts,A) SG, HRO; M1813-1881 CMI
M1605-1837 Boyd; B1605-1837 HBI; Extracts M1813-1876 IGI

WHITCHURCH (Society of Friends) - See ALTON

WHITCHURCH (Baptist) Wood Street, Newbury Street (Official date 1652, but possibly founded 1690 by members of Broughton; Wood Street Chapel erected 1726, Newbury Street Chapel erected c1720, active) (Records 1721+ HRO)

OR   Adult baptisms 1722,1732-1735,1758-1912 Z1759-1836 B1772-1836 D1721,1732-1919, D certs 1880-1928 HRO (46M71/R1) (Deaths and adult baptisms occur in membership lists 1721-1916 in 46M71/B1-B3,B11-B13)

Mfc   Z1759-1836 B1772-1836 HRO

Cop   B1813-1836 HBI

WHITCHURCH (Particular Baptist) Winchester Street (Erected 1875, closed 1949)

WHITCHURCH (Independent) (Existed by 1690, possibly founded 1658, closed) (Records c1760+ HRO, in 127M94)

OR   C1835,1863-1902 D1790,1817-1818,1847-1855,1872-1875 HRO (127M94/96-98) (The death entries occur in membership lists in 127M94/96; a few deaths from 1761 are noted in the church minutes)

WHITCHURCH (Wesleyan) Winchester Street (Southampton Wesleyan Circuit, Winchester Wesleyan Circuit from 1816, Andover Wesleyan Circuit from 1818) (Chapel erected 1812) (Records 1846+ HRO)

WHITCHURCH (Primitive Methodist) (Micheldever Primitive Methodist Circuit) (London Road Chapel erected 1849, moved to London Street 1902, closed 1966) (Records 1897+ HRO)

OR   M1934-1961 HRO (96M72/NMC/R13-15)

Mfc   M1934-1961 HRO

WHITCHURCH Cemetery (Records 1894+ Town Council)

WHITCHURCH Union Workhouse

OR   No registers survive. Other records at HRO.

WHITEHILL (Independent, Bible Christian, Cemetery) - See BLACKMOOR

WHITSBURY St Leonard (183) (Fordingbridge Union) (The parish was transferred from Wiltshire to Hampshire in 1895)
OR   C1714-1811 M1714-1969 B1714-1973,1985-1992 HRO (Gap c1750-1780)
BT   1780-1782,1784,1786-1788,1790,1792,1794-1801,1803-1884 HRO
    (Mfm SLC)
Mfc   C1714-1811 M1714-1969 B1714-1973,1985-1992 HRO
Mfm C1714-1811 M1714-1846 B1714-1812 HRO, SLC
Cop M1714-1837 HMI; M1714-1885 CMI; B1714-1837 HBI
    Extracts M1780-1846 IGI

WHITSBURY (Primitive Methodist) (Woodfalls Primitive Methodist Circuit) (Existed by 1901) (Records 1901+ WRO)

WICKHAM St Nicholas (1,085) (Fareham Union)
OR   C1556-1983 M1556-1990 B1556-1946 Bn1785-1812,1872-1912,1934-1946,
    1963-1987 HRO (Gap 1654-1695)
BT   1707,1741-1742,1755,1780-1818,1820-1861 HRO (Mfm SLC)
Mfc   C1556-1983 M1556-1990 B1556-1946 Bn1785-1812 HRO
Mfm C1556-1950 M1556-1837 B1556-1897 Bn1785-1812 HRO
Cop C1784-1812 B1784-1812 (Ts,I) HRO; M1780-1782 (BT) (Ts) SG
    M1556-1837 HMI; M1700-1881 CMI; B1556-1837 HBI

WICKHAM (Wesleyan Methodist Association) (Existed 1851, probably short-lived)

WICKHAM (Wesleyan) Fareham Road (Fareham Wesleyan Circuit, Gosport & Fareham Wesleyan Circuit from 1908) (Existed by 1877 in the former Wesleyan Methodist Association Chapel, new chapel erected 1906) (Records 1877+ HRO)

WIDLEY St Mary Magdalen (512) (Fareham Union) (Demolished 1953) (See also Cosham, Portsdown)
OR   C1738-1917 M1739-1930 B1738-1934 PCRO
    (For earlier entries see Wymering)
BT   1780-1786,1788-1791,1793-1795,1797-1812,1814-1837,1839-1850,1856 HRO
    (Mfm SLC)
Mfc   C1738-1917 M1739-1930 B1738-1934 HRO, PCRO
Mfm C1738-1876 M1739-1875 B1738-1875 PCRO, SLC
Pc   B1813-1934 PCRO
Cop C1738-1917 M1739-1930 B1738-1934 (Ts,I) HRO, PCRO
    M1739-1799 for Wymering & Widley (Ts,A by grooms) PCRO (CHU15/9D1)
    C1738-1876 M1739-1930 B1738-1934 PCI; M1739-1837 HMI
    M1739-1887 CMI; B1738-1837 HBI; Extracts C1738-1876 M1739-1877 IGI

WIDLEY (Baptist) - See COSHAM

WIELD St James (248) (Alton Union)
OR   C1539-1938 M1539-1970 B1539-1999 Bn1756-1796,1857-1983 HRO
      (Gap in M 1645-1663 and B 1650-1688. For copy entries of C1741-1782
      B1739-1782, and original entries of C and B 1782-1812, see 101M71/PZ1-2)
BT   1781-1810,1813-1833,1836,1838-1853,1855-1869 HRO (Mfm SLC)
Mfc   C1539-1938 M1539-1970 B1539-1780,1813-1988 Bn1756-1796 HRO
Mfm   C1539-1774,1813-1877 M1539-1875 B1539-1780 Bn1756-1796 HRO, SLC
Cop   C1539-1810 M1539-1812 B1539-1814 (Ts) HRO, Inc; M1539-1837 HMI
      M1813-1846 B1815-1981 (Ts) HRO; M1539-1885 CMI
      C1539-1780 M1539-1812 B1539-1781 (Ts,MsI) SG; B1539-1837 HBI

WIELD (Primitive Methodist) Upper Wield (Micheldever Primitive Methodist
      Circuit) (Chapel erected 1848, closed 1948)

WILDHERN (Wesleyan, Primitive Methodist) - See ANDOVER

WILTON [Wiltshire] Primitive Methodist Circuit (Formed 1898 from Salisbury
      Circuit. Included Martin Chapel) (Records 1898+ WRO)
OR   C1897-1940 WRO (1150/314)
Mfm   C1897-1940 SLC

WIMBORNE [Dorset] Wesleyan Circuit (Included chapels at Bransgore,
      Christchurch, and Ringwood for the period 1925-1932 only)
OR   C1841-1932 DRO

WIMPSON (Wesleyan) - See MILLBROOK

WINCHESTER
      The present City of Winchester includes the ancient parishes of Chilcomb, Weeke,
      and Winnall, which are listed separately.

WINCHESTER Cathedral (The Holy Trinity & St Peter & St Paul & St Swithun)
OR   C1599+ M1603+ B1599+ (plus six burials 1485-1598) Cathedral Library
      (No marriages took place 1754-1869; no baptisms 1811-1821; gap in C and M
      c1641-1670. Includes some marriages for the chapel of Wolvesey Palace)
Mfm   C1599-1994 M1603-1754,1869-1973 B1599-1987 HRO
Cop   C1599-1811 M1603-1754 B1599-1812 Phillimore Vol 4
      C1599-1994 B1599-1997 (Ts,I) HRO
      M1603-1754 HMI; M1603-1754,1869-1881 CMI; M1603-1754 Boyd
      B1599-1837 HBI: Extracts C1599-1811 M1603-1754 IGI

WINCHESTER St Bartholomew Hyde (744) (Winchester Union)
OR   C1563-1991 M1563-1990 B1563-1855 Bn1755-1869,1928-1988 HRO
      (Gap in M 1648-1688)
BT   1780-1848,1850-1865,1867-1868 HRO (Mfm SLC)
Mfc   C1563-1958 M1563-1981 B1563-1855 Bn1755-1812 HRO
Mfm   C1563-1958 M1563-1981 B1563-1855 Bn1755-1812 HRO
Cop   M1563-1837 Phillimore Vol 16 and Boyd; M1563-1837 HMI
      C1705-1776 M1705-1753 B1704-1776 (Ts,MsI) HRO, HGS
      M1563-1881 CMI; M1790-1837 Pallot; B1563-1837 HBI

WINCHESTER St Faith with St Cross (394) (Winchester Union)

OR   C1670-1948 M1674-1972 B1676-1977 Bn1755-1812,1824-1987 HRO
(Plus C1631-1632 M1632 B1632)

BT   1780-1790,1813-1825,1827-1836,1852,1867-1882 HRO (Mfm SLC)

Mfc   C1670-1948 M1674-1972 B1676-1977 Bn1755-1812 HRO

Mfm   C1670-1812 M1674-1812 B1676-1812 Bn1755-1812 HRO

Cop   M1674-1837 Phillimore Vol 16 and Boyd; M1674-1837 HMI
M1674-1882 CMI; M1790-1837 Pallot; B1676-1837 HBI

WINCHESTER St John the Baptist (785) (Winchester Union)

OR   C1578-1957 M1578-1980 B1578-1945 Bn1754-1812,1929-1970 (Plus C1553-
1554) HRO (Many gaps, notably C 1596-1602, M 1596-1610, B 1596-1611;
defective 1644-1670. The registers include early entries for St Peter Chesil)

BT   1780-1784,1787,1794,1798-1799,1801,1803-1833,1835-1883 HRO
(Mfm SLC)

Mfc   C1578-1957 M1578-1967 B1578-1945 Bn1754-1812 HRO

Mfm   C1578-1957 M1578-1967 B1578-1945 Bn1754-1812 HRO

Cop   M1578-1837 (Ts,I) SG; M1578-1837 (Ts) HRO; M1578-1825 (Ts,I) HGS
M1578-1837 HMI; M1578-1882 CMI; B1578-1837 HBI

WINCHESTER St Lawrence (331) (Winchester Union)

OR   C1760-1965 M1754-1978 B1760-1952 Bn1754-1814,1824-1987 HRO
(Earlier registers were stolen in 1760)

BT   1780-1787,1792,1794,1797-1801,1803-1809,1811-1812,1814-1818,
1820-1859,1862-1882 HRO (Mfm SLC)

Mfc   C1760-1965 M1754-1978 B1760-1952 Bn1754-1814 HRO

Mfm   C1760-1877 M1754-1876 B1760-1852 Bn1754-1814 HRO, SLC

Cop   M1754-1812 Phillimore Vol 5 and Boyd; M1754-1836 HMI
M1754-1900 CMI; M1790-1837 Pallot; B1760-1837 HBI

WINCHESTER St Maurice (with St Mary Kalendar & St Peter Colebrook) (2,927)
(Winchester Union) (Demolished 1957)

OR   C1560-1955 M1538-1954 B1538-1855,1910-1952 Bn1754-1903,1931-1955
(plus one burial in 1873) HRO (Gap 1659-1677)

BT   1780-1791,1793-1834,1837-1838,1840-1842,1844-1845,1848,1861-1867 HRO
(Mfm SLC)

Mfc   C1560-1955 M1538-1954 B1538-1855,1910-1952 Bn1754-1780 HRO

Mfm   C1560-1876 M1538-1875 B1538-1855 Bn1754-1780 HRO, SLC

Pc   C1560-1652 M1558-1649 B1558-1649 (PR Vol 2) HRO

Cop   M1538-1837 Phillimore Vol 13; M1538-1837 HMI
M1813-1881 CMI; M1651-1675,1701-1725 Boyd; M1790-1837 Pallot
B1538-1837 HBI; Extracts C1661-1876 M1662-1875 IGI

WINCHESTER St Michael (552) (Winchester Union)

OR   C1634-1984 M1632-1972 B1635-1855 Bn1754-1812,1824-1829,1850,1853-
1854,1876-1972 HRO (Gap in M 1643-1652,1653-1659 and B 1644-1656)

BT   1780-1793,1795-1808,1810-1866 HRO (Mfm SLC)

Mfc   C1634-1984 M1632-1972 B1635-1855 Bn1754-1812 HRO

Mfm   C1634-1929 M1632-1972 B1635-1812 Bn1754-1812,1824-1829,1850,1853-
1854,1876-1953 HRO

Cop   M1632-1812 Phillimore Vol 5 and Boyd; M1632-1837 HMI
M1632-1885 CMI; M1790-1812 Pallot; B1635-1837 HBI

WINCHESTER St Peter Chesil (609) (Winchester Union) (Redundant 1950)

OR   C1606-1948 M1597-1948 B1597-1947 Bn1754-1812,1824-1942 HRO
(Gaps in C 1627-1643,1644-1654, M 1627-1632,1643-1648, B 1642-1667.
Some earlier entries for St Peter are in the registers of St John the Baptist)

BT   1780,1783-1784,1787,1798,1801,1803-1871 HRO (Mfm SLC)

Mfc   C1606-1948 M1597-1948 B1597-1947 Bn1754-1812 HRO

Mfm   C1606-1948 M1597-1948 B1597-1947 Bn1754-1812,1824-1942 HRO

Cop   M1597-1837 Phillimore Vol 16 and Boyd
M1597-1837 HMI; M1597-1882 CMI; B1597-1837 HBI

WINCHESTER St Swithun upon Kingsgate (326) (Winchester Union)

OR   C1562-1976 M1564-1925 B1563-1849 Bn1863-1923 HRO
(No marriages after 1925, no baptisms after 1976)

BT   1780-1792,1795-1798,1800-1801,1803-1824,1826-1835,1837-1845,
1847-1861,1864,1866 HRO (Mfm SLC)

Mfc   C1562-1976 M1564-1925 B1563-1849 HRO

Mfm   C1562-1878 M1564-1875 B1563-1849 HRO, SLC

Cop   C1562-1695,1773 M1564-1812 B1562-1695,1773 Phillimore Vol 4
C1562-1695 M1564-1694 B1653-1694 (Ts) SG, HRO
M1564-1837 HMI; M1703-1896 CMI; M1564-1812 Boyd
B1563-1837 HBI; Extracts C1562-1695,1773-1878 M1564-1875 IGI

WINCHESTER St Thomas (with St Clement) (1,665) (Winchester Union)
(Redundant 1970)

OR   C1671-1969 M1685-1969 B1678-1855 Bn1754-1846,1879-1969 HRO
(Plus copy register of C1805-1812 B1806-1812,1816-1823 - 37M82/PZ1)

BT   1762,1780-1864,1866-1867 HRO (Mfm SLC)

Mfc   C1671-1969 M1685-1969 B1725-1855 Bn1754-1846 HRO

Mfm   C1671-1876 M1685-1876 B1678-1855 Bn1754-1846 HRO, SLC

Cop   M1685-1837 Phillimore Vol 16 and Boyd; M1678-1837 HMI
M1813-1881 CMI; M1790-1837 Pallot; B1678-1837 HBI

WINCHESTER All Saints (Chapel to Chilcomb; became the parish church of
Chilcomb in 1950)

OR   C1950-1982 M1902-1970 B1971-1973 Bn1950-1986 HRO

Mfc   C1950-1970 M1902-1970 B1971-1973 HRO

WINCHESTER Christ Church (Formed 1861 from St Faith)
OR   C1861-1956 M1861-1951 Bn1948-1980 HRO
Mfc   C1861-1956 M1861-1951 HRO
Mfm C1861-1956 M1861-1951 Bn1948-1967 HRO
Cop M1861-1881 CMI

WINCHESTER Holy Trinity (Formed 1855 from St Mary Kalendar & St Maurice)
OR   C1854-1949 M1854-1984 Bn1924-1968 HRO
Mfc   C1854-1949 M1854-1984 HRO
Mfm C1854-1949 M1854-1962 HRO
Cop M1854-1881 CMI

WINCHESTER St Barnabas - See WEEKE

WINCHESTER St Luke, Stanmore (District formed 1951 from St Faith & Christ
   Church; separate parish 1961)
OR   C1949-1967 M1952-1984 B1966-1983 Bn1952-1987 HRO
Mfc   C1949-1967 M1952-1984 B1966-1983 HRO

WINCHESTER St Matthew - See WEEKE

WINCHESTER St Martin - See WINNALL

WINCHESTER St Paul - See WEEKE

WINCHESTER Garrison Chapel
OR   C1857-1894 HRO (with St Thomas parish records); C1891-1985 RACD
Mfc   C1857-1894 HRO

WINCHESTER (Roman Catholic) St Peter (Mass from 1579 at the site of the present
   Royal Hotel; moved to St Peter's House c1680; chapel established c1740; replaced
   1792 by the church of St Peter; present church erected 1924-26)
OR   C1721+ M1721+ B1779+ Inc (Includes baptisms 1799-1800 at Botley of
   children belonging to an Irish Regiment)
Mfm C1721-1947 M1721-1961 B1779-1974 HRO
Cop C1721-1855 M1721-1855 B1779-1855 (I) CRS Vol 1 & 42
      M1721-1836 HMI; B1826-1837 HBI; Extracts C1721-1855 M1721-1855 IGI

WINCHESTER (Roman Catholic) French Émigré Priests (Entries for French refugee
   families from Toulon, settled at Romsey, Hardway, and Winchester)
OR   C1795-1801 M1797-1801 B1797-1801 Centre des Archives Diplomatiques,
   Nantes (Includes C1795-1798 for Romsey and C1796 for Hardway) (Entries
   are indexed with other Émigré registers in a separate index volume held at
   Nantes. A microfilm copy of the index volume is held at PCRO)
Cop C1795-1801 M1797-1801 B1797-1801 (I) CRS Vol 42
      M1797-1801 HMI; B1797-1801 HBI

WINCHESTER (Society of Friends) - See ALTON

WINCHESTER (Baptist) Silver Hill (Founded 1817 in a former Wesleyan chapel,
   mission to City Road Chapel from 1861, closed 1942)

WINCHESTER (Baptist) City Road (Founded 1861, active)

WINCHESTER (Independent, later United Reformed) Jewry Street (Founded 1662 in Cheesehill Street, Parchment Street Chapel erected 1704, Jewry Street Chapel erected 1853; united 1974 with St Peter Street and Parchment Street Methodist churches to form the United Church, Parchment Street) (Records 1738+ HRO)
OR C1716-1837 PRO (RG 4/20,726,3562)
  C1860-1974 M1933-1971 D1876-1891 HRO (65M77/1-3,89)
  (The death entries occur in membership lists 1842-1905 in 65M77/4,5)
Mfc M1933-1971 HRO
Mfm C1716-1837 PRO, HRO, SLC
Cop Extracts C1716-1837 IGI

WINCHESTER Wesleyan Circuit (Formed 1816 from Southampton Circuit, but re-absorbed into that circuit in 1818; re-formed in 1862; became part of the South Hampshire Wesleyan Mission in 1900; re-formed in 1936 as Winchester & Eastleigh Methodist Circuit; renamed Winchester Methodist Circuit in 1942. Included chapels at Bishopstoke, Cheriton, Durley, Eastleigh, Hinton Ampner, New Alresford, Owslebury, Romsey, South Stoneham, Timsbury, West Wellow, and Winchester; also Overton, Thruxton, and Whitchurch for 1816-1818 only)
OR C1799-1836 PRO (RG 4/1394); C1848-1975 HRO (79M72/NMR1-2,20)
Mfc C1848-1907 HRO
Mfm C1799-1836 PRO, HRO, SLC
Cop Extracts C1799-1836 IGI

WINCHESTER (Wesleyan) Parchment Street (Southampton Wesleyan Circuit, Winchester Wesleyan Circuit from 1862, South Hampshire Wesleyan Mission from 1900) (Silver Hill Chapel opened 1785, Cross Keys Passage from 1796, chapel sold to Baptists 1817, Parchment Street Chapel established 1816)

WINCHESTER (Wesleyan) St Peter Street (Winchester Wesleyan Circuit, South Hampshire Wesleyan Mission from 1900) (Founded 1865, united 1973 with Parchment Street Primitive Methodist Church) (Records 1864+ HRO)
OR M1912-1974 HRO (79M72/NMR13-17)
Mfc M1912-1974 HRO

WINCHESTER (Wesleyan) Stanmore - See WEEKE (Wesleyan)

WINCHESTER Wesleyan Methodist Association Circuit (United Methodist Free Church Circuit from 1857, United Methodist Circuit from 1907) (Formed 1835 by a breakaway group of the Winchester Wesleyan Society, joined by the Wesleyan societies of most villages in the area. Included chapels at Braishfield, Houghton, Kings Somborne, Kings Worthy, Soberton, Sparsholt, Twyford, and Winchester) (Records 1912+ HRO)

WINCHESTER (Wesleyan Methodist Association, United Methodist Free Church from 1857) Upper Brook Street, Parchment Street (Winchester United Methodist Free Church Circuit) (Founded 1835 at The Close, Upper Brook Street Chapel erected c1839, Parchment Street Chapel erected 1874, closed 1937)
OR C1897-1937 HRO (79M72/NMR5)
Mfc C1897-1937 HRO

WINCHESTER Primitive Methodist Circuit (Formed 1853 From Basingstoke Circuit. Included chapels at Bighton, Easton, New Alresford, Owslebury, Ropley, and Winchester) (Records 1892,1929+ HRO)
OR   C1886-1936 HRO (79M72/NMR4) (For later entries see Parchment Street)
Mfc   C1886-1936 HRO

WINCHESTER (Primitive Methodist) Parchment Street (Winchester Primitive Methodist Circuit) (Founded 1852, chapel purchased from Independents 1853, united 1973 with St Peter Street Wesleyan, and in 1974 with the United Reformed Church to form the United Church; active) (Records 1853+ HRO)
OR   C1938-1972 M1923-1974 HRO (79M72/7-12) (Includes baptisms at other chapels in the circuit)
Mfc   C1938-1972 M1923-1974 HRO

WINCHESTER (New Jerusalem Church) Southgate Road (Established 1841, possibly ceased by 1867)

WINCHESTER College
OR   C1726-1729,1781+ M1699-1745 B1678+ at the College (Only four marriages)
Cop   C1726-1861 M1699-1745 B1678-1903 Phillimore Vol 11
        M1699-1745 HMI; M1699-1745 CMI; M1699-1745 Boyd; B1678-1837 HBI Extracts C1765-1861 M1699-1745 IGI

WINCHESTER Diocesan Maternity Home
OR   C1914-1926,1942-1965 HRO (With St Bartholomew)
Mfc   C1914-1926,1942-1965 HRO
Mfm   C1914-1926,1942-1965 HRO

WINCHESTER Wolvesey Palace - See MORESTEAD, WINCHESTER Cathedral

WINCHESTER West Hill Cemetery (Later records - City Council)
OR   B1840-1918 (consecrated) B1841-1908 (unconsecrated) HRO
BT   1840-1842,1844,1848-1849,1853-1855 HRO
Mfc   B1840-1996 (consecrated) B1841-1977 (unconsecrated) HRO

WINCHESTER Magdalen Hill Cemetery (Records - City Council)
Mfc   B1916-1976 HRO (Includes index 1932-1983)

WINCHESTER Union Workhouse (Winchester Incorporation was replaced in 1837 by Winchester Union; a new workhouse was erected at Weeke)
OR   Z1835-1914 D1835-1914 HRO (PL5/11/58-60,62)
        Z1914-1931 (closed until 2007) HRO; D1914-1938 (closed until 2014) HRO

WINCHESTER St Paul's Hospital
OR   D1938-1951 (closed until 2027) HRO (21M91/3)

WINCHESTER & EASTLEIGH Methodist Circuit - See WINCHESTER Methodist Circuit

WINCHFIELD St Mary (227) (Hartley Wintney Union)

OR   C1660-1966 M1660-1998 B1659-1895 Bn1899-1954 HRO
      (Gap in B 1658-1686; gap in C 1807-1813 and B 1804-1813, but the missing
      entries [except 1808] are in the BT)

BT   1782,1785-1793,1795-1798,1800-1801,1803-1807,1809-1818,1820-1861,
      1864-1867 HRO (Mfm SLC)

Mfc   C1660-1966 M1660-1993 B1659-1895 HRO

Cop   M1660-1812 Phillimore Vol 3 and Boyd; M1813-1837 (Ts) SG, HGS
      M1660-1837 HMI; M1660-1883 CMI; M1790-1812 Pallot; B1659-1837 HBI

WINCHFIELD Union Workhouse (Hartley Wintney Union) - See HARTLEY
  WINTNEY

WINNALL St Martin (115) (Winchester Union) (Demolished c1971)
  (Now within the City of Winchester)

OR   C1680-1965 M1697-1965 B1697-1940 Bn1824-1960 HRO

BT   1780,1782-1784,1786-1789,1791,1794-1797,1799-1800,1802-1885 HRO
      (Mfm SLC)

Mfc   C1680-1965 M1697-1965 B1697-1940 HRO

Mfm   C1680-1965 M1697-1965 B1697-1940 Bn1824-1960 HRO

Cop   M1697-1834 (Ts,I) SG; M1697-1834 HMI; M1697-1887 CMI
      M1697-1834 Boyd; B1697-1837 HBI

WINSLADE St Mary (134) (Basingstoke Union) (Redundant 1978)

OR   C1723-1977 M1723-1973 B1723-1977 Bn1755-1807,1825-1947 HRO
      (Gap in C 1740-1747 and B 1730-1756)

BT   1780,1782-1813,1815-1822,1824-1872,1874-1879 HRO (Mfm SLC)

Mfc   C1723-1977 M1723-1973 B1723-1977 Bn1755-1807 HRO

Mfm   C1723-1877 M1723-1876 B1723-1883 Bn1755-1807 HRO, SLC

Cop   M1723-1807 Phillimore Vol 2 and Boyd; M1790-1812 Pallot
      C1723-1812 M1723-1807 B1723-1812 (Ts) HRO; M1723-1836 HMI
      M1723-1893 CMI; B1723-1837 HBI; Extracts C1723-1877 M1723-1876 IGI

WINSLADE (Independent) (Founded 1887, active 1929, possibly a mission to
  Basingstoke)

WOLVERTON St Catherine (229) (Kingsclere Union)

OR   C1717-1971 M1717-1993 B1717-1996 Bn1761-1820 HRO

BT   1780,1782-1783,1785,1787-1870,1872 HRO (Mfm SLC)

Mfc   C1717-1971 M1717-1993 B1717-1996 Bn1761-1820 HRO

Cop   M1717-1812 Phillimore Vol 8 and Boyd
      C1717-1837 M1717-1840 B1717-1837 (Ts,I) SG, HRO, Inc
      C1717-1837 M1717-1840 B1717-1836 (Ts) HRO; M1717-1835 HMI
      M1717-1908 CMI; M1790-1812 Pallot; B1717-1837 HBI

WOLVERTON (Primitive Methodist) Wolverton Common (Silchester Primitive
  Methodist Circuit) (Existed by 1872, closed by 1982) (Records 1916+ BRO)

WONSTON Holy Trinity (740) (Winchester Union)
OR   C1570+ M1571+ B1571+ Bn1754-1840,1873+ Inc
      (Gaps 1619-1623, 1634-1641; defective 1656-1672)
BT   1724,1780-1792,1794-1858,1861-1863,1866-1867 HRO (Mfm SLC)
Mfc   C1570-1812,1850-1960 M1571-1837 B1571-1812 Bn1754-1812 HRO
Mfm   C1570-1876 M1571-1876 B1571-1875 Bn1754-1812 HRO, SLC
Cop   M1571-1812 Phillimore Vol 9 and Boyd; M1790-1812 Pallot
      C1570-1868 M1570-1870 B1672-1870 (Ms) HGS
      C1570-1718 M1571-1717 B1571-1718 (Ts) HRO, Inc
      C1570-1669 B1571-1661 (Ts) HRO; C1570-1669 (Ts) HGS
      M1571-1769 (Ts,I) HRO, HGS; Index to C1570-1769 (Ts) HRO
      M1571-1837 HMI; M1700-1881 CMI; B1571-1837 HBI

WONSTON (Primitive Methodist) Sutton Scotney (Micheldever Primitive Methodist
   Circuit) (Chapel erected 1864) (Records 1921+ HRO)

WOODCOTT St James (90) (Kingsclere Union)
OR   C1579+ M1579-1755,1843+ B1579+ Inc (BT includes M in 1830 and 1831)
BT   1819-1823,1825-1827,1830-1831,1833-1838,1840,1846-1851,1856-1875 HRO
      (Mfm SLC)
Mfc   C1579-1983 M1579-1755,1843-1969 B1579-1761,1782-1983 HRO
Mfm   C1579-1979 M1579-1755,1843-1969 B1579-1761,1782-1981 HRO
Cop   M1579-1755 HMI; M1843-1902 CMI; B1579-1837 HBI

WOODFALLS [Wiltshire] Primitive Methodist Circuit (Formed 1898 from Salisbury
   Circuit. Included chapels at Breamore, Damerham, Fordingbridge, Sherfield
   English, and Whitsbury) (Records 1897+ WRO)
OR   C1898-1926 WRO (1150/365)
Mfm   C1898-1926 SLC

WOODGREEN (Wesleyan) - See BREAMORE

WOODHAY - See EAST WOODHAY

WOODLANDS - See KINGSCLERE WOODLANDS

WOODMANCOTE St James (92) (Basingstoke Union) (Chapelry of Brown
   Candover; separate parish 1847)
OR   C1762-1986 M1772-1962 B1840-1988 Bn1824-1867,1871-1970 HRO
      (Prior to 1840, burials were registered at Brown Candover)
BT   1780-1781,1785-1796,1798-1800,1803-1832,1834-1849,1851-1861 HRO
      (Mfm SLC)
Mfc   C1762-1986 M1772-1962 B1840-1988 HRO
Cop   M1772-1812 Phillimore Vol 9 and Boyd
      C1762-1812 M1772-1812 (Ms) HRO (Filed with Popham)
      M1772-1837 HMI; M1772-1890 CMI; M1790-1812 Pallot

WOOLMER (Roman Catholic) - See BRAMSHOTT

WOOLSTON - See SOUTHAMPTON Woolston

WOOLTON HILL St Thomas (Formed 1850 from East Woodhay)
OR   C1849-1999 M1850-1991 B1849-1982 Bn1919-1987 HRO
BT   1849-1868 HRO (Mfm SLC) (Filed with East Woodhay)
Mfc   C1849-1941 M1850-1958 B1849-1914 HRO
Cop   M1850-1883 CMI

WOOLTON HILL (Independent) (Existed by 1911; possibly the same chapel as East Woodhay)

WOOTTON (Primitive Methodist) - See MILTON

WOOTTON ST LAWRENCE St Lawrence (847) (Basingstoke Union) (See also East Oakley, Ramsdell)
OR   C1560-1960 M1560-1989 B1560-1960 Bn1754-1812,1816,1823-1972 HRO (Probably defective prior to 1723; entries prior to 1600 were copied partly from an older register and partly from memory)
BT   1780-1793,1795-1807,1809,1812,1814-1862 HRO (Mfm SLC)
Mfc   C1560-1960 M1560-1989 B1560-1960 Bn1754-1812,1816 HRO
Mfm C1560-1876 M1560-1875 B1560-1877 Bn1754-1812,1816 HRO, SLC
Cop   M1560-1812 Phillimore Vol 1, Boyd, Pallot; M1560-1837 HMI
       C1560-1785 M1560-1812 B1560-1785 (Ts,A) HRO; M1560-1881 CMI
       B1560-1837 HBI; Extracts C1560-1876 M1560-1875 IGI

WOOTTON ST LAWRENCE (Wesleyan) Newfound (Basingstoke Wesleyan Circuit, Surrey & North Hampshire Wesleyan Mission from 1900, Basingstoke Wesleyan Circuit from 1917) (Chapel erected 1883) (Records 1909+ HRO)

WOOTTON ST LAWRENCE (Primitive Methodist) Charter Alley (Reading Primitive Methodist Circuit, Silchester Primitive Methodist Circuit) (Existed by 1836, chapel opened 1848, closed 1993) (Records 1836+ BRO)

WOOTTON ST LAWRENCE (Primitive Methodist) (Basingstoke Primitive Methodist Circuit) (Chapel erected 1870)

WOOTTON ST LAWRENCE (Primitive Methodist) East Oakley (Basingstoke Primitive Methodist Circuit) (Chapel erected c1868, active)

WORLDHAM - See EAST WORLDHAM, WEST WORLDHAM

WORLD'S END (Primitive Methodist) - See HAMBLEDON

WORTHY - See HEADBOURNE WORTHY, KINGSWORTHY, MARTYR WORTHY

WORTING St Thomas of Canterbury (120) (Basingstoke Union)
OR   C1604-1913 M1609-1835 B1610-1971 Bn1754-1812,1825-1989 HRO (Fragmentary prior to 1732)
BT   1758,1780-1781,1783-1823,1825-1868 HRO (Mfm SLC)
Mfc   C1604-1913 M1609-1967 B1610-1971 Bn1754-1812 HRO
Cop   M1609-1812 Phillimore Vol 5 and Boyd; M1790-1812 Pallot
       C1604-1733 M1609-1812 B1610-1732 Bn1754-1812 (Ts) HRO
       M1609-1835 HMI; M1609-1921 CMI; B1610-1837 HBI

WORTING (Independent) - See BASINGSTOKE (Independent) Worting Town End

WYMERING St Peter & St Paul (578) (Fareham Union) (See also Cosham, Portsdown)
OR   C1654-1960 M1654-1985 B1654-1971 Bn1954-1987 PCRO
      (Entries prior to 1738 are for both Wymering and Widley)
BT   1780-1850,1856 HRO (Mfm SLC)
Mfc   C1654-1960 M1654-1977 B1654-1946 HRO, PCRO
Mfm C1654-1876 M1654-1876 B1654-1875 PCRO
Cop   M1654-1799 for Wymering & Widley (Ts,A by grooms) PCRO (CHU15/9D1)
      C1654-1895 M1654-1905 B1654-1678,1700-1812 PCI
      M1654-1836 HMI; M1700-1882 CMI; B1654-1837 HBI
      Extracts C1654-1876 M1654-1876 IGI

WYMERING St Barbara, Hilsea (Garrison Church) (Established 1888)
OR   C1877-1966 Bn1933-1962 RACD (Entries prior to 1888 are headed "The Military Chapel, Hilsea" and "The School Chapel, Hilsea")

WYMERING (Methodist) (Portsmouth Wesley Circuit) (Founded 1934 by members of Portsea Arundel Street) (Records 1935+ PCRO)

YATELEY St Peter (1,874) (Farnborough Incorporation; Hartley Wintney Union from 1869) (See also Cove, Fleet, Hawley)
OR   C1636-1975 M1636-1979 B1636-1974 Bn1973-1991 HRO (C and M deficient 1710-1730. Some fire damage in 1979, but most registers are legible)
BT   1732-1733,1780-1811,1813-1815,1817-1820,1822-1884 HRO (Mfm SLC)
Mfc   C1636-1975 M1636-1979 B1636-1974 HRO
Mfm C1636-1975 M1636-1978 B1636-1974 Bn1973-1978 HRO
      C1685-1876 M1754-1876 B1685-1876 SLC
Cop   M1636-1812 Phillimore Vol 2 and Boyd
      C1636-1844 M1636-1837 B1636-1897 (Ms & Ts) HRO; M1636-1837 HMI
      C1785-1844 M1754-1837 (Ts) HGS; M1636-1881 CMI; B1636-1837 HBI

YATELEY (Particular Baptist) Zoar Chapel, Cricket Hill (Chapel opened 1827, Church founded 1832, active)
OR   No information
Pc   B1859-1924 D1860-1882 HRO (Photocopy 530)

ISLE OF WIGHT PARISH LISTING

ADGESTONE (Bible Christian) - See BRADING

APSE HEATH (Wesleyan) - See NEWCHURCH

ARRETON St George (1,864) (Isle of Wight Incorporation) (See also Blackwater, Havenstreet, Wootton Bridge)

OR	C1653-1968 M1653-1966 B1653-1966 Bn1823-1968 IWRO (Gap in M 1740-1754)
BT	1780,1784,1786-1790,1792-1847,1849-1854,1856,1858 HRO (Mfm SLC)
Mfm	C1653-1968 M1653-1966 B1653-1966 Bn1823-1968 IWRO, SLC
Cop	C1653-1900 M1653-1900 B1653-1900 IWCI; M1837-1910 VMI M1654-1837 (Ms) SG; M1654-1837 Boyd

ARRETON (Wesleyan) Wootton Bridge (Newport Wesleyan Circuit, Ryde Wesleyan Circuit from 1861, Newport Wesleyan Circuit from 1878) (Chapels erected 1794 and 1840) (Records 1860+ IWRO)

OR	C1799-1837 PRO (RG 4/713)
Mfm	C1799-1837 PRO, HRO, IWRO, SLC
Cop	C1799-1837 IWCI; Extracts C1799-1837 IGI

ARRETON (Wesleyan) Havenstreet (Newport Wesleyan Circuit, Ryde Wesleyan Circuit from 1861) (Society existed by 1813, chapel opened 1833)

ARRETON (Wesleyan) Hale Common (Newport Wesleyan Circuit, Ryde Wesleyan Circuit from 1861, Ventnor Wesleyan Circuit from 1878) (Chapel opened 1837) (Records 1895+ IWRO)

ARRETON (Wesleyan) Blackwater (Newport Wesleyan Circuit) (Chapel erected 1845, closed) (Records 1941 [only] IWRO)

OR	C1913-1930 IWRO (MDR/21)

ARRETON (Wesleyan) Merstone (Newport Wesleyan Circuit) (Chapel erected 1848) (Records 1889+ IWRO)

Mfm	C1848-1979 SLC
Pc	C1848-1979 IWRO
Cop	C1848-1900 IWCI

ARRETON (Wesleyan) Wootton Bridge (This second Wesleyan chapel at Wootton Bridge existed by 1867; a Wesleyan Methodist Reformers' chapel referred to in 1878 is possibly the same chapel)

ARRETON (Bible Christian) (Isle of Wight Bible Christian Circuit, Newport Bible Christian Circuit from 1845) (House meetings from c1823, chapels erected 1866 and 1879, active) (Records 1929+ IWRO)

ARRETON (Bible Christian) Ebenezer Chapel, Littletown (Newport Bible Christian Circuit) (Chapel erected 1846, destroyed c1897 and replaced by Wootton Bible Christian Chapel)

ARRETON Cemetery (Records - Local Authority)
Pc   B1857-1987 IWRO

ARRETON Cemetery, Gore (Records - Local Authority)
Pc   B1909-1996 IWRO

ASHEY St Matthew (Mission church to Ryde All Saints; closed)
OR   M1922-1946 IWRO
Mfm   M1922-1946 IWRO, SLC

ASHEY Cemetery (Records - Local Authority)
Pc   B1911-1999 IWRO
Cop   Index to B1911-1999 Quigley

BARTON St Paul (Formed 1844 from Whippingham)
OR   C1844-1985 M1845-1972 B1844-1979 Bn1844-1984 IWRO
BT   1844-1874 HRO (Mfm SLC)
Mfm   C1844-1985 M1845-1972 B1844-1979 Bn1844-1984 IWRO, SLC
Cop   C1844-1900 M1845-1900 B1844-1900 IWCI; M1845-1910 VMI

BARTON Cemetery
OR   B1872+ Local Authority; Burial Order Books 1881-1890,1927-1938 IWRO
Pc   B1872-1954 IWRO
Cop   Index to B1872-1954 Quigley

BARTONS CORNER (Bible Christian) - See SHALFLEET

BEMBRIDGE Holy Trinity (Chapelry of Brading; separate parish 1884)
OR   C1827-1976 M1838-1988 B1827-1990 Bn1915-1969 IWRO
BT   1827-1847,1849-1875,1878,1880 HRO (Mfm SLC)
Mfm   C1827-1976 M1838-1983 B1827-1884 IWRO, SLC
Cop   C1827-1900 M1838-1900 B1827-1900 IWCI; M1838-1910 VMI

BEMBRIDGE (Wesleyan) (Newport Wesleyan Circuit, Ryde Wesleyan Circuit from
    1861) (Chapels erected 1826, 1844, 1934) (Records 1867+ IWRO)
OR   C1844-1918 IWRO (MDR/20)
Mfm   C1844-1918 SLC
Cop   C1844-1900 IWCI

BINSTEAD Holy Cross (258) (Isle of Wight Incorporation)
OR   C1708-1943 M1709-1976 B1710-1908 Bn1755-1828 IWRO
        (Few baptisms before 1722)
BT   1780-1782,1784-1786,1788-1805,1807,1809-1823,1825-1830,1832-1833,
        1835-1859,1861-1868 HRO (Mfm SLC)
Mfm   C1708-1943 M1709-1976 B1710-1908 Bn1755-1828 IWRO, SLC
Cop   C1708-1900 M1709-1900 B1710-1900 IWCI; Index to PR 1710-1837 (Ts) GL
        C1708-1796 M1709-1837 B1711-1781 (Ts,I) SG; M1837-1910 VMI
        Index to C1708-1796 M1709-1837 B1711-1781 (Ts) HRO

BINSTEAD (Wesleyan) (Ryde Wesleyan Circuit) (Chapel erected 1866)
    (Records 1866+ IWRO)

BINSTEAD Cemetery (Records - Local Authority)
Mfm   B1857-1978 SLC
Pc   B1857-2000 IWRO
Cop   Index to B1857-2000 Quigley

BLACKWATER (Wesleyan) - See ARRETON

BONCHURCH St Boniface (146) (Isle of Wight Incorporation)
OR   C1734-1958 M1754-1801,1811-1981 B1764-1939 Bn1754-1783 IWRO (For
        other Bonchurch entries, see Shanklin registers of C1724-1783 M1802-1812)
BT   1780-1790,1792-1807,1809,1811-1872,1874 HRO (Mfm SLC)
Mfm   C1734-1958 M1754-1801,1811-1981 B1764-1939 Bn1754-1783 IWRO, SLC
Cop   C1734-1900 M1754-1801,1811-1900 B1764-1900 IWCI; M1837-1910 VMI
        M1754-1836 Bn1777-1783 (Ts) SG; M1754-1836 Boyd
        Index to M1780-1836 (Ts) SG; M1780-1836 Pallot

BORDWOOD (Bible Christian) - See BRADING

BOWCOMBE (Bible Christian) - See CARISBROOKE

BRADING St Mary the Virgin (2,227) (Isle of Wight Incorporation) (See also
    Bembridge, Sandown)
OR   C1547-1954 M1547-1981 B1547-1941 Bn1754-1813,1823-1945 IWRO
BT   1780,1782-1790,1792-1859,1861 HRO (Mfm SLC)
Mfm   C1547-1954 M1547-1981 B1547-1941 Bn1754-1945 IWRO, SLC
Pc   B1941-1987 IWRO
Cop   C1547-1900 M1547-1900 B1547-1900 IWCI; M1837-1910 VMI
        M1547-1812 Phillimore Vol 12 and Boyd; M1790-1812 Pallot

BRADING (Independent, later United Reformed) The Mall (Founded 1832 as a
    village station of George Street Ryde, chapel erected 1847)
Mfm   B1847-1974 SLC
Pc   B1847-1974 IWRO
Cop   B1847-1858 IWCI

BRADING (Bible Christian) Salem Chapel (Isle of Wight Bible Christian Circuit,
    Shanklin Bible Christian Circuit from 1845) (Society founded 1823, rented chapel
    opened 1837, chapel erected 1867) (The 1851 Religious Census also lists a second
    Bible Christian chapel) (Records 1865+ IWRO)

BRADING (Bible Christian) Bordwood (Isle of Wight Bible Christian Circuit,
    Shanklin Bible Christian Circuit from 1845) (Meetings by 1842, chapel by 1882)

BRADING (Bible Christian) Adgestone (Shanklin Bible Christian Circuit) (Meetings
    by 1843) (Records 1903+ IWRO)

BRADING (Bible Christian) Lake (Shanklin Bible Christian Circuit) (Meetings by
    1849, chapel erected 1877, new church erected c1957) (Records 1952+ IWRO)

BRADING (No denomination) Providence Chapel (Chapel erected 1836; 1851
    Religious Census; no other references located)

BRIGHSTONE St Mary the Virgin (641) (Isle of Wight Incorporation)
OR   C1644-1940 M1644-1982 B1644-1889 Bn1824-1963 IWRO
BT   1780-1820,1822-1831,1833-1860,1863-1864,1869-1874 HRO (Mfm SLC)
Mfm   C1644-1940 M1644-1982 B1644-1889 Bn1824-1963 IWRO, SLC
Pc   B1889-1987 IWRO
Cop   C1644-1900 M1644-1900 B1644-1900 IWCI; M1837-1910 VMI

BRIGHSTONE (Bible Christian) Beulah Chapel (Isle of Wight Bible Christian Circuit, Newport Bible Christian Circuit from 1845, Yarmouth Bible Christian Circuit from 1862) (Chapel erected 1836)

BROOK St Mary the Virgin (125) (Isle of Wight Incorporation)
OR   C1653-1977 M1653-1977 B1653-1978 Bn1754-1812 IWRO (Gap 1671-1695)
BT   1780-1861 HRO (Mfm SLC) (Filed with Brading)
Mfm   C1653-1977 M1653-1977 B1653-1978 Bn1754-1812 IWRO, SLC
Cop   C1653-1900 M1653-1900 B1653-1900 IWCI; M1837-1910 VMI
        M1654-1659,1695-1776 (Ts,I) SG; Bn1824-1838 (Ts,I) SG, HRO

BROOK (Bible Christian) Jireh Chapel (Newport Bible Christian Circuit, Yarmouth Bible Christian Circuit from 1862) (Chapel erected 1848) (Records 1848,1859 [only] IWRO)

CALBOURNE All Saints (844) (Isle of Wight Incorporation) (See also Newtown)
OR   C1561-1957 M1559-1980 B1560-1803,1813-1891 Bn1772-1805,1832-1905,
        1926-1941 IWRO (Gap in M 1726-1741; burial register 1804-1812 missing)
BT   1757,1780,1782-1829,1831-1870,1872 HRO (Mfm SLC)
Mfm   C1561-1957 M1559-1936 B1560-1803,1813-1891 Bn1772-1805,1832-1905
        IWRO, SLC
Cop   C1561-1900 M1559-1900 B1560-1891 IWCI (Includes B1804-1812 from BT)
        M1837-1910 VMI; M1559-1812 Phillimore Vol 12; M1813-1837 (Ms) SG
        Index to M1780-1837 (Ts) SG; M1559-1837 Boyd; M1790-1812 Pallot

CALBOURNE (Independent) Porchfield (Founded 1810, new chapel 1846, closed)
Mfm   C1848-1908 B1848-1978 SLC
Pc   C1848-1908 B1848-1978 IWRO (Some baptisms at Porchfield prior to 1837
        were registered at Cowes, Union Road)
Cop   C1848-1900 B1848-1858 IWCI

CALBOURNE (Wesleyan) (Newport Wesleyan Circuit) (Existed by 1882)
        (Records 1882+ IWRO)
OR   C1884-1946,1966-1967 IWRO (MDR/39A)
Mfm   C1884-1946,1966-1967 SLC
Cop   C1884-1900 IWCI

CALBOURNE (Bible Christian) Bethesda Chapel, Porchfield (Isle of Wight Bible Christian Circuit, Newport Bible Christian Circuit from 1845) (Meetings from 1824, chapel erected 1852, closed 1991)

CARISBROOKE St Mary (4,713) (Isle of Wight Incorporation)
OR   C1572-1981 M1573-1992 B1572-1897 Bn1754-1793,1816-1820,1887-1895,
        1940-1951,1968-1990 IWRO (Gap in B 1676-1696)
BT   1727-1729,1780-1792,1794-1808,1810-1847,1857-1861 HRO (Mfm SLC)
Mfm   C1572-1981 M1573-1982 B1572-1897 Bn1754-1793,1816-1820,1887-1895,
        1940-1951,1968-1982 IWRO, SLC
Cop   C1572-1900 M1573-1900 B1572-1897 IWCI; M1837-1910 VMI
        M1572-1837 (Ms) SG; Index to M1780-1837 (Ts) SG
        M1572-1837 Boyd; M1780-1837 Pallot; Extracts M1572-1837 IGI

CARISBROOKE St Nicholas, Carisbrooke Castle (317) (Isle of Wight Incorporation)
OR   C1723-1795,1923-1961 M1723-1754,1769,1922-1988 B1744 IWRO
BT   None
Mfm   C1723-1795,1923-1961 M1723-1754,1769 B1744 IWRO, SLC
Cop   C1723-1795 M1723-1754,1769 B1744 IWCI
        M1723-1754,1769 (Ms) SG; M1723-1754 Boyd

CARISBROOKE St John the Baptist (Formed 1837 from St Mary; formerly known as
    Newport St John the Baptist)
OR   C1837-1965 M1846-1967 B1837-1940 Bn1968-1987 IWRO
BT   1838-1839,1847,1849-1878 HRO (Mfm SLC)
Mfm   C1837-1965 M1846-1967 B1837-1940 IWRO, SLC
Cop   C1837-1900 M1846-1900 B1837-1900 IWCI; M1846-1910 VMI

CARISBROOKE St Michael, Parkhurst Garrison
OR   C1855-1945 B1855-1956 Bn1934-1965 IWRO (Catalogued under Newport)
Mfm   C1855-1945 B1855-1956 Bn1934-1965 IWRO, SLC
Cop   C1855-1900 B1855-1900 IWCI

CARISBROOKE (Baptist) - See NEWPORT (Particular Baptist) Castlehold

CARISBROOKE (Wesleyan) Gunville (Newport Wesleyan Circuit) (Society formed
    c1814, chapel erected 1816, probably lapsed before 1900)

CARISBROOKE (Wesleyan) Parkhurst (Newport Wesleyan Circuit, Ryde Wesleyan
    Circuit from 1861, Newport & Cowes Wesleyan Circuit from 1878) (Chapel at
    Noke Common erected 1836, Parkhurst Chapel c1872) (Records 1882+ IWRO)
OR   M1938-1995 IWRO (AC 96/46)

CARISBROOKE (Wesleyan) Chillerton (Founded c1845)

CARISBROOKE (Primitive Methodist) (Newport & Cowes Primitive Methodist
    Circuit) (Society existed by 1840, Castle Street Chapel 1859, Chapel-on-the-Hill
    opened 1884, closed 1984 and united with Gunville (former Bible Christian) to
    form Carisbrooke & Gunville Methodist Church) (Records 1883+ IWRO)
OR   C1960-1969 IWRO (MDR/22)

CARISBROOKE (Primitive Methodist) Beulah Chapel, Gunville (Newport & Cowes
    Primitive Methodist Circuit) (Existed c1849-1883)

CARISBROOKE (Bible Christian) Chillerton (Isle of Wight Bible Christian Circuit, Newport Bible Christian Circuit from 1845) (Society founded 1823, chapel erected 1860) (Records 1881+ IWRO)

CARISBROOKE (Bible Christian) Bethel Chapel, Gunville (Isle of Wight Bible Christian Circuit, Newport Bible Christian Circuit from 1845) (Chapels erected 1831,1848,1907) (Records 1913+ IWRO)
OR   C1951-1981 IWRO (MDR/53)

CARISBROOKE (Bible Christian) Bowcombe (Newport Bible Christian Circuit) (Chapels erected 1882 and 1908) (Records 1908+ IWRO)
OR   C1951-1989 (MDR/55)

CARISBROOKE Cemetery, Mount Joy
OR   B1858+ Local Authority; Burial Order Books 1859-1863,1864-1884, 1886-1889,1891-1894,1895-1899,1900-1905,1907-1938 IWRO
Pc   B1858-2000 IWRO; Burial Order Books 1858-1859,1863-1864 IWRO
Cop   Index to Burial Order Books 1859-1938 Quigley; Index to B1938-2000 Quigley

CARISBROOKE House of Industry (Workhouse for Isle of Wight Incorporation)
OR   No registers survive. Other records at IWRO
BT   1782-1783,1813-1827,1829-1871 HRO (Mfm SLC) (Photocopy at IWRO)
Cop   1782-1783,1813-1827,1829-1871 (BT) IWCI

CHALE St Andrew (544) (Isle of Wight Incorporation)
OR   C1685-1866 M1699-1989 B1679-1906 Bn1824-1895 IWRO
BT   1780-1785,1787-1790,1792-1861,1870 HRO (Mfm SLC)
Mfm   C1685-1987 M1699-1979 B1679-1906 Bn1824-1895 IWRO, SLC
Pc   C1866-1987 B1907-1987 IWRO
Cop   C1685-1900 M1699-1900 B1679-1900 IWCI; M1837-1910 VMI
        M1699-1837 (Ms) SG; M1699-1837 Boyd

CHALE (Wesleyan) (Newport Wesleyan Circuit, Ventnor Wesleyan Circuit from 1878) (Chapels erected 1833 and 1888) (Records 1842+ IWRO)
Mfm   C1869-1979 SLC
Pc   C1869-1979 IWRO
Cop   C1869-1900 IWCI

CHALE (Bible Christian) Zoar Chapel (Isle of Wight Bible Christian Circuit, Newport Bible Christian Circuit from 1845) (Chapel erected 1840) (Records 1909+ IWRO)

CHILLERTON (Wesleyan, Bible Christian) - See CARISBROOKE

COLWELL (General Baptist) - See FRESHWATER

COWES St Mary the Virgin (Population included in Northwood) (Isle of Wight Incorporation) (Chapelry of Northwood; district formed 1832; known as West Cowes until 1894)

OR   C1679-1703,1761-1977 M1679-1703,1838-1970 B1679-1703,1761-1966 Bn1897-1918,1946-1969 IWRO

BT   1808-1810,1812-1831,1833-1843,1845-1873 HRO (Mfm SLC)

Mfm   C1679-1703,1761-1977 M1679-1703,1838-1970 B1679-1703,1761-1966 Bn1897-1918,1946-1969 IWRO, SLC

Cop   C1679-1703,1761-1900 M1679-1703,1838-1900 B1679-1703,1761-1900 IWCI; M1838-1910 VMI; M1680-1703 (Ms) SG; M1680-1703 Boyd Extracts M1680-1703 IGI

COWES Holy Trinity (District formed 1832 from Northwood; see also Gurnard)

OR   C1833-1913 M1855-1958 B1834-1927 Bn1906-1976 IWRO

BT   1833-1854 HRO (Mfm SLC) (Baptisms only; filed with Cowes St Mary)

Mfm   C1833-1913 M1855-1958 B1834-1927 IWRO, SLC

Cop   C1833-1900 M1855-1900 B1834-1900 IWCI; M1855-1910 VMI

COWES St Faith

OR   C1927-1972 M1928-1965 B1927-1977 IWRO

Mfm   C1927-1972 M1928-1965 B1927-1977 IWRO, SLC

COWES (Roman Catholic) St Thomas of Canterbury (Founded 1796 as Holy Trinity, St Thomas from 1832)

OR   C1796+ M1837+ B1828+ Inc

Pc   C1796-1918 M1837-1839,1849,1860-1942 B1828-1833 IWRO

Cop   C1796-1856 M1837-1839,1849 B1828-1833 (I) CRS Vol 59
C1796-1900 M1837-1839,1849,1860-1900 IWCI
M1837-1839,1860-1942 VMI
Extracts C1796-1856 M1802,1837-1839,1849 IGI

COWES (Baptist) Victoria Road (Founded 1866, active)

COWES (Independent, now Congregational) Union Road or Sun Hill (Chapel opened 1804, Church formed 1805, active)

OR   C1804-1837 B1821-1834 PRO (RG 4/608) (Includes entries for Porchfield [Calbourne] Independent); C1804+ M1870+ Inc

Mfm   C1804-1837 B1821-1834 PRO, HRO, IWRO, SLC
C1804-1901 M1870-1893 SLC (From the photocopy at IWRO)

Pc   C1804-1901 M1870-1893 IWRO

Cop   C1804-1900 B1821-1834 IWCI; Extracts C1804-1837 IGI

COWES (Wesleyan) Birmingham Road (Newport Wesleyan Circuit, Ryde Wesleyan Circuit from 1861, Newport Wesleyan Circuit from 1878) (Bath Road Chapel erected 1804, new chapels opened 1831 and 1901) (Records 1860+ IWRO)

OR   C1832-1837 PRO (RG 4/1108) (Listed as Northwood; includes entries for other chapels); C1837-1908 IWRO (MDR/9) (Includes other chapels)

Mfm   C1832-1837 PRO, HRO, IWRO, SLC
C1837-1908 SLC (Listed as Newport & Cowes Circuit)

Cop   C1832-1900 IWCI; Extracts C1832-1837 IGI (Listed as Northwood)

COWES (Wesleyan Methodist Reformers, United Methodist Free Church from 1857) St Mary's Street, Mill Hill Road (Newport, Ryde, & Cowes United Methodist Circuit from 1907) (Chapel erected 1853, chapel in Mill Hill Road erected 1889) (Records 1861+ IWRO)
OR   M1915-1963 IWRO (MDR/50-51)

COWES (Primitive Methodist) Market Hill, Beckford Road (Newport & Cowes Primitive Methodist Circuit) (Chapel at Market Hill existed by 1850, Beckford Road Chapel erected 1889, possibly closed in 1930s) (Records c1930+ IWRO)

COWES (Bible Christian) Salem Chapel, Cross Street (Newport Bible Christian Circuit) (Chapel erected 1853, probably closed by 1890)

COWES (Spiritualist) Market Hill (Existed by 1939)

COWES Cemetery - See NORTHWOOD Cemetery

EAST COWES St James (Formed 1843 from Whippingham)
OR   C1834-1987 M1836,1844-1984 B1836-1966 Bn1942-1984 IWRO
Mfm   C1834-1915 M1836,1844-1938 B1836-1959 Bn1942-1984 IWRO, SLC
Cop   C1834-1900 M1836,1844-1900 B1836-1900 IWCI; M1844-1910 VMI
       M1836 (only) (Ms) SG; M1836 Boyd

EAST COWES (Roman Catholic) St David (Founded 1906)
OR   1908+ Inc

EAST COWES (Independent) Bridge Square (Founded 1829)
OR   C1829-1837 PRO (RG 4/1107)
       C1829-1917 M1859-1939 B1867-1939 D1834-1912 IWRO (AC 79/17)
       (The deaths occur in membership lists 1829-1929)
Mfm   C1829-1837 PRO, HRO, IWRO, SLC
Cop   C1829-1900 IWCI; Extracts C1829-1837 IGI

EAST COWES (Wesleyan) Adelaide Grove (Newport Wesleyan Circuit, Ryde Wesleyan Circuit from 1861, Newport Wesleyan Circuit from 1878) (Existed by 1855) (Records 1919+ IWRO)
Mfm   C1885-1920 SLC
Pc   C1885-1920 IWRO
Cop   C1885-1900 IWCI

EAST COWES (Bible Christian) Clarence Road, Osborne Road (Newport Bible Christian Circuit) (Chapel erected 1859, new chapel 1897) (Records 1885+ IWRO)

EAST COWES Cemetery (Records - Local Authority)
Pc   B1877-1933 IWRO
Cop   Index to B1877-1933 Quigley

EAST WIGHT Methodist Circuit (Formed 1934) (Records 1934+ IWRO)

ELMFIELD (Independent) - See ST HELENS

FRESHWATER All Saints (1,184) (Isle of Wight Incorporation) (See also Totland Bay)
OR   C1576-1965 M1576-1960 B1576-1956 Bn1754-1816,1865-1907,1938-1975 IWRO
BT   1780-1790,1792-1837,1840-1872 HRO (Mfm SLC)
Mfm   C1576-1965 M1576-1960 B1576-1956 Bn1754-1816,1865-1907,1938-1975 IWRO, SLC
Pc   B1956-1987 IWRO
Cop   C1576-1900 M1576-1900 B1576-1900 IWCI; M1837-1910 VMI
       M1813-1837 (Ms) SG; M1576-1812 Phillimore Vol 12
       M1576-1837 Boyd; M1790-1812 Pallot

FRESHWATER (General Baptist) Ebenezer Chapel, Colwell Road, Colwell (Founded 1834 as a General Baptist Church by seceders from Wellow Particular Baptist Church, Shalfleet; active)
OR   1834+ Inc
Cop   Membership list 1834-1963, adult baptisms 1835-1964, B1837-1907 printed in "A History of the Baptist Church at Colwell, Isle of Wight" by Basil Twyman Cheverton (The "burials" are probably from monumental inscriptions) B1837-1858 IWCI

FRESHWATER (Baptist) Norton Green (Erected c1827, closed 1834, reopened 1838 as a village station of Newport and later of Yarmouth, closed by 1890)

FRESHWATER (Independent) Norton (1851 Religious Census; no other references located)

FRESHWATER (Independent, now United Reformed) Guyers Road (Founded 1882, active)

FRESHWATER (Wesleyan) Providence Chapel, Middleton Green (Newport Wesleyan Circuit) (Chapel erected 1824) (Records 1824+ IWRO)
OR   C1834-1959 IWRO (MDR/23)
Mfm   C1834-1959 SLC

FRESHWATER (Bible Christian) (Yarmouth Bible Christian Circuit) (Chapel erected 1866)

GATCOMBE St Olave (263) (Isle of Wight Incorporation)
OR   C1560-1926 M1560-1955 B1561-1979 IWRO (Gap in B 1769-1782)
BT   1780-1783,1785-1794,1797-1843,1845-1847,1849-1858,1861-1864,1872 HRO (Mfm SLC)
Mfm   C1560-1926 M1560-1955 B1561-1979 IWRO, SLC
Cop   C1560-1900 M1560-1900 B1561-1900 IWCI; M1837-1910 VMI
       C1673-1769 M1674-1751 B1673-1685 (Ts) SG
       M1560-1835 (Ts,I) SG; Index to M1780-1835 (Ts) SG
       M1560-1835 Boyd; M1780-1835 Pallot; Extracts M1560-1835 IGI

GATTEN - See SHANKLIN St Paul

GODSHILL All Saints (1,305) (Isle of Wight Incorporation)
OR   C1678-1956 M1679-1934 B1678-1880 Bn1754-1813,1823-1911 IWRO
BT   1780-1824,1826-1843,1845-1847,1849-1872 HRO (Mfm SLC)
Mfm   C1678-1956 M1679-1934 B1678-1880 Bn1754-1813,1823-1911 IWRO, SLC
Pc   B1881-1986 IWRO
Cop   C1678-1900 M1679-1900 B1678-1900 IWCI; M1837-1910 VMI
        M1679-1837 (Ms) SG; Index to M1780-1837 (Ts) SG; M1679-1837 Boyd
        B1679-1715 (Ts) SG, HRO; M1780-1837 Pallot; Extracts C1678-1837 IGI

GODSHILL (Particular Baptist) Roud (Chapel erected 1830)

GODSHILL (Wesleyan) (Newport Wesleyan Circuit, Ventnor Wesleyan Circuit from
    1878) (Wooden chapel opened 1790, new chapel erected 1838, active) (Records
    1866+ IWRO)

GODSHILL (Bible Christian) Providence Chapel, Rookley (Isle of Wight Bible
    Christian Circuit, Newport Bible Christian Circuit from 1845) (Society formed
    1823, chapels erected c1832 and 1859) (Records 1952+ IWRO, with Cowes
    Birmingham Road)

GODSHILL (Bible Christian) Sandford (Isle of Wight Bible Christian Circuit,
    Shanklin Bible Christian Circuit from 1845) (Society formed 1824 at Godshill,
    chapels at Sandford erected 1848, 1867, 1910, active) (Records 1917+ IWRO)

GUNVILLE (Wesleyan, Primitive Methodist, Bible Christian) - See CARISBROOKE

GURNARD All Saints (District formed 1893 from Cowes Holy Trinity)
OR   C1902-1977 M1931-1969 B1902-1994 IWRO
Mfm   C1902-1977 M1931-1969 IWRO, SLC
Cop   Index to B1902-1994 Quigley

GURNARD (Primitive Methodist) - See NORTHWOOD

HALE COMMON (Wesleyan) - See ARRETON

HAVENSTREET St Peter (Formed 1853 from Arreton & Newchurch)
OR   C1852+ M1853+ B1852+ Inc
Mfm   C1852-1930 M1853-1976 B1852-1979 IWRO, SLC
Pc   C1852-1930 M1853-1976 B1852-1979 IWRO
Cop   C1852-1900 M1853-1900 B1852-1900 IWCI; M1853-1910 VMI

HAVENSTREET (Wesleyan) - See ARRETON

HAYLANDS (Independent) - See RYDE

HUNNY HILL (Wesleyan) - See NEWPORT

ISLE OF WIGHT Wesleyan Circuit - See NEWPORT Wesleyan Circuit

ISLE OF WIGHT Primitive Methodist Mission - See NEWPORT & COWES
    Primitive Methodist Circuit

ISLE OF WIGHT Bible Christian Circuit (Formed 1823; divided 1845 into Newport Circuit and Shanklin Circuit. Included chapels at Arreton, Brading, Brighstone, Calbourne, Carisbrooke, Chale, East Cowes, Godshill, Newchurch, Newport, Ryde, St Helens, Sandown, Shalfleet, Shanklin, Ventnor, and Whitwell)
OR   C1824-1837 PRO (RG 4/2299); C1837-1860 IWRO (MDR/10) (Entries from 1845 are for Newport Bible Christian Circuit)
Mfm   C1824-1837 PRO, HRO, IWRO, SLC; C1837-1860 SLC
Cop   C1824-1860 IWCI; Extracts C1824-1837 IGI

ISLE OF WIGHT Incorporation Workhouse - See CARISBROOKE House of Industry

ISLE OF WIGHT (EAST) Bible Christian Circuit - See SHANKLIN Bible Christian Circuit

KINGSTON St James (83) (Isle of Wight Incorporation) (Closed)
OR   C1647-1984 M1647-1959 B1647-1984 Bn1823-1978 IWRO
BT   1813,1815-1835,1837,1840-1842,1844-1845,1847-1856,1858,1860-1870 HRO (Mfm SLC)
Mfm   C1647-1984 M1647-1959 B1647-1984 Bn1823-1978 IWRO, SLC
Cop   C1647-1900 M1647-1900 B1647-1900 IWCI; M1840-1910 VMI
        C1647-1795 M1647-1747 B1649-1793 (Ts,I) SG, HRO
        M1647-1832 (Ms) SG; M1647-1832 Boyd

LAKE The Good Shepherd (Chapelry of Sandown; separate parish 1930)
OR   C1879+ M1930+ Inc
Pc   C1879-1980 M1930-1975 IWRO

LAKE (Bible Christian) - See BRADING

LANGBRIDGE (Independent) - See NEWCHURCH

LITTLETOWN (Bible Christian) - See ARRETON

MARK'S CORNER (Primitive Methodist) - See NORTHWOOD

MERSTONE (Wesleyan) - See ARRETON

MOTTISTONE St Peter & St Paul (142) (Isle of Wight Incorporation)
OR   C1680-1977 M1680-1977 B1680-1974 Bn1755-1812,1824-1978 IWRO
BT   1780-1783,1785-1835,1837-1852,1854-1861 HRO (Mfm SLC)
Mfm   C1680-1977 M1680-1977 B1680-1974 Bn1755-1812,1824-1978 IWRO, SLC
Cop   C1680-1900 M1680-1900 B1680-1900 IWCI; M1837-1910 VMI
        M1680-1835 (Ms) SG; Index to M1780-1812 (Ts) SG
        M1680-1835 Boyd; M1790-1812 Pallot; Extracts M1680-1813 IGI

NETTLESTONE (Bible Christian) - See ST HELENS

NEWBRIDGE (Primitive Methodist, Bible Christian) - See SHALFLEET

NEWCHURCH All Saints (4,928) (Isle of Wight Incorporation) (See also
Havenstreet, Ryde, Ventnor, Wroxall)

OR   C1692-1845 M1692-1987 B1690-1980 Bn1842-1865 (plus B1884-1933 in the
      new burial ground) IWRO
BT   1724,1780-1868,1872 HRO (Mfm SLC)
Mfm   C1692-1980 M1692-1947 B1690-1980 Bn1842-1865 (plus B1884-1933 in the
      new burial ground) IWRO, SLC
Pc   C1846-1980 IWRO
Cop   C1692-1900 M1692-1900 B1690-1900 IWCI; M1837-1910 VMI
      M1692-1786 (Ts) SG; M1692-1733,1767-1786 (Ts) HRO
      Index to B1865-1980 Quigley

NEWCHURCH (Independent) Langbridge (Chapel opened 1845 as a village station
of George Street Ryde)

NEWCHURCH (Independent) Wroxall (Listed in White's Directory 1878; no other
references located)

NEWCHURCH (Wesleyan) Apse Heath (Ryde Wesleyan Circuit, Ventnor Wesleyan
Circuit from 1878) (Chapel erected c1873) (Records 1875+ IWRO)

NEWCHURCH (Wesleyan) Redhill, Wroxall - See NITON

NEWCHURCH (Primitive Methodist) Wroxall (Ryde & Sandown Primitive
Methodist Circuit) (Chapel erected 1875) (Records 1914+ IWRO)

NEWCHURCH (Bible Christian) Providence Chapel, Wroxall (Isle of Wight Bible
Christian Circuit, Shanklin Bible Christian Circuit from 1845) (Chapels erected
c1838 and 1887) (Records 1897+ IWRO)

NEWPORT St Thomas the Apostle & St Thomas of Canterbury (4,081) (Isle of Wight
Incorporation)

OR   C1541-1964 M1541-1971 B1541-1948 Bn1813-1837,1845-1883 IWRO
      (Gap in B 1751-1775)
BT   1681,1780-1840,1843-1852,1854-1879 HRO (Mfm SLC)
Mfm   C1541-1964 M1541-1971 B1541-1948 Bn1813-1837,1845-1883 IWRO, SLC
Cop   C1541-1900 M1541-1900 B1541-1900 IWCI; M1790-1837 Pallot
      M1541-1837 Phillimore Vol 14; M1651-1675 Boyd; M1837-1910 VMI

NEWPORT St John the Baptist - See CARISBROOKE St John the Baptist

NEWPORT St Michael, Parkhurst Garrison - See CARISBROOKE St Michael

NEWPORT (Roman Catholic) St Thomas of Canterbury (Founded 1791)

OR   C1792-1909 M1785,1807-1855 D1793-1795,1839-1915 (plus Z1793-1800
      M1786,1791 for two families) Portsmouth (Catholic) Diocesan Archives
Pc   M1856-1960 IWRO
Cop   C1792-1856 M1795,1807-1855 D1793-1795,1839-1857,1883,1887 (plus
      Z1793-1800 M1786,1791 for two families) (I) CRS Vol 59
      C1792-1856 M1785,1807-1900 D1793-1795,1839-1857 IWCI
      M1837-1910 VMI; Extracts C1792-1856 M1785,1807-1855 IGI

NEWPORT (Society of Friends) High Street (Meeting House erected 1694 in Pyle Street, demolished c1804, moved to High Street, Meeting House at Castlehold, High Street, erected c1860, used until c1922)

NEWPORT (General Baptist, Unitarian) High Street (General Baptist congregation founded 1726, chapel in Pyle Street erected 1728, High Street Chapel erected 1774, became Unitarian soon after 1800, active) (Records 1726+ IWRO)
OR   Z1739-1837 D1744-1756 PRO (RG 4/36,42) (Listed as Presbyterian) (Entries prior to 1758 are for one family only)
       Z1739-1837 C1826-1854,1885-1975 M1885-1979 B1884-1980 IWRO (NC/U/11A,11B,43) (The birth entries are copies)
       D certificates 1887-1922 IWRO (NC/U/31)
Pc   C1885-1975 M1885-1979 B1884-1980 IWRO
Mfm   Z1739-1837 D1744-1756 PRO, HRO, IWRO, SLC
Cop   Z1739-1837 (Ts,I) SG, IWRO (The IWRO copy is on film)
       Z1739-1837 D1744-1756 IWCI; Extracts Z1739-1837 IGI

NEWPORT (Particular Baptist) Castlehold Chapel, High Street (Founded 1809 at Town Lane, Castlehold Chapel erected 1812, active) (Records 1809+ IWRO)
OR   Z1807-1837 B1853-1858 PRO (RG 4/402,2107) (Births catalogued as Newport, burials catalogued as Carisbrooke)
       Adult baptisms 1810-1887 B1853-1877 D1813-1886 IWRO (Burials are in NEP/BAP/3, other entries in membership lists 1809-1887 in NEP/BAP/1-2)
Mfm   Z1807-1837 B1853-1858 PRO, HRO, IWRO, SLC
       B1853-1877 (from the photocopy at IWRO) SLC
Pc   B1853-1877 IWRO
Cop   Z1807-1837 B1853-1858 IWCI; Extracts Z1807-1837 IGI

NEWPORT (Independent, now Congregational) Lower St James Street (Founded 1662, chapels erected 1699 and 1848, active) (Records 1784+ IWRO)
OR   C1784-1837 PRO (RG 4/124,3563)
       C1784-1953 (many gaps) IWRO (AC 99/37/16)
Mfm   C1784-1837 PRO, HRO, IWRO, SLC
Cop   C1784-1837 IWCI; Extracts C1784-1837 IGI

NEWPORT (Independent) Nodehill (Chapel opened 1804 by seceders from St James Street; closed 1881 and reunited with St James Street) (Records 1804+ IWRO)
OR   C1804-1837 PRO (RG 4/722)
       C1804-1878 M1857-1873 B1806-1879 IWRO (AC 99/37/17)
Mfm   C1804-1837 PRO, HRO, IWRO, SLC
Cop   C1804-1837 IWCI; Extracts C1804-1837 IGI

NEWPORT (Unitarian) High Street - See NEWPORT (General Baptist, Unitarian)

NEWPORT Wesleyan Circuit (The Isle of Wight Wesleyan Circuit, which had existed briefly in 1787 and 1789, was formed in 1809 from Portsmouth Circuit; renamed Newport Circuit in 1833 and Newport & Cowes Circuit in 1878. Included chapels at Arreton, Bembridge, Calbourne, Carisbrooke, Chale, Cowes, East Cowes, Freshwater, Godshill, Newport, Niton, Northwood, Ryde, St Helens, Sandown, Shalfleet, Shorwell, Ventnor, and Yarmouth) (Records 1835+ IWRO)
OR   C1813-1837 PRO (RG 4/1388) (Listed as West Cowes)
       C1813-1850 IWRO (MDR/1) (For 1850+ see Newport Wesleyan, Pyle Street)
Mfm C1813-1837 PRO, HRO, IWRO, SLC; C1813-1850 SLC
Cop   C1813-1850 IWCI; Extracts C1813-1837 IGI

NEWPORT (Wesleyan) Pyle Street (Newport Wesleyan Circuit) (Society formed by 1753 in Node Hill, chapel in Town Lane opened 1781, Pyle Street Chapel opened 1804, closed c1970 and converted to a theatre) (Records 1828+ IWRO)
OR   C1850-1977 M1899-1969 IWRO (MDR/26-38) (Includes baptisms at other chapels in the circuit)
Mfm C1850-1924 M1899-1905 SLC
Cop   C1850-1900 IWCI

NEWPORT (Wesleyan) Hunny Hill (Newport Wesleyan Circuit) (Founded 1901) (Records 1901+ IWRO)
OR   C1926-1956 IWRO (MDR/24)

NEWPORT (Wesleyan Methodist Reformers) Pyle Street (Chapel erected 1852, sold to Primitive Methodists c1878)

NEWPORT Primitive Methodist Mission - See NEWPORT & COWES Primitive Methodist Circuit

NEWPORT (Primitive Methodist) Pyle Street (Newport & Cowes Primitive Methodist Circuit) (Chapel in Holyrood Street erected c1836, moved to Pyle Street by 1855, and to the former Wesleyan Reformers' Chapel in Pyle Street c1878) (Records 1858+ IWRO)
OR   C1873-1896 IWRO (MDR/47)
Mfm C1873-1896 SLC
Cop   C1873-1896 IWCI

NEWPORT Bible Christian Circuit (Formed 1845 from the Isle of Wight Circuit; later known as Newport & Ryde Circuit, then Newport Ryde & Cowes Circuit. Included chapels at Arreton, Brighstone, Brook, Calbourne, Carisbrooke, Chale, Cowes, East Cowes, Godshill, Newport, Ryde, Shalfleet, and Wootton) (Records 1858+ IWRO)
OR   C1861-1983 IWRO (MDR/12-14,54) (For earlier entries see Isle of Wight Bible Christian Circuit)
Mfm C1861-1901 SLC
Cop   C1861-1900 IWCI

NEWPORT (Bible Christian) Zion Chapel, Quay Street (Isle of Wight Bible Christian Circuit, Newport Bible Christian Circuit from 1845) (Chapels erected 1843 and 1880, active) (Records 1878+ IWRO)
OR   C1923-1948 M1949-1968 IWRO (MDR/40-43)

NEWPORT (Catholic Apostolic Church) Holyrood Street (Established by 1867 in a former Primitive Methodist Chapel, possibly ceased by 1890)

NEWPORT Cemetery, Fairlee Road
OR   B1858+ Local Authority; Burial Order Books 1859-1938 IWRO
BT   B1859-1923 HRO (1859-1863 filed with Newport St Thomas)
Pc   B1858-2000 IWRO
Cop   Index to B1858-2000 Quigley; Index to Burial Order Books 1859-1938 Quigley

NEWPORT & COWES Wesleyan Circuit - See NEWPORT Wesleyan Circuit

NEWPORT & COWES Primitive Methodist Circuit (The Isle of Wight Primitive Methodist Mission was established c1836 as a mission of the Hull [Yorkshire] Circuit; renamed Newport Mission in 1862 and Newport & Cowes Mission or Circuit in 1893. Included chapels at Carisbrooke, Cowes, Newport, Northwood, Ryde, and Shalfleet) (Records 1836+ IWRO)
OR   C1838-1872,1882-1884,1916-1934 IWRO (MDR/19)
Mfm   C1838-1872,1882-1884,1916-1934 SLC
Cop   C1838-1872,1882-1884 IWCI

NEWPORT & RYDE Bible Christian Circuit - See NEWPORT Bible Christian Circuit

NEWPORT, RYDE, & COWES Bible Christian Circuit - See NEWPORT Bible Christian Circuit

NEWTOWN The Holy Spirit (Formed 1871 from Calbourne & Shalfleet)
OR   C1872?+ M1872+ B1872+ Bn1872+ Inc
Pc   M1872-1990 IWRO
Cop   M1872-1900 IWCI; M1872-1910 VMI

NINGWOOD (Primitive Methodist, Bible Christian) - See SHALFLEET

NITON St John the Baptist (573) (Isle of Wight Incorporation)
OR   C1560-1986 M1561-1981 B1559-1909 Bn1754-1812,1824-1873,1884-1947 IWRO (Gaps in C 1637-1654, M 1647-1654)
BT   1780-1787,1789-1860,1862-1863,1865-1872 HRO (Mfm SLC)
Mfm   C1560-1986 M1561-1981 B1559-1909 Bn1754-1812,1824-1873,1884-1947 IWRO, SLC
Pc   B1909-1987 IWRO
Cop   C1560-1900 M1561-1900 B1559-1900 IWCI; M1837-1910 VMI
       M1813-1837 (Ms) SG; M1561-1812 Phillimore Vol 12
       M1561-1837 Boyd; M1790-1812 Pallot

NITON (Particular Baptist) St Catherine's Chapel, Institute Hill (Founded 1835, new chapel erected 1849, active)
OR   Records 1835+ Inc
Mfm   Adult baptisms 1850-1946 D1855-1897,1931-1947 (plus a few deaths 1914-1930) SLC (From the photocopies at IWRO)
Pc   Adult baptisms 1850-1946 D1855-1897,1931-1947 (plus a few deaths 1914-1930) IWRO (In membership lists 1835-1946)

NITON (Wesleyan) (Newport Wesleyan Circuit, Ventnor Wesleyan Circuit from 1878) (Society formed c1835 at Redhill, Wroxall, moved to new chapel at Niton in 1864, active) (Records 1904+ IWRO)

NOKE COMMON (Wesleyan) - See CARISBROOKE (Wesleyan) Parkhurst

NORTH ARRETON - See WOOTTON BRIDGE

NORTHWOOD St John the Baptist (4,491) (Isle of Wight Incorporation) (See also Cowes)
OR   C1539-1968 M1539-1983 B1539-1914 Bn1778-1804,1822-1887,1921-1965 IWRO
BT   1709-1712,1727-1729,1780-1783,1785-1870 HRO (Mfm SLC) (1828 is filed with Cowes)
Mfm   C1539-1968 M1539-1970 B1539-1914 Bn1778-1804,1822-1887 IWRO, SLC
Cop   C1539-1900 M1539-1900 B1539-1900 IWCI; M1837-1910 VMI
        C1544-1656 M1607-1655 B1539-1656 (Ts) SG
        M1538-1837 (Ms) SG; Index to M1780-1837 (Ts) SG
        M1538-1837 Boyd; M1780-1837 Pallot; Extracts M1538-1837 IGI

NORTHWOOD (Wesleyan) Tinker's Lane, Pallance Road (Newport Wesleyan Circuit, Ryde Wesleyan Circuit from 1861, Newport Wesleyan Circuit from 1878) (Opened 1820) (Records 1952+ IWRO, some with Cowes Birmingham Road)
OR   C1914-1998 IWRO (AC 2000/75)

NORTHWOOD (Wesleyan) Noke Common - See CARISBROOKE (Wesleyan) Parkhurst

NORTHWOOD (Primitive Methodist) Mark's Corner (Newport & Cowes Primitive Methodist Circuit) (Chapel erected 1833) (Records 1883+ IWRO)

NORTHWOOD (Primitive Methodist) Gurnard (Newport & Cowes Primitive Methodist Circuit) (Existed by 1858, chapel erected 1869) (Records 1858+ IWRO)

NORTHWOOD (Primitive Methodist)
OR   C1870-1921 IWRO (MDR/48) (probably kept at Mark's Corner or Gurnard)
Mfm   C1870-1921 SLC
Cop   C1870-1900 IWCI

NORTHWOOD Cemetery (Records - Local Authority)
Pc   B1856-2000 IWRO
Cop   Index to B1856-1998 Quigley

NORTON (Independent) - See FRESHWATER

NORTON GREEN (Baptist) - See FRESHWATER

OAKFIELD (Primitive Methodist, Bible Christian) - See RYDE

OAKFIELD ST JOHN - See RYDE St John, Oakfield

PARKHURST Garrison - See CARISBROOKE St Michael, Parkhurst Garrison

PARKHURST (Wesleyan) - See CARISBROOKE

PORCHFIELD (Independent, Bible Christian) - See CALBOURNE

REDHILL (Wesleyan) - See NEWCHURCH

ROOKLEY (Bible Christian) - See GODSHILL

ROUD (Particular Baptist) - See GODSHILL

RYDE St Thomas (Population included in Newchurch) (Isle of Wight Incorporation)
(Chapelry of Newchurch, separate parish 1866; became a chapel to the new parish
church of All Saints; closed)
OR   C1719-1957 M1719-1754,1811-1940 B1719-1884 IWRO
      (Gap in C 1787-1829,1865-1876 and B 1805-1840)
BT   1872 (only) HRO (Mfm SLC)
Mfm   C1719-1957 M1719-1754,1811-1940 B1719-1884 IWRO, SLC
Cop   C1719-1900 M1719-1754,1811-1900 B1719-1900 IWCI; M1837-1910 VMI
      C1719-1787 (Ts) SG; C1829-1837 (Ms) SG; M1811-1837 Pallot
      Index to C1829-1837 (Ts) SG, HRO; M1719-1754,1811,1819-1837 Boyd
      M1719-1754,1811,1819-1837 (Ms) SG; Index to M1811-1837 (Ts) SG
      Extracts M1719-1837 IGI

RYDE All Saints (See also Ashey)
OR   C1865-1963 M1874-1966 IWRO
Mfm   C1865-1963 M1874-1966 IWRO, SLC
Cop   C1865-1900 M1874-1900 IWCI; M1874-1910 VMI

RYDE Holy Trinity (Formed 1846 from Newchurch)
OR   C1845-1969 M1846-1987 B1846-1864,1920-1949 Bn1847-1883 IWRO
Mfm   C1845-1969 M1846-1972 B1846-1864,1920-1949 Bn1847-1883 IWRO, SLC
Cop   C1845-1900 M1846-1900 B1846-1864 IWCI; M1846-1910 VMI

RYDE St James (Chapel erected 1829)
OR   M1917-1972 IWRO
Mfm   M1917-1972 IWRO, SLC

RYDE St John the Baptist, Oakfield (Formed 1844 from St Helens)
OR   C1843-1971 M1847-1967 B1896-1985 Bn1911-1968 IWRO
BT   1845,1872 HRO (Mfm SLC) (filed with St Helens)
Mfm   C1843-1892 M1847-1900 B1896-1925 IWRO, SLC
Cop   C1843-1900 M1847-1900 B1896-1900 IWCI; M1847-1910 VMI

RYDE St Michael & All Angels, Swanmore (Formed 1864 from Newchurch)
OR   C1862-1951 M1865-1983 Bn1866-1965 IWRO
BT   1862-1872 HRO (Mfm SLC) (Filed with Newchurch)
Mfm   C1862-1951 M1865-1961 Bn1866-1965 IWRO, SLC
Cop   C1862-1900 M1865-1900 IWCI; M1865-1910 VMI

RYDE (Roman Catholic) St Mary (Chapel founded 1844 in West Street, present church opened 1846)
OR   C1845+ M1856+ B1866+ Inc
Pc   C1845-1906 M1856-1928 B1866-1910 IWRO
Cop   C1845-1900 M1856-1900 IWCI; M1856-1910 VMI

RYDE (Particular Baptist) Christ Church, George Street (Founded 1847, chapel in John Street opened 1851, new chapel erected 1862, active)

RYDE (Baptist) Park Road (Erected 1870, possibly closed by 1931)

RYDE (Independent) George Street (Chapel in Newport Street erected 1802, George Street Chapel opened 1816) (Records 1816+ IWRO)
OR   C1817-1837 PRO (RG 4/1373); C1837-1909 D1824-1848,1875-1902 IWRO (RYD/CONG/1,26; D1875-1902 are in membership lists in RYD/CONG/2)
Mfm   C1817-1837 PRO, HRO, IWRO, SLC
Cop   C1817-1900 IWCI; Extracts C1817-1837 IGI

RYDE (Independent, now United Reformed) Upton Road, Haylands (Founded 1802, chapel erected 1851, affiliated to George Street Chapel, active)

RYDE (Independent) Green Lane (Chapel opened 1839, a station of George Street)

RYDE (Independent) Weeks Road (Wooden chapel opened 1844, permanent chapel opened 1865, a village station of George Street Chapel) (Records 1926+ IWRO, with George Street records)

RYDE Wesleyan Circuit (Formed 1861 from Newport Circuit. Included chapels at Arreton, Bembridge, Binstead, Carisbrooke, Cowes, East Cowes, Newchurch, Northwood, Ryde, St Helens, Sandown, and Shanklin) (Records 1850+ IWRO)
OR   C1860-1930 IWRO (MDR/2-4)
Mfm   C1860-1930 SLC
Cop   C1860-1900 IWCI

RYDE (Wesleyan) Nelson Street, Garfield Road (Newport Wesleyan Circuit, Ryde Wesleyan Circuit from 1861) (Chapel erected 1811, Nelson Street Chapel erected c1844, Garfield Road Chapel erected 1885, active) (Records 1811+ IWRO)
OR   C1838-1860 IWRO (MDR/38A) (One baptism 1836 entered at West Cowes)
Mfm   C1838-1860 SLC
Cop   C1838-1860 IWCI

RYDE (Free Wesleyan) William Street, Swanmore (Erected 1854 [possibly 1836])

RYDE (Free Wesleyan) High Street (Existed by 1867, probably ceased by 1890)

RYDE (Primitive Methodist) Bethel Chapel, Star Street, High Street (Newport Primitive Methodist Circuit, Ryde & Sandown Primitive Methodist Circuit) (Star Street Chapel erected 1841, High Street Chapel 1901) (Records 1902+ IWRO)

RYDE (Primitive Methodist) Oakfield (Ryde & Sandown Primitive Methodist Circuit) (Existed by 1882, closed c1932)

RYDE (Bible Christian) Zion Chapel, Oakfield (Shanklin Bible Christian Circuit?) (Chapel erected c1848, probably short-lived)

RYDE (Bible Christian) Newport Street (Newport Bible Christian Circuit) (Chapel erected 1860, closed by 1945) (Records 1862+ IWRO)

RYDE (Catholic Apostolic Church) Daniel Street (Existed by 1899)

RYDE (Evangelical Protestant) Newport Street (Chapel erected 1893)

RYDE (Christian Spiritualist) Newport Street (Existed by 1939, National Spiritualist Church active)

RYDE (Elim Foursquare Gospel Alliance) Warwick Street (Existed by 1939)

RYDE Cemetery, West Street (Records - Local Authority)
BT   B1863-1881,1883-1884,1886-1893 HRO
Pc   B1862-2000 IWRO
Cop   Index to B1862-2000 Quigley

RYDE & SANDOWN Primitive Methodist Circuit (Formed from Newport & Cowes Circuit. Included chapels at Newchurch, Ryde, Sandown) (Records 1917+ IWRO)

ST HELENS St Helen (953) (Isle of Wight Incorporation) (See also Ryde St John the Baptist)
OR   C1653-1960 M1695-1998 B1695-1992 Bn1877-1979 IWRO
BT   1780-1781,1783-1858,1861-1872 HRO (Mfm SLC)
Mfm   C1653-1960 M1695-1913 B1695-1908 IWRO, SLC
Cop   C1653-1900 M1695-1900 B1695-1900 IWCI; M1837-1910 VMI

ST HELENS (Independent, now Congregational) Elmfield (Preaching from c1845 at Westbrook, Elmfield Chapel erected 1870 as a village station of George Street Ryde, active)

ST HELENS (Wesleyan) St Helens Green (Newport Wesleyan Circuit, Ryde Wesleyan Circuit from 1861) (Chapel erected c1811) (Records 1903+ IWRO)

ST HELENS (Wesleyan) Seaview (Newport Wesleyan Circuit, Ryde Wesleyan Circuit from 1861) (Society existed by 1813, chapel 1828) (Records 1903+ IWRO)

ST HELENS (Wesleyan) (Chapel erected 1823; 1851 Religious Census; no other references located)

ST HELENS (Wesleyan Methodist Reformers, United Methodist Free Church from 1857) Jubilee Chapel, St Helens Green (Existed by 1855, active 1900)

ST HELENS (Wesleyan Methodist Reformers, United Methodist Free Church from 1857) Seaview (Existed by 1878, active 1940)

ST HELENS (Bible Christian) Rehoboth Chapel (Isle of Wight Bible Christian Circuit, Shanklin Bible Christian Circuit from 1845) (Society founded 1823, chapel erected by 1844)

ST HELENS (Bible Christian) St Helens Green (Existed by 1878)

ST HELENS (Bible Christian) Nettlestone (Shanklin Bible Christian Circuit) (Existed by 1903) (Records 1903+ IWRO)

ST LAWRENCE St Lawrence (78) (Isle of Wight Incorporation)
OR   C1746-1985 M1747-1984 B1746-1986 Bn1829-1972 IWRO
BT   1780,1787-1789,1791,1793-1813,1815-1864 HRO (Mfm SLC)
Mfm   C1746-1985 M1747-1984 B1746-1986 IWRO, SLC
Cop   C1746-1900 M1747-1900 B1746-1900 IWCI; M1840-1910 VMI
        M1747-1836 (Ms) SG; Index to M1780-1837 (Ts) SG
        M1747-1836 Boyd; M1780-1837 Pallot

ST NICHOLAS - See CARISBROOKE St Nicholas, Carisbrooke Castle

SANDFORD (Bible Christian) - See GODSHILL

SANDOWN Christ Church (Formed 1847 from Brading; see also Lake, Shanklin)
OR   C1847-1938 M1848-1989 B1847-1988 Bn1849-1968 IWRO
BT   1846-1867 HRO (Mfm SLC)
Mfm   C1847-1938 M1848-1961 B1847-1937 Bn1849-1968 IWRO, SLC
Cop   C1847-1900 M1848-1900 B1847-1900 IWCI; M1848-1910 VMI

SANDOWN St John the Evangelist (Formed 1881 from Christ Church)
OR   C1882-1946 M1882-1981 B1969-1988 Bn1920-1986 IWRO
Cop   C1882-1900 M1882-1900 IWCI; M1882-1910 VMI

SANDOWN (Roman Catholic) St Patrick (Founded 1907)
OR   C1907+ M1909+ B1910+ Inc

SANDOWN (Baptist) Pell Street or Station Avenue (Founded 1882, active)
OR   Adult baptisms occur in membership lists 1882-1935,1964-1981 at IWRO
        (AC 2000/72)

SANDOWN (Independent) Leeds Street (Established 1866 in a former Free Wesleyan chapel in Wilkes Road, Church formed 1872, Leeds Street Chapel opened 1873)
Mfm   D1875-1913 (In membership list 1872-1914) SLC
Pc   D1875-1913 (In membership list 1872-1914) IWRO

SANDOWN (Wesleyan) Pell Street, Station Avenue (Newport Wesleyan Circuit, Ryde Wesleyan Circuit from 1861) (Society existed by 1814, chapels erected 1860 and 1865) (Records 1852+ IWRO)
OR   C1815-1954 IWRO (MDR/5-6) (Includes baptisms at other chapels)
Mfm   C1815-1954 SLC
Cop   C1815-1900 IWCI

SANDOWN (Primitive Methodist) Fort Street, Avenue Road (Ryde & Sandown Primitive Methodist Circuit) (Chapel erected 1866) (Records 1929+ IWRO)

SANDOWN (Bible Christian) York Road (Isle of Wight Bible Christian Circuit, Shanklin Bible Christian Circuit from 1845) (Chapel in Broad Lane erected c1838 [or 1828?], York Road Chapel erected 1882, active) (Records 1863+ IWRO)

SANDOWN (Plymouth Brethren) (Chapel listed in White's Directory 1878; no other references located)

SANDOWN (Undenominational) Avenue Road (Existed by 1939)

SANDOWN Cemetery (Records - Local Authority)
Pc   B1926-2000 IWRO
Cop   Index to B1926-2000 Quigley

SEAVIEW St Peter (Formed 1907 from St Helens)
OR   C1907-1986 M1907-1989 Bn1907-1986 IWRO
Cop   M1907-1910 VMI

SEAVIEW (Wesleyan, Wesleyan Methodist Reformers) - See ST HELENS

SHALFLEET St Michael the Archangel (1,049) (Isle of Wight Incorporation) (Dedicated 1964, original dedication unknown; see also Newtown)
OR   C1608-1988 M1604-1972 B1621-1962 Bn1824-1983 IWRO
        (Several gaps, notably C 1655-1664,1683-1691, M 1650-1656,
        B 1639-1649,1670-1677. Few marriages 1670-1677)
BT   1780-1836,1838-1871 HRO (Mfm SLC)
Mfm   C1608-1928 M1604-1972 B1621-1962 Bn1824-1939 IWRO, SLC
Pc   B1962-1987 IWRO
Cop   C1608-1900 M1604-1900 B1621-1900 IWCI; M1604-1812 (Ts,I) SG, HRO
        C1608-1762 M1604-1754 B1621-1762 (Ts) SG; M1604-1837 (Ms) SG
        Index to M1780-1812 (Ts) SG; M1837-1910 VMI; Extracts M1604-1812 IGI
        M1604-1837 Boyd; M1780-1812 Pallot

SHALFLEET (Particular Baptist) Wellow (Founded 1801, chapel erected c1804, active) (Records 1806+ Inc)
OR   Z1810-1837 PRO (RG 4/1807)
Mfm   Z1810-1837 PRO, HRO, IWRO, SLC
        D1911-1939 (plus a few 1858-1890), church minutes 1806-1902 SLC (From
        the photocopies at IWRO) (Catalogued as East Wellow)
Pc   D1911-1939 (plus a few 1858-1890) IWRO (In membership lists 1838-1947)
        Church minutes 1806-1902 IWRO
Cop   Z1810-1837 IWCI; Extracts Z1810-1837 IGI

SHALFLEET (Particular Baptist) (Erected c1840; 1851 Religious Census; no other references located)

SHALFLEET (Wesleyan) (Newport Wesleyan Circuit) (Society formed c1814, chapels erected 1861 and 1911, closed) (Records 1892+ IWRO)

SHALFLEET (Primitive Methodist) Bethesda Chapel, Ningwood (Newport & Cowes Primitive Methodist Circuit) (Founded c1847, closed c1896)

SHALFLEET (Primitive Methodist) Newbridge (Newport & Cowes Primitive Methodist Circuit) (Established c1860)
OR   C1870-1884,1896-1913 IWRO (MDR/49)
Mfm   C1870-1884,1896-1913 SLC
Cop   C1870-1884,1896-1900 IWCI